Short Lessons in ART HISTORY

Artists and Their Work

Revised and Updated

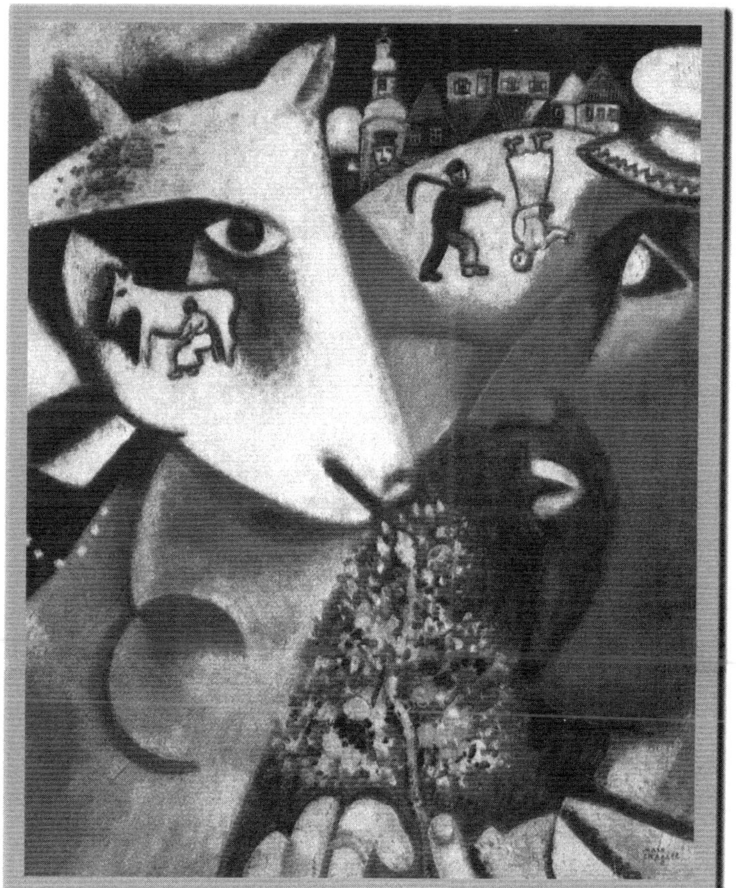

Phyllis Clausen Barker

J. WESTON WALCH PUBLISHER
Portland, Maine

01-1441
ISBN 0-8251-4245-8

J. Weston Walch, Publisher
P.O. Box 658 • Portland, Maine 04101-0658

PRINTED IN THE UNITED STATES OF AMERICA

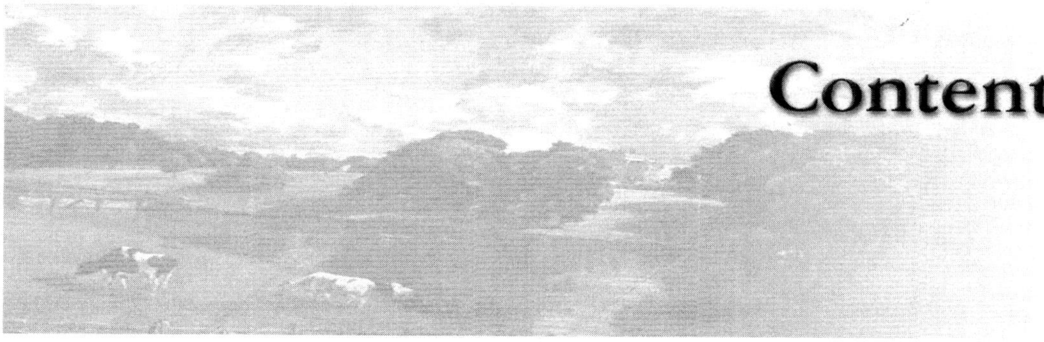

Contents

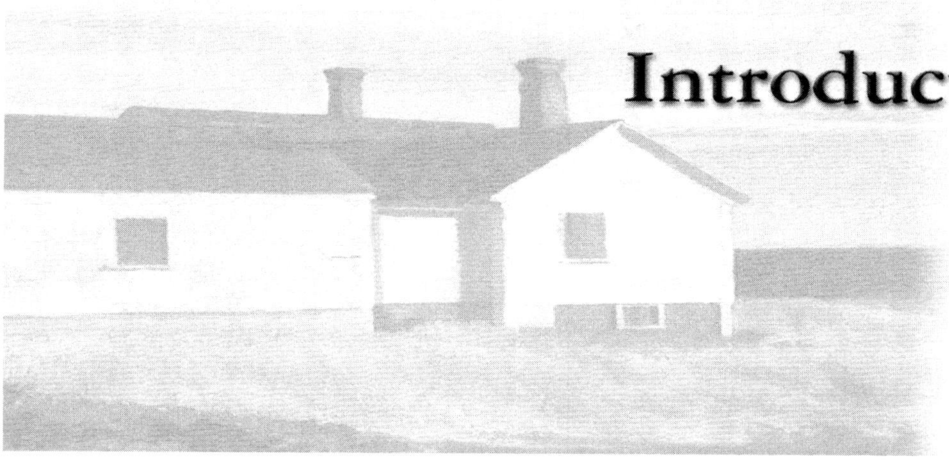

Introduction

People have always had a need to make some kind of art. When very young children are given crayons and paper, they begin drawing lines and shapes. Before long the lines and shapes are given names as the child sees meanings in them. Have you ever "doodled" with a pen or pencil on a notebook, phone book, or textbook? Have you ever written your name with the names of friends, and then added decorative lines and shapes? Have you decorated a T-shirt or sneakers with symbols, shapes, and colors?

People have made art for many reasons. In this book, we will look at artists and their lives. We want to know where and how they lived. It is easy to forget that the world was very different 50, 100, or 500 years ago. Although the world was different, people and their needs have not changed very much. We do not know much about ordinary people who lived 500 years ago. But from their writings we can feel sure that human nature is about the same now as it was in the past. We will explore the world of Western art to try to learn about the kind of art made in different periods of time. Why are some artists remembered and many others forgotten?

The kinds of artwork we will talk about are the visual arts—art you can see. Vincent Lanier, an art educator, has given us an excellent definition for visual art in his book *The Arts We Can See.* He says, "A work of visual art is a made object we see that we value for its own sake." This eliminates things of beauty in nature, since they are not man-made. Learning about a work of art, the artist who made it, and about the times in which the artist lived helps us to understand why we value it for its own sake.

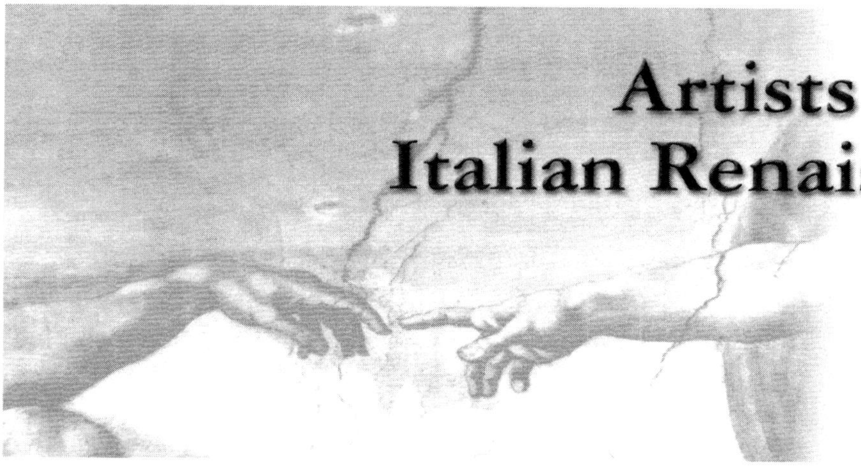

Artists of the Italian Renaissance

THE WORD *renaissance* means rebirth or revival. When capitalized, it refers specifically to a period in Europe that links medieval and modern times. It began in the fourteenth century in Italy and lasted into the seventeenth century in that and other parts of Europe.

The Renaissance was a wonderful era that saw the beginnings of modern science and the flowering of the arts and literature in Europe. To this day, the term Renaissance man (or woman) denotes someone who has wide interests and is an expert on several different subjects. Leonardo da Vinci is often held up as the prime example of a Renaissance man, for reasons we will explore in this unit.

The Italian Renaissance began in the region of Tuscany. Tuscany is a very beautiful part of northwestern Italy that includes the city of Florence, one of the old city-states you may learn about in world history class. The Italians call it Firenze.

Living conditions in the early Renaissance were quite different from those we know today. Since art and artists are products of their times, it might be helpful to briefly look at what life was like during those times. If this arouses your interest, your history texts will have more details.

At the time of the Renaissance, Italy was not a unified nation. It was made up of separate regions and city-states, each with its own customs and leaders. Some of the city-states were sometimes taken over by other countries. Some banded together to form new governmental units. Merchant "princes" developed economic "empires" because of increased trade. The exploration of Asia and the New World were constantly creating new wealth.

Frequent large and small wars were fought by both peasants and mercenaries. The latter group were "hired guns" who fought for pay. While soldiers who fought for a ruler could fight and then go home when the war was over, the mercenaries fought for anyone who paid them. They moved from one ruler to another.

Roads did link cities, but most of them were a far cry from our roads of today. In the cities, however, the main streets were paved by the sixteenth century. Travel was unsafe, particularly for someone traveling alone. Most people walked or rode horses. Sometimes a coach was available. Bandits were a constant threat on the road.

Cities were walled. Closed gates helped control who came in and left. In some cases travelers paid a tax to enter. Walls also helped in the defense of the city. As a city grew, a new wall was built outside the old one to add more land. City streets were no better than sewers. Refuse was simply dumped into the street. This broke down into sludge and was a breeding ground for disease. The wealthy often built fine houses on grounds outside the city.

The Black Death was one of the diseases, or plagues, that spread over Europe during this period. Although rich and poor alike were affected, the poor were more likely to contract disease and die. They were so poorly fed that they had little resistance.

No matter how beautiful and luxurious houses and cities may seem in the paintings we see, we would have found them less comfortable, clean, and private. Personal cleanliness left much to be desired compared to our standards.

The size of a house depended upon the owner's wealth. In towns and cities, the master's workshop was part of the house and workers and apprentices also lived there. It was not until the 1800s that the workplace and home were separate. The shop was on the lower floor; the family quarters were on the middle floor; and the workers lived on the top floor.

Religious faith was an important part of life. Every community had a church and daily attendance was common. The church was also a community center. Often priests were in charge of the village school. The Jesuit order, in particular, wanted to educate children. Girls' education generally fell behind that of boys. Daughters of upper-class families were taught at home and merchants' daughters were schooled at nunneries. Daughters of poor people did not get to go to school, but only learned to do what was needed to run the home.

Religion was important in another way. Many of the artworks created had religious themes, and many were commissioned by and for the Roman Catholic Church, which had a tremendous effect on individual lives and on the destiny of several states in those days. The popes of the Church often favored particular artists. They sometimes demanded that an artist work only for them, regardless of the artist's own desires. This was particularly true in the case of Michelangelo, as we shall see. Some artists enjoyed the pomp and circumstance of the pope's court. Others, like Michelangelo, would rather have had their freedom and a chance to work in peace.

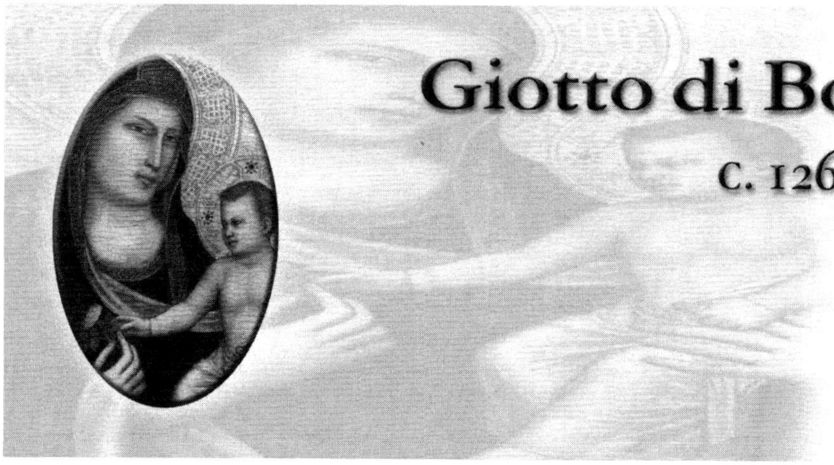

Giotto di Bondone

c. 1266 – c. 1377

Many believe that the Italian Renaissance in art began with the artist named **Giotto di Bondone.** Giotto was born in Tuscany and worked there most of his life. People believed that he was leading a revival of the art of the past. Italians knew of the glories of ancient Rome. They thought he was helping to restore the art styles of Greek and Roman times.

Giotto was born in about 1266 in the valley of Mugello, about 20 miles north of the city of Florence. His father was a farmer. Giotto's name may have been shortened from Ambrogiotto. The legend is that when he was ten years old, he was discovered by a leading painter of the time. Giotto was tending sheep for his father. He liked to draw pictures to help pass the time out in the fields. The artist **Cimabue** was walking past on his way to Vespignano from Florence when he saw the boy's drawings. He was impressed by the boy's skill. He asked Giotto's father if his son could come to Florence to stay with him. This story may or may not be true, but it is a good story nonetheless. A different version tells of the Bondone family moving to Florence when Giotto was a teenager. Giotto worked for a wool merchant, but neglected his job, visiting the workshops of the artists instead. In doing this he met Cimabue and became apprenticed to him.

At that time, the guild system for craftsmen and merchants existed to help set standards for crafts and businesses. A master craftsman ran his own business or workshop. He might become a manufacturer and hire workers to make many items. Such an operation was much like small factories of today. Or, the master might choose to be more involved with the work himself and, therefore, produce fewer things.

To become a master of a craft, a boy began as an apprentice, usually when he was about 12 years old. The boy's parents paid the master who would be training him, or the apprentice himself paid the master when he had finished his apprenticeship. This training period could last as long as seven years. The boy lived with the master and his family. In the workshop he began by doing all sorts of minor chores. Little by little he was given more responsibility and was taught the skills needed for the craft.

As an apprentice, Giotto probably had to learn to prepare the surfaces to be painted, to make and take care of brushes and other tools, and to find minerals from which colors could be made. To make paint, material had to be ground into a powder and mixed with a liquid. This was the job of the apprentices. Next, the apprentice was allowed to begin painting. At first, he painted only the least important parts of the painting. As his skills developed, he was given more important work.

After the apprenticeship was over, the young man became a journeyman. A journeyman painter went from place to place, getting work where he could. When he stopped at a workshop, the master painter was obligated to give him work to do, help him find work, or give him money to go on to the next town. Since the master painter had been helped by the guild system when he was a journeyman, he was supposed to help others. When a journeyman painter or sculptor wanted to become a master, he had to produce a sculpture or painting that was accepted as a good piece of work by the guild. This work was his "masterpiece." That is how we happen to have our term to describe an excellent piece of work. The length of time the young man spent as a journeyman varied, depending upon when he was able to produce his masterpiece.

When Giotto was a young man, the city of Florence was a wealthy, expanding city and a good place for a talented young painter. There were many buildings, particularly churches, to be decorated. The Church was very influential, in both religious and **secular** matters. While an artist *might* have a king as a patron, many artists were given work by churches. A painter had to work within the guidelines of the Church if he was given a commission. He had to make up a contract to present to his patron for a planned work. The contract included a description of the subject matter, the proposed size of the work, and how many figures and colors were to be used.

Giotto's talent enabled him to get many commissions. He was a master storyteller through his paintings. He knew exactly what each picture was to tell the viewer. He often added very human touches. Giotto's paintings of the Virgin may have been suggested to him by the farm women he had known as a child. Giotto's Holy Family seems much more approachable than did the stiff, formal figures in Byzantine-style paintings of the same theme (see Figure 1).

Apparently Giotto was the kind of person who could work well with a variety of people in a variety of situations. By the end of his life he had become very wealthy. He knew how to manage his business of painting to make it pay well. He ran a large workshop in which painters worked for him. He had investments in land that were also profitable.

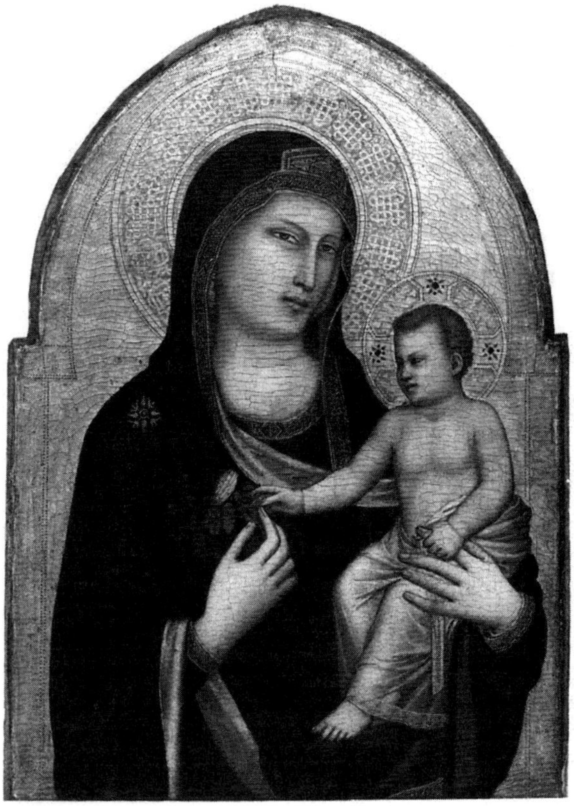

Figure 1
Madonna and Child, c. 1320–1330
Giotto di Bondone

Giotto married Cuita di Lapo del Pela, a girl from Florence. They had eight children, four boys and four girls. One son grew up to be a painter; one son became a priest; one daughter married a painter; and one daughter became a nun. When Giotto had to work in another city, he took his family with him. He was known to have an even temper and a good sense of humor. He wanted to paint and not become involved in the politics of the city in which he worked. He was not vain, and did not want to be called "master."

The first work identified as Giotto's is the crucifix for the choir screen of the Santa Maria Novella Church in Florence. It is almost 19' high. At each end of the crosspiece a small painting was added. At one side is Mary, and on the other side is St. John. This is the only addition to the usual design with only the figure of Christ; there is no decoration other than the lines that serve as a frame. The feeling is that of sorrow and suffering.

Giotto's most famous paintings were frescoes. This painting method is still used today, and was used then for murals (wall paintings). Fresco comes from the Italian word that means "fresh." The painting is done on wet or "fresh" plaster. The wall surface to be painted is given a waterproof coating, then a layer of plaster. Another smoother layer of plaster is applied next. On this layer the design is sketched. The paint used is a mixture of **pigment** and water. The pigment then forms a bond with the plaster as it hardens. For this reason, a mistake can cause problems. To make a correction, the mistake must be chipped out and fresh plaster added. A painter must work quickly to complete the work before the plaster hardens and won't absorb the paint. Even though the painting is done in sections, there is little fine detail in a fresco. There is simply not enough time to paint in a lot of detail.

In Giotto's time, panel painting was done with egg tempera as the medium. The panel was made of thick, solid wood, often poplar. The wood was given a coating of **gesso.** Gesso was made from glue mixed with finely ground chalk. The wood panel was sometimes covered with layers of linen cloth, also coated with gesso, to make a ground, or painting surface. The paint was made of pigment mixed with egg yolk and water. (This may sound strange, but if you have ever tried to remove dried egg yolk from a dish, you will understand what a durable mixture egg tempera is. Later we will talk about the art of a twentieth-century American painter who uses egg tempera as his painting medium.)

Many layers of paint were used to cover the gesso-coated ground. Some painters added a final coating of wax or varnish to create a glossy finish. If gold touches were needed, the painter used gold leaf, which is a very thin sheet of gold glued to the painting.

The Basilica of St. Francis in Assisi was decorated with a series of frescoes of the life of the saint. Some of them may have been done by Giotto. Many artists at this time did not sign their work, and historians can identify it only by comparing individual styles.

The work that is considered Giotto's greatest is in the city of Padua, Italy, about 25 miles from Venice. He was commissioned to decorate the Arena Chapel, so called because it was built on the place where an old Roman amphitheater had stood. It's a brick structure, 67' long and rather narrow. The inside is simple in design; a barrel vault makes a curved ceiling. Six windows are set into the walls below.

Thirty-four frescoes are painted in the three tiers or divisions. The top row of paintings tells of the early life of the Virgin Mary. The middle section consists of paintings of the childhood and ministry of Christ. The lower tier is made up of scenes from the **Passion** of Christ. The ceiling is blue, studded with stars; among the stars are ten medallions in which the Prophets, Mary, and Christ are painted. Below the last tier of paintings is a base for paintings of the virtues and the vices; they are painted to resemble marble relief sculpture. On the wall at the entryway is a painting of the last judgment; opposite this is a painting of God the Father sending the angel Gabriel on his mission to earth. Below this painting are four small frescoes of the annunciation.

Giotto made the pictures easy for the viewer to understand. One scene leads to the next. We recognize the emotions of joy, anger, tenderness, and cruelty in the faces and gestures of those who take part in the drama. Giotto uses only what is needed to tell the story and to express the feelings involved.

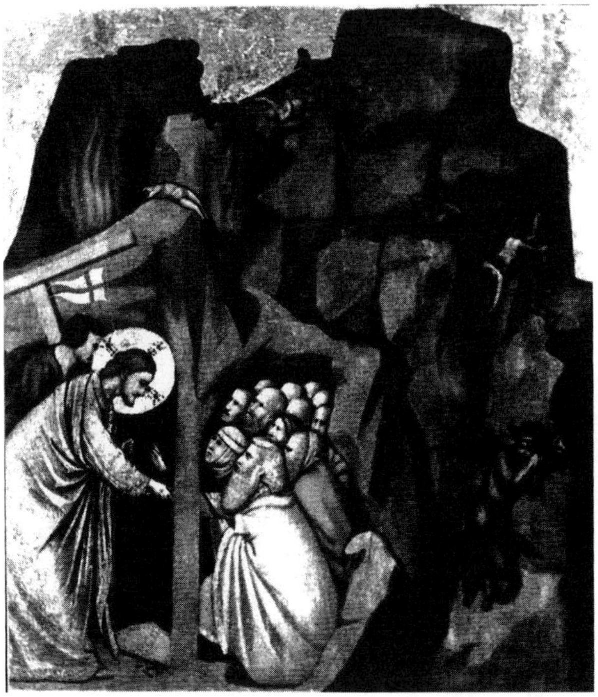

Figure 2
Christ in Limbo, c. 1320–1325
Giotto di Bondone

The Arena Chapel is a forerunner of the Sistine Chapel, in which frescoes by Michelangelo are found. We will study these later. Another well-known commission for Giotto was the chapel of the Church of Santa Croce, which contains a panel featuring *Christ in Limbo* (see Figure 2). Art historian Giorgio Vasari was an artist and writer in the sixteenth century. He wrote that Michelangelo knew and admired Giotto's work. Vasari also said that Giotto decorated churches in Rimini, Ravenna, Verona, Ferrara, and Urbino.

The last of Giotto's surviving works are in two chapels in Florence, the Bardi and the Peruzzi chapels. The commissions came from two rival families; each family wanted to use the art to improve its image in the city. The style of these paintings is that of the mature Giotto, using the best of techniques in developing space. There is a feeling of calm that we will find in later Renaissance paintings.

In 1334 Giotto was appointed chief master of the cathedral building and chief of public works in Florence. During this time he also worked in Milan for its ruler.

The same year he received the new appointments, Giotto was placed in charge of the construction of a bell tower for Florence. It was often referred to as "Giotto's tower." Work began on it in 1334, but he did not live to see its completion. It was finished in 1387, but Giotto died in 1337. The tower was 278' high and 14' wide at the base. The walls were white marble. Delicate inlaid horizontal lines crossed the lower levels. Vertical panels were divided by narrow green stripes. The higher part of the base held vaulted niches deep enough to contain sculpture done later by Renaissance sculptors, including Donatello. Pointed windows with cusped openings were built into the second, third, and fourth levels. Its **campanile** can be seen above the adjacent dome of the cathedral of Florence. He came home to Florence at the end of 1337 and died just as the new year began.

Giotto's contribution to art included the qualities that would be seen again in the art of the Renaissance. Following Giotto's death, the relative calm that he had known disappeared. The Black Death, which swept Europe in the fourteenth century, created an atmosphere of fear in which the arts did not make much progress. By August of 1348, more than half of the population of Florence alone had died of the plague. Along with this contagion, there were business disasters, small and large wars, and bands of paid soldiers pillaging the countryside. Giotto's painting brought about a rebirth of classical art, but more than 50 years would pass before this renaissance would flourish.

On September 26, 1997, an earthquake struck Umbria, the central part of Italy. In the town of Assisi the basilica of St. Francis of Assisi was damaged. The quake registered a magnitude of 5.5. A second quake occurred the next day, collapsing the vaulted ceiling and the frescoes from the main entrance. At least four of the frescoes from the life of St. Francis were damaged.

Glossary

Giotto di Bondone pronounced jot´-tō dee bon-dō´-neh

Cimabue pronounced cheem-a-boo´ay

secular pertaining to things of the world, not to sacred or spiritual things

pigment a powdered substance mixed with liquid to impart a color

gesso a mixture used as an undercoat before painting

Passion the suffering of Jesus from the Last Supper to the Crucifixion

campanile a bell tower, free-standing or built beside a church

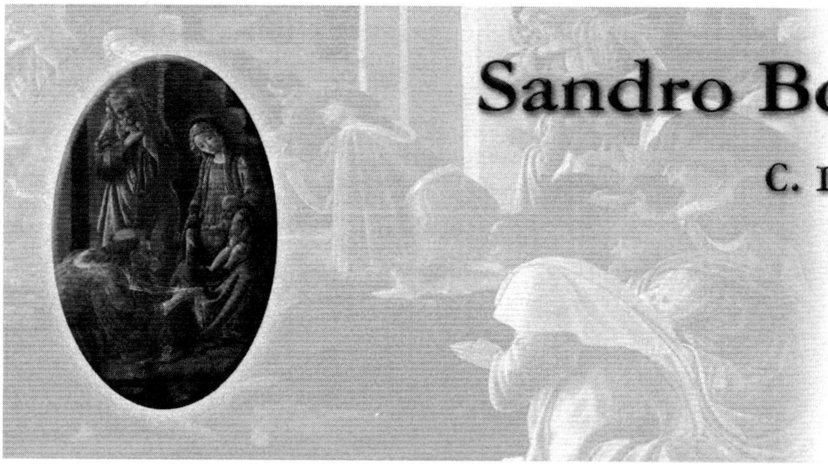

Sandro Botticelli

c. 1444 – 1510

IN THE MIDDLE 1400s, the city-state of Florence was one of the wealthiest in Italy. Commerce, industry, and banking had brought great wealth to Florence. In such times of prosperity, attention can be given to literature, philosophy, and the arts. People began to wonder about things that had been previously considered simply "the will of God." The individual person began to be thought of as self-ruling.

Among the wealthy families who controlled Florence, the most powerful for many years was the **Medici** family. They were patrons of a number of artists, buying their work and giving them commissions to do specific works. **Botticelli** was an artist in Florence during this period. We will look at his life and work.

Sandro Botticelli was born in Florence sometime between 1444 and 1446. He was the last child of a large family. His name was Alessandro di Mariano Filipepi. The name Botticelli was what we would call a nickname. It came from his elder brother, who was called "Il Botticello" (Little Barrel)! Vasari says that Sandro had been "brought up conscientiously." He had been instructed in "all those things usually taught to young children before they are apprenticed."

Botticelli went to the master painter Fra Filippo Lippi when he was 16. He is also thought to have worked with Antonio Poppaiuolo, a painter and sculptor. Botticelli learned ways to portray feminine beauty from Fra Filippo Lippi. From Poppaiuolo he learned ways to show the body in motion.

Botticelli set up his own studio, probably as early as 1470. The Medici family became his patrons. Many of his early paintings are of religious themes.

A famous example of Botticelli's style during this period is *The Virgin Adoring the Child* (see Color Plate 1). Two of his most famous paintings, however, are of subjects from mythology: *Primavera* and *The Birth of Venus*. During this period of his career, Botticelli was in the circle of intellectuals of the Medici; allegory and classic mythology were frequent themes in his work. His style is **linear** and **lyric.** We feel that he loves beauty and grace. The flowing lines create "floating" hair and garments and finely drawn features (see Figure 3).

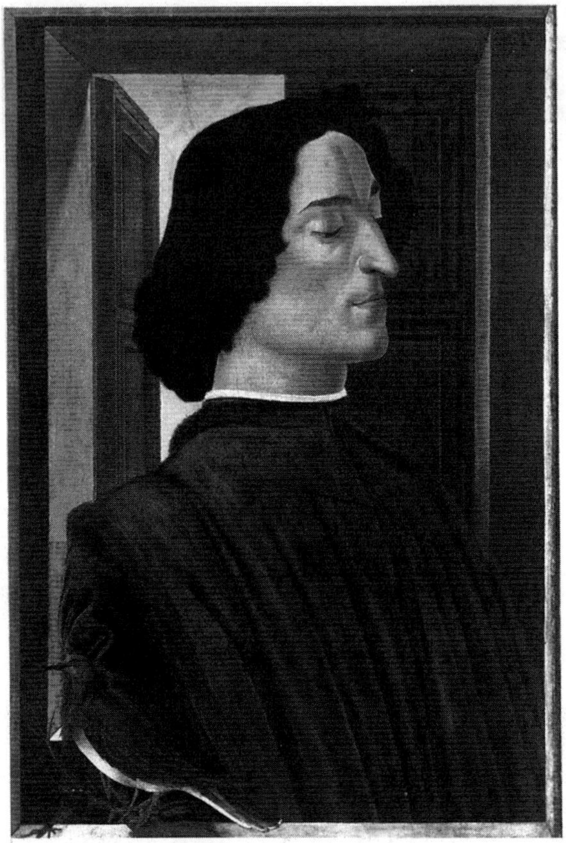

Figure 3
Giuliano de' Medici, c. 1478
Sandro Botticelli

Primavera, which depicts the coming of spring, is now in the Uffizi Gallery in Florence, Italy. It was painted for a member of the Medici family in 1477. There are several interpretations of the theme of this painting. Some believe it is a meeting of lovers; others believe it symbolizes womanhood, or the four seasons. Another interpretation, perhaps most likely, calls the central woman Venus; the figure at the extreme left Mercury; above Venus, Cupid; and the three women dancing together the three Graces.

The Birth of Venus, painted in about 1485, shows the goddess of love gliding to shore on a seashell, blown along by a zephyr, and met by a lady-in-waiting. Figures in either of these paintings may have been inspired by members of the Medici family and their friends. The flowing, graceful figures, the sweet feminine faces, flowers, and the use of lines are familiar qualities in Botticelli's paintings. These qualities are exemplified in another painting of this time, *The Adoration of the Magi* (see Figure 4).

In 1481 Pope Sixtus called Botticelli to Rome to paint three frescoes for the Sistine Chapel. This is the only time he spent away from Florence. When he returned, his work and life were influenced by the religious controversy and strife in the city. A friar, Savonarola, from the Dominican Order, had begun preaching against the worldly and material concerns of the people and the Church. He condemned the pope, the priests, self-indulgence, and human weaknesses in general. He had a large number of followers, among them Botticelli's own brother, Simone, with whom he shared a house. At the same time, the Medici family were at odds with the friar.

When Lorenzo de' Medici died, Savonarola became the most powerful person in the city. Piero de' Medici, Lorenzo's brother, was no match for the friar. Books, luxuries, and artworks were burned in bonfires; Botticelli himself threw some of his art into the flames. For a while Florence accepted the reforms of the friar and his followers. Piero de' Medici was exiled. Then, as often happened in the history of Italy, opposing forces banded together and regained control. Savonarola was put to death.

Botticelli's last masterpiece was a nativity scene painted in 1500. It is the only work signed by him. At the top of the painting a long inscription begins with "I, Sandro, painted this picture at the end of 1500 in the troubles of Italy." The message continues with references to the Book of Revelation in the Bible. The painting rejects the kind of realism popular in Renaissance paintings. The figures have a flat quality, and the sizes of the figures vary. The Virgin and Child, being most important, are larger in scale than the others. The men in the lower section are making a religious pilgrimage and receiving comfort from the angels as they make their way to the Christ Child. Four small devils are held at bay by lances below and at each side. Floating, dancing angels are painted at the top, below the inscription. This painting certainly reflects the effects of the religious controversy and state of the city on the painter.

After 1500 there seem to be no more paintings by Botticelli. This painter, called the greatest artist of linear design in Europe by the art historian Berenson, died in 1510 at the age of 66.

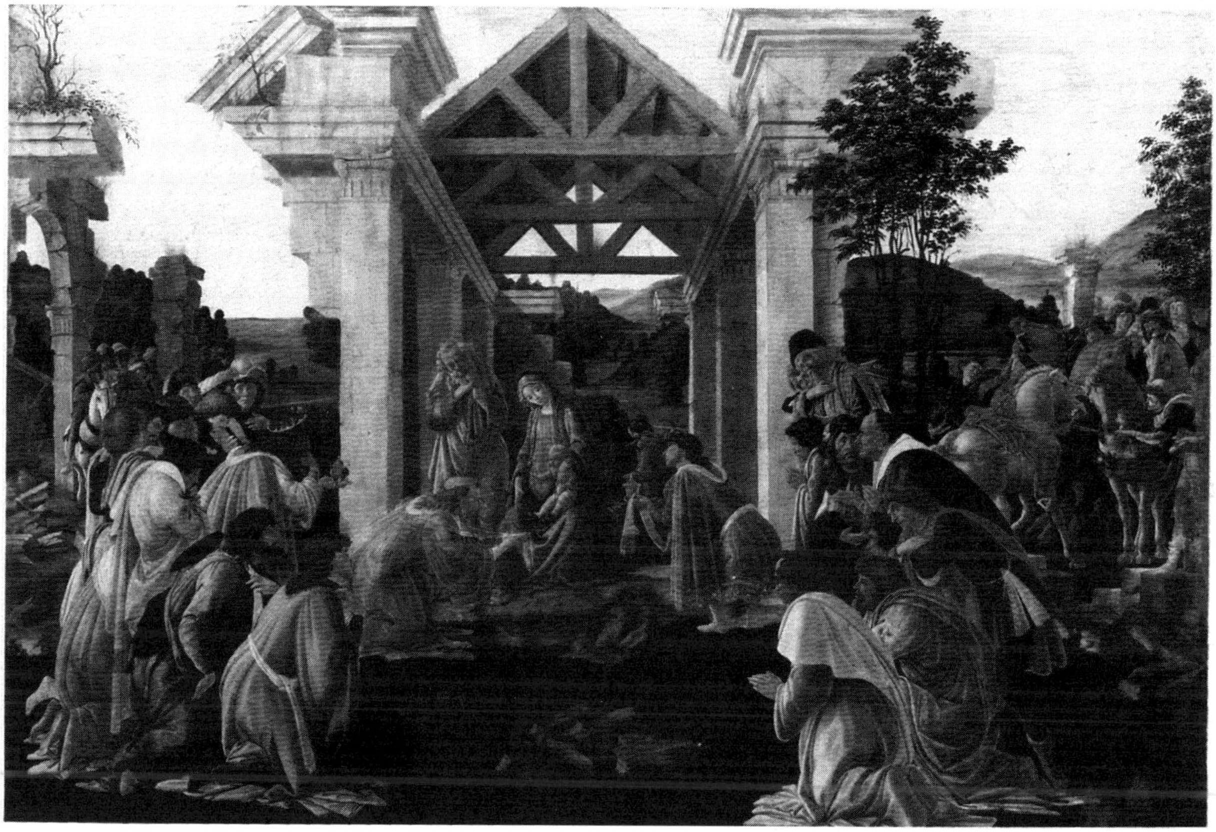

Figure 4
The Adoration of the Magi, early 1480s
Sandro Botticelli

Glossary

Medici pronounced med´-e-chē

Botticelli pronounced bot-ti-chel´-li

linear refers to the use of line. In art, linear means using line in drawing, or design in which line is emphasized.

lyric expressing feelings

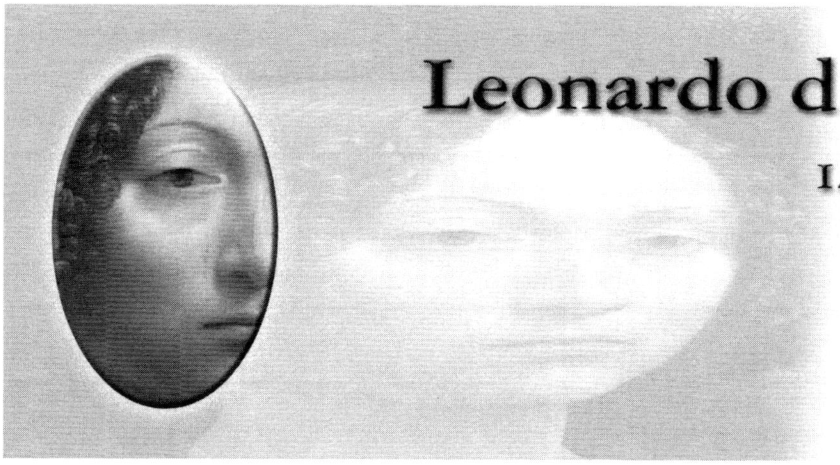

Leonardo da Vinci

1452 – 1519

LEONARDO DA VINCI was born on April 15, 1452, in the town of Vinci, about 60 miles from Florence, Italy. The family name came from the town of Vinci. His father, Piero, was a notary, which was the equivalent of an attorney or lawyer today. Leonardo went to the local school and excelled in music, drawing, and mathematics. Even then he was interested in all of nature and made drawings to help him understand the things that caught his attention.

When he was about 15, his father talked to the artist **Verrocchio** about his son's ability in drawing, and took a portfolio of drawings for the artist to see. Verrocchio took Leonardo into his workshop as an apprentice. The earliest painting we know from this period is *The Baptism of Christ,* which was done in the workshop. The angel at the lower left-hand section is said to be Leonardo's. Another story goes with this painting. Vasari says that when Verrocchio saw the excellence of Leonardo's work and use of color, he never painted again. Whether or not that's true, Verrocchio did turn to sculpture at about that time.

It was characteristic of Leonardo to explore in great detail whatever he worked on, or whatever interested him. His genius led him into explorations of the human body, the ways of nature, machines for war, and a model of a flying machine. He was an engineer, an inventor, and a scientist as well as an artist. His notebooks described his ideas, plans, and research. He was left-handed and wrote in a kind of backwards script; some believe this was to protect the information. Drawings were included in his notebooks. He did dissections and made drawings of a baby in the womb, the human eye, and the structure and workings of bones and muscles.

Only about 19 of his paintings have survived. Many art projects that had been commissioned were begun and not finished. This habit irritated his patrons. His friends could not understand why work was not completed, nor why he moved restlessly from one city to another.

Vasari says that "Leonardo's disposition was so lovable that he commanded everyone's affection." He loved animals, and often bought caged birds in order to let them go free.

Leonardo's painting and drawing techniques were helped by his observation of detail. His depictions of folds of drapery indicate that he was looking at real cloth folds as he worked. Angel wings show his investigation of real feathers from birds' wings. Flowers were painted from real flowers, not from the imagination. This attention to detail can be seen in his portrait of *Ginevra de'Benci* (see Figure 5). A painting method that the Italians called **sfumato** was one of his ideas. Sfumato is the blurring of outlines of forms so that the edges blend into spaces beside them. This was much different from the sharply outlined forms of other artists working at that time.

One of Leonardo's most famous paintings is *The Last Supper,* which he painted in the refectory of the Monastery of Santa Maria delle Grazie in Milan. This painting was copied by other artists of the time and has been reproduced many, many times since. It is very familiar to most people.

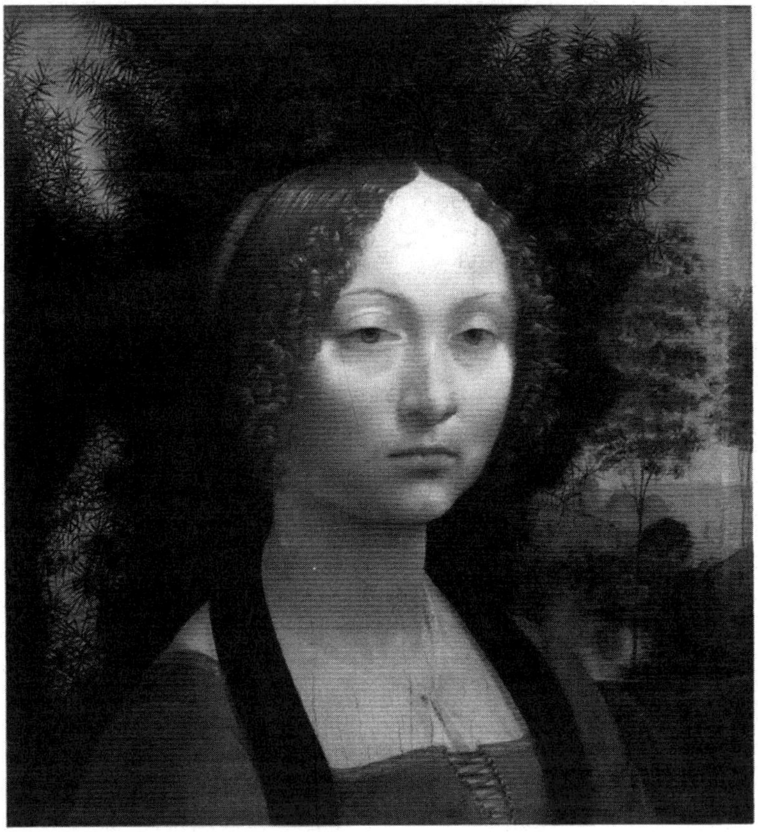

Figure 5
Ginevra de'Benci, c. 1474
Leonardo da Vinci

Leonardo had gone to Milan at the invitation of **Lodovico,** the ruler of Milan. Leonardo had written a letter to the duke describing the many kinds of work that he, Leonardo, was able to do: sculpture, painting, architecture, engineering, and the design of war equipment. He arrived in Milan in 1482, and he made paintings of several people of the court. He was then asked to paint *The Last Supper* for the room in the monastery where the Dominican friars took their meals. The painting tells of the drama of Christ's statement to his disciples. He has told them that one of them would betray him. The composition arranges the men into groups of three with Christ in the center. All of them, except Judas, who did betray Christ, gesture and react to Jesus' words.

Although it is a wall painting, it is not done in the usual fresco technique. This wall had been given a coat of leaded white primer paint and allowed to dry. Leonardo, ever wanting to experiment with new ideas, decided to mix egg, linseed oil, and pigments together. This mixture became the paint he used for his latest work. He brushed it on the dry plaster for *The Last Supper* figures. Because the new paint dried more slowly than painting on wet plaster, as in true fresco, he was able to achieve more detail, allowing careful, painstaking work. The paint had begun to flake off as early as 1517, even though it had been finished around 1490. Fresco paintings are normally long-lived and have been found dating to very ancient times; an example is a Minoan **sarcophagus** dated 1450–1400 B.C.

This painting has undergone at least seven restoration attempts, sometimes causing further damage to the paint and changes to the figures. When Napoleon's troops were in Milan in 1796 they used the refectory as a stable. The soldiers did further harm to the painting.

The latest restoration began in 1977. It was directed by art restorer Pinn Brombilla Barcilon, using the most modern equipment. The workers carefully chipped away layers of oil, varnish, glue, and paint to get down to the painting beneath. Powerful magnifying equipment was used to remove the layers centimeter by centimeter. Places where the original paint was gone were painted with brush strokes of beige color to help distinguish the original from what had been added by earlier restorations and was now removed. Long-covered details came to light, including food items, tableware, and sharper details of facial features of the disciples. The results are much lighter, vibrant pastels. Previous restorers had painted over past accumulations of all kinds of soil, resulting in darkened areas. Some art historians feel that the current restoration went too far and removed important traces of the original; others said that Leonardo's use of sfumato, the blending of one shade into another, was responsible for the darkened places and should not have been removed. Those who favored the restorations pointed out that almost 50 percent of the true painting remained and revealed the original work and brilliant colors of Leonardo. In June 1999, after 22 years of supreme effort, the painting known by millions is now much closer to its original state.

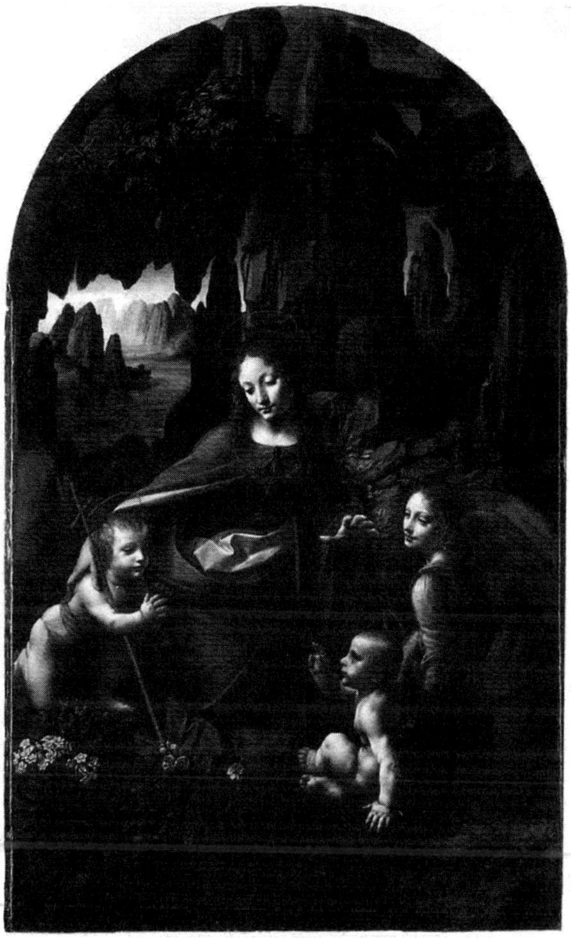

Figure 6
The Virgin of the Rocks, c. 1506
Leonardo da Vinci

Leonardo lived well when he was in Milan with Lodovico as his patron. He had beautiful clothes, servants, and musicians in his household. Sometimes he became so interested in his investigations that he fell behind in the work that he was supposed to do. At times his patron threatened to bring in other artists to finish Leonardo's planned pieces. This caused hard feelings. The situation resolved itself when Lodovico fled the city as it was being captured by the French. Leonardo went on to Mantua, then to Venice, and then back to Florence. He had been away for 17 years.

In Florence, Leonardo was hired by the Servite friars to design an altar picture. He made a plan (a drawing called a *cartoon*) for a painting of the *Virgin and Child with St. Anne and the Infant St. John.* Vasari says that when the cartoon was finished "for two days it attracted to the room where it was exhibited a crowd of men and women, young and old, who flocked there . . . to gaze in amazement at the marvels he had created." This marvel, however, was not to be finished by Leonardo. The friars had to find another painter to finish it.

Leonardo spent most of the year of 1502 away from Florence working as a military engineer for the notorious Cesare Borgia. Borgia served Pope Alexander in many capacities, from diplomat to leader of military assaults on small city-states and countries for the **Vatican.** Corruption was widespread in both government and the Church; the Borgia family is said to have participated in much of it. Cesare Borgia became ill and floundered politically, and Leonardo came back to Florence. It was at this time that he painted his best-known work.

The *Mona Lisa* is familiar to most of us, and thousands of words have been written about the painting. To some, the woman seems to be smiling secretly, to others sadly, and to others mysteriously. Her features and the softness of her face are reminiscent of the *Virgin and St. Anne* drawing. The sfumato technique is found in the *Mona Lisa,* adding to its lifelike quality. Vasari says that Leonardo worked for four years on this painting, and that he brought in jesters, musicians, and singers to entertain the model while he worked. She was not a famous or noble person, but the wife of an official of Florence. She was Elisabetta, the third wife of Francesco del Giocondo. Leonardo kept the painting, saying that it was still not finished. Eventually it was bought by Francis I, King of France, and now is in the Louvre in Paris.

In 1505 Leonardo went to Milan again to work for the viceroy of the city. Around that time he painted *The Virgin of the Rocks* (see Figure 6). In 1516 he moved on to France and became a painter and engineer for the king. He was 64 years old and his health was failing. The king admired Leonardo's intelligence and enjoyed conversations with him. In 1519 Leonardo suffered a stroke and died on May 2.

Glossary

Verrocchio pronounced ver-ō´-kee-ō

sfumato pronounced sfū-mah´-tō

Lodovico pronounced lō-dō-vee´-kō

sarcophagus a stone coffin

Vatican the group of buildings that make up Vatican City, the residence of the pope and the seat of government of the Roman Catholic Church

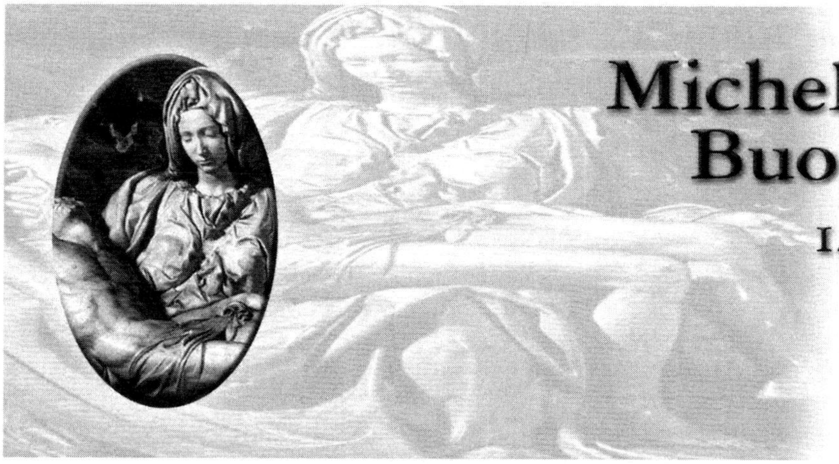

Michelangelo Buonarroti
1475 – 1564

MICHELANGELO BUONARROTI was born on March 6, 1475, in the town of Caprese, Italy. The art historian Berenson calls him perhaps the greatest of the artistic giants of whom so many were born in the fifteenth century. The artist's family may have come from nobility, though it was a distant relationship and not proven. His father was the mayor of the town. When Michelangelo was six years old, the family moved to Florence.

Michelangelo was a small, not particularly handsome or happy child. He liked to draw more than he liked going to school. Since being an artist was considered just a step above being a common laborer, his father was not pleased at his son's penchant for drawing. Finally, when Michelangelo was 13, his father brought him to be an apprentice to Domenico **Ghirlandaio,** a well-known painter in Florence. The boy was to stay in that workshop for three years, and to be paid a total of 24 florins along with food and a place to live.

Since many art students were allowed to study sculpture and architecture in the Medici gardens, Michelangelo probably spent time there and copied some of the art. When Lorenzo de' Medici, whose family were rulers of Florence and patrons of the arts, decided to start a school of sculpture, Michelangelo was one of the apprentices sent to him by Ghirlandaio. Soon he was making statues, and Lorenzo took note of his ability and the quality of his work. He took Michelangelo to live in the palace. The student lived as one of the family, having meals with them and meeting the important people who were Lorenzo's guests. Michelangelo heard about literature, art, political discussions, and important new ideas.

Lorenzo de' Medici died in 1492 and Michelangelo went back to live with his family. During this time he studied anatomy by dissecting corpses at the hospital of Santo Spirito. Many artists were competing for work in Florence, so Michelangelo moved to Rome in 1496. He hoped to find more work there.

The artist's first known commission in Rome was to carve figures of Bacchus and Cupid for a banker named Iacopo Gallo. His most important work at this time is the famous *Pietà,* which is now in St. Peter's Basilica in the Vatican (see Figure 7). In this sculpture the Virgin Mary holds the body of Jesus, which has been taken down from the cross. She looks at him with gentle grief, love, and sorrow. Her beautiful face seems to be very young. Criticized for this, Michelangelo explained that Mary in her purity would not show the effects of aging. Her body and the drapery of her gown are exaggerated in size to hold the body of Christ. This remarkable sculpture brought fame and wealth to the artist. Since Michelangelo was now the chief means of support for his parents, the money was needed.

Michelangelo returned to Florence in 1501 and received a commission from the cathedral. A block of marble $13\frac{1}{2}'$ in length but irregular in shape was available. Another sculptor had already done tentative work on the block. That commission was for a "male statue called Il Gigante." Michelangelo carved his *David* from this marble, using its entire length. When it was finished two and a half years later, the decision of where to place it was left to the artist. He chose a spot in front of the Palazzo Vecchio. Moving it from his workshop near the cathedral took 40 men four days; 21 were needed to put it in place. (In 1873 it was moved to the Accademia delle Belle Arti in Florence to protect it from erosion.)

The sculpture shows us David ready to face the giant Goliath. His sling is over his shoulder. Michelangelo talked of removing the stone on which he worked to release the figure within the block. The figure he found within this block does not have the larger, more bulging muscles we see in the artist's later work.

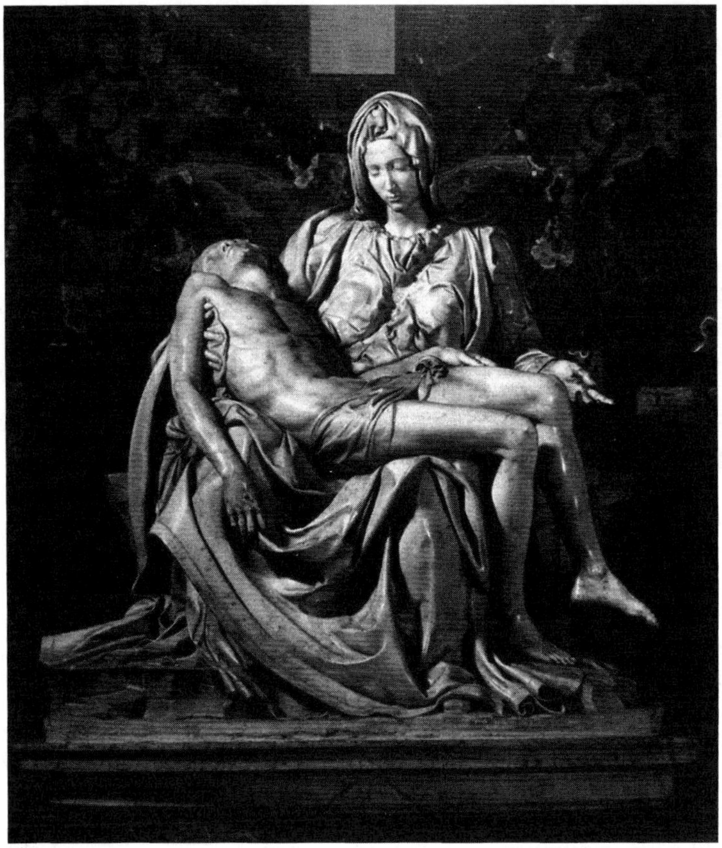

Figure 7
Pietà, 1498–1500
Michelangelo Buonarroti

During the two and a half years that Michelangelo worked on the *David,* he also worked on other, smaller statues. His first commission as a painter is thought to have been the *Holy Family,* painted in a round format. He was invited to paint a mural in the Hall of the Great Council of the Palazzo Vecchio, just opposite a space where Leonardo da Vinci was also to paint a corresponding mural. Since Michelangelo did not like Leonardo, it was probably with great satisfaction that he left this assignment undone. Instead, he went to Rome to do sculpture for Pope Julius II.

Michelangelo and Pope Julius II had much in common. They both had bad tempers, were difficult to work for or with, did not like to compromise, and were proud men. The pope wanted to plan for a tomb to hold his body when he died. Michelangelo suggested a monument 27 feet long and 18 feet wide with space for 40 statues. It would use a great amount of marble and cost a lot of money. When the money to pay him was not available, Michelangelo went back to Florence and worked on the mural he had agreed to paint. By 1508 the pope had recalled him to Rome and insisted that he now paint the ceiling of the Sistine Chapel, leaving the monument sculpture for the time being. Michelangelo did not want to do this new work. He considered himself a sculptor, not a painter. He suspected his enemies were responsible for his being chosen for the ceiling painting.

However, Michelangelo needed the money, and also felt that he should obey the pope. He hired five men to help put up the **scaffolding** and to measure and plan the spaces where the paintings would be done. A cartoon, which is the drawing or plan for a painting, was made for each segment of the ceiling. The cartoons were placed face down on the wet plaster to transfer the lines, and then each part was painted. The men hired to help were only kept long enough to get the work begun. Michelangelo did not work well with others and preferred to follow his own ideas. He worked on the ceiling for over four years. The ceiling is part of a barrel **vault** construction with flat space at the top. It is believed that the painter had to work lying on his back, though some scholars now believe he painted while standing on the scaffold, his head tilted upward. In any case, it had to have been very uncomfortable. The lighting was poor. It was a very difficult task, both physically and artistically.

The Chapel is like a large hall with a curved ceiling, flattened at the top; when the painting was completed, however, the ceiling appeared to be higher and more open to the sky. The architecture and window spaces created sections for the paintings. The lower walls had been decorated by other artists earlier, using themes from the life of Christ and of Moses. Michelangelo used stories and people from the Old Testament, from the creation of man onward (see Figure 8). In both his sculpture and his painting, he used the human body as the focus for his art. The figures in the Chapel ceiling show his genius and his unsurpassed skill in portraying the human body.

When the Sistine Chapel was finished, Michelangelo returned to the task of the sculptures for the tomb of Julius II, who died a few months after the chapel ceiling was completed. The project was reduced in size; the final version was a wall tomb featuring the figure of Moses in the center surrounded by other biblical figures.

Each succeeding pope wanted this famous artist to work for him. Besides the churchmen, there were princes and others with wealth competing for Michelangelo's services. Only the man's great genius could have made people put up with his ill temper and impatience. Michelangelo really cared only for his work. He often ate only whatever was lying about and often slept in his work clothes. Even though he was believed to be wealthy, he seemed miserly. He wore his clothing until it was old and falling apart. He was suspicious of others. He felt he had more enemies than probably was the case, even in that city of competing artists.

In 1535 Michelangelo was appointed chief architect, sculptor, and painter at the Vatican. A fresco behind the altar of the Sistine Chapel was one of his last works. He was then 60 years old. The size of the painting was to be 66' by 33'. This painting was done while reforms were taking place in the Catholic Church. There were some criticisms of the number of nude figures in the painting. Michelangelo responded by painting likenesses of some of the critics into the section of souls in eternal damnation! The tumult of the *Last Judgment* may tell us of the painter's increased religious concerns as he grew older. In this painting, as in his other works, the human body is the

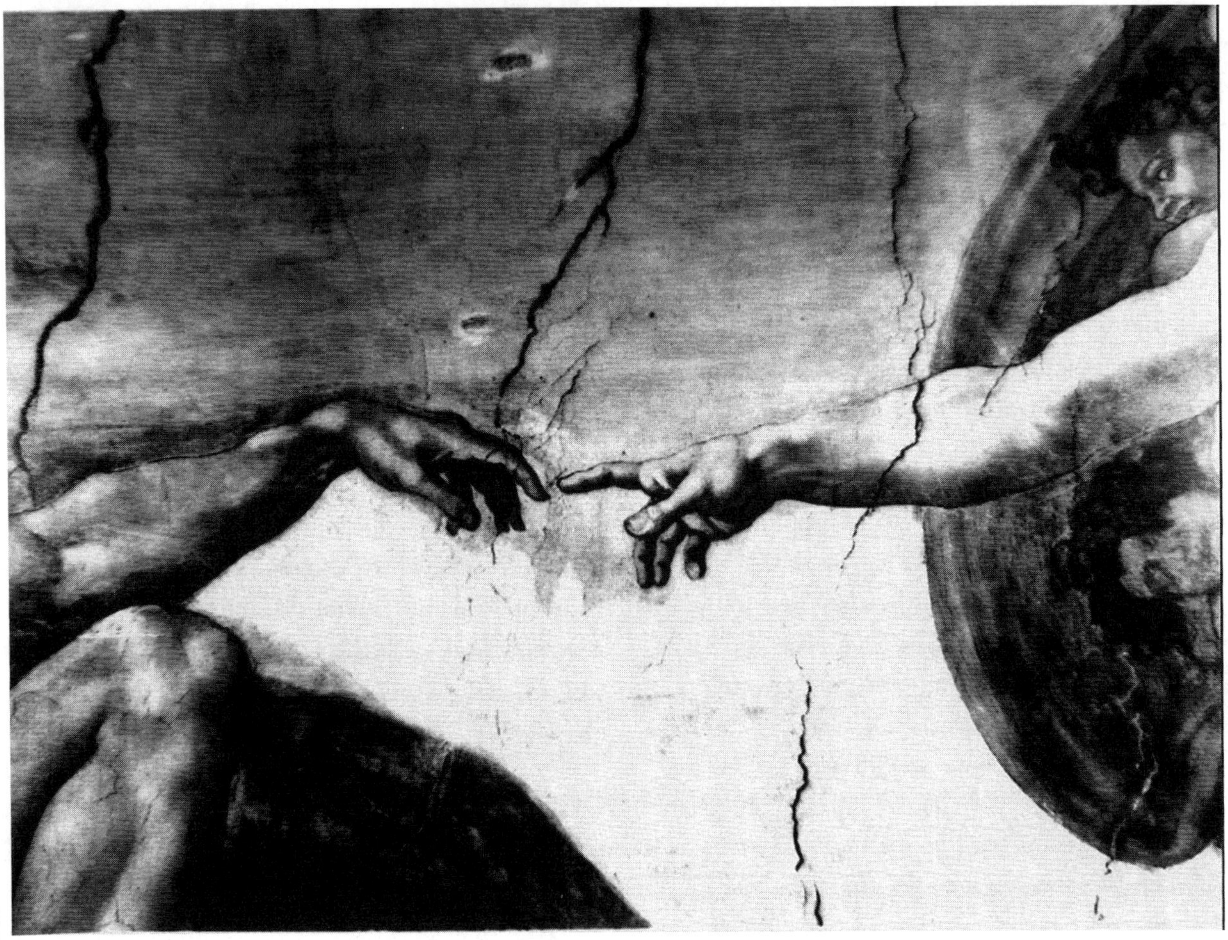

Figure 8
The Creation of Adam (detail), 1508–1512
Michelangelo Buonarroti

medium of expression. He used the human form to tell of the joys and terrors that people experienced in the final judgment.

Michelangelo stayed on at the Vatican until his death. His last sculpture was the *Pietà Rondanini*. Some believe it shows a new sculpture style. However, its unfinished appearance may simply show us the work of a very tired, 89-year-old man who would die within a few days. He died in February 1564, and was buried in the Church of Santa Croce in Florence.

On June 16, 1980, the restoration of the frescoes in the Sistine Chapel began. The work began on the ceiling. Next came the wall where the *Last Judgment* was painted. On that first morning in June, a scaffolding was put up. Gianluigi Colalucci, the head of the restoration team, touched a small area of the painting with a moist cloth. To everyone's amazement, a strong yellow color was visible through the gummy layer of dirt!

Colalucci had worked at the Vatican Museums for 20 years. Then he was assigned to lead a small group in restoring Michelangelo's paintings in the Sistine Chapel. There were different opinions about doing the project. In the past, other attempts to restore the paintings had been made. The paintings had ended up the worse for it. Some believed the natural process of aging should be allowed to continue. Others thought the latest scientific methods should be used. Then the original appearance of the paintings could be restored.

Three men worked with Colalucci. Each worked on a separate section. The technique used by Michelangelo was *buon fresco.* This means painting on wet plaster with water-based paint. Painting on dry plaster is called *secco*. Most of the Chapel paintings were done on wet plaster. The plaster mixture was made up of three parts volcanic ash and one part lime. Only enough plaster for one day's work was mixed at a time. This was because it was essential for the paint and the plaster to dry together. In some areas, Michelangelo had used *secco.* Perhaps the paintings came through time and abuse so well because the fresco technique was used; fresco is one of the most durable of methods.

Some areas of the *Last Judgment* were allowed to remain in their repainted state. The Council of Trent, under Pope Pius IV, had convened to reform problems within the Church. The Council objected to the unclothed figures in the Sistine Chapel, a religious setting. In 1564 a commission was appointed to see that the "indecent nudes" and a "thousand heresies" be corrected. Clothes or draperies were painted over the offensive areas. In the restoration process, there was a question as to whether these later cover-ups should be removed. It was decided to leave the sixteenth-century draperies, since they were a part of the history of the Chapel, but to remove any later ones. Chemical analyses of the pigments determined the dates of the later painted drapes.

Laboratory tests were done at every stage. The work was very slow and detailed. Layers of dirt, animal glues that had attracted black fungi, and tiny tears in the film of the ancient pigments were only a few of the problems. A data bank was set up to keep a record of any future substance damage. An air-conditioning system was installed to regulate incoming air. It changes the 10,000 cubic centimeters of air 1.7 times an hour. The air coming from the outside is filtered to remove pollutants. The temperature is kept to 18–25°C. The relative humidity is kept at 50–60 percent. The extensive information accumulated throughout the restoration will be invaluable in other restoration work, and should result in better ways to prevent damage to other precious art.

The original colors have appeared in the Sistine Chapel as though a veil had been removed, as indeed it had.

Glossary

Michelangelo Buonarroti pronounced mik-el-an´ge-lo bwo-nar-ro´ti

Ghirlandaio pronounced geer-lan-dah´yo

scaffolding a raised platform or framework placed as a temporary structure for workers

vault a space covered by an arched structure

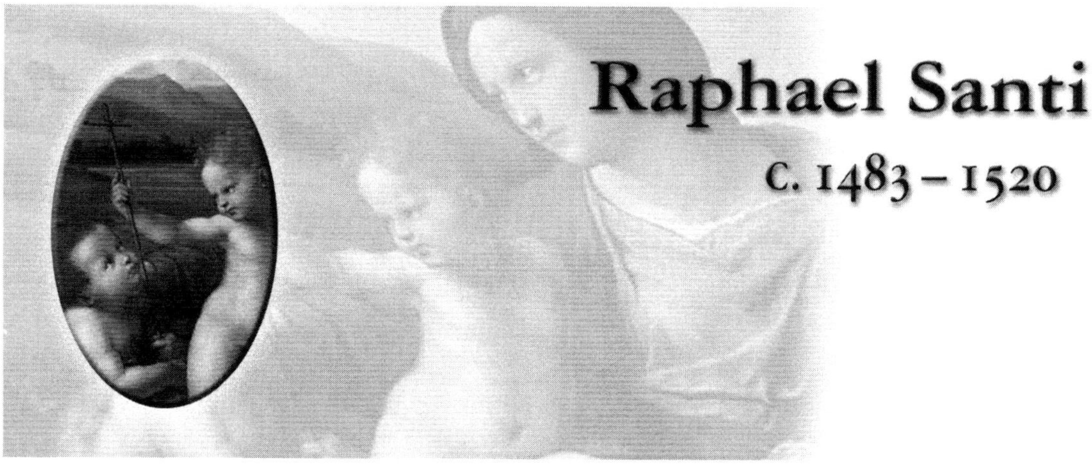

Raphael Santi

c. 1483 – 1520

Raffaello Santi, whom we know as **Raphael,** was born in **Urbino,** Italy, in 1483. His father, Giovanni Santi, was a painter who was probably popular in Urbino. Raphael must have met and known other painters who came to his father's workshop. The city of Urbino and the palace of its duke were gathering places for people interested in literature, arts, and learning. Giovanni Santi was often a guest at the palace, and it is thought that his son went with him. The young Raphael was exposed to some of the best art of the period and to the ideas of those who gathered for discussions. His father is thought to have been Raphael's first painting teacher. He died when Raphael was 11.

At 17 Raphael went to Perugia, the capital of the province of Umbria, to work as an apprentice. His master was Pietro Vannucci, known as **Perugino.** The artist was a friend of Raphael's late father, and had also been an apprentice in the workshop of Verrocchio with Leonardo. At this time he had a busy and popular painter's workshop with several apprentices and other painters to help get commissions done. Raphael did the usual work of an apprentice. He had to help prepare the paints and the panels, copy drawings, and perform other chores. He learned the styles of other artists quickly. Vasari says that Raphael could paint so much like Perugino that it was not possible to tell one from the other. Such was the job of an apprentice; the more he could paint as his master did, the better.

Raphael began to get commissions, most of which were from churches. Two from this period are the *Assumption* and *Coronation of the Virgin,* which now hangs in the Vatican, and the *Crucifixion,* now at the National Gallery in London. His painting style at this time imitated and reflected Perugino's quiet, rather sweet and graceful figures.

By 1503, Raphael had worked on commissions in Perugia and Urbino and had been to Florence. In the fall of 1504, however, he apparently decided to establish himself in Florence to study. Florence was a center of art. All the latest ideas about the use of color, new methods for using oil paint instead of egg tempera, the use of composition, new methods of perspective, and more were discussed and argued. Young Michelangelo's giant statue of David was being set into place. Raphael must have seen works by Leonardo, Michelangelo,

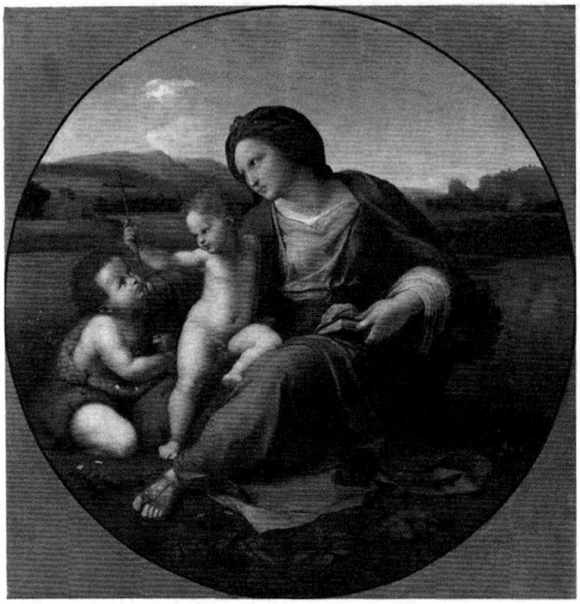

Figure 9
The Alba Madonna, c. 1510
Raphael Santi

and other artists whose work and ideas were the talk of the art community. He studied anatomy, using dissection to help him learn how the parts of the body worked. He made sketches of other artists' work. Sometimes he went back to Perugia or Urbino to finish work or to begin new commissions. One of the first paintings Raphael did in Florence was *Saint George and the Dragon* (see Color Plate 2).

Raphael's personality contributed to his professional progress. While Michelangelo was aloof and suspicious, and Leonardo was preoccupied with his many ideas and inventions, Raphael was friendly and comfortable with people. Perhaps his childhood in Urbino, meeting artists and nobility as he accompanied his father, helped him to find his place easily with others. He was modest about his abilities and eager to learn more. He was able to work while avoiding involvement in the political problems, violence, and turmoil in Italy, which continued throughout this time.

During these early years in Florence, Raphael began his series of many paintings of the Madonna and Child. Among these were the *Madonna del Granduca, La Belle Jardiniere,* the *Madonna of the Meadow,* the *Madonna del Cardellino,* the *Madonna del Baldacchino,* and *The Alba Madonna* (see Figure 9). He had seen the use of sfumato by Leonardo, and adopted that technique for his own work. He worked with the problem of color and its use in softening the edges of forms to avoid a sharp edge. Raphael was able, since his apprentice days with Perugino, to copy the style of other artists. But he was also able to take those techniques, sort out the ones that suited him, and make them a part of his own style.

The art historian Berenson calls Raphael a great "space-composer" because of his arrangements and groupings of forms. The two best examples of this skill are the *Disputa* and the *School of Athens,* which are among the paintings done in the Vatican's Stanza della Segnatura.

When Raphael was about 26, Pope Julius II commissioned him to decorate a series of rooms in the Vatican. The theme was to unite the Church, religious teachings, classical ideas, the humanism of the Renaissance, literature, and philosophy. The two paintings mentioned above are part of this commission. In the *Disputa,* the figures represent God the Father at the top in a heavenly group with Christ, Mary, and John the Baptist at the next level. Below them and on both sides are angels, saints, and biblical figures. The groups at the lower part of the mural are made up of various Christian figures, popes, saints, and writers. The message of the painting tells of the teachings of the Church concerning the **Eucharist.** Steps are used as a device for moving the figures back into space in the lower part. The heavenly groups are arranged on cloud-like forms, curved to fit, and repeat the curve of the frame around the whole mural.

In the *School of Athens,* the philosophers of the Golden Age of Greece are arranged in an architectural setting. Steps are used here also to help compose the groups of people. Plato and Aristotle occupy the center, framed by an arch. Others are in clusters of four or five, separate, yet part of the whole.

The style of the figures in these murals reminds us that at this time Michelangelo was also in Rome working on the Sistine Chapel. There is a story of Raphael's being taken secretly to see the Sistine paintings while the work was in progress. Michelangelo is said to have been very angry. The legend is that the two were enemies, but others say that they probably admired each other's work.

As Raphael worked in Rome, he collected friends and admirers. He lived well and was stylishly dressed. Sometimes he gave away paintings to friends, and he helped struggling artists. He liked beautiful women and once said that the women he painted were a composite, or combination, of the best features of many women he'd known.

When Pope Julius II died, he was followed by Leo X. Both men had found Raphael's good temper and easy disposition far more pleasing than Michelangelo's prickly temperament. Leo X spent the Church's money more extravagantly than did his predecessor. He loved art and continued to fund commissions for various artists' work. Before long, however, the vast treasury of the Church began to disappear. Leo X was ready to use almost any means to collect funds. Raphael's portrait of him, done in 1518, is not a flattering one; it may reflect the problems the pope was experiencing.

Raphael had become the leading artist of Rome. His commissions came from wealthy private citizens as well as from the Church. At the same time that he worked on the murals for the Vatican, he also did a number of other paintings. His portrait *Bindo Altoviti* (see Figure 10) dates from this period. He had a well-organized workshop and many assistants. Art historians debate the later works of Raphael. Some may have been done with quite a bit of help from his assistants. Raphael was also assigned less serious work by the pope, such as painting a portrait of the pontiff's pet elephant.

Raphael's last years were busy ones. His last work was left unfinished. It was the *Transfiguration* for the Cathedral of Narbonne. He began work on it in 1517. In the spring of 1518 he became very ill with a high fever and died on April 6. He was only 35 years old. All the people who knew him mourned his death. He was considered the greatest painter of his time.

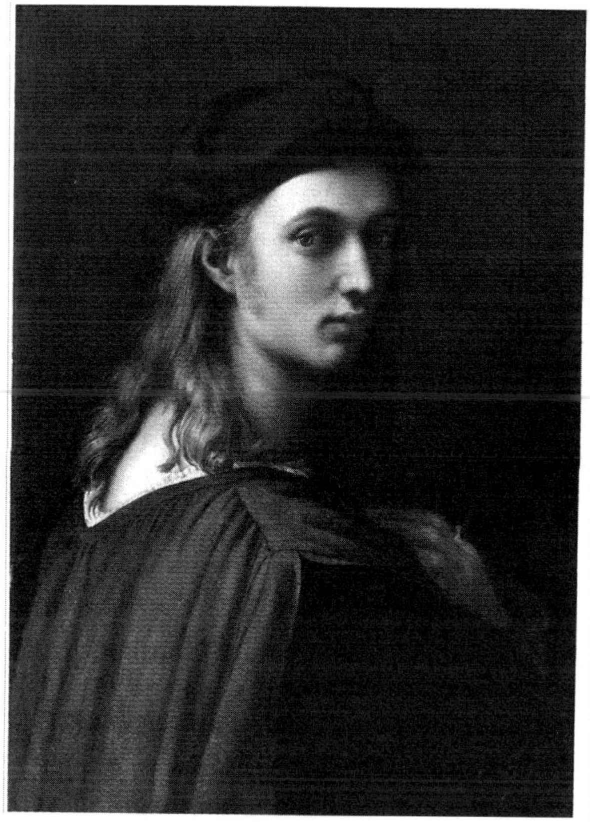

Figure 10
Bindo Altoviti, c. 1512
Raphael Santi

Glossary

Raphael pronounced raf-a-el´

Urbino pronounced ur-bee´-no

Perugino pronounced pear-oo-ge´-no

Eucharist the sacrament of the Lord's Supper, or the Mass, in Christian faith

Great Artists of Northern Europe

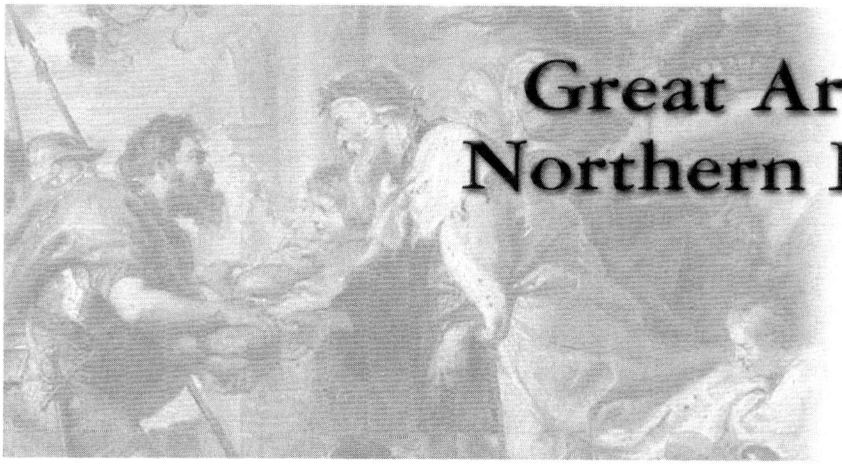

From Italy at the height of the Renaissance we will now move back to the early fifteenth century and to northern Europe. Just as art flourished in the south, new styles and new artists were developing in the north.

In the north of Europe, growth of trade and commerce, small and large wars, political turmoil, and recurrent plagues were occurring just as in the southern countries. The duchy of Burgundy occupied about the same area that we know as the Netherlands and Belgium today. It was part of France. The king gave the territory to his son as a reward for bravery in battle. The Duke of Burgundy added to the land by marriage. (Marriages of kings and the nobility were usually arranged in order to benefit a country. The bride's father had to give land or money or both to the groom. This was known as a *dowry.* This custom was carried on in the lower classes as well. If the couple were in love, so much the better; but that wasn't important then. Marrying for love is a relatively recent custom.)

The cities of Bruges, Brussels, Tournai, and Ghent became centers of art as well as centers of trade and banking. Philip the Good became Duke of Burgundy in 1419. His government was one that encouraged the arts just as the Medici family had done in Florence.

Men who worked in manufacturing, trade, and banking belonged to guilds that regulated such businesses. Artists were organized into similar groups in order to regulate their products and the training of apprentices. We've studied such systems in the Italian cities. At the beginning of the Renaissance, an artist was considered to be a craftsman, and ranked with other craftsmen on the social scale. By the end of the Renaissance many artists were considerably higher in rank than this and were highly respected. You will notice that many of the artists we study were also good businessmen. They expected their work to earn money as well as respect. They ran workshops, trained apprentices, and usually lived well. The image of the "starving artist" who lived in a garret does not always apply to the great artists included in this book.

In the north, too, artists were commissioned to do work with religious subject matter for churches. Often, however, the commissions came from wealthy laymen and not from those directly connected with the Church. If the painting was a gift to a church, the donor who was paying for the work would ask to have his portrait included in the picture. This practice was much more common in the north than in Italy. Both laymen and churchmen were often painted beside the Madonna and Child. Besides religious commissions, sources of work for artists included portraits ordered by wealthy bankers, merchants, and the nobility.

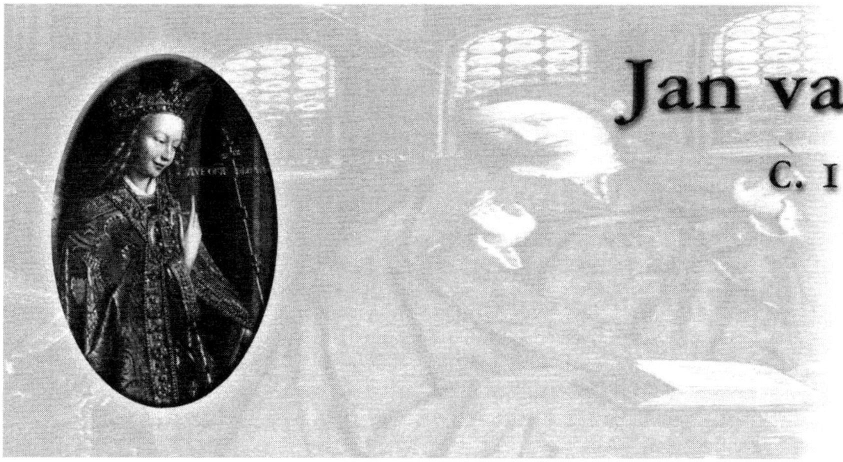

Jan van Eyck

c. 1390–1441

ONE IMPORTANT PAINTER of this period in northern Europe is **Jan van Eyck**. Jan is better known than his brother, Hubert (c. 1370–1426), who was older and also a painter. Information about Hubert's work is sketchy. Some art historians do not believe he existed. Jan's paintings, however, are usually signed and dated.

For many years the van Eyck brothers were given credit for inventing oil painting methods. Now, many historians believe that oil painting had been used during late medieval times in northern Europe. The van Eycks did use it and developed glowing, exciting color. Painting at this time included a new realism. Forms were carefully detailed. Edges were smooth and visible. Michelangelo knew of the northern style and did not like it.

As with other artists, we learn much about the van Eycks through documents: letters, tax records, and other legal records. In May 1425, Jan settled in **Bruges** and was given the job of court painter to the duke, Philip the Good. He was given assignments other than painting by the duke. He became a trusted friend and served as a kind of ambassador, making trips to other countries. On two trips he made paintings of women with whom the duke was considering marriage. The second of these assignments was apparently successful, for the duke married Isabella of Portugal in July 1429.

As in the south, artists who were employed by rulers or other officials had many kinds of chores. Any decorative work needed was the artist's job. Festivals, pageants, processions, and the costumes and objects used for these activities were his job.

We don't know much about Jan van Eyck's personal life. He is believed to have been born in 1390. He did set up his own workshop in Bruges in about 1430, working on commissions for the duke and other patrons. He bought a comfortable house there and lived in Bruges until his death in 1441.

Some of the qualities of the painting done at this time should be considered. The van Eycks, as well as other artists, used a great deal of symbolism, especially in religious paintings. These symbols were understood by the people who came to church or saw the paintings in other places. Many of these symbols are visible in Jan van Eyck's *The Annunciation* (see Figure 11). For exam-

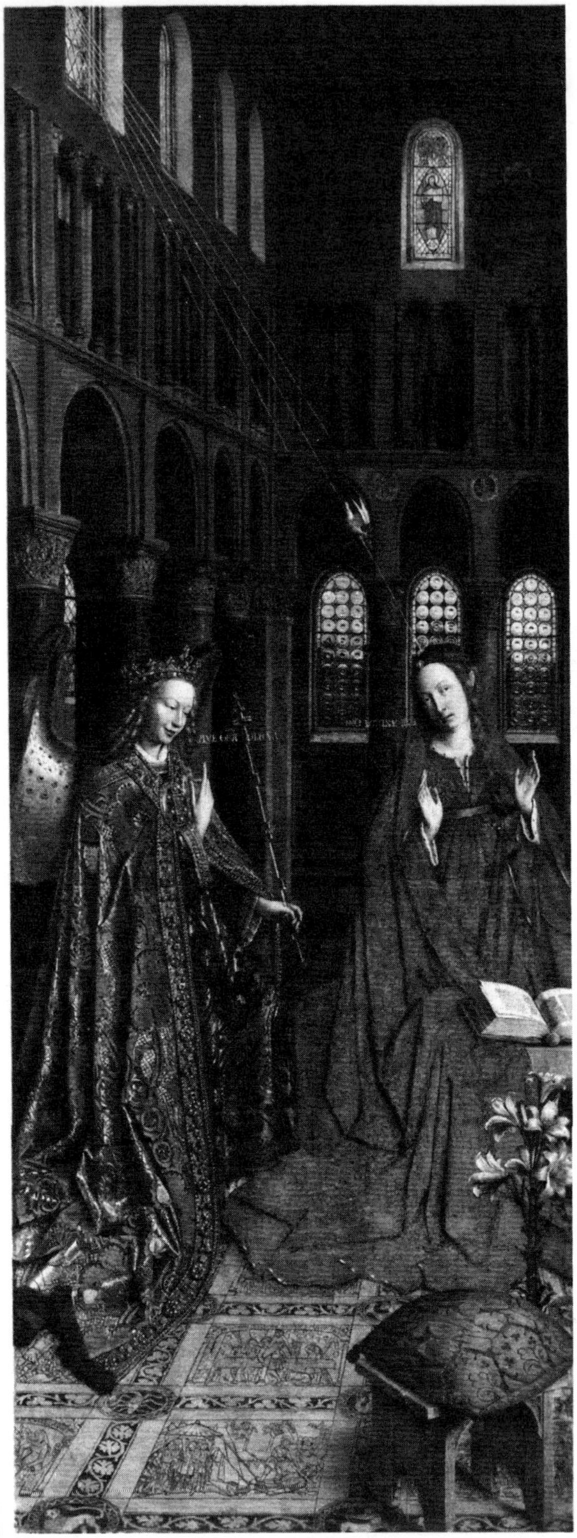

Figure 11
The Annunciation, c. 1434–1436
Jan van Eyck

ple, white lilies symbolized the Virgin Mary. The Virgin herself was a symbol of the Church. Three windows or arches in a religious painting stood for the Trinity. The direction of light or the use of a stream of light could mean light from heaven. A dog was the symbol of faithfulness. There were other symbols, some quite complicated. Our understanding of them is not always complete.

The use of oil paint made possible richly colored garments and elegant interiors. Broadly flowing fabric spilled out around the feet of human figures, particularly that of the Virgin. Landscapes became more realistic, with carefully worked details. Under Jan van Eyck's brush, the Christ Child became a more realistic baby, reaching for a book held by his mother, perhaps, or turning in her arms to look about. He looked much as babies do today. Northern painters before this time often painted the Christ Child as though he were a small, unclothed doll lying at Mary's feet.

The greatest work done by the van Eyck brothers is the Ghent Altarpiece. There is a message on its frame that calls Hubert the "greatest and most skilled artist" and says that Jan is "second in art" and was the one who finished the painting. It also gives credit to Jodocus Vyd for a donation that paid for completing the work. It is believed that Jan finished the painting after his brother died. The altarpiece is made up of panels that are hinged so that the outside panels can fold over the inner ones. (A group of three such panels is called a **triptych**; these were often used for paintings behind church altars.) When it is folded, one sees paintings on the outside panels; when it is unfolded, new scenes are visible. The painting is in the Cathedral of St. Bavon in Ghent, Belgium. The inscription gives May 6, 1432, as the date it was completed.

The outside panels are thought to have been done by Jan. They contain paintings of the donor,

Jodocus Vyd, and his wife Isabella. There is an Annunciation scene with Mary on one panel and the announcing angel on another. Two figures, John the Baptist and John the Evangelist, are painted in **grisaille.** (Grisaille is a painting style in which values of gray are used, making pictures that resemble relief sculpture.) In the upper panels other biblical figures are found.

There are twelve inside panels, five below and seven above. The lower panels contain saints, martyrs, officials of the Church, holy hermits, religious pilgrims, knights of Christ, and judges. The upper six panels are arranged three on each side of the center panel, which contains God the Father. The Virgin Mary is to his right and John the Baptist is on the left. The remaining sections feature angels, musicians and singers, and Adam and Eve.

One of Jan van Eyck's most famous paintings is a wedding portrait of Giovanni Arnolfini and his wife (see Figure 12). It has been called a marriage document because an inscription on the wall above a mirror reads "Jan van Eyck was here, 1434." In the mirror we see the artist; thus the painting features him as a witness to the marriage. Arnolfini, a wealthy merchant of Lucca, stands in the center with his wife. Symbols in the painting include: a dog for faithfulness, a burning candle for Christ, who sees all, the groom having taken off his sandals because he stands on holy ground, and the chair with a carving of St. Margaret, who is the patron saint of childbirth. The actual size of the painting is 23½" × 32¼". The exquisite detail in so small a space is extraordinary. It hangs in the National Gallery in London.

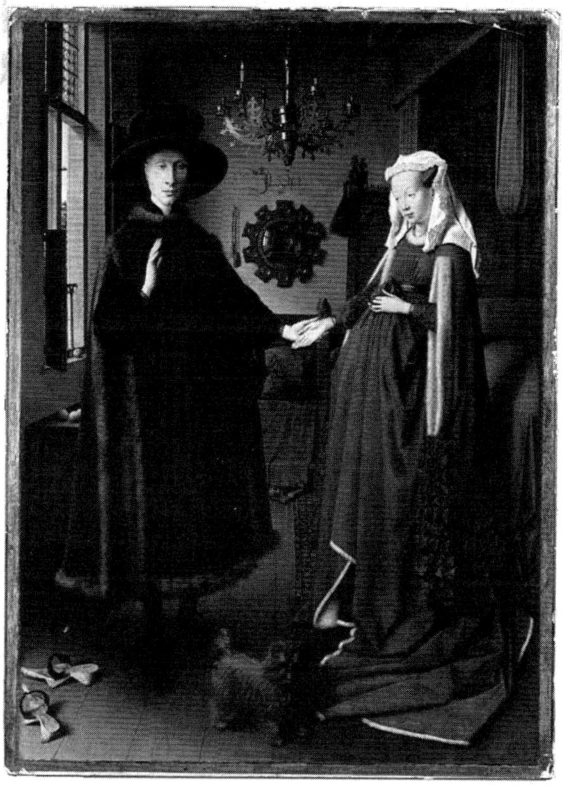

Figure 12
The Arnolfini Marriage, c. 1434
Jan van Eyck

Two other well-known paintings by Jan van Eyck are *A Man in a Turban* and a portrait of Margaret van Eyck, Jan's wife. The strong resemblance between the people in these two paintings makes one wonder if the man was his wife's brother or another relative.

During his lifetime, Jan van Eyck's work was known and appreciated in many other countries. It is still admired for the astonishing detail, the glowing color, and the expressiveness of the portraits. Van Eyck contributed to the increased use of landscape and detailed interiors, and the further development of oil as a painting medium.

Glossary

Jan van Eyck pronounced yahn vahn ike
Bruges pronounced broozh
triptych pronounced trip´-tik
grisaille pronounced gree-zī´

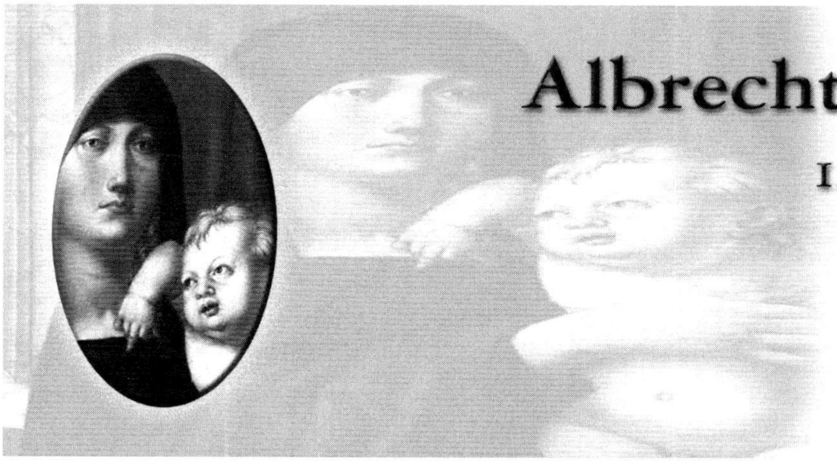

Albrecht Dürer

1471 – 1528

To learn about the next northern painter, we must move ahead to the late 1400s. The artist is Albrecht Dürer, considered to be Germany's finest artist. He is ranked with Raphael, Michelangelo, and Leonardo as one of the best of the Renaissance artists. Dürer was both a painter and a printmaker. He was born in Nuremberg in 1471.

Dürer's father, a goldsmith, came to Nuremburg in 1445. The city had become a free city some 20 years before that. It was located at about the center of what was then the Holy Roman Empire. It occupied the areas we now know as Germany, the Netherlands, and Belgium. At the time Dürer's father came to Nuremberg, the emperor was Frederick III. He was not a strong leader and there was much strife in many parts of the empire. It was a Roman Catholic country. The peasants who made up most of the population had to contend with recurring plagues, poor harvests, and political conflict. There were periodical peasant uprisings, but they left the people worse off than before. Many believed that on New Year's Day in 1500 the world would come to an end. Readings from accounts of the Last Judgment lent support to this belief.

The walled towns and cities gave people the most protection. Nuremberg was surrounded by a triple wall. The houses were small and the streets were narrow. However, it was a prosperous city for those times. It was a center for trade and commerce, and arts and crafts. The elder Dürer found work with the goldsmith Hieronymus Holper.

Later he married Holper's daughter, Barbara, and inherited the workshop. Goldsmithing required a variety of skills. A good goldsmith was not only a craftsman, but a designer. He designed not only jewelry but large and elaborate objects that were like sculpture. Expert ability in drawing and draftsmanship was necessary. Designs had to be carved on metal with the **burin,** an engraving tool. Dürer's father was an excellent craftsman, and became a prosperous goldsmith in his own right. He had commissions from the emperor as well as other important citizens.

Albrecht Dürer's parents had 18 children, many of whom did not survive past childhood. This was not unusual for those times. Albrecht was the second son, born on May 21, 1471. He went to school at St. Lorenz grammar school, and when old enough he was taken into his father's workshop as an apprentice. His older brother had died and it was up to Albrecht to learn the family craft. The family had bought a house not far from the busy workshop of Michael Wolgemut, a painter. It was also close to the printing shop of Anton Koberger, Albrecht's godfather. We can imagine the young Albrecht visiting both shops as he played in the neighborhood.

As his father's apprentice, Albrecht learned quickly and had great aptitude. At 13 he made his first existing self-portrait. It is done in silver-point—literally a pencil of silver—with which no erasing is possible. This work indicates what was to be expected in the future from this youngster. Folds of cloth, textures, and facial detail are done with remarkable clarity. Perhaps his father was not too surprised when Albrecht asked to be sent to a painter's workshop to be apprenticed. The work-shop of Wolgemut, just down the street, seemed the logical place. Dürer spent three years there, and wrote that he "learned well," though he had to "endure much from the shop boys." Wolgemut was a popular painter, and had a mass production system in his shop, with many workers making many paintings from his designs. Dürer learned the usual skills that painters' apprentices were taught, and also learned about woodcuts. This training, along with the experience in his father's shop, was to be valuable to him later. Both of these printmaking methods became true art forms in Dürer's hands.

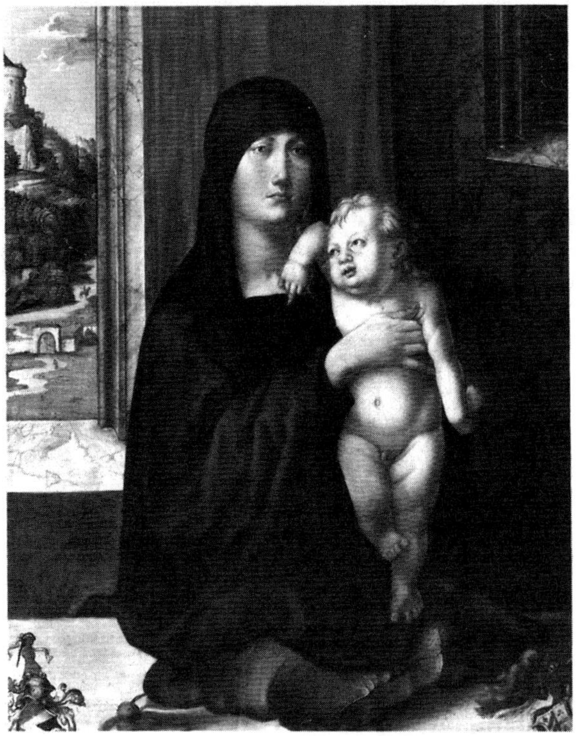

Figure 13
Madonna and Child, c. 1505
Albrecht Dürer

Printmaking was first known in Europe in the stamping of designs on fabrics. When papermak-ing came to Europe through Spain, printmakers discovered that both pictures and words could be printed on paper. The pictures (with or without words) were carved into wood blocks. Johann Gutenberg is credited with making individual movable letters. This made it possible to make many prints, rearranging the letters to make new pages. Printing the written word became a much faster process. Religious prints, hand-colored, were popular and sold well in the early fifteenth century. People who could not afford to buy paintings could easily afford printed pictures for their homes.

Since printmaking is an important part of Dürer's art, we will look at the different kinds of printmaking that were done in his time and are still used today. Woodcuts are a relief method by which the lines that are to print are left as a raised surface. The space around the area to print is cut away. The printing plate is then inked. Paper is laid on the top and it is run through a press.

Intaglio methods of printing include engrav-ing, drypoint, and etching. *Intaglio* means that the material to be printed is cut or carved *below* the surface of the printing plate, unlike the raised image of a woodcut. The early printmakers used lead for a printing plate. Later that metal was replaced by copper. The lines of the picture are cut into the metal plate in the engraving method, using a burin. The plate is inked and the ink is worked into the cut lines. The surface is then wiped clean, leaving the ink in the lines. The plate is put into a press. Damp paper is laid on the plate. The press forces the paper into the lines, where the inked picture is picked up. In drypoint the method is essentially the same, except that the lines are cut into the plate with a needle. In the etching process, the plate is first covered with a waxy coating. The lines are scratched through the coating to expose the metal. Then the plate is soaked in an acid solution long enough to allow the acid to eat into the metal where it is not protected by the coating. The plate is then cleaned, inked, and printed as an engraving.

Look carefully at a Dürer print. Think how difficult it must have been to cut those many, many delicate lines into either a metal plate or a piece of wood!

Among early engravers, Martin Schongauer was probably best known to Dürer. Schongauer was both a painter and an engraver. His workshop was in Colmer. He was one of the foremost engravers of the fourteenth century. Dürer knew and admired his work.

After four years in Wolgemut's shop, Dürer began the wandering phase of his career. He spent over a year and a half traveling. His route is not really known but his final destination was Colmer. He wanted to visit Schongauer. When he arrived he found that the man had died. His brothers were still in the workshop. They sent Dürer on to Basel, Switzerland, where another of the brothers lived. George Schongauer, who was a goldsmith, welcomed Dürer and gave him work. A woodcut block from this time still survives. The print shows St. Jerome pulling a thorn from the paw of a lion. It was used for the cover of a book of the saint's letters. From Basel, Dürer went on to Strasbourg. We do not know for whom he worked there. Some paintings are known to have been done while he lived there: a self-portrait in oil, and one in pen and ink.

Meanwhile, back in Nuremberg, Hans Frey, a prosperous metalwork craftsman, was talking to Dürer's father about arranging a marriage between Albrecht and his daughter Agnes. The Freys were a prominent family, and her **dowry** was generous. Such a marriage must have seemed to be a good thing to the elder Dürer. Albrecht returned to Nuremberg and married Agnes in July 1494.

From all accounts, it was not a happy marriage. Agnes was said to have had a sharp tongue, and she probably did not keep up with her handsome husband as he climbed the ladder of success. She may have expected a different, more ordinary husband, one more like her father in his metal workshop. Dürer's best friend, Willibald Pirckheimer, called Agnes "nagging, jealous, and shrewish." Agnes is said to have disliked Willibald as well.

At any rate, two months after his marriage, Dürer left Nuremberg alone to visit Italy and see Italian art and artists. He walked to Italy. His plan was to go to Venice, which was an important center of art at that time. We can be sure that he carried his sketching materials with him as he walked. He must have made hundreds of sketches of everything that caught his attention and interest. Some sketches and watercolors from this trip have survived. He loved animals and loved to draw them. He has been compared with Leonardo da Vinci. They had many interests in common. Both were interested in nature, and their drawings from nature reflected this interest. Both made studies of anatomy and of ways to develop systems for drawing people. Both looked for answers all their lives. Dürer has been called the "northern Leonardo."

The young man from Nuremberg was charmed and fascinated by the Venice he saw in October 1494. This city, built over water with canals as streets and with brightly decorated houses, brought people from many lands to its docks. Dürer filled his notebooks with sketches of people in oriental dress, animals, strange shellfish in the fish market, slaves, landscapes, and St. Mark's Cathedral.

In addition to the other wonders of Venice, Dürer saw the art of such Italians as Mantegna, and visited the studio of Giovanni Bellini and his brother Gentile. The two men ran their workshop with many assistants. Titian and Giorgione, two famous artists of the High Renaissance, were apprentices there at this time. Dürer may have also met them. He was allowed to sit in and work, making paintings and studying what others were doing. During this time Dürer became interested in landscape, both by itself and as a background for paintings and prints.

Dürer returned to Nuremberg in 1495 and opened his own workshop. An important new patron was the elector of the district of Saxony, Frederick the Wise. He commissioned a portrait and an altarpiece. Following these successful works, Dürer was asked to paint a Madonna for the chapel of the Haller family in Nuremberg. This was a very productive time for Dürer. Besides painting commissions he continued to make woodcuts and engravings. He made for himself a series of woodcuts illustrating the biblical story of the Apocalypse. It is one of his best-known works. The prints were published along with the biblical texts. Dürer was a religious man and was surely affected by the fears and events of the time. The Reformation, in which the Roman Catholic Church was divided, had not yet come about, but the storm clouds were on the horizon. Remember that many expected the world to end soon, and plagues often swept through parts of the country. These woodcuts may have been Dürer's reaction to the uncertainty of his world.

The Apocalypse series was popular and was sold throughout Europe. Dürer's fame spread. This was the first time that an artist had produced work without the help of a patron and had sold it through his own shop. After this he marketed other prints. His wife and even his mother sold his prints at local fairs.

Dürer's workshop was never short of work or of young men who wanted to work with him as apprentices. In addition to making prints, they were also busy designing articles for customers, including book illustrations. Dürer also worked on ways to show perspective, space, and depth in pictures.

Dürer was a popular citizen of Nuremberg and had friends among the most learned and sophisticated. A self-portrait done when he was 27 shows him as an elegant and fashionable gentleman. He was an affectionate son and wrote of his parents with great love and respect. He made several portraits of each of them. His father died in 1502 after a period of poor health. Dürer's own health had caused him some problems, and his father's death added to the burden.

In 1505 the artist went to Venice again, traveling in a more comfortable way this time, with horses, baggage, and prints to sell. On this visit he was received by the wealthy and the nobles. Some of the Venetian artists were plainly jealous of this now famous northerner. He was still warmly welcomed at Bellini's studio, however. Bellini greatly admired Dürer's work.

While in Venice Dürer received a commission for an altarpiece for a church that most of the Germans in Venice attended. The painting is called *The Feast of the Rose Garlands* (rose garlands were used to symbolize the **rosary**). The Virgin and Child are putting crowns of roses on the heads of Emperor Maximilian and Pope Julius II. Other

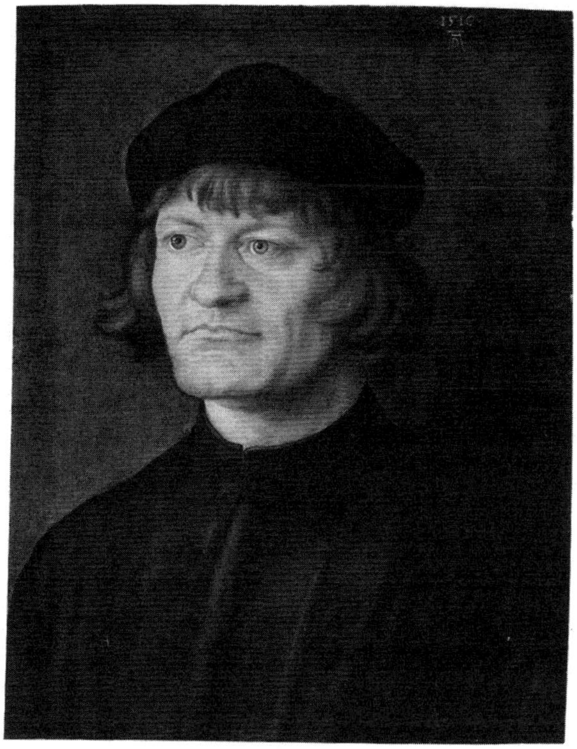

Figure 14
Portrait of a Clergyman, c. 1505
Albrecht Dürer

local figures are in the picture, Dürer himself included. Cherubs distribute garlands to them as they kneel around the throne.

Because Dürer wrote letters that have been saved and also kept notebooks recording his business dealings and activities, we know much more about him than we do about some other artists. Letters to his friend Pirckheimer from Venice tell us about his work in Venice, about shopping for items to bring home, and about his pleasure in living and working there. He enjoyed the mild climate. When he was offered a pension to become a resident of Venice it must have been difficult to refuse. Dürer said, "Here, I am a gentleman. At home, a nobody." In Nuremberg, artists were still regarded as craftsmen, not gentlemen.

Dürer was influenced by the art he saw in Venice—the art of the Italian High Renaissance. In particular he was influenced by the Venetians' use of color as a way to model a form. In a painting of a young woman done in Venice, we see the face modeled with soft color, instead of with the sharper edges and shading seen in northern art. His *Madonna and Child* and *Portrait of a Clergyman,* painted about this time, show this influence as well (see Figures 13 and 14).

When Dürer returned to Nuremberg in 1507, he had earned enough money to clear up some major debts and to buy a large house, which still stands in the city. He lived there with his wife and his mother, and spent the rest of his life there. He was chosen to be a member of the Grand Council, a group of city leaders who served as advisors. Though they had no real power, it was an honor to be a member. He was hardly a "nobody" in Nuremberg.

He had earlier done a woodcut called *The Martyrdom of the Ten Thousand,* and now he was commissioned to make a painting of the same subject. It is now in Vienna. The artist and his friend Pirckheimer are shown in the center, acting as observers of the massacre of 10,000 Christians by a king of Persia. It was a popular theme at this time. The landscape of rocks and cliffs is covered with the victims and the soldiers, much more full of forms and activity than usual Dürer compositions. This certainly gave him ample opportunity to work on his formula for drawing the human form.

In 1507 he began work on *Ascension and Coronation of the Virgin,* in which we find the famous "praying hands." This image has been taken from the painting and reproduced in many sizes and colors and on countless kinds of objects. The hands were first drawn as a **study** for the painting and were used in the same form in the painting. The original painting was lost in a fire, and only a copy is left.

After painting the *Adoration of the Trinity* in 1511 for a chapel in Nuremberg, Dürer did little more painting and turned back to engraving and woodcuts. He may never have developed his painting as he might have; he continued to include elements of etching and engraving.

In his prints he did not have the advantage of color values, and he looked for ways to develop tones and values through the use of line. He had become a court painter for Maximilian I. While serving him, Dürer was in charge of a monumental print: a triumphal arch. It was made of 192 blocks of wood and measured 11½' × 9¾'. Like a Roman arch, it contains story pictures. But while Roman arches were actually pieces of architecture, this arch was a giant woodcut print. The emperor wanted pictures of his life and his ancestors. All the surfaces are covered with complicated symbols, pictures, and decoration. Assisted by other artists, Dürer added a procession print. The entire work combined was on a sheet 60 yards long.

Dürer had some difficulty collecting payment from the emperor. The pension and additional money promised him were to be paid by the Nuremberg government. The city refused to pay both. Dürer worried about money (particularly money for his old age), and he had counted on the pension. A new emperor, Charles V, was to be crowned in Aachen. Dürer decided to go to see him and ask for payment of the debts.

For the first time, Dürer took his wife with him. He also took woodcuts and engravings to sell. They were gone for a year. Dürer kept a record of the trip: places he visited, purchases made, and gifts that were given to him. He made sketches, of course, of people, animals, and other things he wished to remember. (The modern traveler carries a camera, but Dürer carried his sketchbook. Probably a modern artist does the same.)

The Dürers traveled down the Rhine River and arrived in Aachen for the coronation of Charles V in October 1520. Dürer was recognized as a celebrity wherever he went and met the famous people in each city. He succeeded in his goal: The new emperor renewed his life pension and paid the money owed him. He met other artists and saw well-known works of art, including some by Jan van Eyck and some by Michelangelo that had been bought and brought north. He was home in 1521.

At this time Martin Luther was protesting practices within the Church that would lead to the Reformation. While Dürer had sympathy for Luther's beliefs, he did not break with the Roman Catholic Church.

In what were to be his last years, Dürer's work included two panel paintings of the four apostles for the city of Nuremberg. The paintings show the slow change in painting style from his early works. The forms are more softly modeled by the use of color tones, influenced as we saw earlier, by the Italian style. Nuremberg had become Protestant, and there are quotations below the apostles in Luther's translation from their writings.

The last year or two of his life were spent on his writing. He published a book on the teaching of measurements, and was working on *Four Books of Human Proportions* when he died. Pirckheimer completed the books. They were published in seven languages and were a popular text for artists.

Dürer died on April 6, 1528. He left a great number of prints, known and enjoyed by rich and poor alike in his lifetime and in the centuries since. Besides his paintings, over a thousand of his drawings remain.

Glossary

burin an engraver's steel cutting tool

intaglio pronounced in-tal-yo; method of print-making

dowry property, money, or goods that the bride's family provides for the man whom she marries

rosary a set of beads used in the Roman Catholic faith for counting a prescribed number of prayers. In Dürer's painting *The Feast of the Rose Garlands,* rose garlands symbolized the rosary beads.

study drawing, sketch, or painting of an idea or of objects that the artist may use in a final work

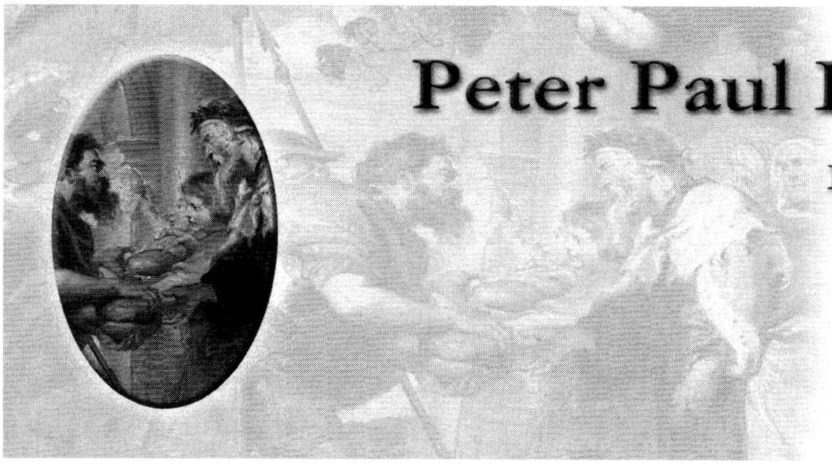

Peter Paul Rubens

1577–1640

Now we'll move ahead another hundred years to June 28, 1577. On that day Peter Paul Rubens was born in Westphalia, Germany. His family had come there to escape religious persecution. This was the time of the Reformation, and his father, Jan, had been interested in the ideas of a Protestant leader, John Calvin. The family had come from Antwerp, which was under Spanish (and therefore Roman Catholic) rule. When Rubens was a year old, the family moved to Cologne, where they lived until the death of the father when Peter Paul was ten years old. The mother then moved with her children back to Antwerp, where the Rubens' ancestors had lived for two centuries.

The Netherlands had been torn by a revolution against Spain since 1555. The northern provinces had broken away under the leadership of William of Orange and had formed a confederation of provinces. The southern part remained under Spanish rule. For years Spain tried to recapture the northern provinces. When Maria Rubens and her family came back to Antwerp in 1587, the city still showed the ruin of the earlier war. There were destroyed houses and buildings. The countryside was dotted with deserted farms. The trade that had made Antwerp a wealthy city had gone to safer ports.

Gradually things became better. Spain contributed by making Antwerp the center for financing its armies in the north. The Dutch cooperated by allowing more ships to reach Antwerp, so shipping began to come back. Farmers began to work the land, and even the arts were called upon to help restore the beauty of the destroyed churches.

The Rubens home was one in which love and affection, learning and literature were provided along with food and clothing. When trouble came, the family worked together to help each other. Peter Paul attended the school of Verdonck, who was a well-known scholar. When he was 13, his sister Blandina was to be married. She needed a dowry, which created a financial problem for the family. To help out, both Peter Paul and his brother Philip stopped their schooling and looked for work. Peter Paul was placed as a page in the house of the countess of Lalaing. For a boy from a good family, this was an opportunity to work his way up, going on to service with a nobleman and to government work. While the time spent there was of value to Rubens later when he served as a **diplomat,** he knew even then that he wanted to be a painter.

It was agreed that Peter Paul should be apprenticed to Tobias Verhaecht, a painter of small landscapes. Rubens moved on to the workshop of Adam van Noort, where he stayed for four years. Next he went to Otto van Veen, who took the Latin form of his name, Vaenius. Vaenius had studied in Italy and was a member of a group of artists called the Romanists who had all studied there. Through this master Rubens was introduced to the themes and techniques of Italian painting. Vaenius was also famous for his knowledge of the symbols used in paintings. Early in van Eyck's paintings, we saw his use of symbols in art. In Rubens' time, symbols were still used extensively to give a message, or lesson through pictures. People enjoyed the challenge of figuring out what the symbols meant.

Rubens apparently was not a child prodigy. There are no early self-portraits like those of Albrecht Dürer. He knew he wanted to be an artist and patiently worked to acquire the skills needed. When he was 21, he was made a member of the Guild of St. Luke, an artist's guild, though he stayed on in the Vaenius shop.

In May 1600 Rubens left for Italy. His older brother, Jan-Baptist, had studied there. His master, Vaenius, had spent time in Italy. Many artists considered study in Italy an important part of their training. Rubens spoke Italian fluently and also read and wrote Latin.

While Rubens lived in Venice, the Duke of Mantua heard of his work. Rubens was offered and accepted the job of court painter to the duke. As usual with this job, artists were to be available for any kind of creative work the court needed. It was common practice for paintings to be copied by other painters. (It was quite acceptable to do this. In our time the camera can make copies of paintings; perhaps making copies served the function of a camera. Also, making copies of good art has long been considered a way for a beginning artist to learn.) As Rubens traveled about making copies of paintings the duke wanted, he had the chance to see Italian art and study it firsthand. Rubens' own work was forever influenced by the Renaissance and **Baroque** art that he studied during his early years in Italy.

Rubens' first large church commission was for the Church of Santa Croce in Gerusalemme. Archduke Albert of the Netherlands asked him to paint three altarpieces for the chapel of St. Helena at the church. Rubens used the themes of the elevation of the cross as Christ is crucified, Christ with the crown of thorns, and St. Helena. The paintings are dramatic, full of movement and expression: the beginning of Rubens' Baroque style.

In March 1603 Rubens was sent to Spain by the duke to present gifts to the king. While there he was asked to paint the portrait of the Duke of Lerma. It was much admired at the court.

After his return from Spain, Rubens moved to Rome to share a house with his brother, Philip, who was to be the librarian for Cardinal Ascanio Colonna. It was an opportunity for Peter Paul to study the ancient Roman ruins with the help and information his brother provided. He also made illustrations for a book Philip was writing on Roman life. The book was later published by their friend Balthasar Moretus at the Plantin Press in Antwerp.

Rubens continued to receive commissions for work and his fame continued to spread. However, in the fall of 1608, his mother became ill, and Rubens immediately went back to Antwerp. His brother had gone back the summer before. While Rubens thought that he would surely return to Italy, this turned out to be his last stay. Arriving in Antwerp, he found that his mother had died. Before he could make the decision to go back to Italy, other events kept him at home. His brother Philip was to be married and he wanted to be there for the wedding. Then, the archduke of the Netherlands asked Rubens to take the position of court painter. Rubens did not want to move to the palace; he was allowed to work in Antwerp so that he could also open his own workshop.

A third reason for staying in Antwerp was that Rubens had met a beautiful and charming young woman. Her name was Isabella Brant. They were married after his appointment to the court. They had 17 happy years together. Rubens described her as "all goodness, all sincerity." He painted a wedding portrait of them. In it they are fashionably dressed, and Isabella sits beside Peter Paul, holding his hand. They look pleased to begin their life together.

Rubens' career moved on with few problems. He chose themes from his Catholic faith and also from mythology. Churches were being rebuilt after the war and there were many commissions to redecorate them. Protestant churches at this time rejected pictures and statues. It was a part of their rejection of the Roman Catholic faith. However, since the days of the early Church, pictures and statuary had been used to tell the story of Christianity. So the Roman Catholic churches saw no reason why such objects should not still be used to inspire and teach. During the Counter-reformation, some Catholic officials thought the Protestants might be right on this issue. Some even tried to persuade the pope to have the nude paintings in the Sistine Chapel painted over. Luckily for the world of art, they did not succeed. Rubens was a devout Catholic. He is said to have attended Mass every morning before beginning work. He surely must have believed that his talent was a God-given gift and that his religious paintings were done for the glory of God.

Rubens' paintings were usually on a large scale, meant for walls with lots of space to display and view them. He was a Baroque painter. His style was one of exciting and dramatic action. Figures are in motion. Light and dark dramatize the story. Horses leap, swords wave, and animals snarl. The women's forms are not what we might expect. Not only were well-rounded female forms the ideal of Rubens' time, but probably a kind of form that he liked to paint. Unlike the female forms of Michelangelo, which often resemble a muscular male body, the Rubens female nudes are moderately curved. While the males have obvious muscles, they are less emphasized than in Michelangelo's paintings.

Paintings with religious themes usually show less violent action than secular works, but illustrate a dramatic emotional state. Rubens painted the various stages of the Crucifixion and Deposition, the Adoration and Holy Family, as well as numerous paintings of the saints and their stories. He painted loving portraits of his children and of his two wives. He spent time in careful thought about parts of a painting, but after he began, he worked quickly.

The large studio attached to his home in Antwerp had space for his students. As with other artists, Rubens had help from his best students in making his own paintings. He kept a strict record as to how much of each painting was his own and made sure that purchasers knew this. The composition was always his, as were the final touches. Sometimes Rubens asked someone to read to him as he painted. Sometimes he dictated letters as he painted.

During Venice's heyday as a center of art, Venetian painters were known for their use of color. Rubens learned much about color from them and he learned about dramatic use of light and shade from High Renaissance and early Baroque painters. The problems of painting textures challenged him. He developed ways of using varying shades of a color to bring out the texture of human skin, animal skin, or fur. Probably no painter has ever been able to paint human skin with the same realistic glow. As Dürer had enjoyed painting animals, so did Rubens. Some of his most dramatic action paintings are the *Lion Hunt,* the *Hippopotamus Hunt,* and the *Wolf and Fox Hunt.*

Rubens became famous throughout Europe and Britain. He was called "a prince of painters and a painter of princes" by the English ambassador. While other artists were trying to be recognized as better than craftsmen, Rubens had made such a success of himself that he could modestly call himself a craftsman who worked with his hands.

The loosely organized states and cities called the Holy Roman Empire were under the control of the Hapsburg dynasty. Through intermarriages and other political and financial dealings, their control reached from one end of Europe to the other. Included were Spain, Portugal, parts of Italy, and central and southern Europe. The countries in which Protestant religion dominated were uneasy about the power of the larger, Roman

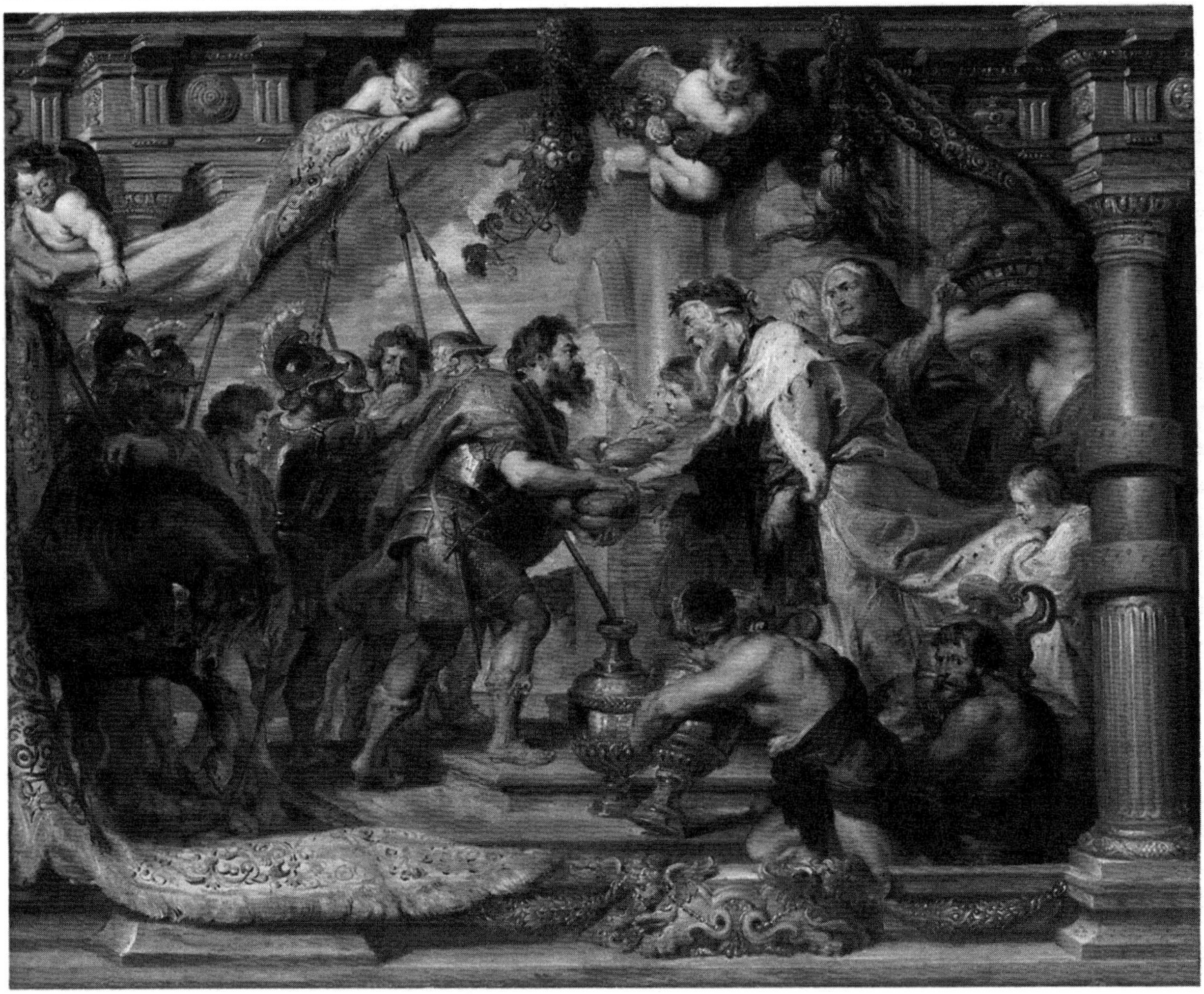

Figure 15
The Meeting of Abraham and Melchizedek, c. 1625
Peter Paul Rubens

Catholic countries. The Dutch Republic had made a 12-year truce with Spanish Netherlands, which was to come to an end in 1621. (To put this into perspective, remember that the Pilgrims landed on Plymouth Rock in 1620.) The Archduke Maurice and Archduchess Isabella were anxious to settle on another truce before war began again. They knew that Rubens was well-known and had contacts in the Dutch Republic. He could travel as a diplomat under the guise of a visiting artist. So Rubens was sent with a proposal to the Prince of Orange, the Dutch leader. However, it was one that the prince could never accept. To come under the control of Spain again was something the Dutch would never tolerate. So the war began again. Although Rubens' diplomatic venture was not successful, he functioned in the same role several times later. Meanwhile, the war came closer to Antwerp.

The same year Rubens visited Paris and received commissions for a large series of paintings and designs for **tapestries.** The paintings, 21 in all, were to decorate the walls of the new Luxembourg Palace. The tapestries were to portray the story of the Emperor Constantine. Also dating from this period is *The Meeting of Abraham and Melchizedek* (see Figure 15).

In 1626 Isabella Rubens died, three years after their only daughter, Clara, had died. Rubens missed them sorely. Isabella had been an excellent manager of their busy home and a loving mother to their children. Theirs had been a particularly happy marriage. Rubens had great difficulty accepting his loss. Though he kept up his painting, he produced less.

He made more diplomatic trips. First, he went to Holland to negotiate with the Dutch, but without success. In 1628 he was sent to Madrid, Spain, to discuss ways to bring about peace with England. He waited six months for the Spanish leaders to come to a decision. While he waited, he met and talked with the Spanish painter Velázquez. Rubens had not been favorably impressed by Spanish paintings, though, and urged the king to send him to Italy for study.

Next Rubens was sent to England. Not only was his diplomatic mission successful, since the king of England was ready to end the war, but Rubens was given a commission to paint a ceiling to decorate the Banqueting House in Whitehall for the king. Rubens was knighted by King Charles, and returned to Antwerp after having been away for a year and a half.

In getting settled back into his work as a painter once more, Rubens, urged by his friends, decided he needed a wife. He chose a young woman, 16 years old, who had grown up in the neighborhood and who was a niece of his late wife, Isabella. Her name was Hélène Fourment. His good fortune followed him. This was another happy marriage. They had five children, and once again Rubens' work became more lighthearted with his new happiness. He painted many portraits of Hélène after their marriage, and also of their children. At about this time, he bought a country home outside of Antwerp. He wanted to lead a more quiet life and to give up diplomatic work. Here he could continue to paint and to enjoy the company of his wife and children in a more peaceful spot. He began to notice the ordinary people who lived and worked in the countryside. In his last years he painted many landscapes, some of them filled with peasants working or playing. Many of his drawings are left, though unsigned. Rubens was increasingly bothered by attacks of gout and his health became a problem. He died on May 20, 1640.

Three centuries after his death, Rubens' work is still known and appreciated. He had been fortunate in every aspect of his life. He worked easily and pleasantly with others; every home he knew, from his childhood through his marriages, had been full of warmth and happiness. He enjoyed his fame and success during his lifetime but was not spoiled by the admiration of others.

Glossary

diplomat a person who conducts the business of his or her government with the governments of other countries

Baroque an art style that flourished from the middle 1500s to the middle 1700s in which there was much emphasis on curving lines, decoration, and movement

tapestries heavy cloths, either handwoven or machine-woven, with pictures or decorative designs that are used for wall hangings

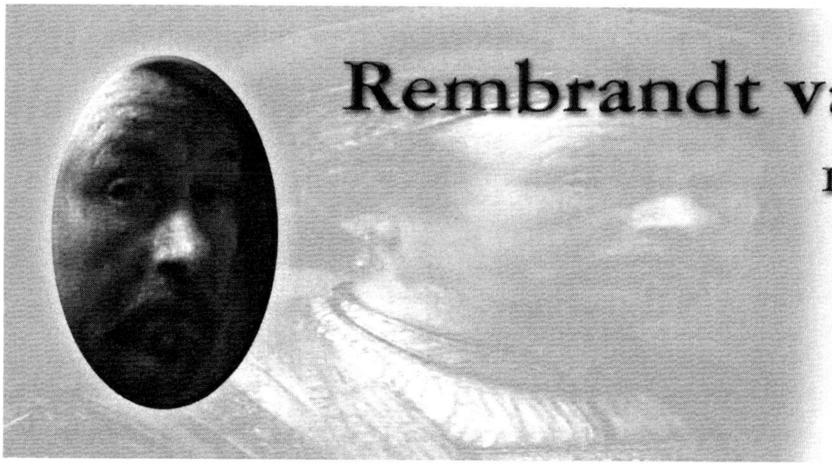

Rembrandt van Rijn

1606 – 1669

YOU MAY REMEMBER that the United Provinces, the parts of the Netherlands that had freed themselves from Spanish rule, were joined together under the House of Orange. During the Reformation this area had adopted Calvinism, which was a branch of Protestantism. During the seventeenth century the most important kind of business for this new country was shipping. Much of the trade in Europe used ships from the United Provinces. Many ships were also built there. The Dutch ships sailed to the Pacific, China, and Japan. A lot of money was earned by buying rice, spices, and other goods to sell upon return to Europe. The Americas were also on their trading routes. Furs, sugar, and wood were brought back from the New World. The upper-class merchants experienced great prosperity. The lower classes were poorly housed, clothed, and fed. Children were even taken from orphanages or from the street to work in textile factories for long, 14-hour workdays.

This is the world into which Rembrandt Harmenszoon van Rijn was born in Leiden on July 15, 1606. Leiden is 25 miles from Amsterdam. It was the second largest city after Amsterdam. There were about 50,000 people living there. Rembrandt's father was a miller. The words "van Rijn" had been added to the family name to mean that the family had lived by the Rhine River. Rembrandt was the second of eight children.

Rembrandt grew up in Leiden and attended the Latin School. He entered this school when he was seven and finished at fourteen. Although his brothers were ordinary workers, his parents must have seen something in this boy that seemed special. They wanted him to have an education. The Latin School was a preparatory school for the university. Students learned Latin, read the classics in Latin, and spoke in Latin. Following the Latin School, Rembrandt spent some time at the University of Leiden. Some sources say one year, while others say he was there only a month or two.

Since painters were ranked with other craftsmen, it may have been a disappointment for Rembrandt's parents when he dropped out of the university to become an apprentice with a local painter. After a time with this man, Rembrandt was next apprenticed to Jacob van Swanenburgh. Here he learned the basic methods of painting, etching, and drawing. When he had made as much progress under this teacher as seemed likely, his father sent him to Amsterdam to work with Pieter Lastman. This master had studied in Italy, and was much influenced by Caravaggio and his use of light and dark (**chiaroscuro**). Rembrandt was in Lastman's studio for six months and developed his own techniques for chiaroscuro. His dramatic use of light became an important quality of his painting style.

The young painter left Amsterdam in 1625 to return to Leiden, where he started his own workshop. An early painting from this period was *The Stoning of St. Stephen*. It is the first of many biblical paintings that Rembrandt was to make. Using contrast of light through the action in the center with the darker areas to the left, he used Caravaggio's lighting techniques.

Other early paintings were *The Money Changer, Christ at Emmaus, The Angel and the Prophet,* and *Tobit and Anna.* At this point his paintings were on a small scale. The light sources were often a bright fire, candles, or light coming from a biblical figure, replacing the halo so often seen in the paintings of the past.

Figure 16
Self-Portrait, 1650
Rembrandt van Rijn

The use of light not only provided dramatic touches, but also helped explore the emotions of the persons involved. Rembrandt felt especially drawn to the common people he saw about him and often used them in his paintings and etchings. Recurrent themes were the stories from the Old and New Testaments. He thought that people in Bible stories were likely to have looked like the people he saw every day. He preferred to paint them in that way instead of painting them as idealized, beautiful people as Renaissance painters might have done. Rembrandt had the opportunity to discuss biblical passages with scholars, with Jews, and with Mennonites whom he knew and painted.

Most artists and art teachers collect works of other artists, objects that interest them, and miscellaneous materials that could be used in their art or classes. Rembrandt was no different. He was fascinated by exotic

Far Eastern clothing, lush decorative fabrics, armor, and weapons. He is said to have gone to auctions where he bought interesting-looking clothing, seashells, and other bizarre or exotic objects. He collected art from everywhere. While he did not travel far from Amsterdam or Leiden, he made up for it by collecting from distant lands. (Later, his enthusiasm for gathering these materials contributed to his financial woes.) Meanwhile, many of his paintings feature models and even himself dressed in luxurious garments. Since at the time clothing styles for both men and women consisted mainly of black outfits with white collars, Rembrandt probably enjoyed the colorful clothing even more.

Rembrandt's early twenties were years of success. He moved back to Amsterdam in 1631. He lived and worked in the house of Hendrick van Uilenburgh. This man ran a workshop in which paintings were copied for selling; he also bought and sold the art of others. Some of Rembrandt's paintings were copied here, though he was too well-known to have worked as a copier. He began a profitable series of portraits. The group portrait *The Anatomy Lesson of Dr. Nicolaes Tulp* was done in 1632. This painting brought much attention to Rembrandt. At this time the group portrait was a popular way to commemorate the members of a guild, militia company, or other organization. (You will see some similarity here with group pictures in the school yearbook.) Each person in the group paid for his section. The difficulty for the artist was to infuse the group picture with some interest beyond the simple likeness. Since Rembrandt was able to make these group portraits more interesting than those by other artists, his skills were in demand.

At about this time Rembrandt began his courtship of Saskia van Uilenburgh, the cousin of his landlord. She was from a wealthy family and brought the painter entrance to a higher rung of society. These were probably his happiest years in terms of wealth, success, and personal relationships. He and Saskia were married in 1634. He bought a large house, paying for most of it and getting a mortgage for the rest. He had many students and had set up a workshop for them.

Rembrandt's own body of work is among the largest of any known artist. Surviving works include 300 etchings, 600 paintings, and 1,400 drawings. Many drawings were not dated or signed. These were probably made during the process of working out ideas for paintings or etchings, or to record an idea for later use. At least 90 are self-portraits, many of which seem to be studies in ways to portray various emotions (see Figure 16). What are some good ways to show anger, joy, or puzzlement on the human face? From his middle years, the self-portraits show a certain amount of self-satisfaction, since things were going well. Later, as misfortune occurred again and again, his self-portraits show a more solemn, thoughtful man with the changes of old age appearing.

Rembrandt has been called a rebel. He rebelled against the subject matter and artistic styles popular in Holland. Because of his pity for the common people who worked so hard and lived so poorly, he used them in his pictures. He showed us the good in people. He rejected the idealized people painted by many others. However, despite his sympathy for the poor, Rembrandt himself liked to live well. He spent money freely, and when a debt came due, he often borrowed more money to pay the original debt.

Saskia's health was poor. Their first three children all died in infancy. The fourth child, a boy named Titus, was the only one to live to adulthood. Some paintings of Saskia show her state of failing health, while others portray her in the early days of their marriage (see Figure 17). Later paintings of her seem to be a loving memory of those times. She died in June 1642.

Tradition has placed Saskia's death and the painting of *The Night Watch* as the beginnings of Rembrandt's downhill slide. Research has proved these stories wrong. The painting of a company of militiamen with Captain Frans Banning Cocq was commissioned to Rembrandt. As he'd done in the painting of *The Anatomy Lesson of Dr. Nicolaes Tulp,* he decided to make a composition different from the usual lineup of figures. The company is assembling not for a battle, but for a parade or some social gathering. The men carry weapons, one man plays a drum, and a barking dog and little girl run through their midst. All these figures make a Baroque composition with drama, action, and rich color. The name *The Night Watch* has been given the painting because it had darkened so much by the nineteenth century. It was thought to be a night setting. Efforts to seal and restore it have brought back its original color and strong contrasting lights. It is one of Rembrandt's largest paintings, 13' × 16', and hangs now in the Rijksmuseum in Amsterdam. The stories that members of the company refused to pay their share because they did not like the painting are untrue. It was hung in the designated place, and the captain had a watercolor made of it to keep in an album.

Many of Rembrandt's paintings had been varnished as people sought to preserve them. The varnished surfaces darkened with age. Now, the restored paintings show us much brighter colors.

While Saskia's death was undoubtedly a tragic loss for Rembrandt, he did continue to work and his work continued to sell. As tastes changed in Holland, other artists made work more popular than Rembrandt's. Some of the artists had been his students. However, until the year he died, he was selling work and had friends who were in contact with him. His inability to manage his money problems was more likely the reason for his financial state than the lack of popularity of his paintings.

Saskia's will left half of their joint holdings to their son and half to Rembrandt. The interest from Titus' share was to go to Rembrandt, also. However, if he remarried, Titus' inheritance was to go to Saskia's sister. With his money affairs always difficult, this last provision probably prevented Rembrandt from remarrying. A household maid, Hendrickje Stoffels, was his common-law wife until her death in 1663. They had one living child, a daughter, Cornelia. Hendrickje was a warm and loving mother to Titus, and made a home for them all. She was a comforting companion to the artist. He made paintings and drawings of her, also.

Many of Rembrandt's drawings and etchings were made working outdoors in the countryside around Amsterdam. He drew with chalk, especially in his early years. Later, he preferred pen and ink. He also used brush and ink as a drawing medium, finishing with an ink wash. His simplicity of line has caused some retouching in the past by people who felt a drawing was not finished. Besides landscapes, Rembrandt drew many of the poor as they worked, visited together, or sat in thought.

Etching was Rembrandt's favorite printmaking method. Remember that the artist draws with a sharp needle-like tool onto a waxy coating on a metal (usually copper) plate. The plate is then put into an acid bath so that the acid eats into the metal through the drawing. Corrections and changes can be made on copper by pounding out the mistake, coating it again, drawing, and putting it back into the acid. Artists have their own "recipes" for mixing the acid bath, as well as the amount of time to leave the plate immersed. Rembrandt often made changes in prints over a period of years. He sold the prints from the beginning as well as the ones in which changes were later made. Collectors of his work tried to find prints from different stages of his development.

Rembrandt worked rapidly with his etching needle, and many of the lines are incredibly tiny and close together to create dark tones. He experimented with the use of different sizes of tools to add lines to an etching. One of his best-known prints is called the "hundred guilder print" because it sold for that price. It shows Christ healing the sick, the **Pharisees** arguing, and the young man whom Jesus told to give away all his wealth. Three Bible stories are combined in one print. Again—light! It seems to radiate from the figure of the Christ. The shadows help create drama.

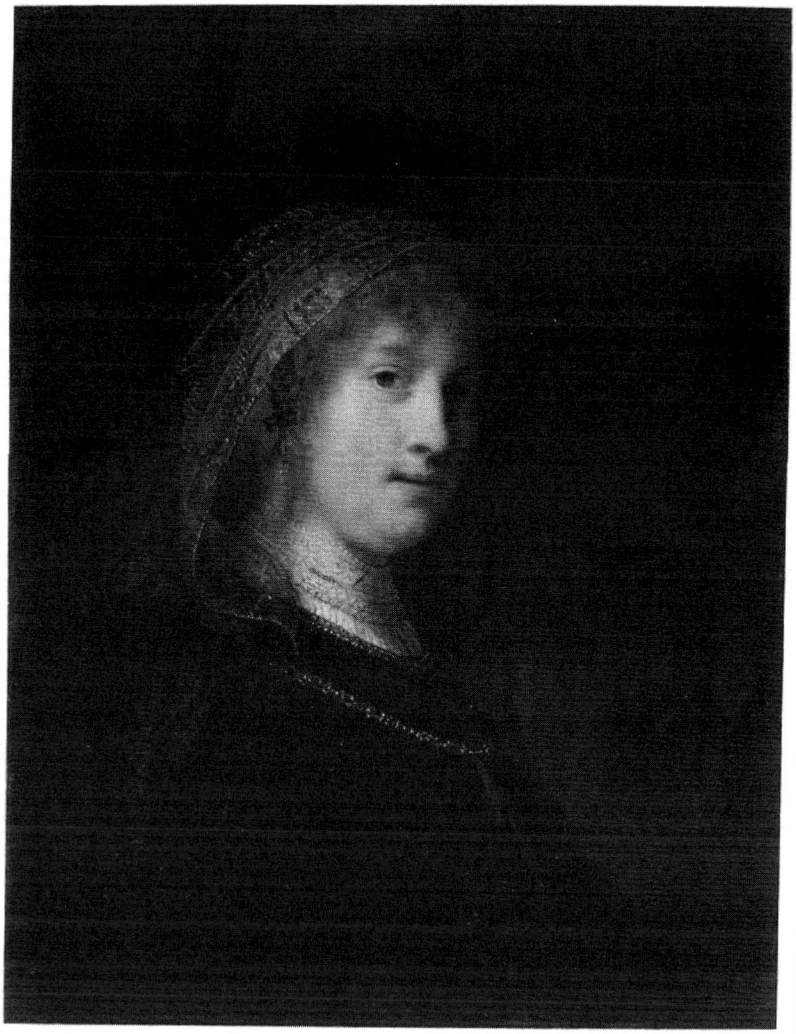

Figure 17
Saskia van Uilenburgh, the Wife of the Artist, c. 1633
Rembrandt van Rijn

During the last 20 years of Rembrandt's life, he lived quietly. Commissions still came in, some from as far away as Italy. He still had students, and his etchings were selling well. Many of his possessions, his collections of interesting objects, and his and others' art pieces had been sold to satisfy a **bankruptcy** judgment against him. He moved at least twice more, each time to a poorer section of the city. Since he and Hendrickje were not married, the Council of the Reformed Church complained about their lifestyle. He was now on a lower social level than in the old days.

In his last years he turned more and more to paintings of biblical figures when he was working for his own enjoyment. He had come from a religious home and had always been a religious man. His faith seems to have been a continued comfort to him in his troubled years. Some historians believe that he was drawn to the Mennonite sect. These people were followers of the Dutch **theologian** Menno Simons. They did not accept sacraments or ceremonies not found in the New Testament and begun by Christ or his apostles. Rembrandt must have been comfortable with their Bible reading, silent prayer, and charity to others.

The art of Rembrandt's last years increasingly portrayed the inner life, the thoughts and feelings, of his subjects. Their faces, especially in the religious paintings, express the depth of their faith (see Color Plate 3).

During 1661 and 1662 Rembrandt was commissioned to paint another group portrait. *The Syndics,* as it is known, shows the five Staalmeesters of the Cloth Hall of Amsterdam. The artist did not compose the kind of dramatic picture he did in *The Night Watch*. The figures are not lined up in a row. Their attention is focused at some point in front of them as they gather informally around a table. Each face is an honest portrait of the man. The light seems to come from the faces and the white collars, with some reflected from the bright red table cover. We see a calm, dignified group.

In the years after Hendrickje's death, Rembrandt took care of their daughter, but his next loss was his son, Titus. The young man had married just seven months before. Rembrandt died in October 1669. He had always been in control of his own artistic style and short of patience with those who wanted to direct him to other paths. He was able to withstand the depression that his often troubled life must have produced. Perhaps his art became the way to save himself.

Glossary

chiaroscuro pronounced kyah-ro-scur-o; the method of using light and dark values to create form

Pharisees members of an ancient Jewish group in which religious laws were rigidly observed

bankruptcy occurs when a person is unable to pay just or legal debts

theologian a person who studies systems of religious beliefs; usually refers to Christian beliefs

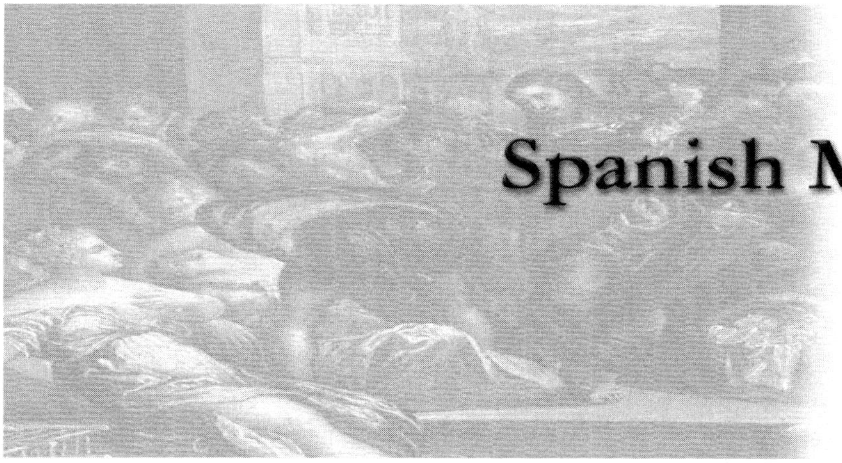

Three Spanish Masters

El Greco, Velázquez, and Goya are three great painters whose work spans two and a half centuries of Spanish history. They did not all paint in one "Spanish" style; they are separate, unique representatives of Spain's rich cultural tradition.

It is interesting to note that El Greco was not even Spanish. He was born in Greece and spent the early part of his life training in Venice. He was attracted to Spain because it had been a crossroads for people from the British Isles, Europe, and Africa for thousands of years. Its culture reflected all those influences. To this day, the Prado in Madrid is thought to have one of the best collections of any art museum in the world. There is also a great amount of Islamic architecture in Spain, a rarity in other parts of western Europe.

During the century in which El Greco and Velázquez began working, Spain was at its peak as a world power. Spanish explorers had colonized parts of Africa and the New World and riches were pouring in. Holland and later Portugal were seized as Spain continued to seek territory.

Then, Spain began to crack under the strain of all its ambitions. The treasury was bankrupted at least twice. In 1588, when the English defeated the Spanish armada, or navy, it was the beginning of the end.

Yet during this time, much was accomplished in the arts. El Greco and Velázquez benefited from royal patronage. El Greco expressed his inner vision, which still appeals to us today, and Velázquez served as the Spanish representative of the Baroque style popular elsewhere in Europe.

One hundred years later, Goya worked in a Spain still in turmoil. The country was reacting to the revolutions in North America and France and the revolution that gained independence for the Spanish colonies in Latin America. During this period Spain also went to war against England again and was occupied by Napoleon's troops.

Goya's art is aligned more with the Romantic movement and English painters Turner and Constable than the neoclassic art that was still being taught at the time. Goya and others were inspired to use strong colors and dramatic subjects to express their feelings.

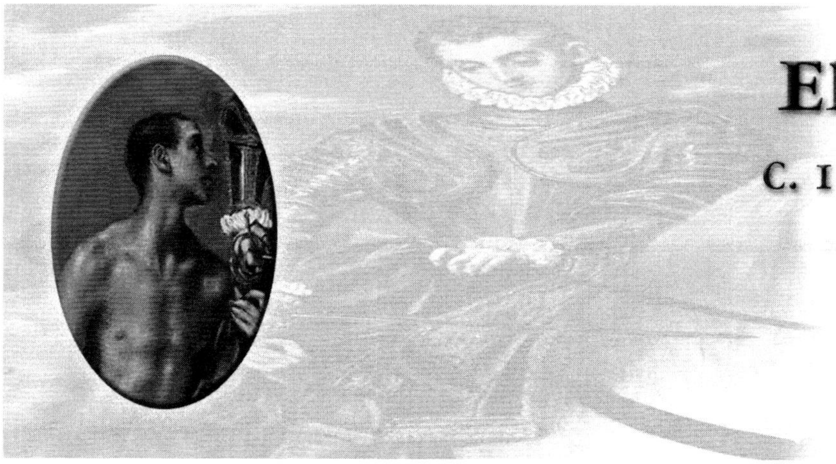

El Greco
c. 1541 – 1614

His name was Domenikos Theotokopoulos. He was born in 1541 on Crete, a Greek island then under the control of Venice. We know him as the Spanish painter, El Greco. "El Greco" means "the Greek" in Spanish.

When El Greco was 20, he moved to Venice. We have read about other artists who traveled to Venice to learn about the kind of art being made there. Venetian painting was known for the use of color as an important part of form. Light and airy landscapes became as important as the objects or people within the painting. Color was at once rich and mellow, and was used to unify the parts of a picture.

In Venice El Greco learned about the Venetian use of color by working in the workshop of the painter Titian. Then he moved on to Rome. He had help from influential friends in the city, but had little success there. He seems to have been a man who spoke his mind very forcefully without thinking of the consequences. If his painting style did not catch on in Rome, some of his statements may have had something to do with it. A well-known painting made during his stay in Italy is *Christ Cleansing the Temple* (see Figure 18).

Following the High Renaissance, many artists adapted a style now called "**Mannerism**" for lack of a better term. It encompasses art made from the early 1500s to about 1600. Some art historians ignore the term altogether. The style is identified by its anticlassical, dramatic, and overly emotional feelings, and by the human forms that tend to **distortion.** El Greco is the best known among the Mannerist painters.

In 1577 El Greco went to Spain and settled in Toledo. This city had become a religious center for Roman Catholic Spain. The Counter-Reformation was sweeping the country. Church officials sent many commissions his way. They apparently appreciated his work more than King Philip II did, who may not have liked El Greco's style. In Toledo the painter was considered a great master and a prize for the city.

The first paintings El Greco made in Toledo were eight altar paintings for the new Church of Santo Domingo el Antiguo. For the Cathedral of Toledo, he painted the *Espolio,* in which Christ's robes are about to be stripped from him. Many figures and expressive faces add to the drama. He was criticized by cathedral officials because of the arrangement of some of the figures. Christ was placed lower than other figures, and the painter had included the three Marys. El Greco refused to make any corrections. His fee for the painting was cut, and paid in small amounts over a two-year period.

The *Martyrdom of St. Maurice* was painted for the king, but, as noted above, El Greco's style did not get a favorable reception. He saw that he was better off staying in Toledo, where he was sure to have many commissions, and did not try to establish himself in Madrid.

The Burial of Count Orgaz is one of El Greco's best-known paintings. Its story is from the legend of a miracle in which St. Augustine and St. Stephen appeared to help lower the count's body into his grave. The very large painting is divided into two sections, the earthly and the heavenly. The earthly scene below is mournful, while the heavenly scene is one of rejoicing. Both are crowded with figures and faces, many of which were probably portraits of people known to the people of the sixteenth century. In the heavens, the soul (in infant form) is being received, borne

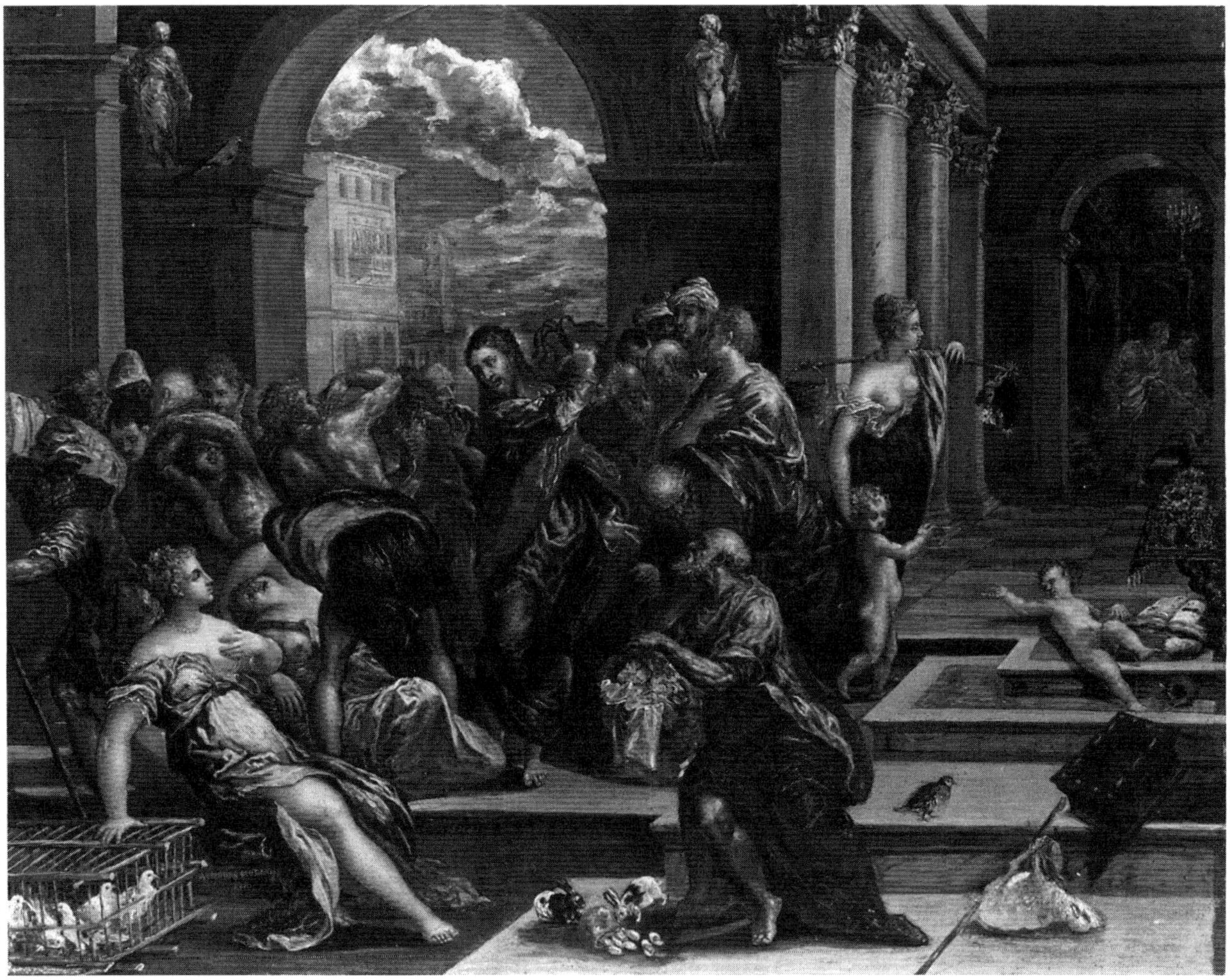

Figure 18
Christ Cleansing the Temple, c. 1570
El Greco

up by an angel. The canvas fills a large opening that looks like a curved, domed window. Since the bottom of the opening is six feet above the floor, El Greco painted to give the viewer the feeling of actually looking up into the picture space. Also dating from this period is *Madonna and Child with Saint Martina and Saint Agnes* (see Color Plate 4).

In the Mannerist style, the human forms painted by El Greco were elongated. That means they appear to be stretched out into a longer form than usual. This style grew more his own as the years passed. It is evident in his painting *Saint Martin and the Beggar* (see Figure 19). A devout Catholic, he tried to use his art as a part of his own worship and as a means to help others worship.

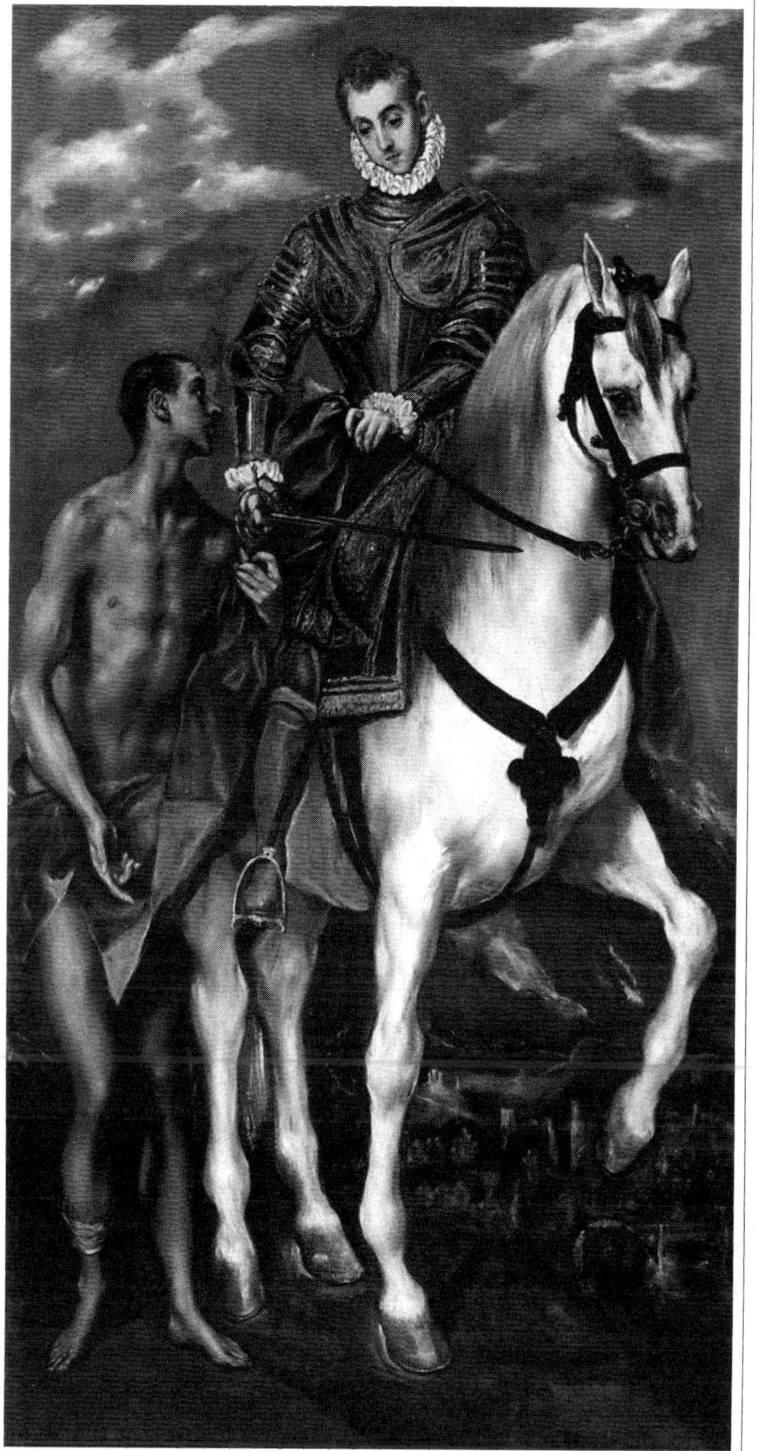

Figure 19
Saint Martin and the Beggar, 1597–1599
El Greco

Though religious themes dominated this painter's work, he did landscapes as well. The best-known and most dramatic is the *View of Toledo.* The clouds gather above the distant city and create the drama of the coming storm. El Greco is said to have kept small copies of all of his paintings so that customers could select ones they liked. A copy was then made. He did not mind repeating whatever had been successful.

The argument over the *Espolio* was neither the first nor the last disagreement he had about one of his paintings. He refused to suffer without protest what he thought was injustice. He remained popular during his lifetime, but other painters and styles took his place shortly after his death in 1614. The late art historian Kenneth Clark said that El Greco "was the first European painter to reject the main premises of the classical tradition." Clark continued, "He thought surface more important than depth . . . he thought color more important than drawing, and he sought to communicate his emotions by **pictorial** means, even if it involved distortion." El Greco was determined to make his own decisions and break away from the traditions of classical art that had charmed Western artists for so long.

Glossary

Mannerism an artificial "mannered" style, revolting against the classical work at the peak of the Renaissance

distortion twisting out of normal shape; also stretching out or elongating

pictorial related to the drawing of pictures; graphic

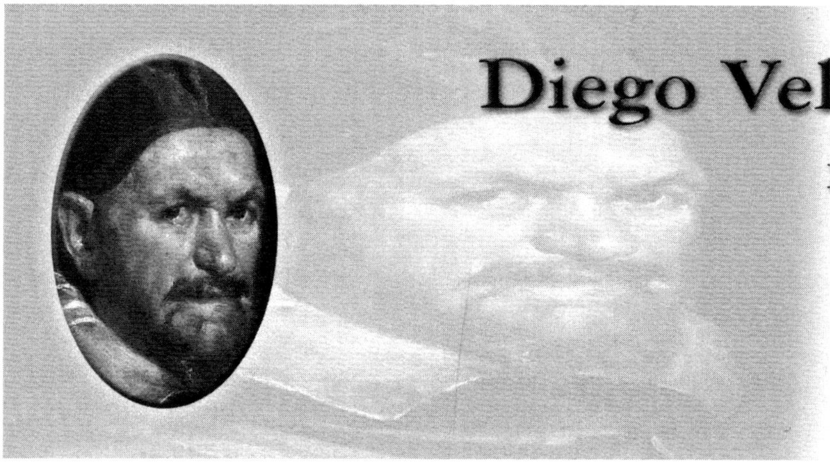

Diego Velázquez
1599–1660

DIEGO VELÁZQUEZ was born in Seville, Spain in 1599. His parents came from the **hidalgo** class (the lower class of nobility). People of this class felt that they were above being craftsmen. If they did not inherit money or land, it was often difficult for them to find work that was not "beneath" them.

At the age of 11, Velázquez was apprenticed to Francisco de Herrera and subsequently to Francisco Pacheco. Pacheco is better known today for his writings than for his painting. He was an art critic, a painter, a teacher of painting, and a writer. His writings are not valued as much for their information about how to paint as for the information they contain about the artists and paintings of that time. In *The Art of Painting* he set out exactly how religious paintings should be done. Thus it seems that Velázquez received a very exacting education. Students in the studio had to work hard. Soon Velázquez was moving ahead of the rest, and before long, ahead of his master. Pacheco must have approved of Velázquez, for he allowed his daughter to marry the young student.

Velázquez's early paintings were **genre paintings** set in kitchens or on the streets, featuring common street people and servants (see Figure 20). His painting style was full of detail. He used bright, golden light and dark shadow to create strong contrast. Some early paintings are: *The Old Woman Frying Eggs, The Waterseller, Christ in the House of Martha and Mary, The Immaculate Conception, St. John,* and *The Crucifixion*. Browns, yellows, grays, greens with light tones, and whites are used. Some of the rules laid down by his teacher, Pacheco, were followed, although Mary and Martha and the figures of the Virgin and the saint could have been found on the streets of Seville.

Velázquez may have been influenced, as many painters at this time were, by the work of Caravaggio, an Italian painter who painted everyday people in a realistic manner. He discarded the traditions. When he painted religious figures, he wanted them to look like real, not idealized, people. He also used strong lights and darks.

Velázquez traveled to Madrid for the first time in 1622 when he was 22. He made some contacts at court and then returned to Seville. Meanwhile, the court painter died, and Velázquez was called back to the capital. The young king's chief advisor was the Count of Olivares, who held that powerful post until he was dismissed in 1643. It was the good fortune of Velázquez that Olivares liked his work and brought him to Madrid.

Velázquez's artistic career was tied to the fortunes of the Spanish court. Spain at the beginning of the seventeenth century was not a strongly unified country. The peninsula that we know as Portugal and Spain today was divided into three parts: Portugal, Castile, and Aragon. These in turn were divided into provinces with the capital in Madrid, in the center of Castile. Philip IV had just come to the throne at the age of 16. People hoped that this would be a new beginning, and for good reason. The country was having many problems. The economy, the treasury, and the armed forces were all in serious condition. The common people were bearing the brunt of the extravagances of the wealthy and the royalty.

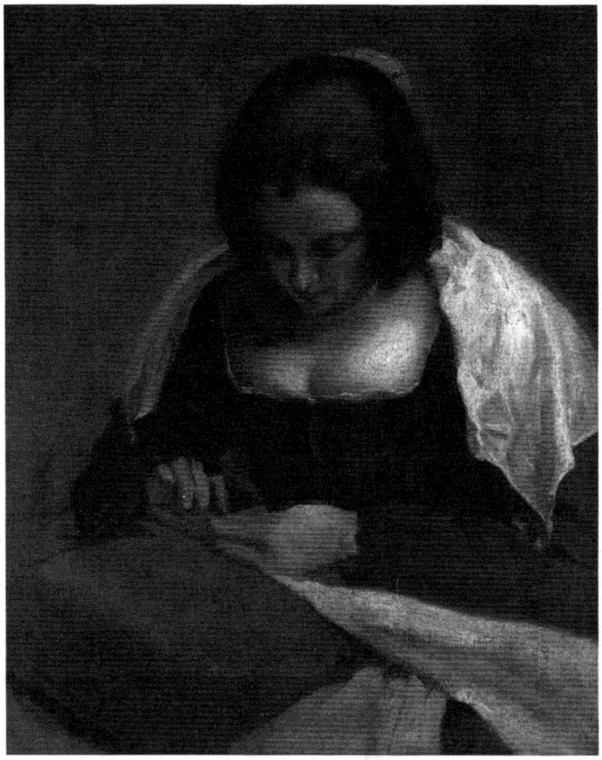

Figure 20
The Needlewoman, c. 1640
Diego Velázquez

We know the kind of work usually expected of a court painter. Paintings of the royal family and courtiers were a way of keeping a visual record over the years, just as a family photo album is kept today by means of a camera. After being given the post, Velázquez spent his entire career as court painter. He portrayed the royal family with the same kind of sympathy and insight we see in paintings of common people. The king was not a handsome man, nor did he have a strong personality. Velázquez painted his portrait many times, each time with increasing idealization. We see him looking more as a king ought to look, and perhaps less as Philip actually looked. The same kind of idealization is seen in portraits of Olivares.

Velázquez was given freedom to paint as he liked and was also given other duties at court. In 1627 he was made an Usher of the Chamber, for which he was allowed an apartment, free medical care, and an allowance. Other promotions brought him to a point at which he was considered a friend of the king and traveled with him. He was evidently devoted to his ruler.

Velázquez painted many portraits of the royal children. The first was that of 16-months-old Baltasar Carlos. Beside him was one of the dwarfs who were kept at court much as we would keep an animal as a pet to amuse us. There were also "fools," like comedians, at court to help entertain. Both dwarfs and fools apparently provided entertainment because of their size, physical deformity, or low intelligence. They were allowed to say and do things that would have been disrespectful or forbidden had others done them. Velázquez painted several portraits of dwarfs and included them in some group portraits of the royal family. He portrayed them with sympathy and compassion, helping us to understand how they might have suffered in their situation.

Philip was a **shallow** young man when he became king. From time to time he tried to overcome his natural weakness, but was never really able to do so. He depended on Olivares to help him govern for many years. Even though Spain had explored and conquered a lot of territory in the New World, the money the colonies brought in was wasted in one war after another. What was left was used by the royal family and the aristocracy for lavish living. The common people were taxed far beyond what they could pay. Both the king and the queen loved to be amused and entertained.

A new palace was built in 1634. Velázquez and other artists were busy making paintings to decorate it. One vast room, called the Hall of the Realms, was to honor Philip's reign. There were plans for 12 military scenes and ten paintings illustrating the labors of Hercules. Velázquez was to paint five portraits of the royal family.

One of the artist's most famous paintings was done for this palace. *The Surrender of Breda* tells the story of the heroic Dutch and their year-long defense of the town of Breda. The leader of the Spanish troops was Ambrosio Spinola. He admired the Dutch and let them leave the city without further harm. The painting shows the Dutch general presenting the keys of the city to Spinola. The faces of troops of both sides express their exhaustion, resignation, and the calm end of the long siege. In the background are shown the fires still burning in parts of the city.

Velázquez's painting techniques changed over the years. In his early days in Seville he used paint more thickly and with such careful brushwork that the paint surface is smooth. Textures are built up while the edges of forms are well defined. Later he used paint more thinly, building up layers that showed more evident brushwork and edges that seem blurred at close range. Viewed at a distance, the shapes and edges are distinct.

In 1635 France declared war against Spain. There were still unpaid debts from the old war, and now money would be needed for the new one. Even the aristocrats were in financial trouble. The next year Velázquez himself had to ask for two years' back wages owed him, plus money due for paintings he'd done. Olivares confiscated the money and goods on ships coming in from the Americas.

Despite these difficulties it was decided to remodel and redecorate the king's hunting lodge. Hunting was his favorite sport, and it was thought this would cheer him up. Velázquez was in charge of this job. Rubens made 40 oil sketches for it; many were actually done by assistants. Velázquez painted portraits of Baltasar, Fernando II, and the king. Paintings from mythological stories also decorated the lodge.

Philip's first queen, Isabel, died in 1644. Within the next two years his sister and the heir to the throne, Baltasar Carlos, both died. The king began to believe that he was being punished by God for his sins and failures. During this decade plague swept through Castile, Valencia, and Andalusia, where it killed half the population of Seville. The Spanish colony of Naples revolted and a conspiracy in Aragon was also put down. A peace treaty with the Dutch was signed after 80 years of war.

It is difficult to understand how the royal family and their courtiers could maintain such distance from the troubles of their country. It is difficult to understand how Velázquez could continue to paint in his restrained, calm style. He must have known of the hardship in the lives of the ordinary people, the kind who appeared in his early paintings in Seville. But he was an hidalgo. Social rank was very important. In the tight class structures of the time, people could ignore the condition of others if their own lives were going well.

Velázquez met Rubens when the northern painter and diplomat made trips to Spain for his government in the Spanish Netherlands. Rubens made paintings while in Madrid. Velázquez, then, knew of the turbulent scenes that Rubens delighted in painting. Rubens encouraged King Philip to send Velázquez to Venice and Rome, and Velázquez did spend a year and a half in Italy. First he went to Venice, but he spent most of the time in Rome. He made two paintings there: *The Forge of Vulcan* and *The Bloody Coat of Joseph*. On his way back to Spain, he stopped in Naples to paint a portrait of the king's sister, Maria, who was on her way to be married to the king of Hungary.

The second trip to Italy was made in 1648. The king had decided to have a new picture gallery built. Velázquez took the opportunity to ask permission to go to Italy to buy paintings for the new gallery. In the travel party were Velázquez's assistant and several noblemen who were going to fetch the king's new bride, Mariana. She was a Hapsburg cousin of the king. Originally she had been promised for marriage with Prince Baltasar Carlos before his death.

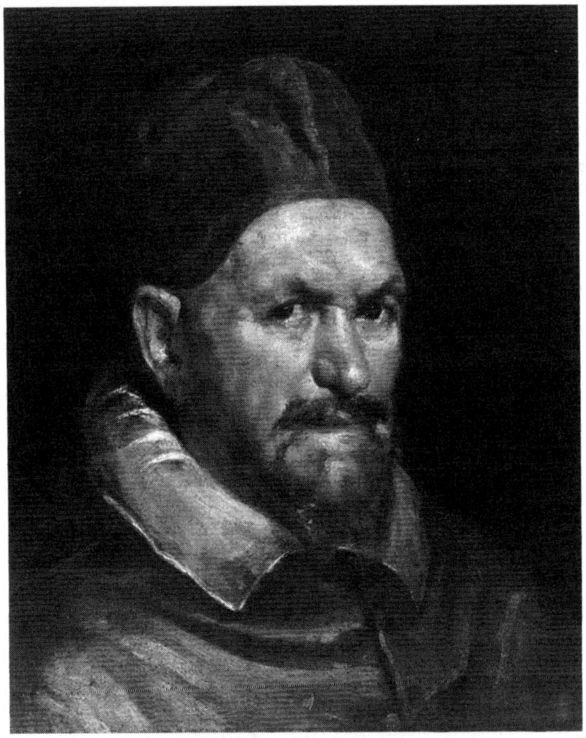

Figure 21
Pope Innocent X, c. 1650
Diego Velázquez

Velázquez went to Venice, where he bought paintings. As he traveled through other parts of Italy, he was received with honor, perhaps because he represented the Spanish court and perhaps because of his own reputation as a painter. This was a year of celebration in Rome. Many visitors were coming, among them many painters. Velázquez stayed more than a year. He painted at least ten portraits, including one of Pope Innocent X (see Figure 21). It was said that he was now using long-handled brushes and could work at a greater distance from his painting. However, in a later painting, in which he included himself in the process of painting, the brushes appear to be of average length. Fellow painters noticed that he used fewer brush strokes.

The portrait of the pope won a great deal of acclaim. Velázquez was honored with an invitation to membership in the painters' guild, and in another group of artists who exhibited their work each year. The pope sent a gold medallion to Velázquez and helped to promote the artist to membership in a Spanish military-religious group, the Order of Santiago. Later Velázquez was made a knight in the Order.

Philip became impatient with his painter for staying so long in Italy. He was ordered home. Velázquez took his time in starting back. Since he had not been away from Spain in 20 years, he was enjoying seeing his fellow artists, painting with them, and developing new techniques.

It would have been comfortable and easy for the painter to have stayed with the same styles and techniques that brought him to Madrid in the first place. In the safe, luxurious palace studio the king had a chair in which he liked to sit to watch Velázquez paint. But Velázquez preferred to experiment and grow. In the last ten years of his life, Velázquez painted some of his best-known works. The Prado, an art museum in Madrid, contains a room in which the painting ***Las Meninas*** (Ladies-in-Waiting) is displayed by itself. The walls of the room repeat the color of the walls in the painting. The viewer feels that he or she is walking into the room where the artist stands painting the little princess. On either side of her and behind her are her ladies-in-waiting, a dwarf, and a large dog. The mirror on the wall behind them reflects the king and queen, who have looked into the room from the viewer's position.

Just as Jan van Eyck recorded his presence in the Arnolfini painting, Velázquez has painted a self-portrait in the process of making *Las Meninas*. His late brushwork techniques are used in this work. At close range, one sees the brushwork and the soft edges of the figures. Viewed from a distance, the brushwork becomes the figures and detail of the painting. How different from the early Seville paintings!

A painting of the new queen, mother of the little princess in the painting above, was done in 1653. Here we see a sulky, petulant young woman. The painter had to make a decision here. Should he flatter her? Should he paint her as a beautiful, pleasant person? He chose to paint an honest, though dignified, work. Having married the king at 15, she had not yet produced a male heir, and was more at home frolicking with her young stepdaughters. The last portrait of the king also shows us an unhappy man; the government had gone bankrupt twice in the last six years. While Velázquez paints his king in a rather idealized way, we still see an expressive work.

We will not see a happy ending for Spain in the story of Velázquez. We do see the artist as having achieved most of the goals he probably had as a young man. He died in August 1660, of malaria; his wife died one week later.

Glossary

hidalgo pronounced ē-dahl´-go

genre paintings pronounced zhon´-rə; paintings in which everyday things or persons are used as subject matter

shallow having little depth of thought or intellect

Las Meninas pronounced lahs may-nee´-nas

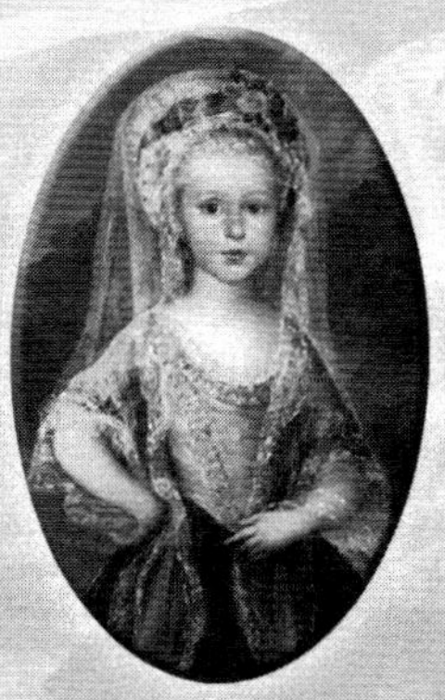

Francisco de Goya

1746–1828

THE NEXT SPANISH ARTIST whose work we will examine is Francisco de Goya, who was born in 1746. Conditions in Spain were not much better than they were at the end of Velázquez' life. The son of Philip IV and the unhappy Mariana was Carlos (Charles) II. He was both physically and mentally handicapped, but he lived until he was 35. He was the last ruler from the Hapsburg dynasty to sit on the Spanish throne. Just before his death, Charles II needed to name his successor, since he had no children. He chose Philip of Anjou, the grandson of the French king, whose grandmother was Spanish. The family was of the Bourbon dynasty. Thus Philip V became king of Spain.

Goya was born in Fuendetodos in the province of Aragon. The area is dry and hot and produces little. Goya's father was a gilder. His mother was of the hidalgo class. When she inherited land in Fuendetodos, the family moved there from Saragossa. Probably Goya's father thought it would be a step upward for the family; they would be landowners. Apparently they were not much better off, and the family moved back to Saragossa, which was the capital of the province. There trade prospered, as did the arts. Goya attended the parish school. His friend for many years, Martin Zapater, was also a pupil there. Much of what we know of Goya's life comes from letters to his friend.

Some persons seem to realize early in life that they are meant to be artists, while others are "discovered" or encouraged in that direction. A Jesuit priest suggested that Goya study with one of the painters in Saragossa. The painter was Jose Luzan y Martinez. He was Goya's teacher for four years. Goya also studied with a local sculptor.

When he was 17, Goya went to Madrid. There he studied with Francisco Bayeu. From there he found a way to go on to Rome. He was 23 at the time. As had many other artists before and since, Goya found new inspiration in the new and old art styles he saw. His own skills were developing. He had entered painting competitions in Madrid and in Rome, but was unsuccessful in both places. When he returned to Spain, he settled back in Saragossa. He was burning with ambition and must have been disappointed in his progress at this point. However, he started a workshop and soon was commissioned to make a series of paintings for the Sobradiel palace chapel. Other work followed, and in three years he was the leading painter in Saragossa.

Goya's painting style at this point was Baroque. But he was open to change. The neoclassic style had been brought to Spain by the artist Raphael Mengs, and was beginning to displace the Baroque and **Rococo** styles, which had been popular. Those bright and airy styles were being replaced by carefully painted figures, based on the idealized forms of Greek and Roman art. The neoclassic style had become popular and Goya did not intend to spend his life in his hometown as a provincial painter. He tried to develop a style that would please.

In 1773 Goya married the sister of his former teacher, Bayeu. Her name was Josefa. They lived in Saragossa until 1774, then moved to Madrid, where Goya was to help design tapestries. Bayeu was in charge of appointing artists to design cartoons (actually large paintings) for the Royal Tapestry Manufactory of Santa Barbara. The paintings were then to be turned into weaving patterns. This job could provide connections with the artists of the court, so it was a good opportunity.

The tapestry designs by Goya are not thought of as his best work. He was not interested in landscape painting and was not comfortable with the problems of painting animals, except for bullfights. The king, however, was interested in hunting, fishing, and country life. Pictures of country life, peasants, and landscapes were assigned for the tapestries. Goya is better remembered for his tapestry cartoons of the **majas** and **majos**—people dressed in the styles of the lower-class street people. Their songs, dances, and style of dress had become popular with the upper classes.

In 1780 Goya submitted a painting of the crucifixion to the Royal Academy of San Fernando. He painted in a style that he knew would be approved, and he was admitted as a member of the Academy.

In 1781 he shared a commission with his brother-in-law and a younger brother, Ramon Bayeu, for fresco paintings in the dome of the Cathedral of Nuestra Señora del Pilar in Saragossa. There was a disagreement about Goya's part of the work. He refused to make changes at the time, though he did so later. The experience was never forgotten by Goya.

In the fall of the same year, Goya became acquainted with the king's brother, the Infante Don Luis de Bourbon. In painting portraits for this man and his family, Goya gained the recognition and position for which he had longed. In an unusual painting of the family of the Infante, servants are included, the wife is having her hair done, and Goya himself is visible in the left corner as he paints the group. This composition bears some similarity to Velázquez' *Las Meninas*. Surely he was familiar with that painting. Another portrait dating from this period in Goya's career is *Condesa de Chinchón* (see Figure 22).

The Duke and Duchess of Osuna were important patrons of Goya. He painted many portraits of family members and family groups. In their country home, Alameda, aristocrats and intellectuals were entertained. The duchess was a leader in style, entertainment, and whatever was fashionable in society. She and her husband purchased more of Goya's paintings than anyone except the king.

A rival in society to the Duchess of Osuna was the Duchess of Alba. Goya first painted her portrait in 1795. She had been married at the age of 13 to the duke, who was then 19. By the time she was in her twenties, she was famous for her beauty and charm, for her good works, and some of her cruelties as well. She was ever at odds with Queen Maria Luisa and the queen's favorite, Prime Minister Godoy. Somehow, Goya managed to stay on the middle ground, making paintings for both.

Some historians think that Goya and the Duchess of Alba carried on a short love affair, while others do not think the evidence supports this notion. At any rate, Goya painted several portraits of her, including two full-length paintings, *The Naked Maja* and *The Clothed Maja*. Some believe they were painted for her rooms in her country home. Prime Minister Godoy acquired them, probably after the duchess' death. Others think that Goya painted the two majas for Godoy.

At any rate, the affair between Goya and the duchess, if it happened at all, did not last. She was known to flit from one affair to the next. Goya was evidently more unhappy than the duchess. Shortly before this time he had been seriously ill, had been paralyzed, and when he regained his health, had been left totally deaf. He was bothered afterward by some sort of noise or ringing in his ears.

Perhaps as a distraction, he began experimenting with etching. He took a separate studio, hardly more than a loft, in Madrid. In two years he had produced over 80 plates, most of which we know as "Los Caprichos" ("The Caprices," or fanciful notions). These etchings express Goya's troubled feelings about the life he saw around him: the vices and **follies** of the people and the corruption in the government and the Church. These works seem to be an indictment of them all. He adds fantasies from the theories of witchcraft, which were much discussed at that time. There are humans with animal heads, monsters of all sorts, bird-man creatures, and weird figures from nightmares. Some of these etchings criticized the Church. Trouble was avoided by turning over the plates to the king's collection. The "Black Paintings," so called for their similarly frightening and puzzling themes, were painted later, as were other series of etchings. The etchings were printed 36 years after Goya's death. One group is called the "Disparates" ("Follies") and "Proverbios" ("Proverbs"), and another is "The Disasters of War." The latter series, for the first time in art, shows the horror of war for both soldiers and the people. War is not shown as romantic, glamorous, and exciting.

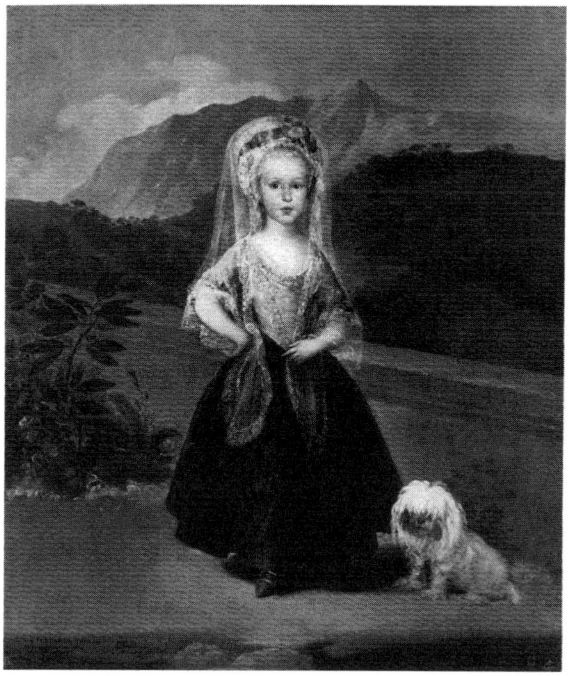

Figure 22
Condesa de Chinchón, 1783
Francisco de Goya

In 1807 Spain was ruled by Charles IV with his wife Maria Luisa and Prime Minister Godoy. France was at war with England. Napoleon wanted to get to Portugal in order to blockade England. Godoy gave permission to Napoleon to move his troops across Spain. For this, Portugal was to be divided among France, Spain, and Godoy himself. By the time the French troops moved in, the Spanish realized that the French had come to conquer, not to protect, Spain. Charles IV abdicated the throne to his son, Ferdinand. Napoleon agreed to this since he planned to turn Spain over to one of his own anyway. Some Spaniards were deeply unhappy with the reign of Charles IV and thought that France would help the country. Goya was in a difficult spot. While he, too, thought Spain might be helped, he wanted to stay in the favor of whoever ended up on the throne so he could retain his position with the court. He had worked long and hard. He did not want to lose what he had gained.

Two paintings by Goya show us the beginnings of the revolution by the people against the French: *The Second of May, 1808* and *The Third of May, 1808.* As the last member of Charles IV's family was to be taken away in exile, the people in the palace plaza rioted. They were fired on by the Spanish. Throughout the night and the next day people were rounded up and shot. The word "guerrilla" comes from this war. The Spanish used it to identify the people who fought against the French from behind the lines. They were not regular soldiers, but were fighting in secret to constantly harass the invaders and make them nervous. Country roads became dangerous and food supplies may have been poisoned. Eventually the Spanish did drive the French out. In fact, his losses in Spain were the beginning of Napoleon's downfall.

The Second of May is reminiscent of a Rubens composition, but it does not succeed with the same kind of believable action. *The Third of May* is one of Goya's masterpieces. By lantern light, the soldiers of a firing squad execute the Spanish people. The light concentrates on the figure in the center, whose arms are raised in horror. Others at his side know they are next, as the dead pile up in the left of the picture. No romantic adventuring here, but war at its most deadly.

Goya's painting style, adjusted enough to be accepted by the courtiers who preferred neoclassicism, still remained his own. When he painted the royal family of Charles IV, he did not flatter them (see Figure 23). They are portrayed as neither very attractive nor very intelligent. Goya

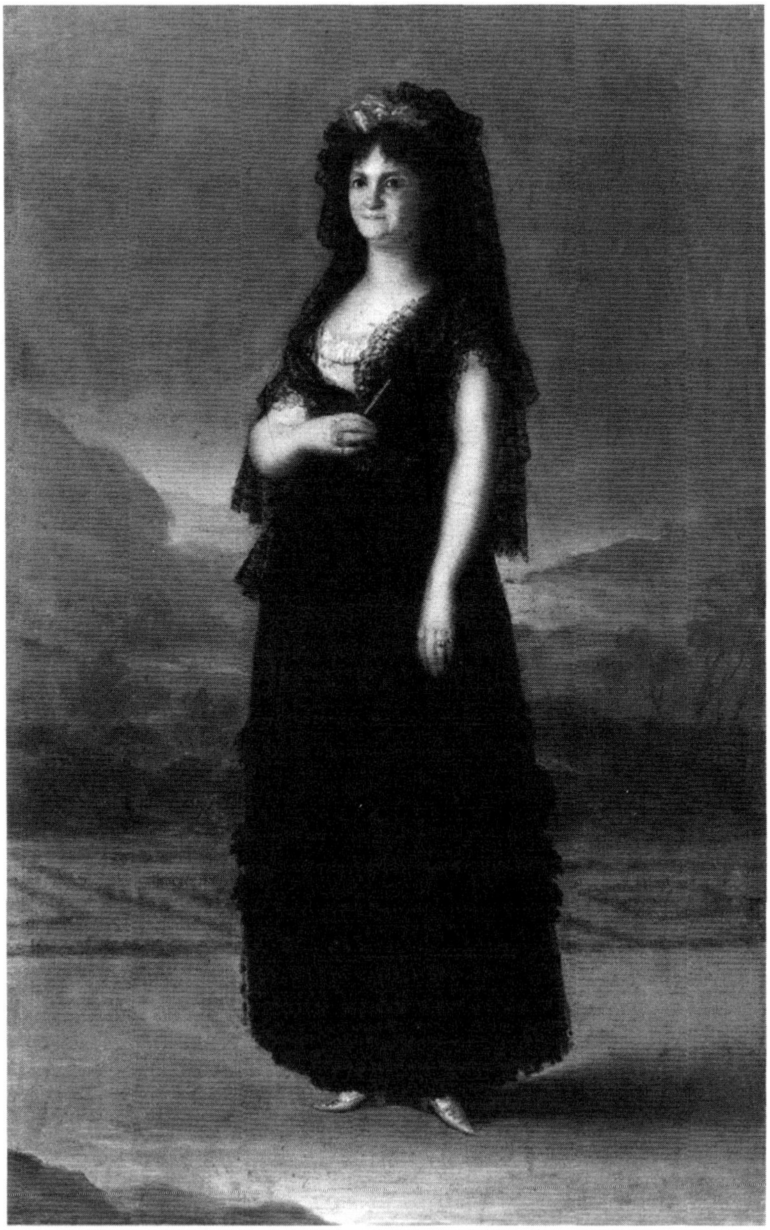

Figure 23
Maria Luisa, Queen of Spain, c. 1799
Francisco de Goya

has been called aggressive, tough, obstinate, and opinionated. He came from a part of Spain in which life was not easy and people had to be tough to survive. He produced at least 350 portraits (including the well-known *Bartolomé Sureda y Miserol,* Color Plate 5), plus etchings, engravings, and paintings of many kinds of subject matter including war, love, bullfighting, and landscapes. He also did tapestry designs and frescoes.

We do not know much about his life with Josefa. Some historians think they may have had twenty children; others believe they had four or five. At any rate, only one child (a son, Xavier) grew to adulthood. A sensitive portrait of the son in his late teens shows us a boy trying to look quite grown up, but with a boy's still slightly childlike face. Goya painted his son in about 1804. One portrait thought to be of Josefa has survived. She died in 1812.

The new king, Fernando VII, who ascended to the throne after the French were driven out, restored Goya to his position at court and increased his pension. Goya was in his seventies. He had periods of illness, dizziness, and depression. He had never been a man of patience; now he was even more easily angered and had to work to keep his temper in check. He moved to a country house outside Madrid with his housekeeper, a woman named Leocadia Weiss, and her daughter Rosarita. She may have been his mistress and the little girl his daughter. Goya was very fond of the child. She had some ability in painting and he gave her painting lessons.

Goya continued to experiment and learn. Late in his life he tried **lithography,** an exacting kind of printmaking. Earlier he had tried using a reed palette knife instead of a brush. The painting *City on a Rock* is said to have been painted with such a tool. His last work, which is unfinished, is a portrait in which we can see how he produced a portrait. He must have been 82 at the time.

In 1824 there was more unrest in Spain. Goya decided to move to France. After visiting Paris, he settled in Bordeaux with Leocadia Weiss and her daughter. He felt at home there in a colony of other Spaniards. He had leave from the king to migrate to France for his health, and in 1826 went back to apply for an extension of the leave. It was granted. He continued to make drawings and to paint. In 1828 he suffered a stroke and died on April 16. He was 82.

Glossary

Rococo a decorative art style that followed the Baroque style, borrowing from the Baroque and emphasizing its most elaborate elements of line and curving forms

majas, majos beautiful and perhaps showy women and men, perhaps dressed as though from the lower classes

follies foolish behaviors or beliefs

lithography a printmaking technique using a stone or metal plate. The picture is drawn with a greasy substance that absorbs the ink for printing.

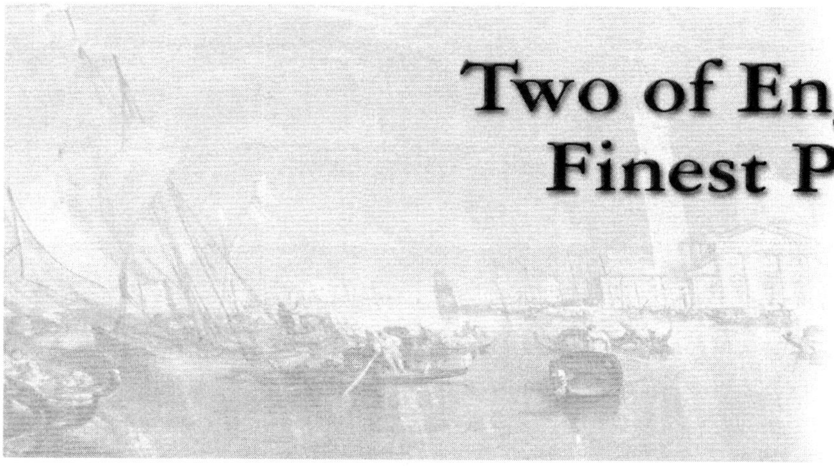

Two of England's Finest Painters

JOHN CONSTABLE AND WILLIAM TURNER became well-known at a time when genius in music, literature, and art was in full flower all over Europe. The gist of much of this new work was romantic. When used to describe art or music, "romantic" means concerned with color and passion and heroism. Whether people were conscious of it or not, Romanticism was a reaction to the Age of Reason that dominated the eighteenth century.

The Age of Reason, or the Enlightenment, emphasized rational, scientific, logical thought. The machine, which made possible the Industrial Revolution that began in England in 1750, was a sort of symbol for this way of thinking.

The Industrial Revolution changed many lives and actually began to form the world we know today. Many English people left the countryside to move into towns and work in the textile mills, which were powered by steam. The modern capitalist society was born and the rationalist thinkers came up with economic and political theories to match it.

Forces were working against rationalist thought, however. The early Romantic movement began with individuals who cared more for portraying the drama and beauty of a subject in a personal way than for following the rules of an academy or other organization. The Romanticists reversed all the previous rules of style and subject matter, and renewed our interest in the natural world. They valued sensuality and emotion over reason and intellect. They also believed that history was still powerful and moving. The French Revolution's ideas about liberty and equality inspired them.

The Romanticists were able to get people to "sit up and take notice." As a result, we now think art and artists are important socially and spiritually. These creative people of the early nineteenth century also managed to make the public accept the idea that many different styles can exist at the same time. Since then, we have come to expect that each new wave of art should be different from the last and that every artist should be original in some way. This was to become very important in the twentieth century.

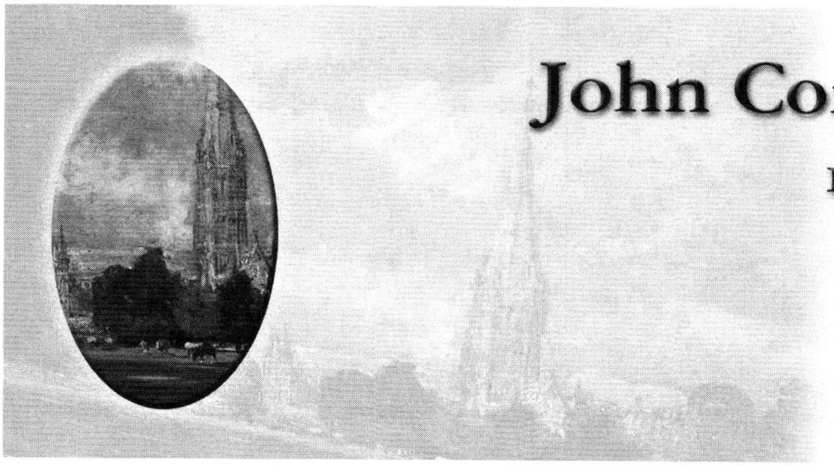

John Constable
1776–1837

JOHN CONSTABLE was born on June 11, 1776, at East Bergholt in Suffolk. His father was a miller, just as Rembrandt's father had been. Golding Constable owned several mills and was a respected member of the community. He had planned for his son to be a minister of the Church of England, but John showed no aptitude for or interest in the kind of study required for that career. His father then hoped that the milling business could be passed on to John. Instead, his youngest son eventually ran the mills and John became one of England's foremost landscape painters.

John loved the countryside in which he grew up. He liked to look about him and plan the kind of painting he would make of it even before he learned to paint. The fields, trees, streams, clouds, hills, meadows, and farmers working the land all seemed to call him to record their beauty.

From the time Constable was a schoolboy he had dabbled in painting. His interest was encouraged by a local man, John Dunthorpe (an amateur painter) and by Sir George Beaumont (who collected art and was also an amateur painter). The latter introduced Constable to paintings in his collection of oils and watercolors. Another early influence was a printmaker and painter, John Thomas Smith, who encouraged Constable to become a professional artist. Through these men, Constable had acquired a rather sketchy knowledge of painting methods and the work of other artists. By 1799 his father agreed to let him try his luck in London.

Constable applied for admission to the Royal Academy and was accepted in 1800. He studied anatomy, made drawings from models and casts, and copied the works of the masters. However, he resisted following the painting styles of the past. He was determined to find his own style. When he was not at the Academy he spent time on walking tours, making sketches and watercolors of the countryside he loved. Landscape painting had become somewhat profitable for artists at that time. Landowners wanted paintings of their homes and the surrounding land. Just as portraits had always been commissioned, landscapes were now the subject of frequent commissions. *Wivenhoe Park, Essex* is a fine example of Constable's landscape style (see Figure 24).

Constable developed a style that influenced such French painters as Géricault and Delacroix. His free, paint-charged brush strokes may also have influenced the Impressionists. For Constable, painting nature was related to his feeling about his religion. He recognized God as the creator of the beauty he saw around him. His paintings were an expression of that feeling. Although he admired the work of the old masters, he did not imitate them. To paint nature as he saw it, he tried to understand the forms found in nature and how they worked together for a poetic whole. A splendid example of Constable's talent for composition is *The White Horse* (see Color Plate 6). Remember that some artists of the past had also striven to understand and paint nature: Leonardo and Dürer, for example.

Constable's work was recognized in France before recognition came to him in his own country. ***The Hay Wain*** attracted the attention of French critics and of the artist Géricault. Delacroix heard of it from Géricault. An art dealer in Paris began to buy Constable's works and had an entire room devoted to them. During Constable's lifetime no English dealers gave him this kind of support, though commissions for paintings sometimes came through such dealers. When Delacroix visited England, he took the opportunity to visit Constable, to see his work and talk with him about painting. This led Delacroix to change his own painting techniques and to introduce more light into his paintings.

Constable also loved the sea and many of his paintings included elements of the seaside. The dramatic movement of the sea was like the dramatic movement of a heavily clouded sky. Both are often found in Constable's paintings. After the death of his beloved wife, to whom he had been married for 12 years, his paintings became more troubled and melancholy. His good friend John

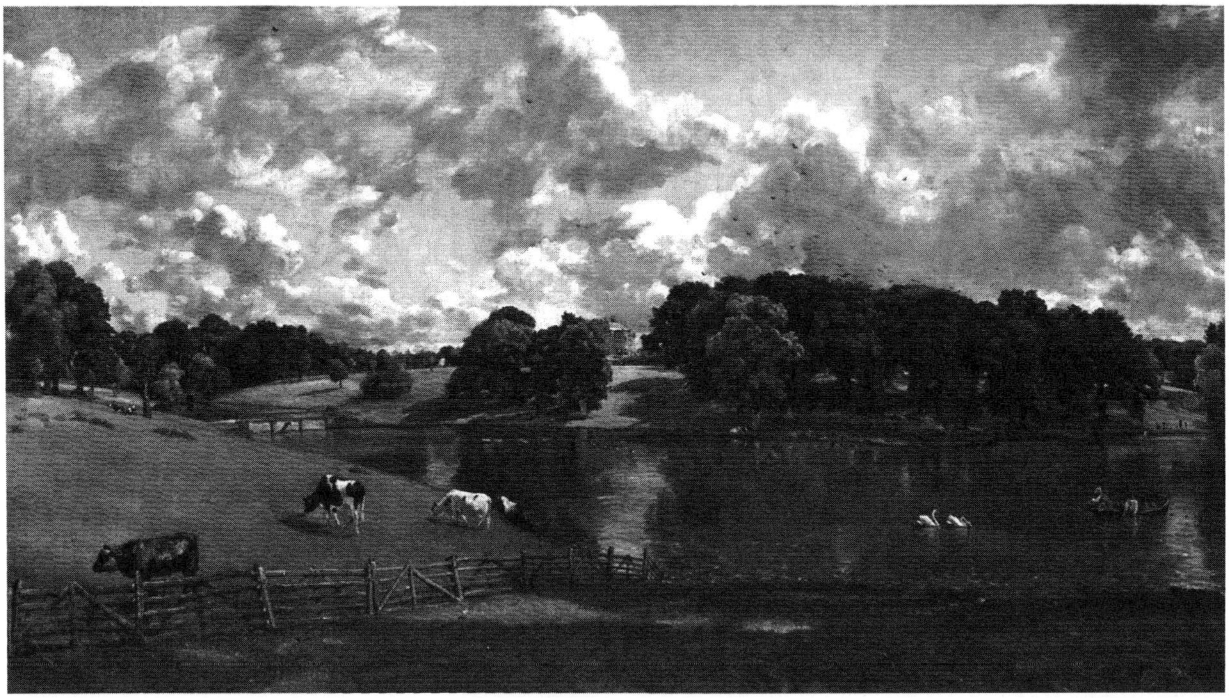

Figure 24
Wivenhoe Park, Essex, 1816
John Constable

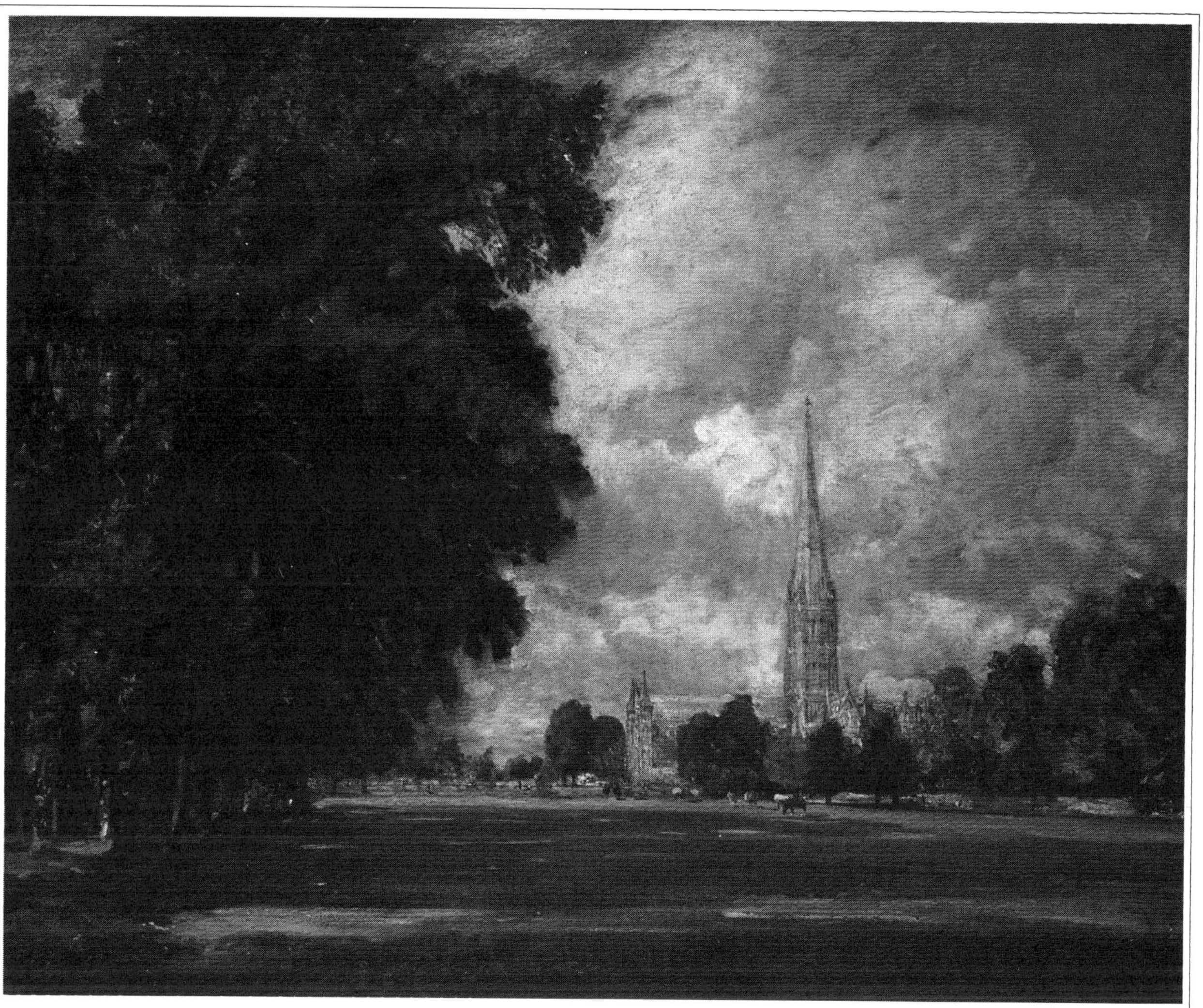

Figure 25
A View of Salisbury Cathedral, c. 1825
John Constable

Fisher advised him to "Calm your mind and your sea at the same time and let in sunshine and serenity." Later a rainbow became an added theme in several of his paintings.

Constable seems to have lived a careful and deliberate life. He did not rush into things. He reached for recognition but it came slowly. He courted his wife for several years before the way was cleared for them to marry. When she died he wore **mourning** for the rest of his life. He was left with children to raise and his work to continue. He loved children and, though he could and did use a sharp and sarcastic tongue with adults, he could never find it in his heart to be unkind to a child. He did not have financial problems. Through an earlier inheritance, his brother's good management of the family milling business, and income from his paintings, he provided well for his children.

For a number of years Constable was refused membership in the Royal Academy, though his paintings had been exhibited there frequently.

Landscape painting was not considered as important as portrait painting. He was admitted to membership at last in 1829.

Many copies of the drawings in Constable's sketchbooks were made into prints by engravers. A series of engravings was done by David Lucas, who copied Constable's paintings for a book entitled *English Landscape Scenery.* He had continued to move about the countryside in the parts of England he loved best. He spent two or three months at a time in an area making drawings and watercolors. Many of these he then made into oil paintings. Salisbury Cathedral appears in many drawings and paintings (see Figure 25).

Constable's work had gained moderate acceptance in England toward the end of his life, but lost popularity after his death in March 1837. By 1888, when his daughter Isabel contributed 100 paintings and 300 drawings to the Victoria and Albert Museum, people were again becoming aware of his work. From that time onward Constable's work has gradually achieved its present position.

Glossary

hay wain a wagon for carrying hay from the fields

mourning black clothing worn for a period of time after the death of a family member

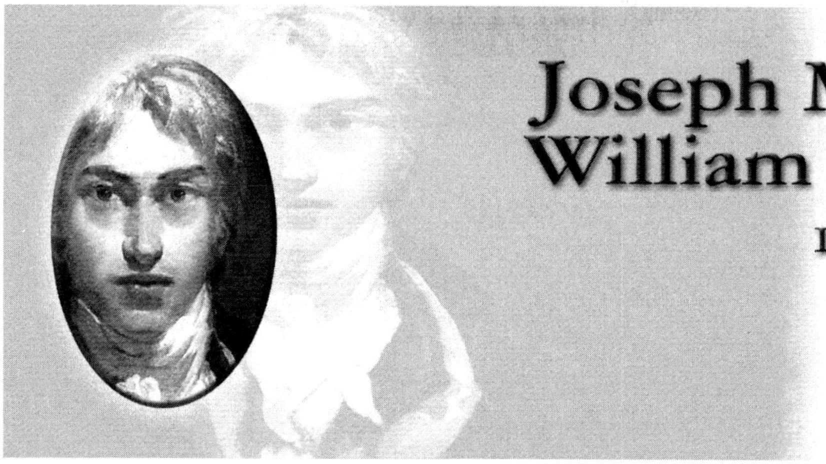

Joseph Mallord William Turner

1775 – 1851

JOSEPH MALLORD WILLIAM TURNER was born in London in 1775. He began drawing when he was very young, and his great talent soon became apparent. It is said that Turner was just a boy when he displayed his drawings in his father's barbershop—and sold some!

When Turner was just 14, he was admitted to study at the Royal Academy's greatly respected art school. Here he began his career devoted to painting.

Every year, the Royal Academy exhibited the works of outstanding artists, both new and established. The Royal Academy was very influential. It was considered by most people to be the judge of what was good art. Its approval could advance an artist's career—and its disapproval could make it difficult for an artist to earn his living.

Artists whose work was most highly thought of were elected to the Academy. Turner was elected an associate of the Academy at 24, the minimum age allowed. He became a full member, or academician, three years later, in 1802. To mark this honor, Turner painted a series of large works inspired by the masters of classical art.

Turner was active in the Royal Academy for most of his life. He was regularly seen at its functions, and taught perspective in its art school for 30 years. On his death he left £20,000 to the Academy.

So Turner was not a rebel against the establishment—the Royal Academy and its artistic standards. But, as his painting developed, his work took him far from the old masters of art.

Turner's early painting was representational. Things looked just like what they were. But in his later works, he captured his impressions of scenes and events. He was painting in impressionistic ways at least 40 years before the Impressionist movement began.

John Constable, the English landscape painter, called the color in Turner's later works "tinted steam." Think how airy that sounds, how fleeting.

A critic who disliked Turner's later works called them "pictures of nothing, and very like." He thought the paintings had no substance, no value; they were like nothing.

Both Constable and the critic were referring to what have become Turner's most famous and best-loved works, paintings such as *The Burning of the*

Houses of Parliament, The Fighting Temeraire Tugged to Her Last Berth to Be Broken Up, and *Rain, Steam, and Speed.*

J.M.W. Turner's work is divided into three major periods.

His first period was conventionally representational. He painted well, but showed things much as people would expect them to look. He continued a habit he formed as a boy—traveling the countryside with a sketchbook, looking for inspiration, making quick drawings to record things of interest. The observations he made on these tours were the basis of many paintings.

This first period lasted from about 1800–1820. During this time, Turner painted subjects from history and mythology. The accurate details of architecture and nature in these paintings show how carefully Turner studied his surroundings.

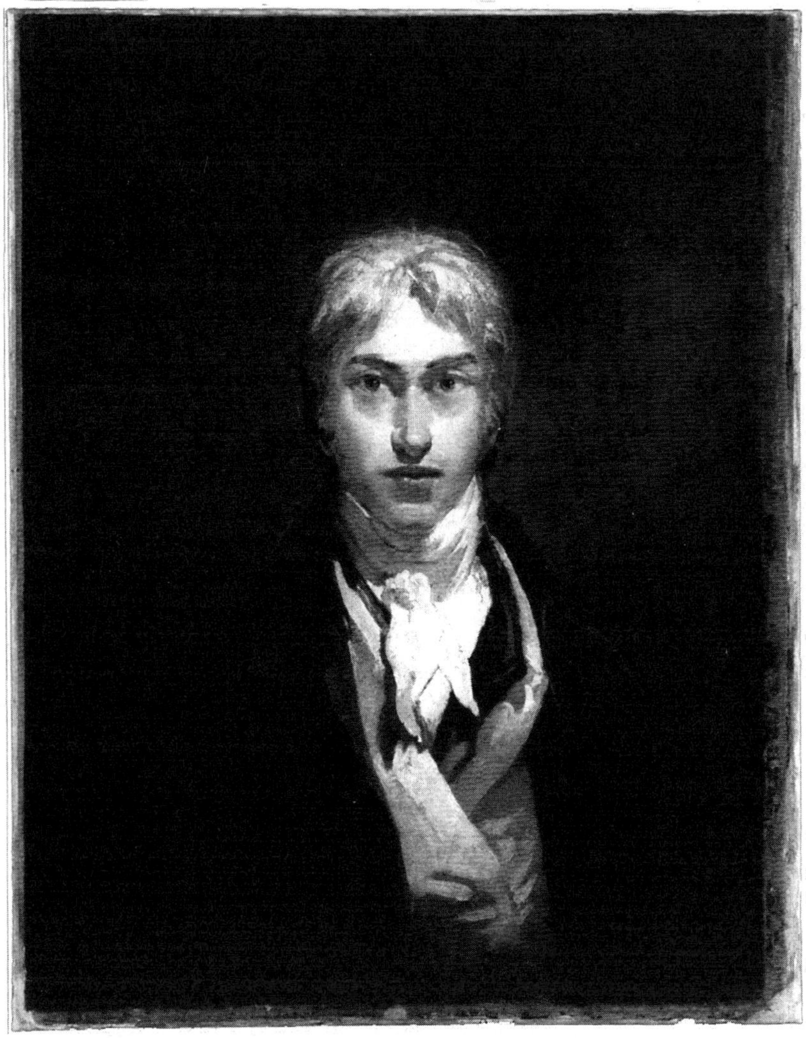

Figure 26
Self-Portrait, c. 1800
Joseph Mallord William Turner

During this period, Turner often imitated the painting styles of well-known, popular artists. He painted this self-portrait (see Figure 26) during this period.

Also during this period, Turner left England for the first time. He went to Paris, where he saw the paintings Napoleon had brought back from Italy. He was impressed by the great Venetians of the sixteenth century, and tried his hand at painting in the Venetian manner.

Then, in 1819, Turner visited Italy for the first time. His second period could be said to begin with this visit. He became more interested in the power of light and atmosphere. He imitated other artists less, and the scenery he painted became more and more idealized. He made the scene look more perfect than it really was. The quality of the light in his paintings changed, and became more luminous. Their subjects seem veiled by films of color.

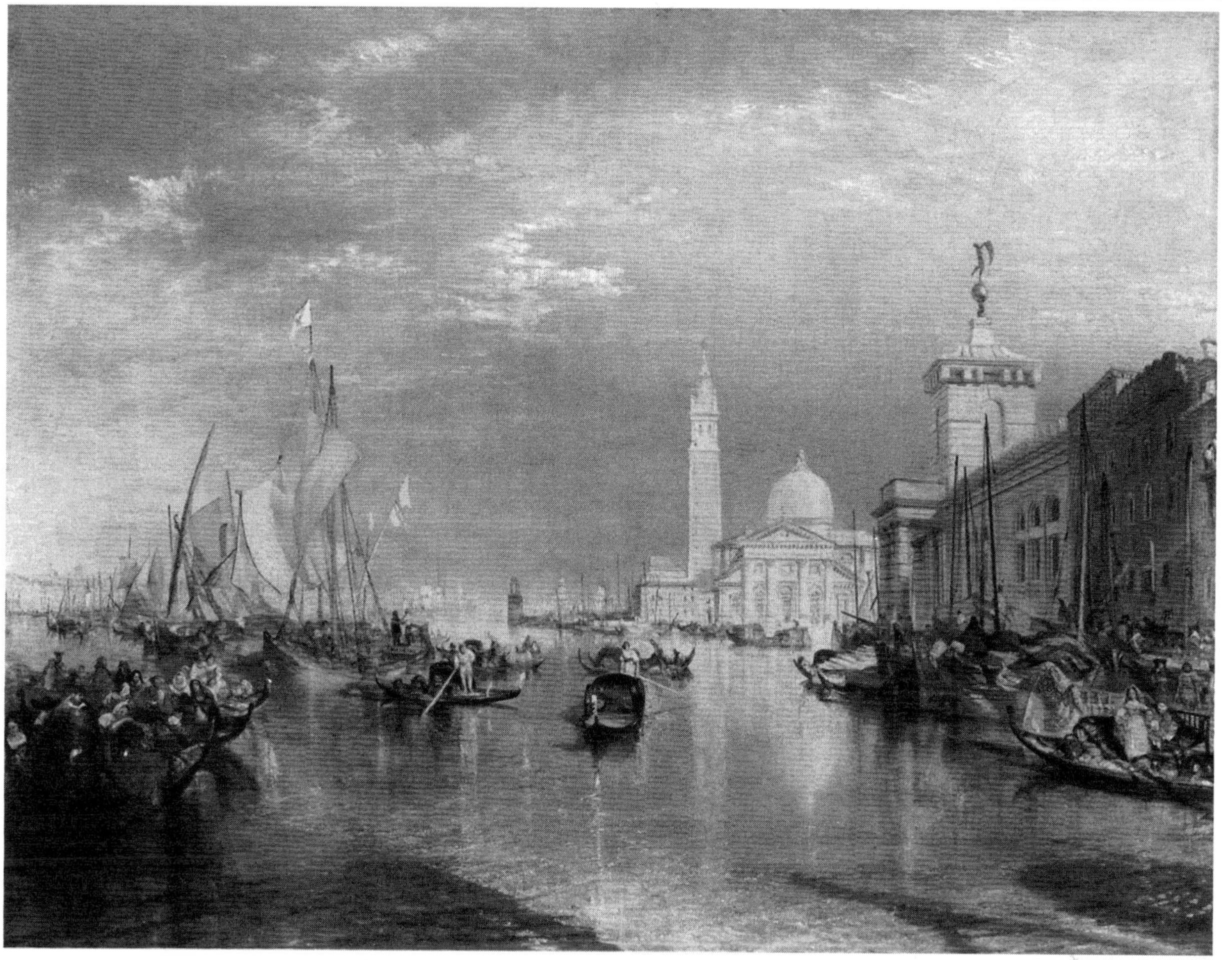

Figure 27
Venice: Dogana and San Giorgio Maggiore, c. 1834
Joseph Mallord William Turner

This can be seen in *Venice: Dogana and San Giorgio Maggiore* (see Figure 27).

In his third and final period, this fascination with light and atmosphere became more and more evident. His compositions from this period are fluid, suggesting movement and space. He was willing to sacrifice detail to achieve a general effect.

In his painting *The Burning of the Houses of Parliament,* Turner transformed an actual current event into a clash between fire and water. In an age when many painters tried to depict, or show, an event as it happened, Turner depicted how it felt to watch the event. He gave viewers an impression of the scene, as opposed to a record of it. The color and light in his paintings grew even more brilliant than before.

In one way, these effects were influenced by his early work with watercolor. By its nature, watercolor is very suitable for improvisation, for quick sketches. Since watercolor is transparent, mistakes can't be painted over. Watercolor painters learn to make instant decisions, and to work quickly before the paint dries.

Turner's method of handling oil paint grew from these qualities of watercolor. He used watercolor often, and adapted some of these skills to painting with oils. After his first visit to Italy,

Turner's use of color became purer. His treatment of his subjects suggested the transparency of watercolor. His painting techniques included using **washes** of oil color to build up layers.

His work with watercolor may also have influenced him in other ways. Turner was one of the first artists to make improvisation, or work done on the spur of the moment, an important aspect of his work. He often sent works to exhibitions unfinished, and completed them on the walls during the three or four days allowed for varnishing. This varnishing time was meant to let artists make last-minute changes to suit the light in the area where their work hung. Turner sometimes took unfair advantage of this time to adjust his works in relation to other works hanging nearby. For example, at the Royal Academy exhibition of 1832, Turner enlarged a red buoy in his seapiece *Helvoetsluys,* which overpowered the reds in Constable's *Opening of Waterloo Bridge.*

Even before his work moved toward what we would consider abstraction, Turner's paintings were a shock to the public of the time. We must remember that people were used to seeing very conventional, highly finished works. Most paintings followed certain accepted rules, and looked quite formal. Turner's paintings looked unfinished by comparison. The colors were too bright, and weren't the "real" colors viewers expected for particular parts of a picture. A critic described Turner in 1816 as making "pictures of the elements of air, earth and water. The artist delights to go back to that first chaos of the world . . . . All is without form and void." (See Color Plate 7.)

These critics would have been even more shocked if they could have seen Turner's experimental works, the paintings he never tried to exhibit. In fact, many of his paintings were not exhibited until the 1960s. The vivid color and apparent abstractness of his late works appeal to modern tastes, but they would have been horrifying to the public of his own time. While Turner pursued a private vision, he was also a practical man. He depended on the public for his living. So although he experimented in the studio, he only incorporated certain aspects of these experiments into the work he exhibited.

Throughout his career, we can see that Turner was fascinated with nature. Even in his early work, he did not focus on human subjects but on overpowering natural phenomena He painted thunderstorms and blizzards on the sea or in the mountains, sunrises and sunsets, descending darkness and moonlight. Once, he had himself fastened to the deck of a ship to watch an actual storm. He spent four hours there, not sure he would survive. In his work, he recorded the most extreme and fleeting effects of weather, time of day and night, light and atmosphere. One of his last works *Rain, Steam, and Speed,* shows a train speeding over a bridge in a heavy rainstorm. The solid form of the machine disappears in mist and spray.

At his death in 1851, he left some 300 oil paintings and more than 19,000 watercolors and drawings to the British nation, a legacy to Turner's devotion to his art.

Glossary

washes in painting, thin mixtures of paint and water or oil

French Painters on the Edge of Change

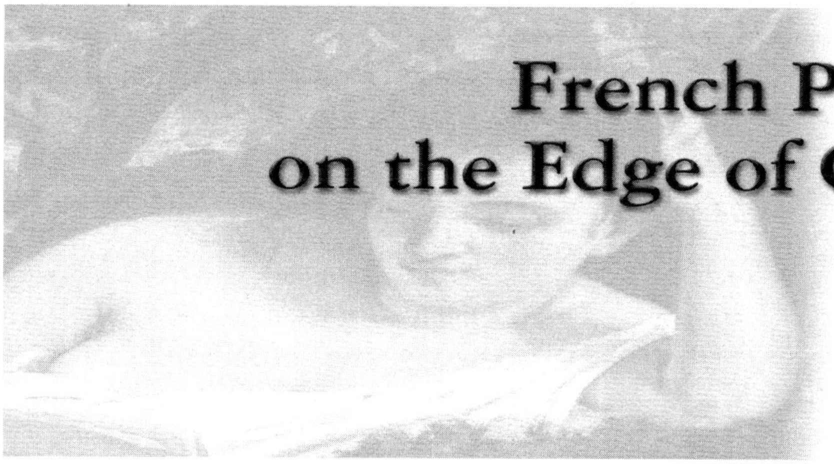

THE French Royal Academy of Painting and Sculpture was established in Paris in 1648. Its purpose was to reward and so to continue the kinds of art its members considered the best. The Academy only accepted works of art that were done according to standards set up at a particular time. Artists sent their work to be judged for inclusion in the Salon, or exhibit, which was first held every second year, and then yearly. In the nineteenth century increasing numbers of artists asked to exhibit. As many as 5,000 pieces might be accepted and just as many rejected. Paintings were often hung in crowded galleries from floor to ceiling. For a long while the only way art could be sold was through the Salon. Rejected work was actually stamped "rejected" on the back, and was difficult to sell afterwards. No one wanted to buy a rejected piece of art. An artist whose work was usually rejected had a hard time getting established in the art world of France. Because the Academy controlled the work of artists, new styles were not always encouraged.

The French people were as interested in art during the nineteenth century as we are in sports today. They knew which styles were accepted by the Academy. They visited the annual Salons to see the new paintings and sculptures. News about the artists who had been awarded medals of merit by the Academy spread rapidly. People knew what the Academy approved and so they felt confident that they knew about art.

The Academy system might have helped art more if it had not restricted the styles it accepted. Today we realize that there are many approaches to art. There are many kinds of media, many kinds of subject matter (or themes), and many styles. Artists have the freedom today to produce their own individual styles and to experiment with many kinds of materials. But in nineteenth-century France, it was not "safe" for an artist to be inventive.

The style favored by the Academy in the early 1800s was neoclassical ("new classical"). Classical art is the art of ancient Greece and Rome. The classical style was discovered again in the Renaissance, and now the French Academy, led by the artist Jacques Louis David, made classic art its pet. In 1757 the ruins of Pompeii were first excavated.

People were fascinated by the idea of the discovery of an ancient civilization. Books were written about this ancient culture and about the art of Greece. David's paintings illustrated ancient Greek myths and stories of heroism, often with a message that could be applied to France at the time. Artists often found inspiration in sculptures from this period and portrayed these ideals in their paintings. The ideas of bravery, beauty, and purity were expressed in static forms. Even an "action" painting such as David's *The Battle of the Romans and the Sabines* seems made up of figures frozen in time, never to move again from their fixed positions.

As the nineteenth century progressed, Napoleon fell from power and David was exiled to Brussels, where he died. The style of art favored by the Academy continued to be neoclassical: cool, controlled, and smoothly painted.

The next leader of neoclassicism was painter Jean Auguste Dominique Ingres, whose drawing skills were truly outstanding. Ingres painted large historical paintings in addition to his many sensitive portraits.

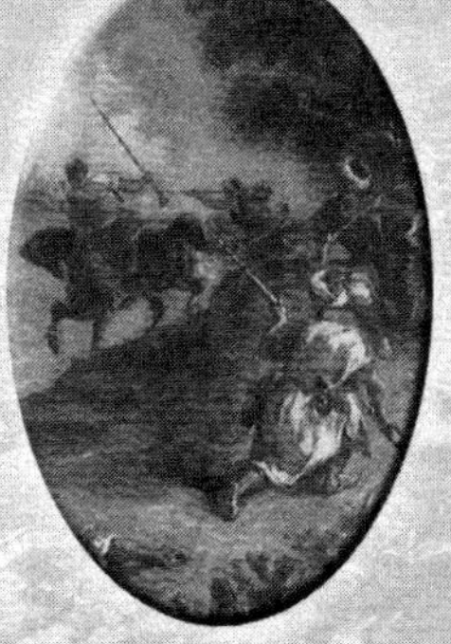

Théodore Géricault

1791 – 1824

Eugène Delacroix

1798 – 1863

THE FIRST REAL CHALLENGE to neoclassicism came with the art of Théodore **Géricault**. He was a painter in the style called Romanticism. Using "romantic" in this way doesn't necessarily mean love and kisses. Instead it means a style that shows emotion, strong feelings, chaotic situations, and dramatic beauty. It seemed quite the opposite of the classic style, which featured **stabile,** idealized people and situations.

Géricault's painting *The Raft of the Medusa,* which is now in the **Louvre** in Paris, was exhibited in the Salon (Academy exhibit) of 1819. The picture shows survivors of the ship *Medusa* on a raft, pleading for rescue. There was a furor about this incident, since many people died in the shipwreck and government corruption was suspected. The public crowded in to see the painting partly because of the gossip and accusations. The painting is dramatic and grim. We see the dead and dying, as well as the living crying for help. As artists before him such as Rubens had, Géricault used vivid color and strong contrast of light and dark. While the Academy had allowed the painting to be placed in the show, it was not among those bought by the government. (The painting was thought to be critical of the government.) In addition, the Academy was not enthusiastic about the new and dramatic style.

Géricault continued to paint in this exciting style. He loved horses and often used them and horsemen in his paintings. Ultimately he died as the result of an injury sustained while riding a horse. Among some of his surviving paintings are portraits of mental patients in which he tried to interpret their confused states of mind.

Following Géricault is Eugène **Delacroix,** considered by some to be the greatest Romantic painter. He was born in Paris on April 26, 1798. His father was a government official who died when Eugène was seven. The boy was a good student who liked to make sketches in his notebooks as well as to study. After a visit to the Louvre when he was ten, it is said that he decided then and there to become an artist. He may have been influenced by his uncle, Henri Riesener, who was a portrait painter and had been a pupil of David.

Delacroix went to study with the painter and teacher Guerin when he was 17. Guerin taught in the conventional manner. His students learned the usual methods of drawing from ancient sculpture and the classic methods of composition. Guerin, however, also allowed students to try their wings in their own styles. It was a busy school and a gathering place for artists.

Delacroix left Guerin's school after a few months to study at the school of the Academy. He may have had money problems at this time, and the Academy school cost less to attend. Delacroix's parents were now both dead, as was his older brother Henri. His first commissioned painting, *The Virgin of the Harvest,* helped his financial situation. It was for a village church in Orcemont. He also did some lithographs for newspapers in Paris.

Delacroix painted *The Bark of Dante* to submit to the Salon. It was the first of many paintings that would be acclaimed by many and scorned by others. He learned from Rubens to suggest water droplets by painting dabs of rainbow colors side by side to look like water drops at a distance. The painting was accepted in the Salon of 1821 and bought by the government. Although many of his paintings were intensely disliked by many members of the Salon juries, they were often bought. Some historians believe that Delacroix

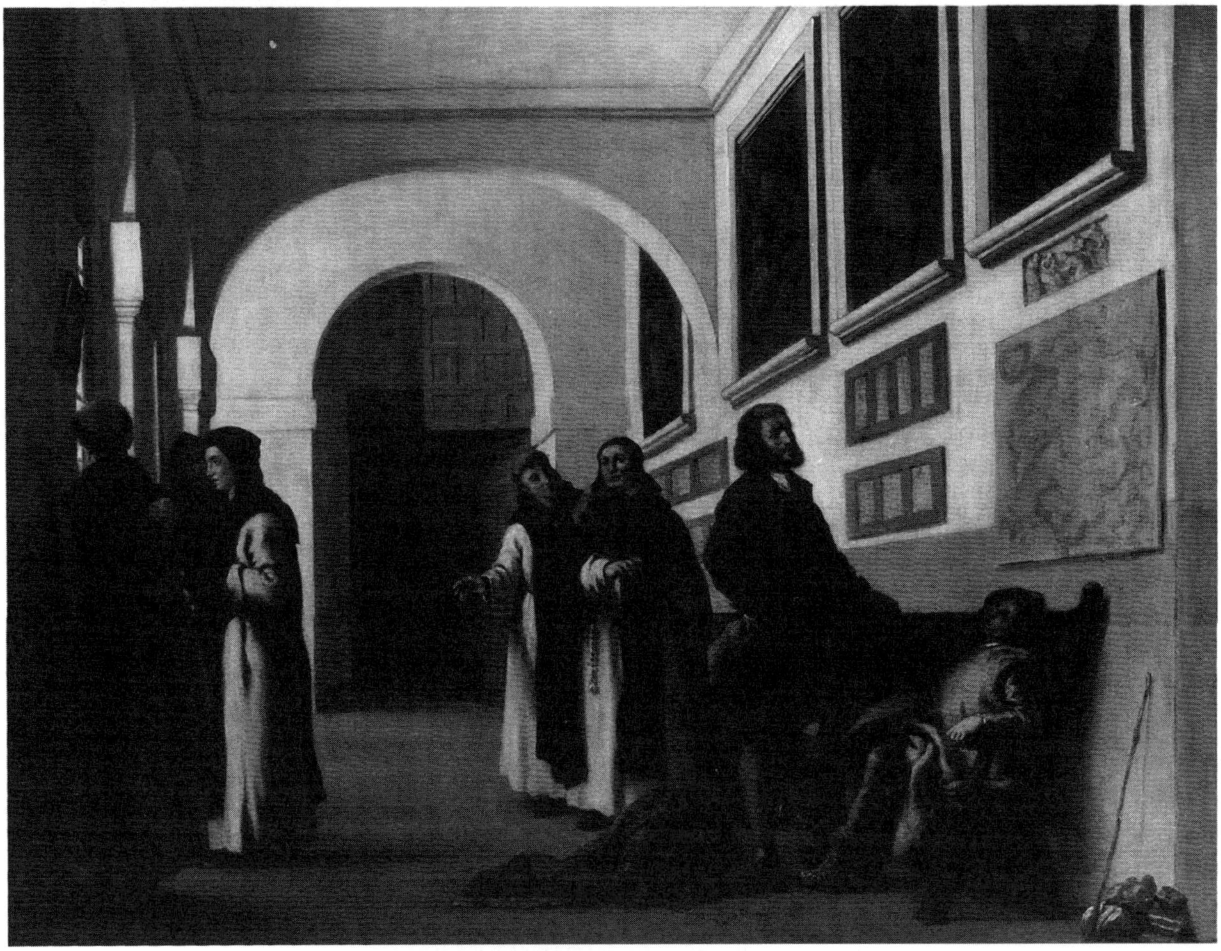

Figure 28
Columbus and His Son at La Rabida, 1838
Eugène Delacroix

was related to a highly placed official who pressured for acceptance of his work. In any case, the government ended up with a collection of masterpieces.

Delacroix was a hardworking painter. His work totals some 12,000 pieces: paintings, watercolors, drawings, and prints. Although he borrowed some classic themes, he did not treat them in the idealized classical way. He personalized the characters to dramatize their stories.

Just as Géricault had used a current story for the *Medusa* painting, Delacroix often used current happenings for the themes of his paintings. *The Massacre at Scio* was based on an actual massacre of Greeks on the island of Scio by the Turks. The 100,000 Greeks living on the island were cut to 9,000. In this painting he used some of the techniques he had admired in Constable's work. Colors brushed on close to one another, not mixed together, gave a more natural effect. The colors reflected light. In the composition a horse and rider rear at the upper right, while the people in the center and at the left seem to be in numb horror.

Delacroix was influenced by artists of the past and those working in his own time. John Constable, mentioned above, was an English painter of landscapes who was able to create natural-looking light and an open, airy feeling in his paintings. Rubens' dramatic paintings and rich color had impressed Delacroix, as had Géricault's. Rembrandt's use of light and dark shadow and Goya's style were additional influences.

In 1827 Delacroix submitted 14 paintings for the Salon; all but one were accepted. He was then almost 30, and a recognized painter, confident of his ability. From this group of pictures one was particularly disliked by the public, even those who usually approved of his work. It was *The Death of Sardanapalus,* the story of an Assyrian king who was planning to kill himself. His riches, his courtiers, and his horse were to be burned with him. In the painting, the first smoke and flames are visible in the upper right. The king lounges on a couch, upper center, seemingly unconcerned with the terror below him. Even though the public was fascinated by things oriental at this time, the painting was too sensational and too violent for most.

We have read of artists who visited Italy. Delacroix was one who never did. He did spend time in England, and certainly knew of the Italian masters. He made a trip to Morocco in 1832 that influenced his later paintings. He was invited to accompany the Count Charles de Mornay on a diplomatic mission. France had just gained control of Algeria, and wanted to establish good relations with the Sultan of Morocco, whose country was next to Algeria.

It was an exciting trip for Delacroix. He began making sketches as the boat crossed the Mediterranean. He left France in January and returned in July. He was able to see something of Spain, including paintings by Velázquez and Goya. He marveled at the golden light, the flowing robes worn by the people, the bright colors, and the Moorish architecture. He filled sketchbook after sketchbook with drawings and watercolor sketches, noting other information that he would want to use later for paintings. *Columbus and His Son at La Rabida* (see Figure 28) dates from this period. He drew animals, faces, deserts, mountains, and charging warriors on horses. He was able to be slipped secretly into a **harem.** One painting done on his return was *Women of Algiers,* from the harem venture. He admired the composure and dignity of the Arabs, though he was not taken by the dramatic exhibitions of horsemanship and shooting. He was not too sure who the victim was to be!

Other paintings Delacroix made on his return were *The Sultan of Morocco, Moroccan Caid Visiting*

His Tribe, and *Jewish Wedding*. Later the painters Cézanne, Renoir, and Picasso were to admire the *Women of Algiers*. Picasso made some 15 copies of it.

Travel to other countries and other cultures always opens our eyes and minds to other parts of the world. The Morocco trip was important for Delacroix. He felt that he had been transported into the ancient past. He could see that some of the classical past could be combined with his Romantic style. He developed more confidence in himself and in his art.

Commissions now came for murals to decorate government buildings. Murals had been somewhat overdone in the recent past and were losing popularity, but Delacroix gave them new life and excitement. He used biblical themes and Greek mythology as well as current ideas. Some projects involved ceiling paintings with all the problems these present to the artist. Delacroix was bothered by illness from time to time, and the mural commissions were exhausting. He painted murals for the Salon du Roi, a hall in which the king received ministers, followed by murals for the Palais Bourbon. There a library of the Chamber of Deputies was decorated.

The nineteenth century in France saw many famous artists not only in the visual arts, but in literature and music as well. Delacroix knew and was a friend of many: Chopin, Baudelaire, Hugo, Berlioz, Dumas, Balzac, and George Sand. He kept journals for many years, recording his thoughts, feelings, activities, and the progress of his work. He wrote well, and toward the end of his life was working on a dictionary of art terms. He never married, but had many romances and romantic involvements with a variety of women.

Delacroix delighted in animals, and spent time in the zoo of the Jardin des Plantes sketching the animals, especially the tigers and lions. In 1848 the American painter George Catlin brought a group of Ojibwa Indians from Iowa to tour Europe. They appeared on exhibition in Paris. Delacroix was as enchanted with them as he had been with the Arabs in Morocco, and made many sketches of them.

Delacroix enjoyed the company of the artistic and intellectual people in Paris and had problems balancing his work with his socializing. Toward the end of his life, however, he wanted more quiet and less social activity. He moved to a small but comfortable house in Champrosay, a suburb of Paris. It was wooded and secluded, and offered a quiet retreat. He still enjoyed his friends, but wanted to be able to escape Paris. He had tried to avoid becoming involved in politics. Though his painting *Liberty Leading the People* had been painted in the excitement of the revolution of 1830, and had been exhibited from time to time depending upon who was in power, it was put away again. He found it hard to be enthusiastic about some of the new inventions such as railways, steamships, or the telegraph. He felt they were simply used to speed up life. He did like photography, however, for he felt it could be useful for an artist, though it was too late for him.

The last, long-overdue honor came to Delacroix when he was finally elected to membership in the Academy. He had been passed over six times before, and now, two years before his death, it did not mean a great deal to him. He had achieved status without it.

Though his life had slowed down in some respects, he continued to paint and to plan paintings until his death on August 13, 1863. One of his last works was *Arabs Skirmishing in the Mountains* (see Color Plate 8). He left special drawings and objects to friends; the rest of his work, 6,000 prints, drawings and paintings, was sold to the public.

Glossary

Géricault pronounced zher-e-cō´

stabile fixed in position; stationary or steady

Louvre pronounced loov´-rə; a former palace that was made into a museum in the 1700s

Delacroix pronounced del-ah-kwoh´

harem in Muslim households, a section of the house in which women are segregated

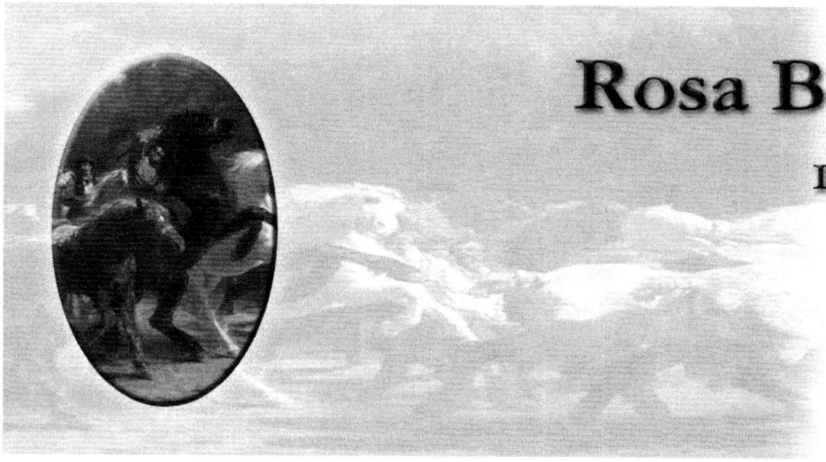

Rosa Bonheur

1822 – 1898

SHE WAS KNOWN and admired on both sides of the Atlantic Ocean. She was a rarity—a nineteenth-century painter who was a woman. She painted Buffalo Bill's portrait. Her name was Rosa **Bonheur,** though she was christened Marie-Rosalie. She was born on March 16, 1822, in Bordeaux, France, where she lived in early childhood. Remember that Goya had moved to Bordeaux at about that time, and lived in the Spanish community there. It is believed that Rosa's family had met Goya through a mutual friend. As a child Rosa loved to draw, and was encouraged by her mother and also by her father, who was a painter and drawing teacher. The family was poor. The father, Raymond, was caught up in various idealistic and **socialistic** movements and devoted much of his time to working for them. The mother, Sophie, found it a struggle to raise four children: Rosa and her sister and two brothers.

In 1829 the family moved to Paris, where the father found work teaching drawing. Rosa missed the freedom she had had in Bordeaux to roam and play. Her mother died when Rosa was 11, leaving everything in her father's hands. Rosa was very upset by her mother's death, and perhaps always felt the unfairness her life had known: hard work and few rewards. To help the family Rosa was apprenticed to a dressmaker. The situation was not to her liking. Next, she was left with friends who did ceramic paintings. Rosa accepted this more easily, but her father thought she should go to school and placed her in a boarding school. She was what we would call a tomboy, mischievous and rebellious. She did not last long in the school.

By that point Raymond Bonheur decided to let her stay home and to train her as an artist. She spent her days doing drawing and painting exercises and her evenings reading. A common teaching method for student artists was the copying of paintings. This Rosa did in the Louvre, joining other young students making copies of the masters' works. She was small and one of the youngest. Her two younger brothers, Auguste and Isadore, and her sister Juliette soon joined in the family schooling venture, making a close-knit unit. While the sister did not make a career of art, both brothers did become painters along with Rosa. Her father followed the neoclassicism of David, and did not approve of the new romantic style.

The reading assigned to the young Bonheurs included the writings of some of Raymond's socialist heroes. It was an unsettled time in France, particularly for the lower classes. An artist like Delacroix, for example, could go ahead with his life and work, skirting the political unrest. For someone like Raymond Bonheur, with little money, and no more than average talent, it was difficult to get ahead. It is no surprise that he looked to a movement that was intended to help the poor.

Rosa's interest in animals was encouraged. She kept birds, small animals, and even a goat at home. She drew the animals, made paintings of them, and even dissected them to learn how they were put together. When her father remarried she was probably relieved of many of the chores that fell to the eldest daughter, and could spend more time with her art.

Beginning in 1840 Rosa sent art to the Salon. A drawing of goats and sheep and a painting, *Rabbits Nibbling Carrots,* were accepted. It was a good beginning, and by 1845 she was given a third-class medal by the Salon. Soon she was selling her work and receiving favorable comment from some of the critics.

When Géricault studied animals, he spent time in slaughterhouses. Rosa found a slaughterhouse in which she was allowed to sketch and observe. At this time she began wearing trousers, and was criticized for both actions. A slaughterhouse was no place for a young woman and trousers were not proper attire. She was small and boyish in appearance and wore her hair cut short; the men were protective of her.

Rosa admired George Sand, a writer mentioned before in connnection with Delacroix. George Sand was a woman who had taken a man's name in place of her own, which was Aurore Dupin. She wrote in the Romantic manner, was interested in politics, and dressed as a man. Her writing was popular during much of the century in which she lived. She was notorious not only for her manner of dress but also for her free style of living. She would have been happier in the late twentieth century, when her lifestyle would have scarcely caused a ripple.

Rosa, however, was never able to throw aside all the customs of her day. She wore trousers while she painted or went out drawing, and rode astride instead of sidesaddle. Where long, wide skirts would have been a nuisance she wore trousers, boots, and a long, smock-like blouse also commonly worn by men who were painters. Sometimes her blouses were embroidered to look more feminine. She never allowed herself to be photographed in her "working clothes." She seems to have been pulled both ways, wanting the freedom that men had, but wanting also to live conventionally as a woman. In order to wear her trousers in public she had to have written permission from the police that was renewed twice a year.

George Sand had written a novel, *The Devil's Pool*, in 1846, that told of peasants' lives and the country setting in which they lived and worked. Rosa Bonheur was possibly influenced by the book as she painted *Ploughing in the Nivernais*. The painting shows oxen, hitched in pairs, pulling plows while guided by the farmers. The painting had been commissioned by the government of the Second Republic, which had decided to encourage painting of landscapes and animals, and thereby to honor common people and their way of life. The painting served to make further connection between Sand and Bonheur, for it illustrates a description of a plowing scene in the novel.

Bonheur was becoming popular with the public and also with some artists of the period, including Delacroix. Her considerable knowledge of the animals she painted resulted in realistic and appealing paintings that were much appreciated by animal lovers. Her best-known painting, *The*

Horse Fair (see Figure 29), was her largest work. She began by making studies of horses over a period of several years. She was known to have made copies of some of Géricault's studies of horses. She made drawing after drawing of Percherons, the same breed that Géricault used in some prints. Among the prints was *Horses Going to a Fair,* in which Percherons were herded along. Bonheur's *The Horse Fair* shows realistic movement as the horses are led or guided by riders from the left to the right side of the canvas. The focus on the group to the center and right is created with lighter, brighter color that contrasts with the rich browns and flecks of red in the surrounding space. The road beneath offers more light, with stirred-up dust contrasting with the blue clouds in the left corner. Some of her best human forms appear in this painting. On the whole she was more comfortable portraying animals than people.

The Horse Fair was exhibited at the Salon of 1853. It was a huge success. Delacroix commented in his journal about her progress as a painter. The emperor and empress, who visited for a private showing the day before the opening, were enthusiastic about *The Horse Fair.* Rosa became famous and was now even recognized as she vacationed in the south of France.

Now financially secure, with her work in demand, Rosa built a new studio with a courtyard, stables, and space for all sorts of animals and birds.

Rosa Bonheur visited Britain in 1855. She was enthusiastically welcomed by many who admired her work. She met Edwin Landseer, a fellow painter who also specialized in animal pictures. She traveled as far north as Scotland, and was charmed by the mists, the mountains, and the animals. She made many drawings of landscapes and was to remember and comment on this trip years later.

Although she was less popular among the artists in France, she still had a following. In 1860 she moved to the country to have more privacy and time for her work. The village of By is at the edge of the Forest of Fontainebleau. Bonheur

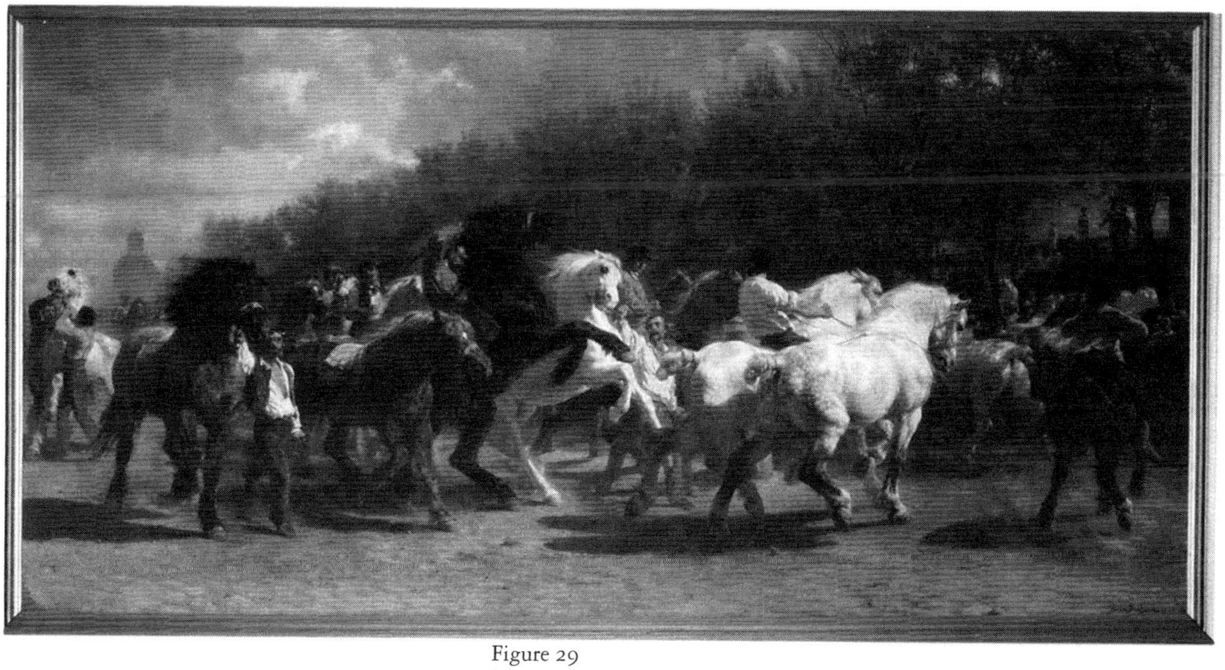

Figure 29
The Horse Fair, 1853–1855
Rosa Bonheur

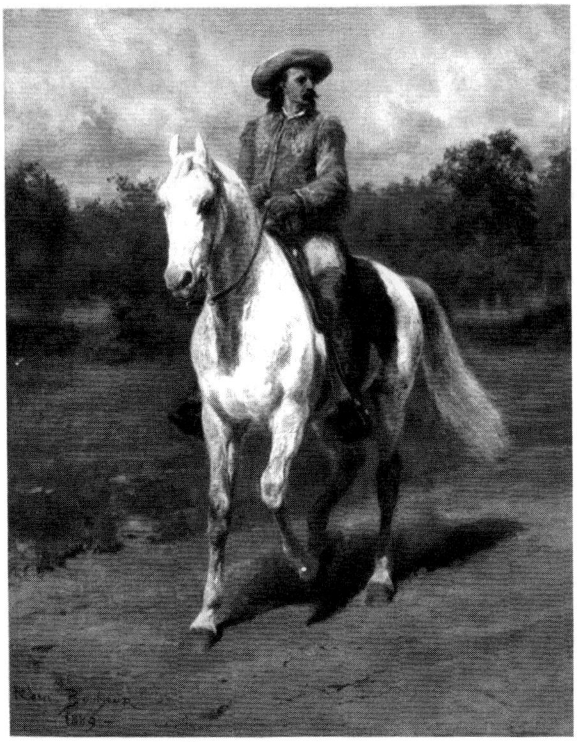

Figure 30
Colonel William F. Cody, 1889
Rosa Bonheur

bought a chateau there, added a studio and other buildings, and settled in. She stayed there the rest of her life. Although the village of Barbizon on the other side of the forest had attracted a new "school" of painting, there is no evidence that she had contact with these painters. Collectors and art dealers frequently visited, and the Empress Eugenie called twice, inviting Rosa to lunch at Chateau de Fontainebleau. Both visits were memorable occasions for Rosa Bonheur.

Later in her life, Rosa became interested in drawing and painting cats, visiting a zoo to observe and sketch them. She took pairs of lions into her house and kept them as though they were dogs. She loved all the animals and birds she kept, but allowed them the dignity of being animals. She did not expect them to behave as people do, or as the kinds of cartoon animals we see on television. Perhaps her love and admiration of her creatures helped her to portray them so beautifully.

One of the most exciting events of her life was the visit of William Cody, America's own Buffalo Bill. She had long been interested in the American West, an interest that was perhaps sparked by the visit of George Catlin and his troupe of American Indians. Buffalo Bill's traveling show included Indians, cowboys, buffalo, mustangs, and Wild Bill Hickok. The Indians fought the scouts; the cowboys rode and roped. Rosa made many drawings and paintings including Buffalo Bill on horseback (see Figure 30), Indians on horseback, and an Indian on horseback bringing down a buffalo.

Although Bonheur continued to be very popular in Britain and America, she was less so in France. While other artists took up new styles, she remained in the same pattern that had brought her acclaim and that continued to sell. After 40 years of not sending art to the Salon, she did send work just before she died. It was unnoticed.

Rosa Bonheur died on May 25, 1899. She had gained recognition in a difficult field, and one especially difficult for a woman in her era. She had lived a long and comfortable life, and had made her own way doing the thing she loved best to do. Most of us could not ask for more.

Glossary

Bonheur pronounced bō-nur´

socialistic reflecting the beliefs of a political movement in which the wealth of the country is distributed and property controlled by its members, who also share in the work and production of goods

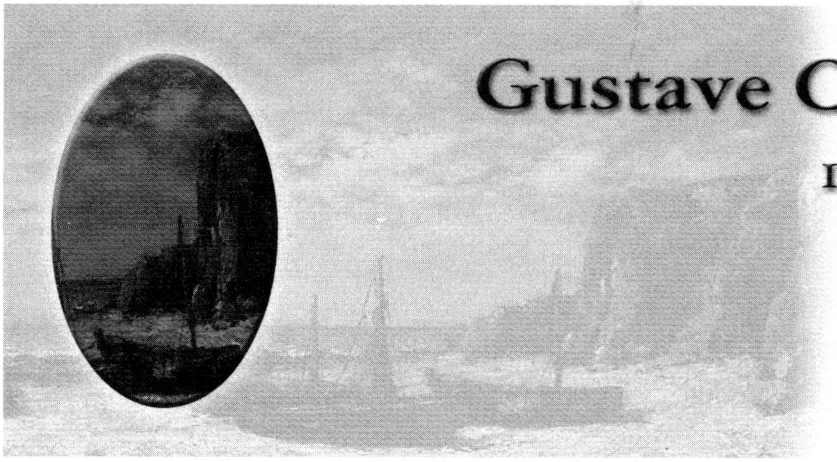

Gustave Courbet
1819–1877

ALONG WITH THE DISRUPTIONS of wars and revolutions, another kind of change entered the picture in the nineteenth century. In the Industrial Revolution, machines were invented that were able to make more objects faster and more cheaply than humans could. The skill of the craftsman lost value. Artists were often looked upon with some suspicion. People sometimes thought that they asked more money for their art than was reasonable. They were getting used to the lower prices of machine-made art objects. In addition, some artists wanted to shock the public with their art and their unconventional lifestyles and dress.

During the nineteenth century France produced an unusual number of artists, musicians, and writers, whose work we still enjoy. At the same time, it was a century of great political upheaval ending with the Franco-Prussian War. Did these artists create because of the chaotic conditions or in spite of them?

Gustave **Courbet** lived and worked at the same time as Delacroix. He was born in 1819 and became a leader in the style of painting known as Realism. He was probably what people call a "born rebel." As a young man in school he stirred up trouble by writing a proposal for six rules of outrageous conduct for his fellow students. His father was a wealthy landowner who fully expected his son to become a lawyer. Courbet had other plans and, though he was supposed to be studying law, slipped off to study art. His realistic style developed because he believed things should be painted as they exist. At the same time his pictures had such an element of the romantic that there is still disagreement as to whether Courbet was a realist or a romantic. In his work we find the dramatic, the lush fabrics and surrounding landscapes, and the kinds of nudes that remind one of Rubens (see Figures 31 and 32). He was a large, handsome man and did not hesitate to include self-portraits in his works.

We find Courbet painting himself as a troubadour, as a sculptor, as a painter, and in a landscape with his dog. He was caught up in the socialist thought of the time and several paintings take jabs at the government. Peasants and workers symbolize the need for socialism and priests symbolize Courbet's **anticlerical** feelings, which date from his school days. Some of his paintings were controversial, such as *A Burial at Ornans, Proudhon and His Daughters,* and *The Painter's Studio.*

Courbet was probably the first artist to use the palette knife as a painting tool. Such a knife has a flexible blade and is used to mix paint on an artist's palette (the tray-like surface used to hold the paint). Courbet's thick paint was sometimes applied to the entire painting with the knife.

Other artists who shared Courbet's political and artistic ideas looked to him as a leader. Courbet's own success came early with the Salon and the medal awarded to him in 1849. The Salon had been somewhat liberal at that time; it soon became more conservative and his paintings were criticized. In 1855 he built the Pavilion of Realism to conduct his own showings. Now there were three dominant styles competing: neoclassical, romantic, and realistic. Each style borrowed from the others somewhat, but many painters were

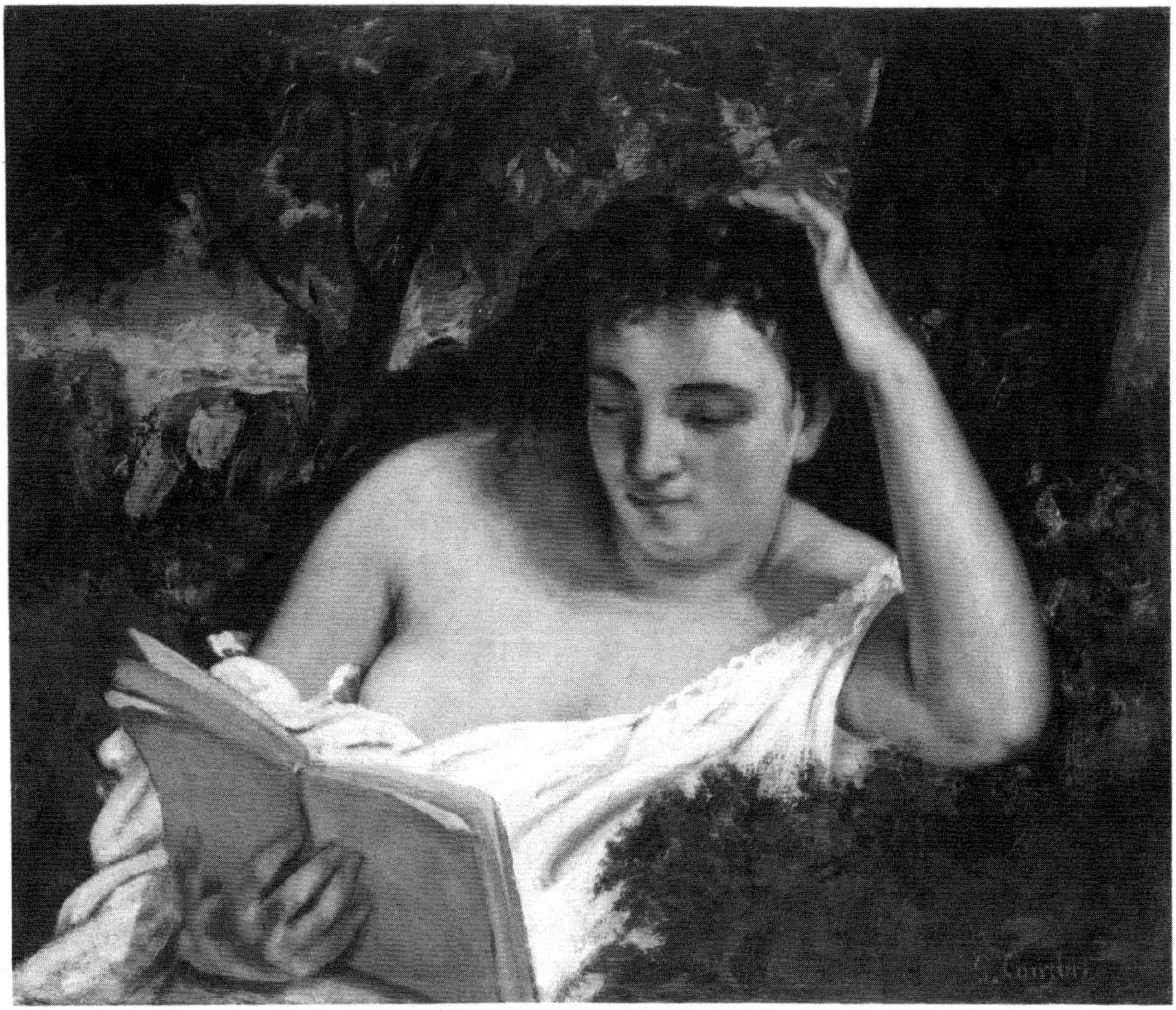

Figure 31
A Young Woman Reading, 1868–1872
Gustave Courbet

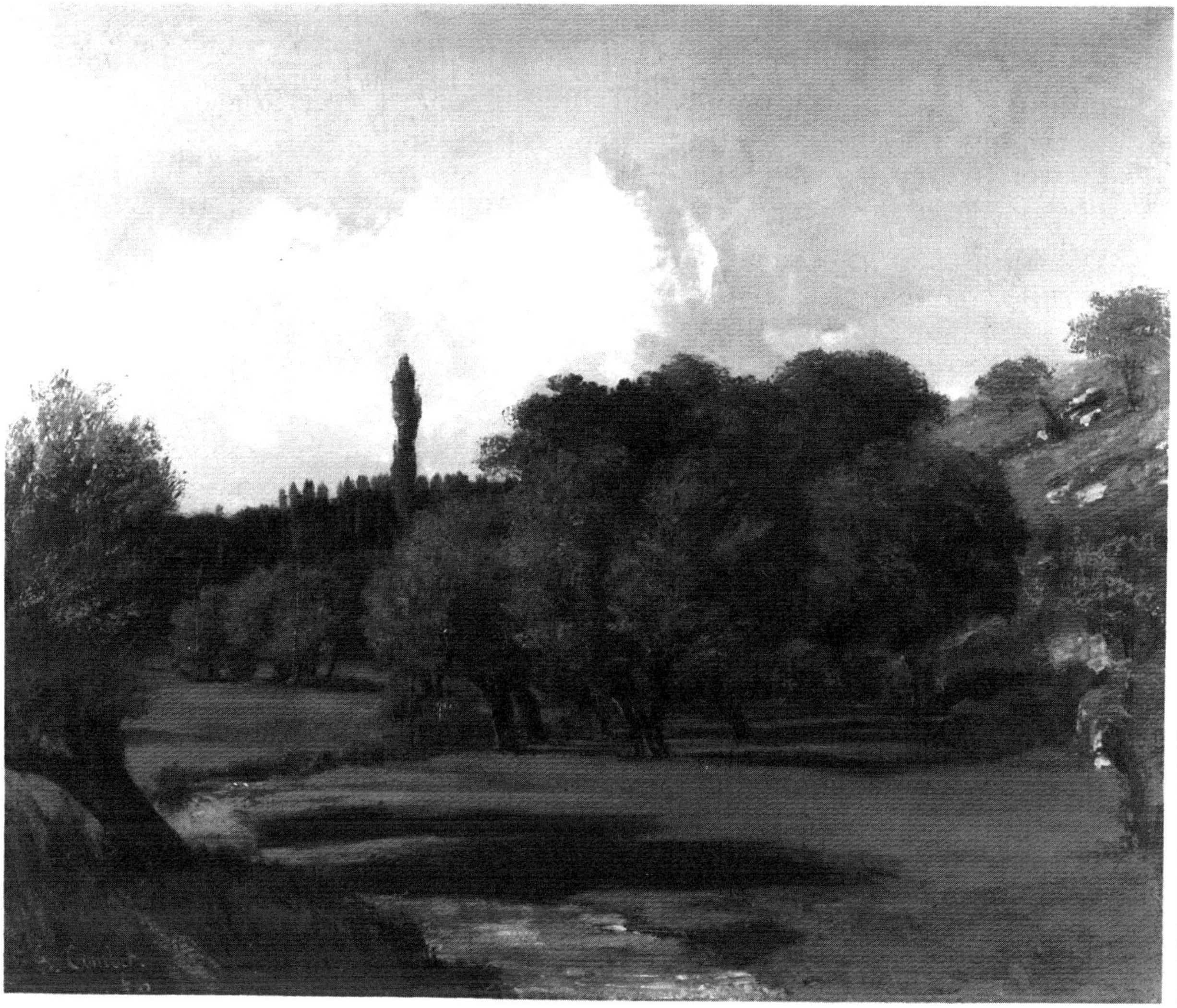

Figure 32
Landscape Near the Banks of the Indre, 1856
Gustave Courbet

most concerned with painting a piece that the Salon and therefore the general public would approve. Courbet was interested instead in shaking them up a bit and painting as his conscience directed him. He was often the center of artistic as well as political controversy. The famous landscape *Boats on a Beach, Etretat* (see Color Plate 9) dates from this period in Courbet's life.

A final political disaster struck Courbet toward the end of his life. After the Franco-Prussian War, there was an uprising in Paris during which a monument, the Colonne Vendôme, was destroyed. Courbet had been appointed to head an artists' group. Before he could begin, he was blamed for the destruction of the column. He could not raise the money to pay for the monument, and fled to Switzerland. He spent the last six years of his life there and died in 1877 at the age of 58. He had paved the way for the next revolution in art, which would be led by Édouard Manet.

Glossary

Courbet pronounced cour-bay´

anticlerical relating to opposition to the clergy and officials of the Church and their influence on public life

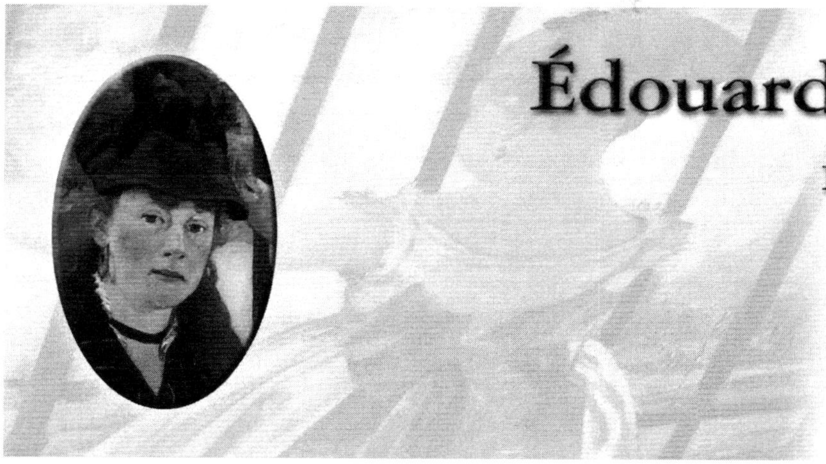

Édouard Manet
1832–1883

Édouard Manet was born in Paris on January 23, 1832. His parents were from well-to-do upper-class families. His father was a civil servant who had become a judge. His brothers were to be civil servants also; the plan was for Édouard to become a lawyer. His father, Auguste, was a stern, unbending man; his mother was quite the opposite. She was interested in the arts and loved to sing. She liked entertaining friends with music, and saw to it that her sons had lessons on the piano. We will see characteristics of both parents in Édouard.

Young Manet was not a very serious student. Only his father's position kept him from failing in school at least twice. It was finally decided, in a compromise, that Édouard would have a career in the navy. After a few months at sea, he knew that the navy was not for him. From drawing class in school and the encouragement of his mother's brother, Édouard knew that he wanted to be a painter. His father disliked the idea; no doubt his mother supported her son's wish. At 18, Édouard began studying at the studio of Thomas Couture. Couture was a vain man and a harsh teacher. He had had some successes in the past and never forgot them, nor did he let others forget. His style and the style he taught was that of the Academy. Manet had many arguments with his teacher about the work he was doing. It is surprising that he stayed six years. He wanted his own success, to be recognized by the critics and the public. He continually switched from a style that he hoped would please the Salon to the style he felt was right for himself (and that he felt almost compelled to use) and back again.

Manet's first painting to be rejected by the Salon was sent there in 1859. It was called *The Absinthe Drinker.* He had found a **ragpicker** near the Louvre who modeled for the painting. The paintings of Velázquez in the Louvre had inspired him to paint a man from the streets as honestly as he could. Couture criticized it sarcastically. Manet was furious. He left Couture and did not come back.

In 1861 Manet sent two paintings to the Salon that were accepted. One of these, *The Spanish Guitar Player,* won an honorable mention. The other painting was a portrait of his parents. The public liked paintings that told a story they could understand. Both of these filled the bill. At this time all things Spanish were popular, perhaps partly because Napoleon III had married a vivacious Spanish woman in 1853.

People were sometimes shocked by the subject matter in Manet's paintings. Sometimes they rejected the way he handled the paint, since it was different from the traditional methods they knew. Color was often applied in dark and light extremes with little middle tone. The forms often appeared flat instead of having curves built up with middle tones. The effect was like that of a quick glance, when we see an object or person but do not take the time to look carefully for details. Part of the time Manet painted in a more conventional style, as though he were trying to please critics. Some paintings are made up of carefully painted parts in the conventional style, and other parts painted in flatter tones, using quick brush strokes, making the paint as important as the objects painted. In *Concert in the Tuileries,* painted in 1860, people are gathered in a wooded area, listening to a concert. Some are seated, some are standing. Distant

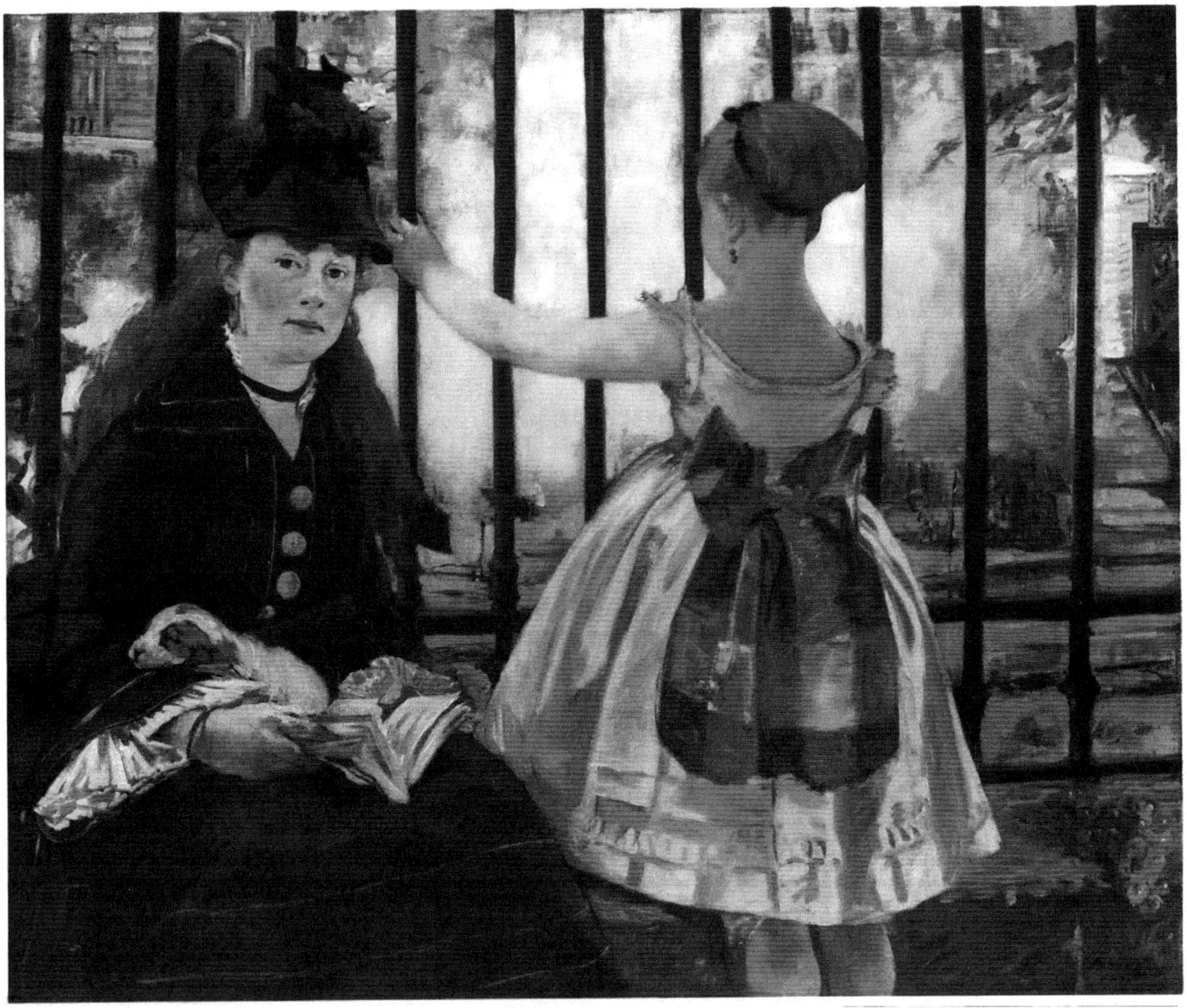

Figure 34
Gare Saint-Lazare, 1873
Édouard Manet

figures are simply suggested with brush strokes. Some of the people near the front are actually little portraits of people Manet knew, with the artist himself at the left. This painting can be classified as one of the first really modern paintings, though it received little notice in Manet's time.

Two paintings by the artist caused a great furor and made it impossible for Manet's other work to receive fair evaluation for many years. Both pictures show a female nude, which in itself should not have shocked the public, since they were accustomed to the nude in art. After all, the classical art that they loved certainly presented many nudes. But the women in *Le Déjeuner sur l'Herbe* (Luncheon on the Grass) and in *Olympia* were not classical nudes in a classical setting, but women of 1863 Paris, and they appeared completely shameless. To make it worse, there was no visible story or moral message in either. Both paintings contain a mixture of the painting styles Manet used.

Luncheon on the Grass was submitted with two other paintings by Manet to the Salon of 1863; all three were rejected. Manet was in good company: of the 5,000 works of art submitted that year, 2,800 were rejected. The artists complained bitterly. Remember that the Salon made a big difference in an artist's career. Napoleon III decided that the best way to quiet them was to give the rejected artists a show of their own. The Salon des Réfusés was opened two weeks after the regular Salon. Fewer than half of the rejected artists brought their work. Manet and Cézanne decided to show their paintings. The public packed the showing, laughing at the art to show that they knew poor art when they saw it. The *Luncheon* certainly came in for more than its share of laughter. Many critics thought that Manet was deliberately trying to cause a scandal in order to call attention to himself.

The Salon des Réfusés was not repeated with the next Salon. Perhaps the Academy was uneasy because much of the work in both Salons was about equal in quality. It did not put the Academy in the best light when thoughtful people noticed this fact. In the Salon of 1865, Manet's *Olympia* was accepted, and the uproar was far worse than the previous one. Crowds became so unruly that two guards were placed in front of the *Olympia,* and the painting was soon moved to a high and inaccessible spot.

People who knew how Manet worked said that he did not seem to have a firm plan as he began a painting, but worked it out as he went along, not sure how it would turn out. He painted quickly, almost instinctively, with a total involvement in the process. He once said that each new painting was like jumping into the water without knowing how to swim. He was always trying to catch the present moment in a painting. Manet was probably a naturalist, not a realist. A realist painted life as it was seen, with some attempt to include an idea. A naturalist painted life as it was seen, both the beauty and the ugliness, and felt that anything was worthy of being painted well. Scenes from everyday life were common themes for Manet, as we can see in *Gare Saint-Lazare* and *The Plum* (see Figures 33 and 34).

The frequent and bitter criticism to which he was subjected hurt Manet deeply. It caused a rift between his father and himself. The father surely expected his sons to bring credit to the family name. Nothing would have given Édouard more pleasure than just that. Although his mother was more supportive, she too was hurt by the public insults. Manet loved Paris. He loved to stroll its sidewalks and visit the cafes. He was always fashionably dressed and enjoyed conversation with friends and especially with beautiful women. Part of him wanted to be an elegant gentleman painter, while the other part resisted being put into the kind of mold that lifestyle would have forced upon him.

At least three times he left Paris hoping to find some relief from the public. He went to Spain, where the food did not agree with him. He went to the country to paint with the Impressionists, and later went to England. He was sure he would be happier there, but he was back in a week. He was simply a city person and the city in which he belonged was Paris.

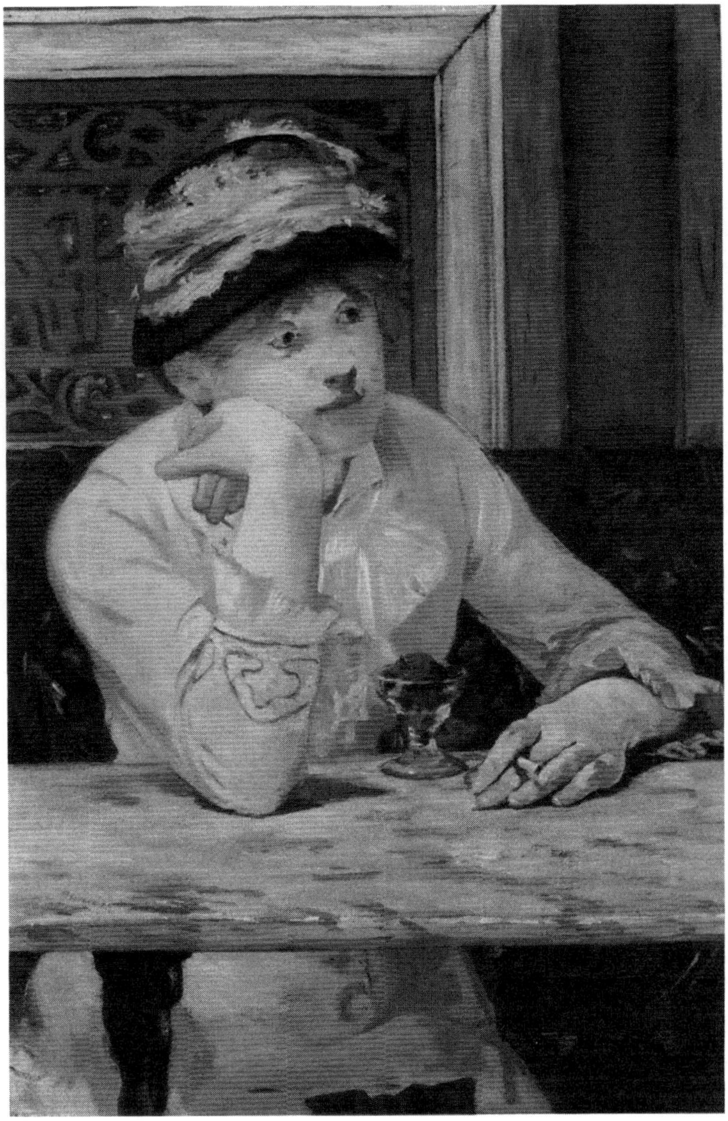

Figure 34
The Plum, 1877
Édouard Manet

Manet continued to paint and to try to win acceptance. In 1872 an art dealer, Durand-Ruel, saw some of his work in a friend's studio. He bought two paintings, then came back the next day to see Manet and bought 23 more. The man also bought and sold some of the new impressionist paintings being done by some of Manet's friends. Then economic crisis caused financial problems for Durand-Ruel. He had to stop buying paintings.

The impressionist painters mentioned above were at the core of a new movement in painting. Their style included using colors in complementary dabs to achieve brightness. They did not mix the colors on the palette, but put the strokes of paint next to each other and let the viewer's eye mix the colors. Black was not used. They did not use middle tones for shading, either. These painters loved landscape and painting outside. They gathered at Argenteuil on the Seine River outside of Paris. Manet spent time there painting with these artists. He never completely adopted their style, though some of his brushwork came close. He did not use their theories of color. He painted *Claude Monet Painting on His Studio Boat, Argenteuil,* and then a cityscape, *Rue Mosnier Decked with Flags*. In these paintings the texture and brushwork are those of impressionism. However, it was not far removed from his own free style. Manet believed that painting was more than just painting what one saw; the act of painting itself was very important.

The artist experienced a flicker of Salon success in 1873. He painted *Le Bon Bock* a picture of a bewhiskered

Dutchman with a long pipe and a glass of beer. It reminded the jury of conventional painting and perhaps of the work of the Dutch school of Frans Hals. It was accepted and given favorable comment. This, along with the purchase of Manet's paintings by Durant-Ruel the year before, was indeed a bright spot in Manet's career. He moved to a larger studio in which he held after-five gatherings for his friends. His wife (his former piano teacher) entertained with music frequently, even during the bad times. It cheered Manet to be surrounded by people.

Le Bon Bock was followed by *Resting* (in which the young woman artist Berthe Morisot was the model), *The Laundress,* and *At the Races* (see Color Plate 10). Manet was turned down again by the Salon, and in 1876 held his own exhibit in his studio. Over 4,000 people came during the two weeks of the show, and many critics praised his work. There was so much noise that his landlord refused to renew his lease.

Manet had developed an illness that was to take his life. In 1881 he was in remission and was painting again. Two paintings were sent to the Salon, and at the insistence of the artist Alexandre Cabanel, a jury member, Manet was awarded a second-class medal. In the winter of 1881–82, the minister of fine arts, Antonin Proust, added Manet's name to the list for the Legion of Honor. Thus, very near the end of his life he was given two honors that he had long coveted; unfortunately, he was too ill to really enjoy them.

His last and largest painting was *A Bar at the Folies-Bergère*. It's a picture of a barmaid, the mirror behind the bar and the reflections in the mirror. The back of the girl, a customer, bottles, flowers, fruit, a distant balcony full of people, and even the feet of a trapeze artist are shown in the mirror. The brushwork is Manet's style, with more control than one might have expected, since Manet had to stop to rest often as he worked. It was finished for the Salon of 1882. The reviews were mixed, but not insulting.

Manet died on April 30, 1883, at the age of 52. After his death his paintings began to sell and within a year a memorial show of his work was held.

Glossary

Manet pronounced mah-nā´

ragpicker a person who makes a living collecting junk and rags

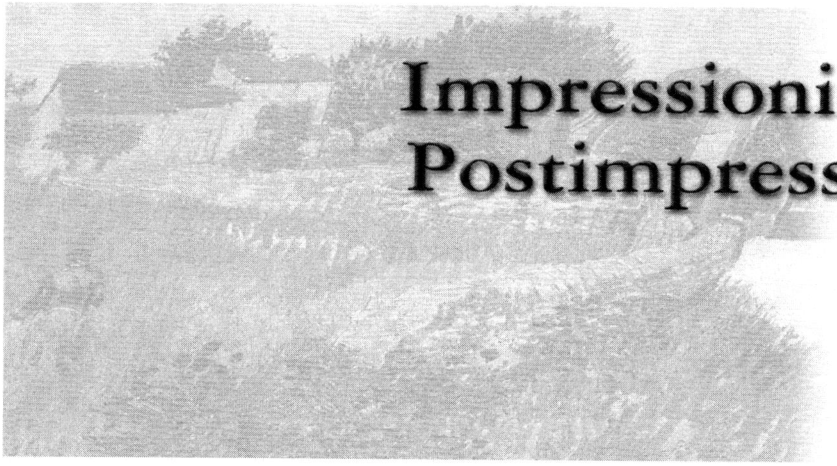

Impressionists and Postimpressionists

From Delacroix came ideas about the use of color including the use of brush strokes side by side, with the colors mixing as they are viewed. A group of painters who chose to paint landscapes, working near Barbizon in 1830, found new ways to use color. The painters, called Impressionists, worked to catch the effect of light and sunlight out-of-doors. They found that the sfumato of Leonardo did not work well outdoors. The effect of strong sunlight did not create that kind of dark shadowing; it was also too slow. They wanted to catch a scene that was changing from minute to minute, as the wind blew, the water formed waves, and a cloud darkened the sun. The brush strokes were quick and detail was left out.

Two other influences at this time were the invention of photography and the new interest in Japanese color prints. Since painters had long been the ones who recorded likenesses, photography eliminated a good portion of the work they normally did. They needed to look for profitable new directions for their art. The Japanese prints showed Western artists that less detail and flatter forms could be used in pictures. Manet's flatter forms are connected with this idea

People discovered they had to step back from an Impressionist painting to see the daubs and loose brush strokes become recognizable forms. The reasons the public was so angry over Impressionism were the lack of detail and the "unfinished" look, as well as the subject matter. With ever-increasing public exposure to the style and subject matter, Impressionism finally won acceptance.

Another factor in the bright Impressionist palette was the development of new pigments. Until that time pigments were made from organic materials and minerals. Chemistry then created new ones: zinc white, cobalt blues, greens, yellows, reds, magenta, and ultramarine blue. Some of the new mixtures were not satisfactory and others were made in their place. Though the old pigments were still used, the new colors certainly must have contributed to the brightness of the Impressionist paintings.

Claude Monet

1840 – 1926

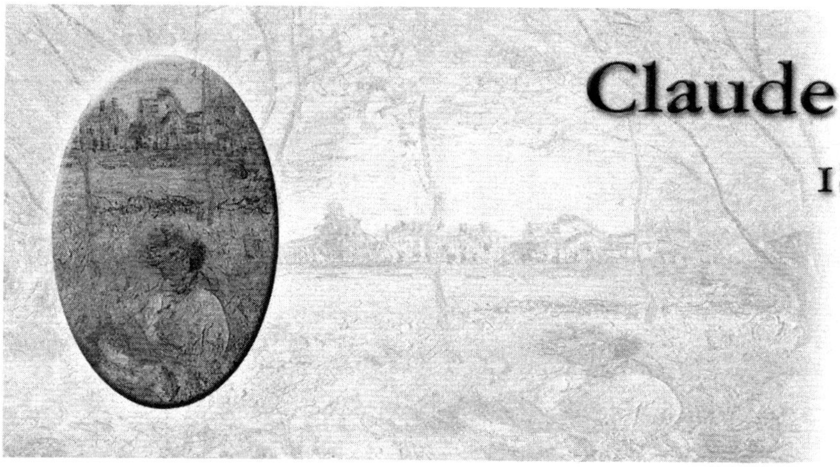

OSCAR CLAUDE **MONET**, known to us as Claude, was born in Paris in 1840. His father, Adolphe, moved the family (consisting of Claude, an older brother Leon, and his wife) to Le Havre, a seaport on the French coast, in 1845. The father was in business with his brother-in-law, supplying materials to ships in port. His wife died when Claude was 12, and the family moved into the home of the brother-in-law, Dr. Lecadre, and his wife, Sophie.

Claude grew up an undisciplined, willful boy. School was a trial to him. He was a trial to his father and the rest of his family. He delighted in annoying others, roaming the seashore, and avoiding schoolwork. He found that his drawing skills could be used to draw **caricatures,** which he used to taunt others. He began with caricatures of his teachers, to the despair of his drawing teacher. However, by the time he was 15, he was well-known in the community for his drawings. His caricatures were displayed in a local picture frame shop, and he began to earn pin money making drawings for others. His opinion of himself and his work was excessively high at that point. He overdressed his five-foot seven-inch frame and took part of his earnings to his Aunt Sophie to save for him. By the time he was 18 he had decided on a career in serious art, and on moving to Paris to pursue that career.

Monet had made the acquaintance of some of the local artists, who gave him some encouragement. His Aunt Sophie dabbled in painting also, and understood his enthusiasm for art. The rest of the family did not entirely approve of his plans. Though his father saw that his drawings had brought in some money, he was not willing to finance his study in Paris. He applied for a grant from the city for Monet's study. Le Havre had made such grants before. Monet grew impatient waiting for word from the city. He wanted to be in Paris for the Salon exhibit of 1859. His father reluctantly allowed him to go.

Paris in 1859 was exciting. Much rebuilding was underway. Monet spent time looking at the art in the Salon show, as planned. He took introductory letters to a few artists and received some encouragement from them. Meanwhile the city of Le Havre apparently felt that his father was able to pay for his son's study and refused to make the grant. Adolphe Monet refused to support his son in Paris. He wanted him to come home and to get into a more serious kind of career (preferably the family business). Claude then had only the savings from his caricatures to live on. He found an inexpensive place to live and painters who would let him paint in their studios. There were places where painters gathered to discuss art and socialize. Monet could sit in on the fringes of such gatherings and feel that he was really a part of the Paris scene.

At that time in France young men were drafted into the army at the age of 20. They were called up if their names were drawn in a lottery and they served seven years. It was possible to buy out of this system simply by hiring someone to serve in place of the draftee. Monet knew that he might be drafted and suspected that his family would offer to buy him off on the condition that he come home to work. His name was drawn and his father did offer to buy a substitute, but Monet joined the army instead.

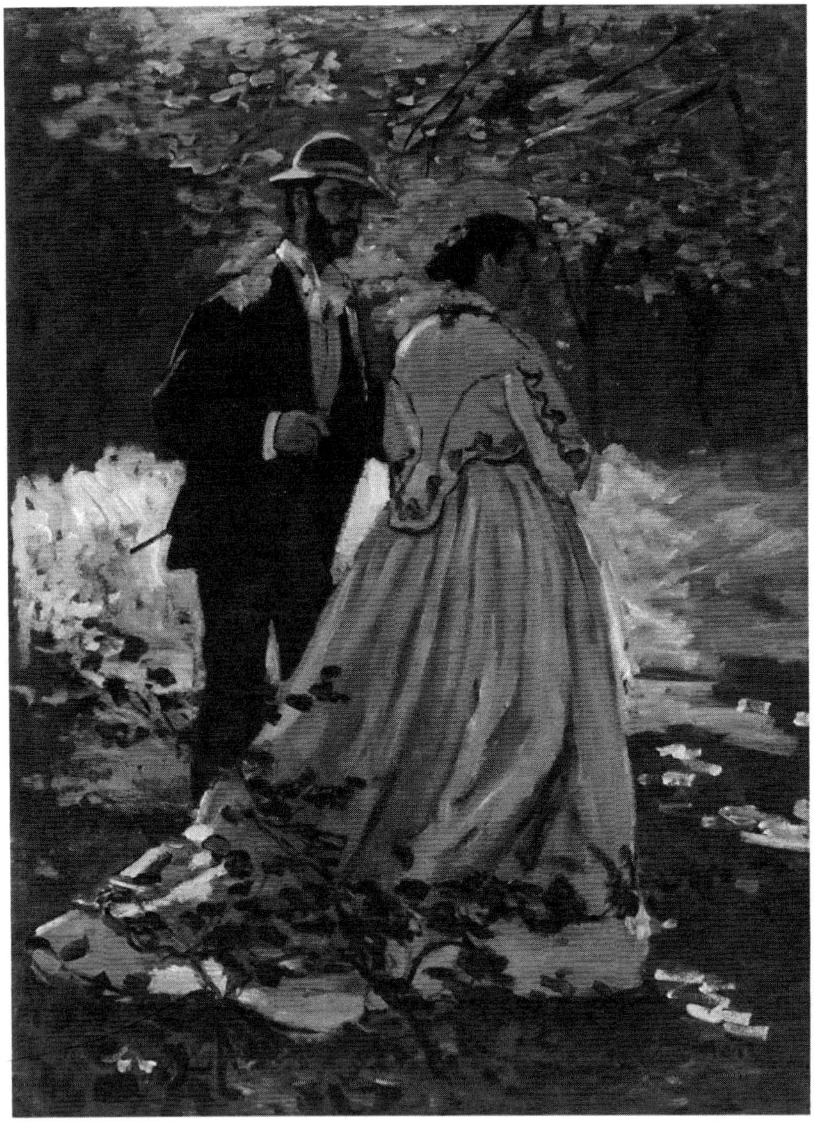

Figure 35
Bazille and Camille, 1865
Claude Monet

He was sent to Algeria. After 11 months he became ill and was sent home on leave to recover. His behavior led his family to think that there was nothing to do but buy him off and send him back to Paris. This time, however, he was to get into the studio of a known artist, and his activities would be checked on by a relative living in Paris. His allowance was to be doled out to him by the relative. Though all this was not much to his liking, he accepted it as something he could tolerate.

Monet had talent, but he still needed to learn basic art skills as well as discipline. He began in the studio of Charles Gleyre, a painter who was a master at the École des Beaux-Arts, who also had his own group of students. Monet did not understand Gleyre's approach to painting

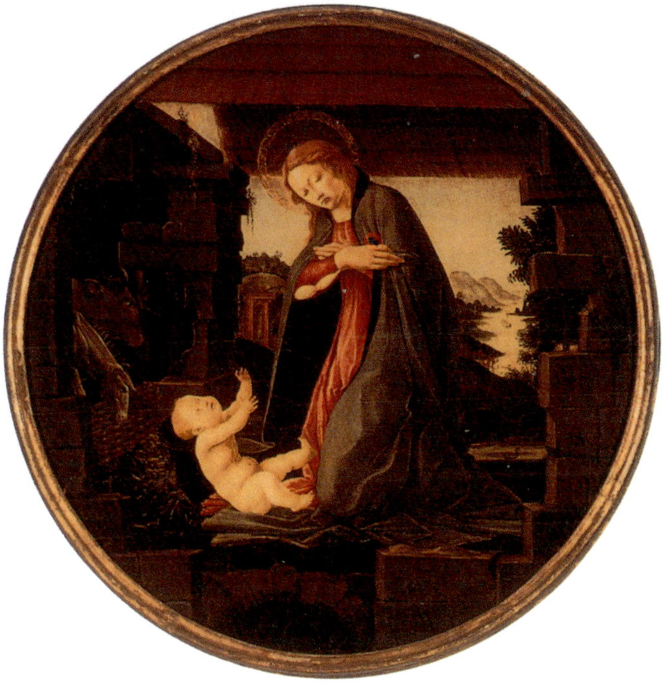

Color Plate 1
The Virgin Adoring the Child, c. 1480–1490
Sandro Botticelli

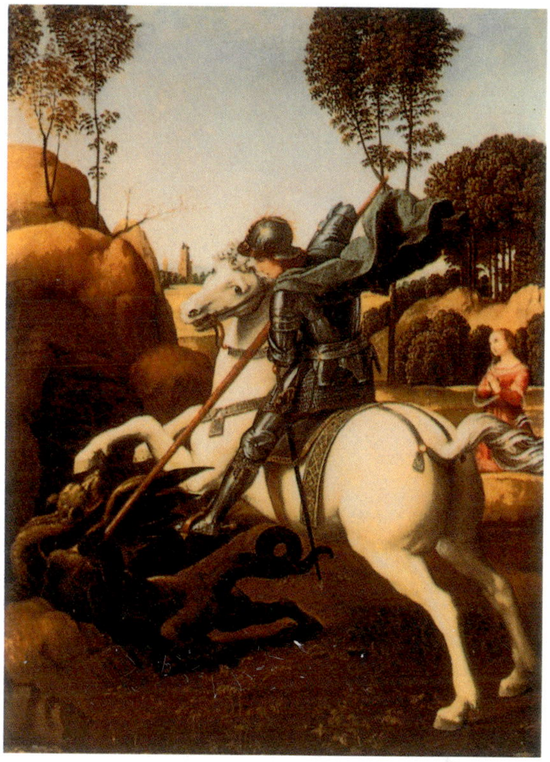

Color Plate 2
St. George and the Dragon, c. 1506
Raphael Santi

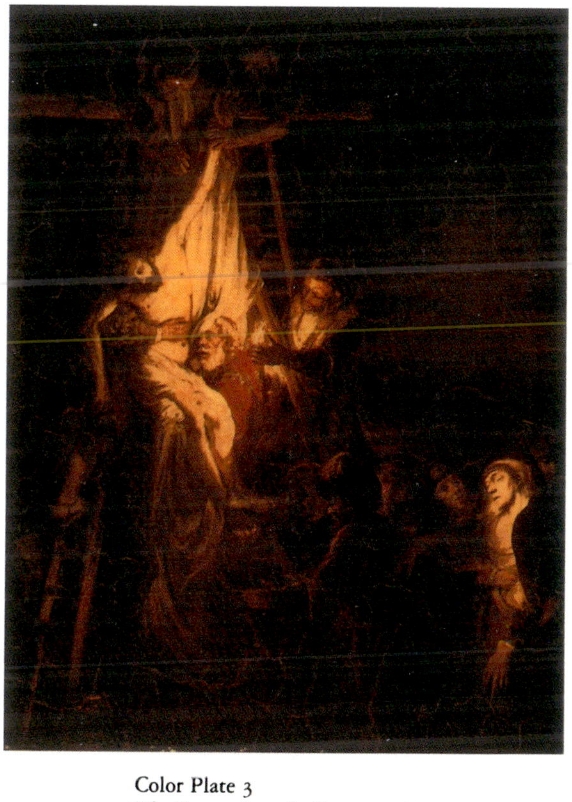

Color Plate 3
The Descent from the Cross, c. 1655
Rembrandt van Rijn

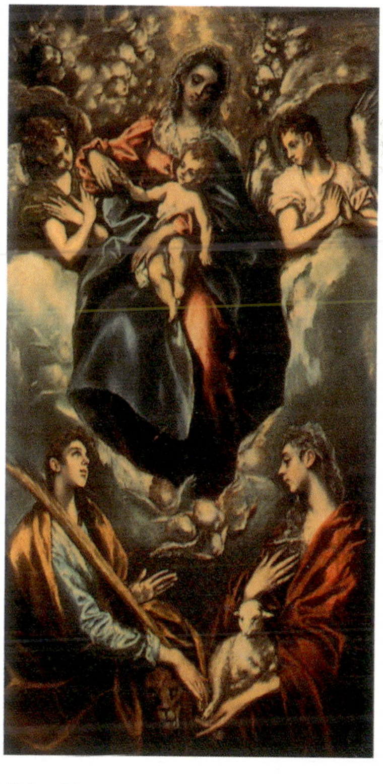

Color Plate 4
Madonna and Child with St. Martina and St. Agnes, c. 1597–1599
El Greco

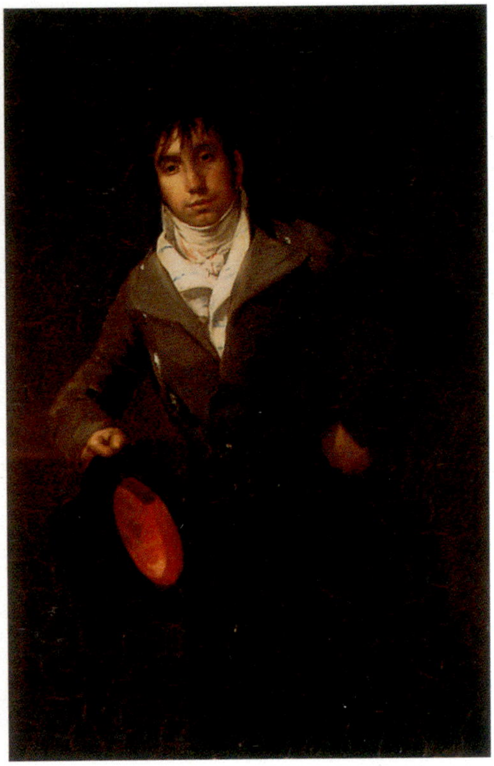

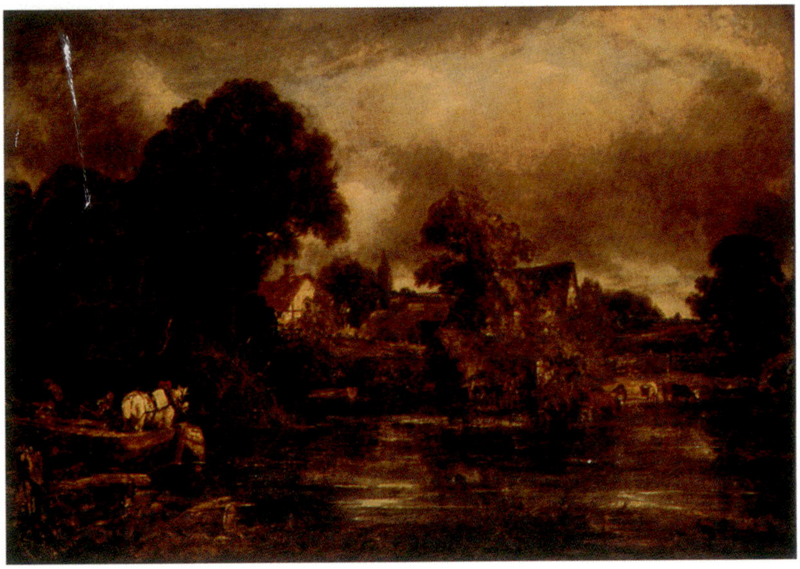

Color Plate 6
The White Horse, 1819
John Constable

Color Plate 5
Bartolomé Sureda y Miserol, c. 1803–1804
Francisco de Goya

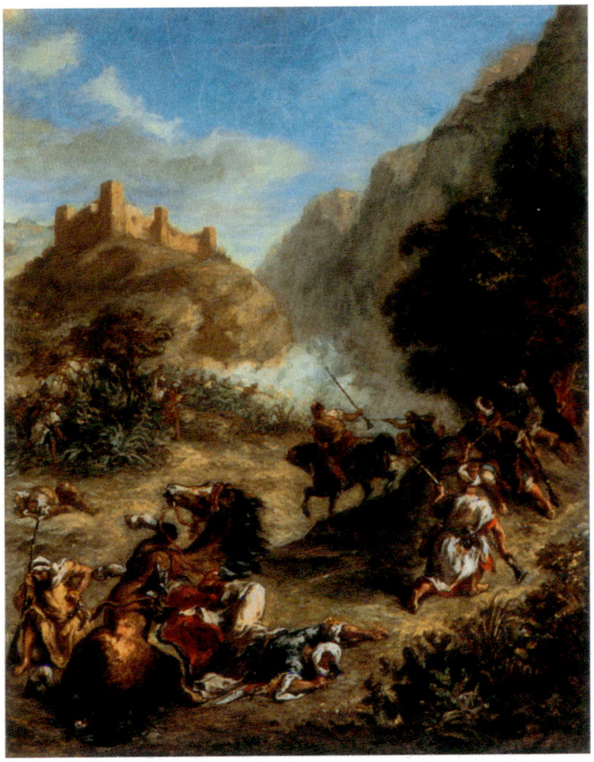

Color Plate 7
Norham Castle: Sunrise, c. 1835–1840
Joseph Mallord William Turner

Color Plate 8
Arabs Skirmishing in the Mountains, 1863
Eugène Delacroix

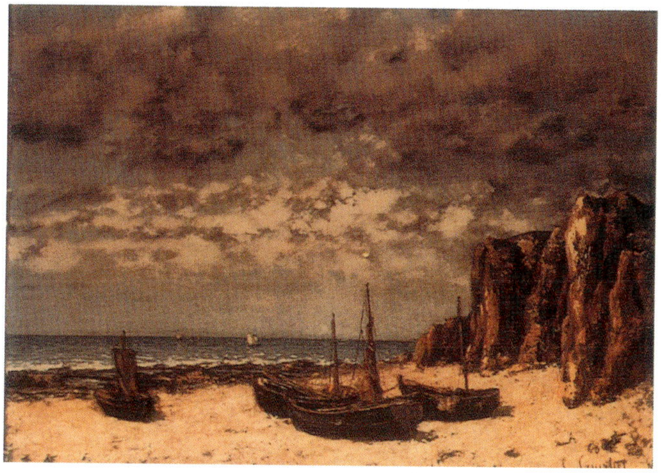

Color Plate 9
Boats on a Beach, Etretat, 1869
Gustave Courbet

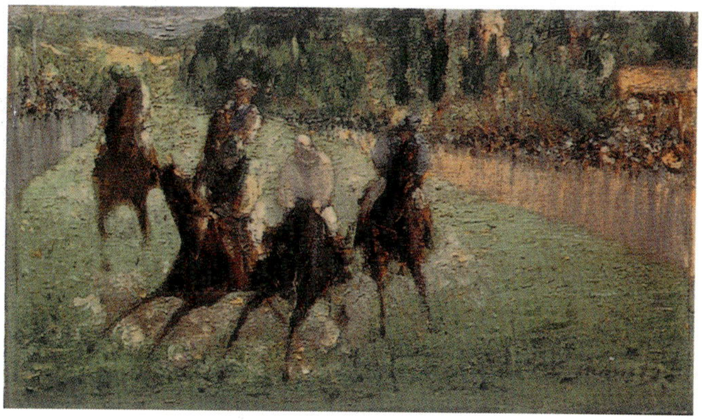

Color Plate 10
At the Races, c. 1875
Édouard Manet

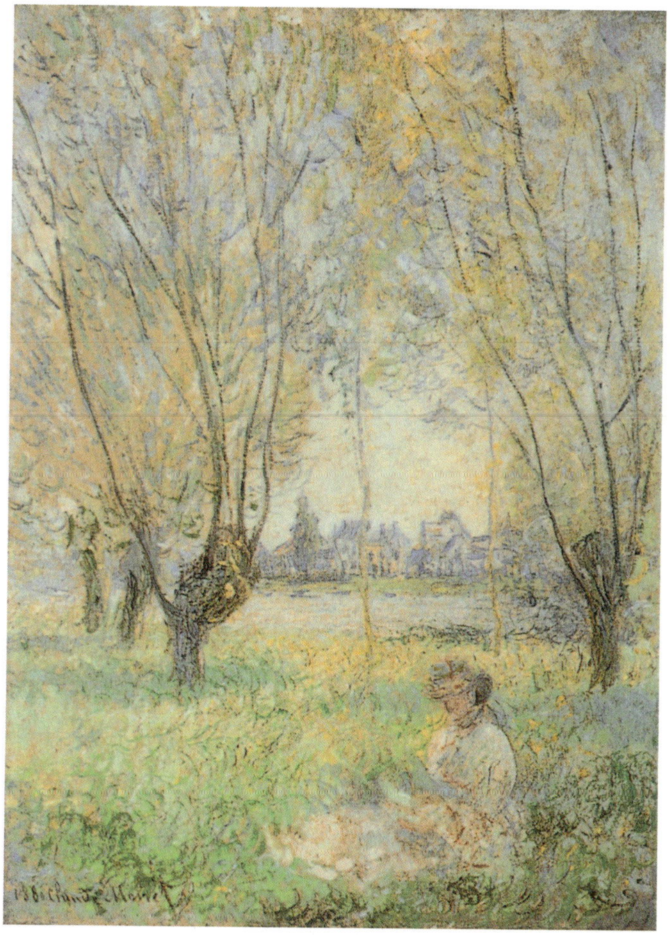

Color Plate 11
Woman Seated Under the Willows, 1880
Claude Monet

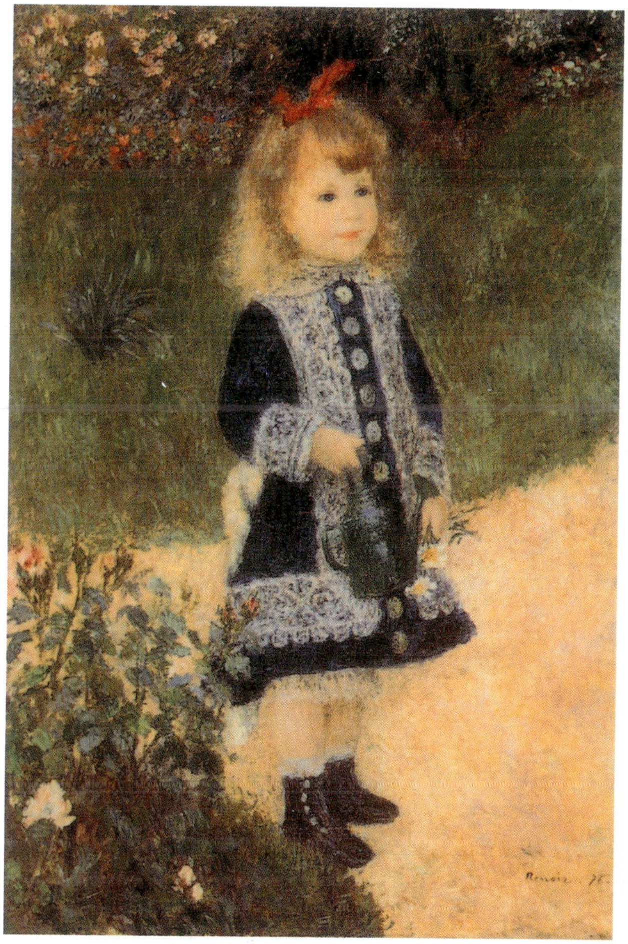

Color Plate 12
A Girl with a Watering Can, 1876
Auguste Renoir

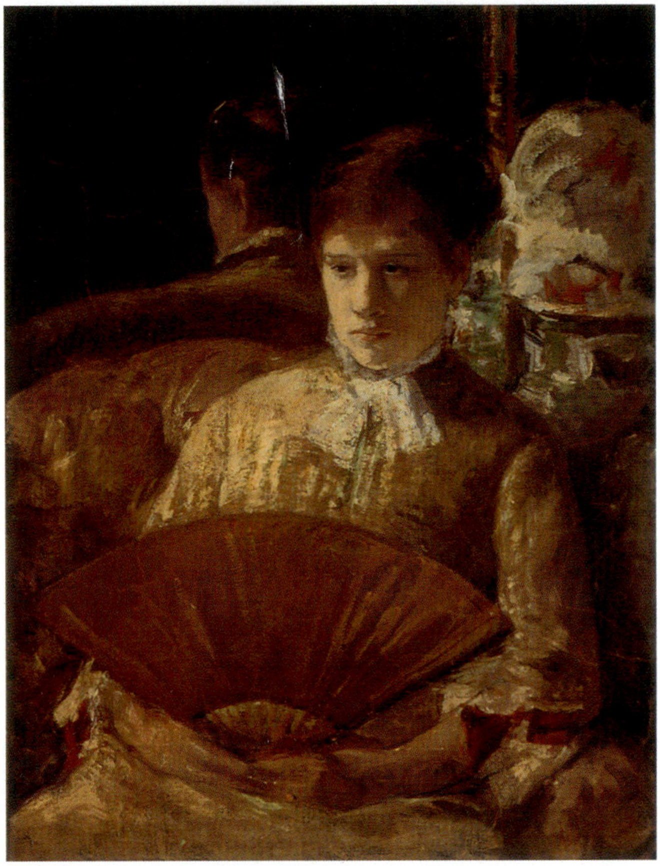

Color Plate 13
Miss Mary Ellison, c. 1880
Mary Cassatt

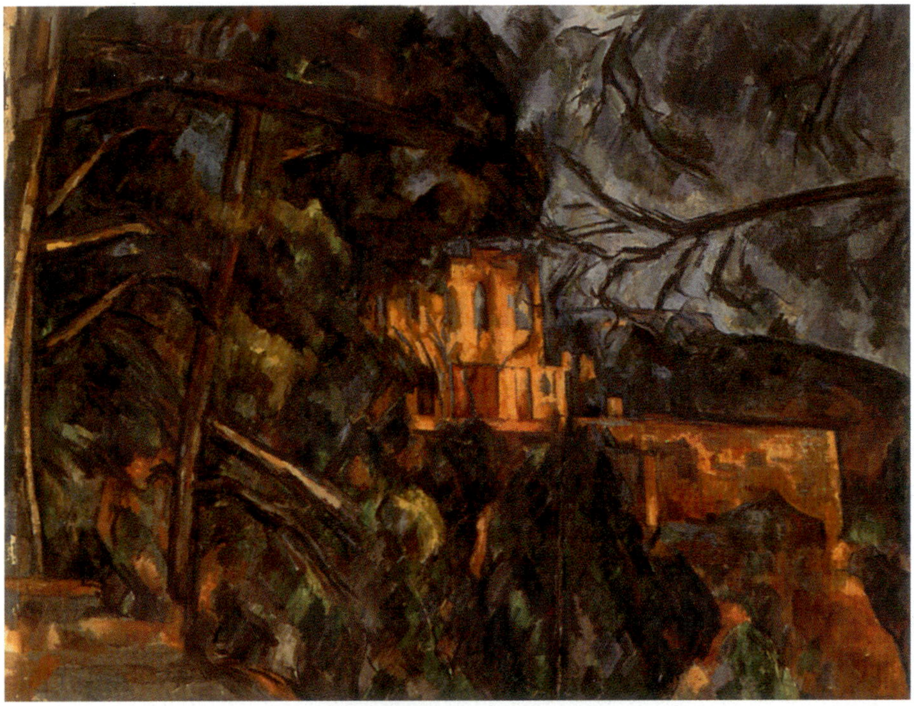

Color Plate 14
Le Château Noir, 1900–1904
Paul Cézanne

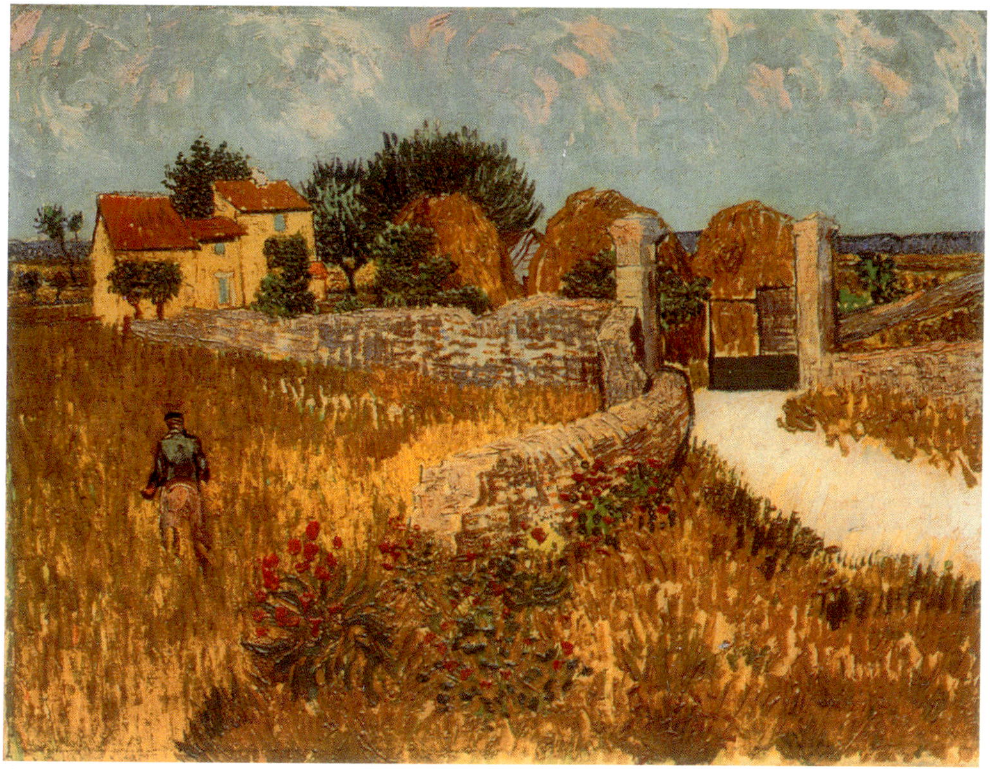

Color Plate 15
Farmhouse in Provence, Arles, 1888
Vincent van Gogh

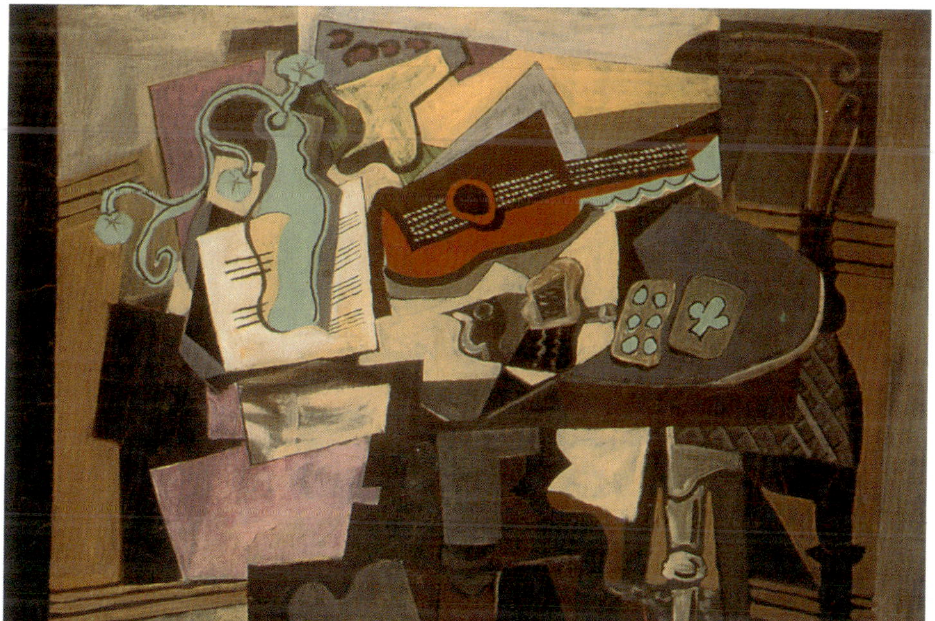

Color Plate 16
Still Life, 1918
Pablo Picasso

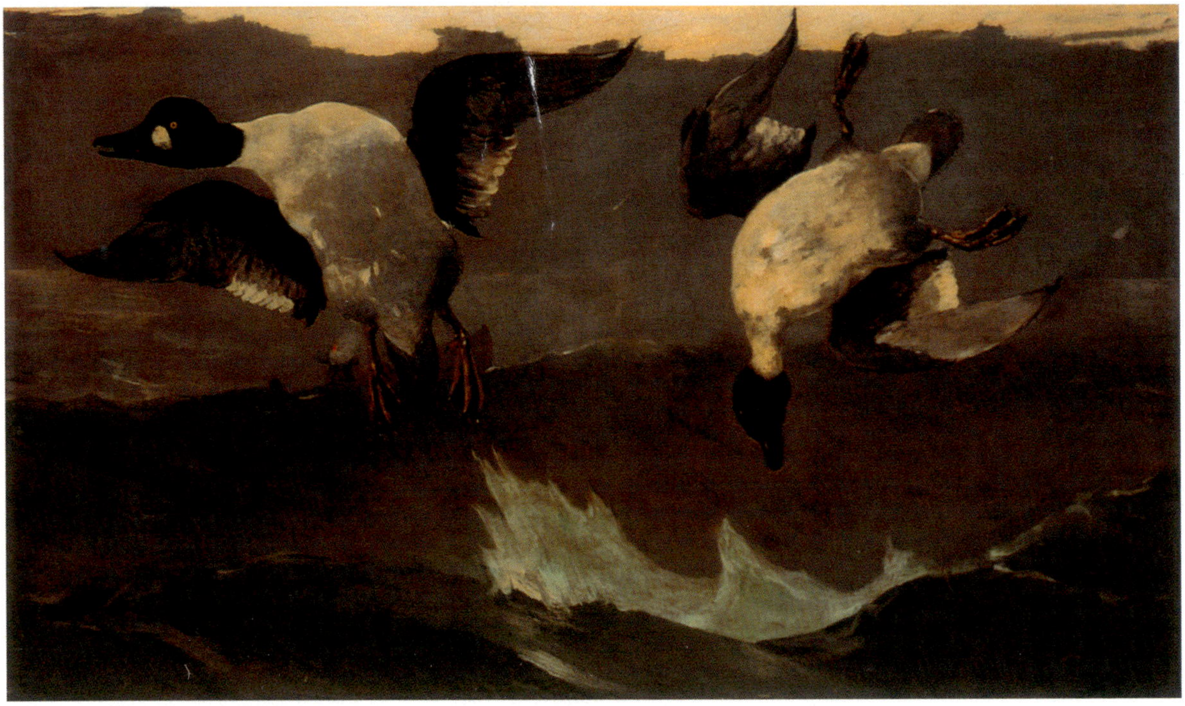

Color Plate 17
Right and Left, 1909
Winslow Homer

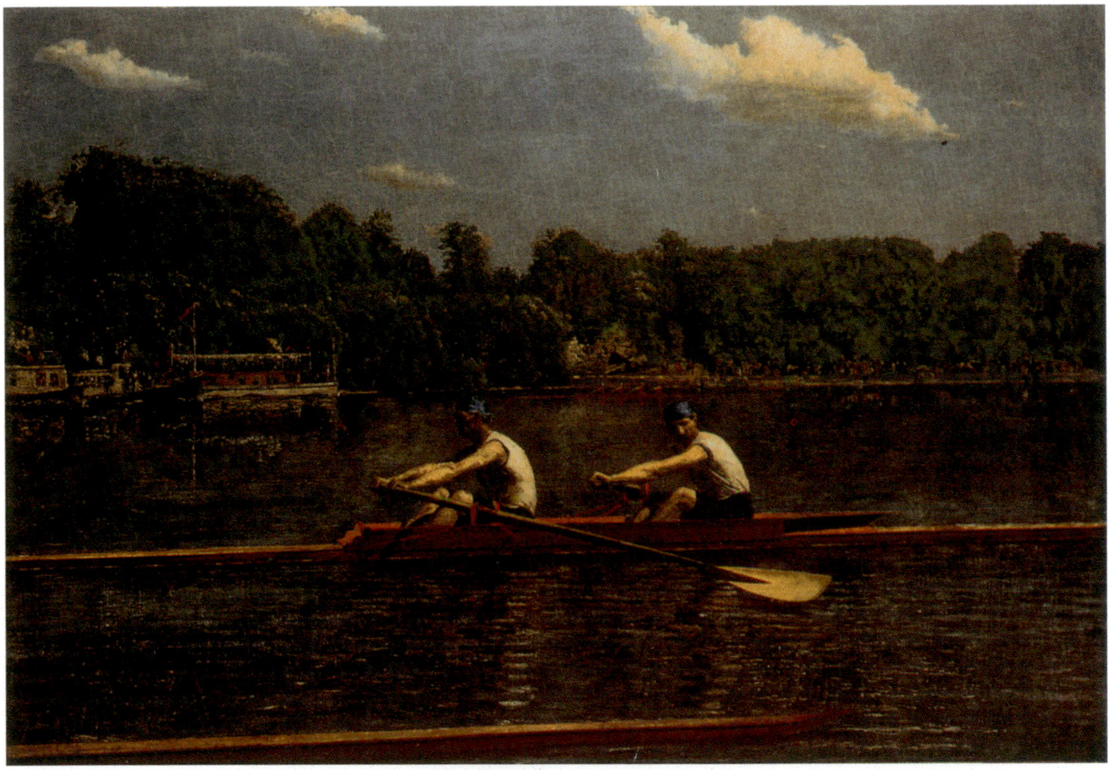

Color Plate 18
The Biglin Brothers Racing, c. 1873
Thomas Eakins

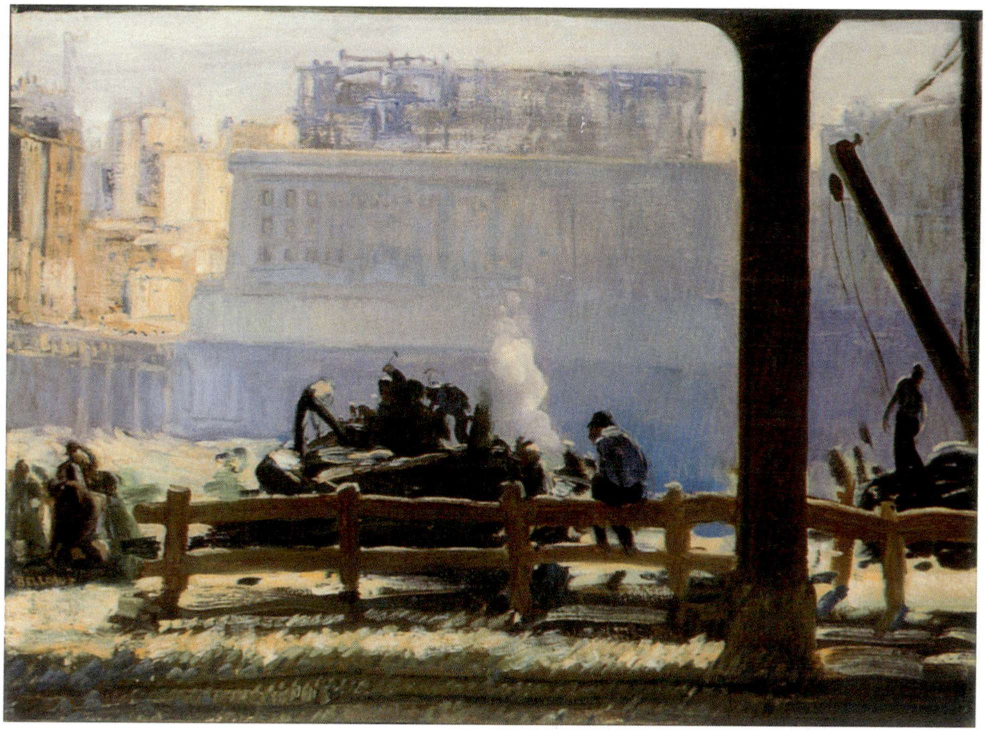

Color Plate 19
Blue Morning, 1909
George Bellows

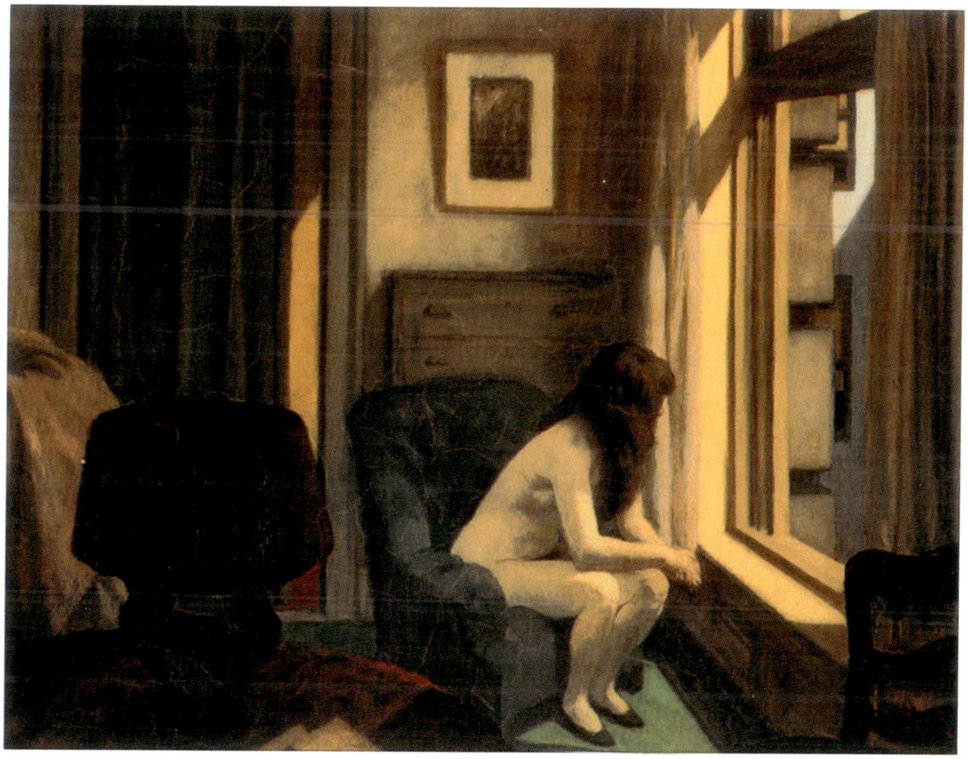

Color Plate 20
Eleven A.M., 1926
Edward Hopper

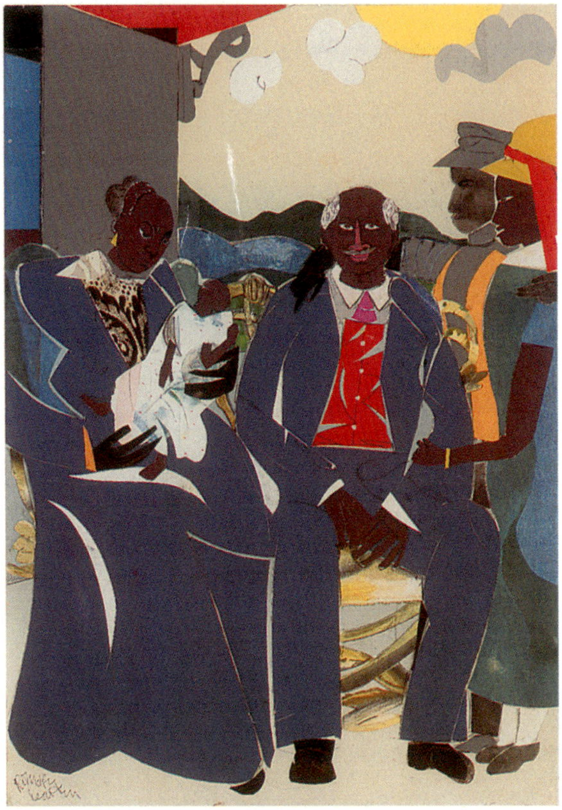

Color Plate 21
Family, 1986
Romare Bearden

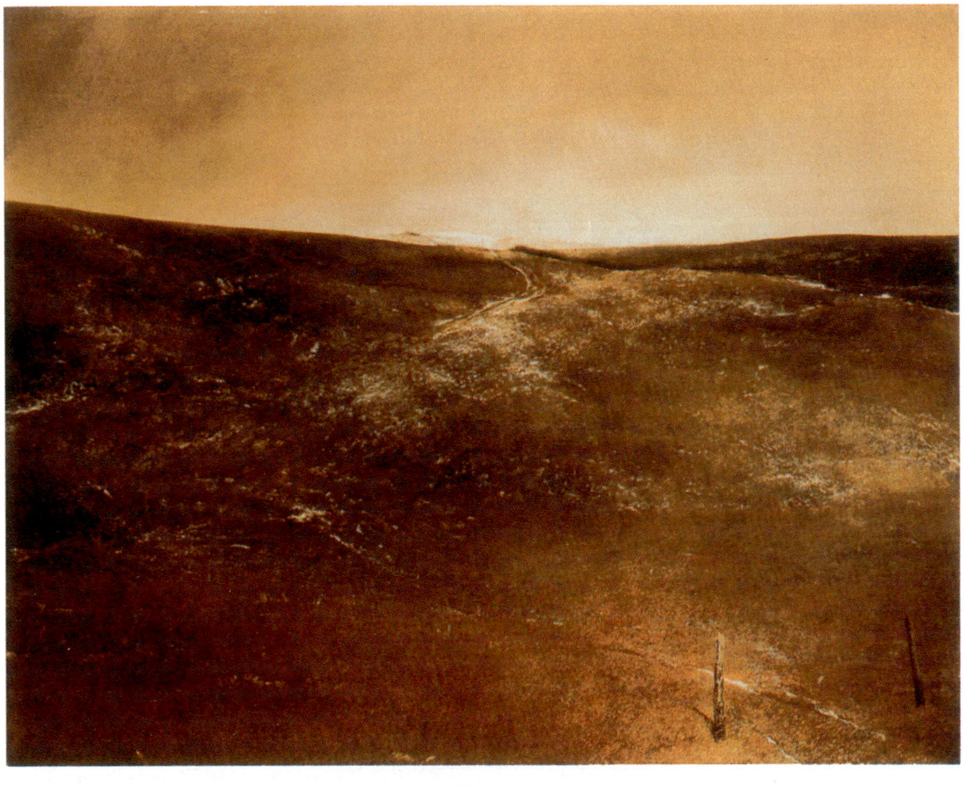

Color Plate 22
Snow Flurries, 1953
Andrew Wyeth

and resented having to study in the studio in order to collect his allowance. He did a minimum of work each week and then left. His use of color was already too free to suit his teachers. Among other students there who became his friends were Renoir, Sisley, and Bazille, all of whom would become painters in the Impressionist style.

Gleyre's studio closed down after Monet had been a student there for a year and a half. This left Monet free to discover outdoor painting with some of his fellow students. They went to Barbizon, where painters had discovered painting nature on the spot. Monet was entranced with the process of capturing air and sunlight with color.

Returning to Paris, Monet, facing possible problems with his allowance, decided to try for acceptance at the next Salon exhibit. He now shared a studio with sleeping space with fellow student, Bazille, who was more mature and self-disciplined than Monet.

Camille Doncieux was a beautiful dark-haired girl of 18 from a well-to-do family when she fell in love with Claude Monet. Perhaps she provided Monet with long-absent warmth and filled the empty emotional spaces in his life. They did not have a relationship in which a lack in one person was supplied by a quality in the other; both Camille and Claude seemed to share the same kinds of immaturities.

Camille had broken with her family and had come to live with Monet. His family had finally cut him off from further money. He also no longer shared the studio with Bazille. Monet and Camille began to experience the continual lack of money that haunted them until her death and the middle of Monet's life. The pattern was repeated over and over: first a little money would turn up when Monet sold a painting or got a commission for one; like delighted children, they spent the money as soon as it came to them. Debts went unpaid, while the money was spent for a holiday at the beach, pretty clothes, or whatever interested them. When very low on funds, Monet wrote whining, begging letters to friends and acquaintances asking for money. If the money that passed through their hands had been added up, they would have had as much to live on as many others at the time. But they were totally unable to manage their lives. There is no account of Monet's ever looking for work to earn a little money to keep them going. He simply begged, and eventually the people who knew him became quite weary of it.

Monet submitted two seascapes to the Salon. It was the same year that Manet's *Olympia* caused such a stir. Both paintings were accepted and brought in a bit of money for him. In the Salon of 1866, two paintings were received favorably; one was a full-length portrait of Camille, who had become a frequent model for Monet. Another work featuring Camille was *Bazille et Camille* (see Figure 35). The next year the jury had tightened up its admissions and Monet as well as many others painting in the "new style" were rejected. Monet's work was rejected regularly by the Salon in the years to follow.

In 1874 the first Impressionist exhibit was organized independently of the Salon. Thirty artists' work was displayed. The organization was a rather loose one, with Monet, Renoir, Pissarro, Degas, and Berthe Morisot among the artists who put it together. One story says the name Impressionist came from the title of one of Monet's paintings (*Impression: Sunrise*). The public picked up the term, and, to the group, it seemed a suitable name. The exhibit received the same kind of ridicule as the work at the Salon des Réfusés. Monet, since he had been a chief organizer and since his painting had contributed the title for the group, was seen as the leader of the new "school."

Monet had married Camille, partly in order to gain the money from her reluctant family for a dowry. At that point they had already had a son, Jean. Monet rented a house in Argenteuil on the Seine River, about 20 minutes from Paris by train. Several of his fellow Impressionists came to the area to work during the summer. Camille served as a model not only for her husband's paintings but also for those of the other artists, especially Renoir. Manet had relatives in the town across the river and also spent time with Monet's group. Here they enjoyed painting nature, the river, trees, flowers, and sunlight. The art dealer Durand-Ruel had bought a number of Monet's paintings and the future looked very promising. Camille could buy new dresses for herself and outfits for Jean. She was able to live for the first and only time in her life with Monet as she had with her family—comfortably. She was a happy young French housewife, and it was a beautiful summer.

But the summer ended, the paintings were not selling well, and not all of Camille's dowry was being paid to them. The winter on the river was difficult, and the letters begging for money began. They moved back to Paris and then to Vétheuil. This setting is the subject of *The Artist's Garden at Vétheuil* (see Figure 36). By the summer of 1879, following the birth of a second son, Camille died. She was 32.

Monet was distraught by her death. His two sons were taken in by Alice Hoschede, the wife of a merchant who was also a collector of art. Financial losses had forced her husband to move to Brussels to start over again. Madame Hoschede stayed in Paris, worked as a dressmaker, and raised their six children.

Monet was truly at the lowest point of his life, emotionally and financially. It is to his credit that he was able to make a new start, and to develop, for the first time, maturity and purpose. Many of his contacts, acquaintances, collectors, and friends were weary of his frequent begging for money in the past, and were rather cool toward him at this point. Even though he was truly in need now, he had worn them out.

Alice Hoschede was now raising Monet's sons as well as her own children. She used her own money, which she had put away from her dowry, and her earnings. Her relationship with Monet was more than just friendly now, and by the year after Camille's death, she had moved into the little house in Vétheuil, children and all. Her husband was still alive and she never sought a divorce (divorce was a rarity then). She was a practical person, warm and cheerful. She organized a stable household for Monet and their combined brood. With the finances in her hands, Monet could tend to his paintings and cease to be the pleading, obnoxious figure he had been for the past ten years. He had written his last begging letter. In 1882 they moved to Giverny, where they spent the rest of their lives.

Durand-Ruel and other dealers now took his work on a regular basis. *Woman Seated Under the Willows* (see Color Plate 11) dates from this period in Monet's career. In 1881 Monet refused to exhibit with the Impressionists, for there seemed no need. By 1889 his work was also selling well in America.

Monet's famous haystack paintings were painted in Giverny. He first noticed the haystacks for their interesting, hut-like shapes. Then he began painting one. When he came back the next day, he saw how their colors seemed to change as the light and atmosphere changed. He continued to paint the haystacks in various seasons and degrees of light. The series created a sensation in Paris—this time, a favorable one. The haystacks were the paintings most in demand from Monet. Pictures in a series became popular.

After a few years Monet and his household were accepted in the village of Giverny. In 1892 Alice's husband died. She and Monet were then quietly married. Shortly afterwards Alice's daughter, Suzanne, married an American. Monet's son, Jean, and Alice's daughter, Blanche, were married in 1897. Monet was fortified by a comfortable home, warm family ties, wealth, and the role of patriarch of the close-knit family. He traveled a little, going to Spain, Britain, Norway, and Venice with Alice.

The next series of paintings was of poplar trees. The ones he planned to paint were due to be chopped down, and Monet had to buy a reprieve for them until he finished his paintings. The poplars series was very well received, even more so than the haystacks.

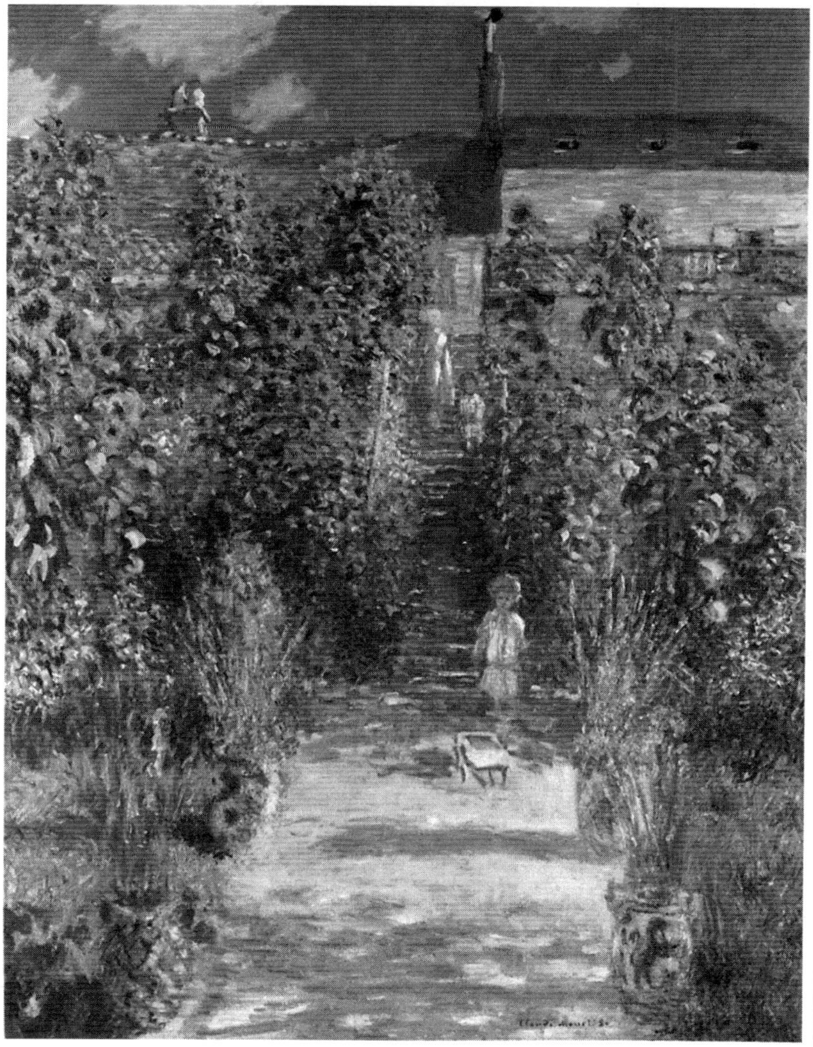

Figure 36
The Artist's Garden at Vétheuil, 1880
Claude Monet

His famous paintings of Rouen Cathedral were begun as he sat in the second floor in the building across from it. He made more than 30 paintings from that spot, as the light changed from one part of the day to the next. He worked there from February 1892 until late that spring. Then the paintings went home with him and he continued to work on them for the next two years.

Monet saw form as color and variations of color, not line. In his later life he was unhappy at being called the father of Impressionism. He thought that those who were painting in what they thought was the Impressionistic style really didn't understand it.

Monet's last painting was of the water lily pond at his home. The French government had commissioned a work from him. He had begun to have problems with his vision, but nothing could stop his painting. A new, larger studio had to be built, for the panels for this painting were huge. Each morning the canvas, set on wheels, was moved outside by the pond so that he could paint, and at night it was wheeled back into the studio. He did not add any medium to the paint, but used it as it came from its container. He was also learning to use the new bristle brushes instead of the softer sable brushes. He began *Water Lilies* in 1916 when he was 76 and continued to work on it until his death in 1926.

Monet died at 86. His painting style had become broader and his brush strokes larger. Color was difficult for him to work out. During the middle 1900s, at the height of the Abstract Expressionism movement, many felt there was a strong connection between Monet and that style. Others feel the style of the *Water Lilies* is the result of Monet's struggle with his loss of vision.

Monet refused to turn *Water Lilies* over to the government during his lifetime. He was uneasy about the work and did not want to know the public reaction. During the fall of 1926, his eyesight failed entirely and he looked forward to death. He died on December 5 and was buried beside Alice in the churchyard at Giverny.

Glossary

Monet pronounced mō-nay´

caricatures in art, deliberately distorted pictures of persons or things

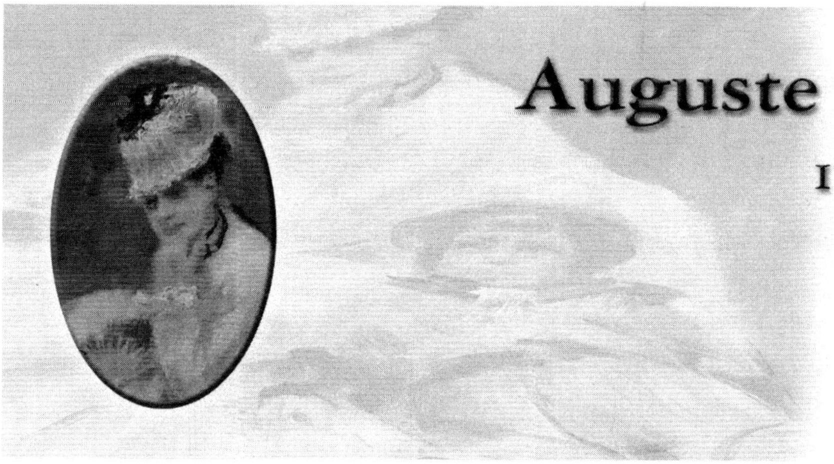

Auguste Renoir

1841 – 1919

LIMOGES, FRANCE, was the birthplace of Auguste **Renoir** in 1841. His father was a tailor. When Renoir was four years old the large family moved to Paris, hoping to make better lives for themselves. In the Renoir family the legend was that the grandfather had been of noble birth. He was said to have been orphaned in the revolution of 1789, left by his family, who were of the nobility. They were killed or fled the country. A cobbler adopted him. The records do not support the story; it was not uncommon for such stories to be repeated in those days, when the chaotic conditions might have made them seem true.

Like other budding artists have done, Renoir drew pictures in his copy books at the government-run school he attended. When he was 13 he took a job, or was apprenticed, in a china factory, where he learned to paint decorations for the porcelain dishes. Having come from Limoges, a name associated with fine china, such a job must have seemed to his parents to be an excellent beginning. He painted colorful flowers that required him to develop skill and control of the paint. Sometimes he painted motifs from nineteenth-century French painters such as Boucher, Watteau, and Fragonard. The Louvre was close to the factory and Renoir spent time there after work studying the paintings. He especially liked the work of these men.

When the china factory closed down, Renoir found work painting the same kinds of courtly figures on ladies' fans. He also worked for a supplier of missionary materials, and painted stained-glass pictures of religious stories. Because of these experiences and the encouragement of a fellow worker, he decided to make a career of art.

Renoir was a thin, somewhat nervous, slightly-built young man with light-brown hair. He had a pleasant disposition and made friends easily. When he had put aside enough money to get started, he enrolled in the studio of Gleyre, where he learned the classical style. He also aquired life-long friends: Monet, Sisley, and Bazille. With these men he could share ideas about painting, especially the use of color. They were all influenced by Delacroix, Courbet, Corot, Degas, Manet, and the English painter Constable.

Renoir's early style was that of the Impressionists, yet he kept it **compatible** with current tastes so he could pick up commissions. His early years as a painter were no easier financially than Monet's. Sometimes he went back to live with his parents; sometimes he could not eat every day. One story tells of his filling pockets with bread from his parents' table to take to Monet. They encouraged each other in their art. Renoir said that without Monet's help he might not have continued. Both of them found help from Bazille and stayed in his studio at times. During the short war with Prussia, Bazille enlisted and was killed; Renoir enlisted but did not see action.

Renoir was active with the group of painters who became the Impressionists. In fact, he had been one of the chief organizers of the first show in 1874. It had been his plan to take ten percent of the money they earned to keep as a fund for the group, instead of dividing it all among them equally. The art dealer Durand-Ruel, whose name comes up so frequently during these years, had had financial problems in 1874, and the independent exhibit was a way to bring their work before the public.

After the disaster that was the exhibit, Monet, Manet, and Renoir found painting at Argenteuil that summer particularly comforting. Renoir simply loved to paint. It is said that a day never passed that he did not paint, even when ill. The

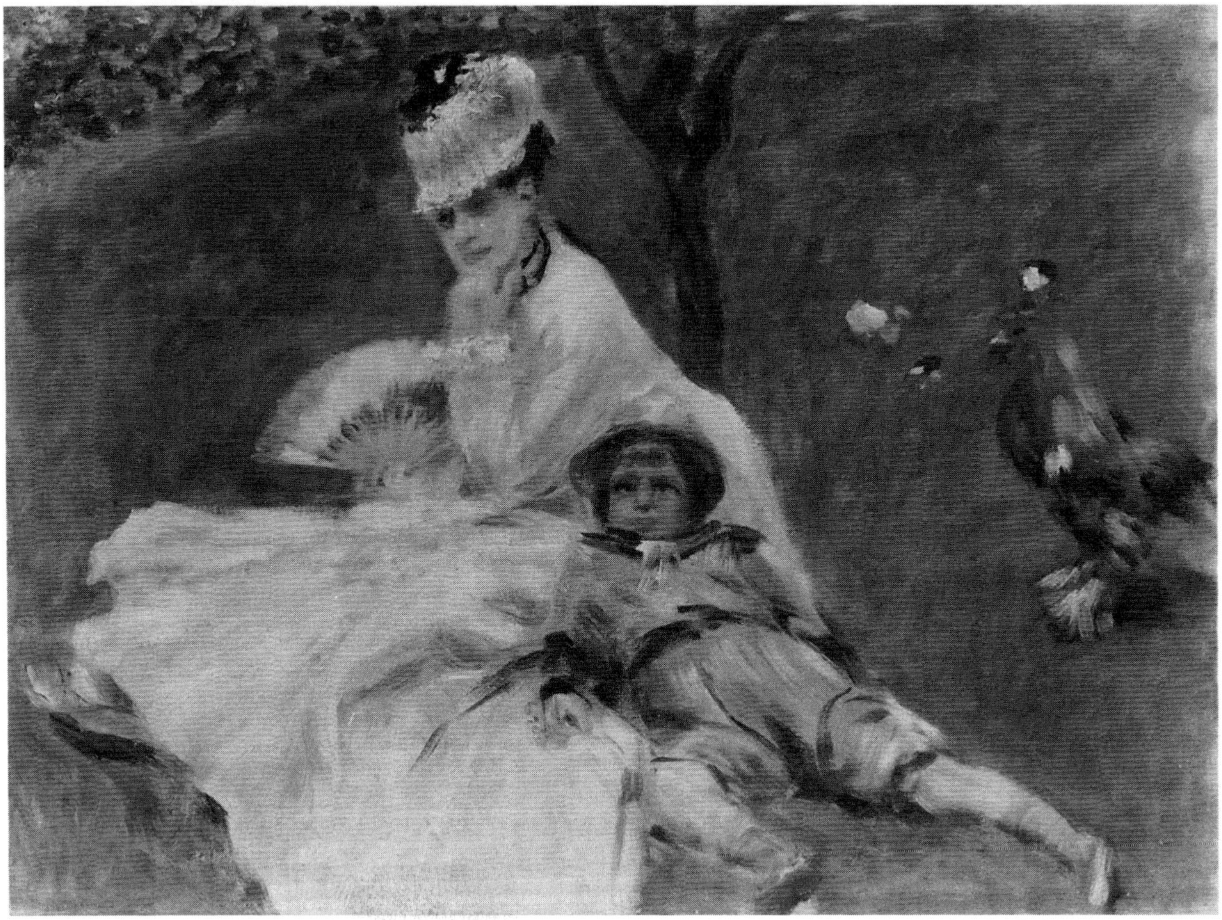

Figure 37
Madame Monet and Her Son, 1874
Auguste Renoir

artists painted each other and they painted Camille Monet. Renoir particularly liked to paint Camille; he particularly liked to paint women. The painting *La Loge* shows Camille with another figure in a theater balcony. He painted her sewing; in another picture she is wearing an oriental robe. At this time in France, boating was a popular activity. People spent as much time as they could on the rivers, men in their shirtsleeves and straw hats, and women in colorful summer dresses. Trees and flowers on the banks, sailboats and rowboats, and colorful people—no wonder these artists found so much subject matter for their paintings.

Renoir found an early patron in the publisher Charpentier. The painting *Madame Charpentier and Her Daughters* was accepted by the Salon for the 1879 exhibit. The painting *The Swing* was painted in the Charpentier garden. A *Girl with a Watering Can* dates from this period of Renoir's career (see Color Plate 12). Other paintings in his early

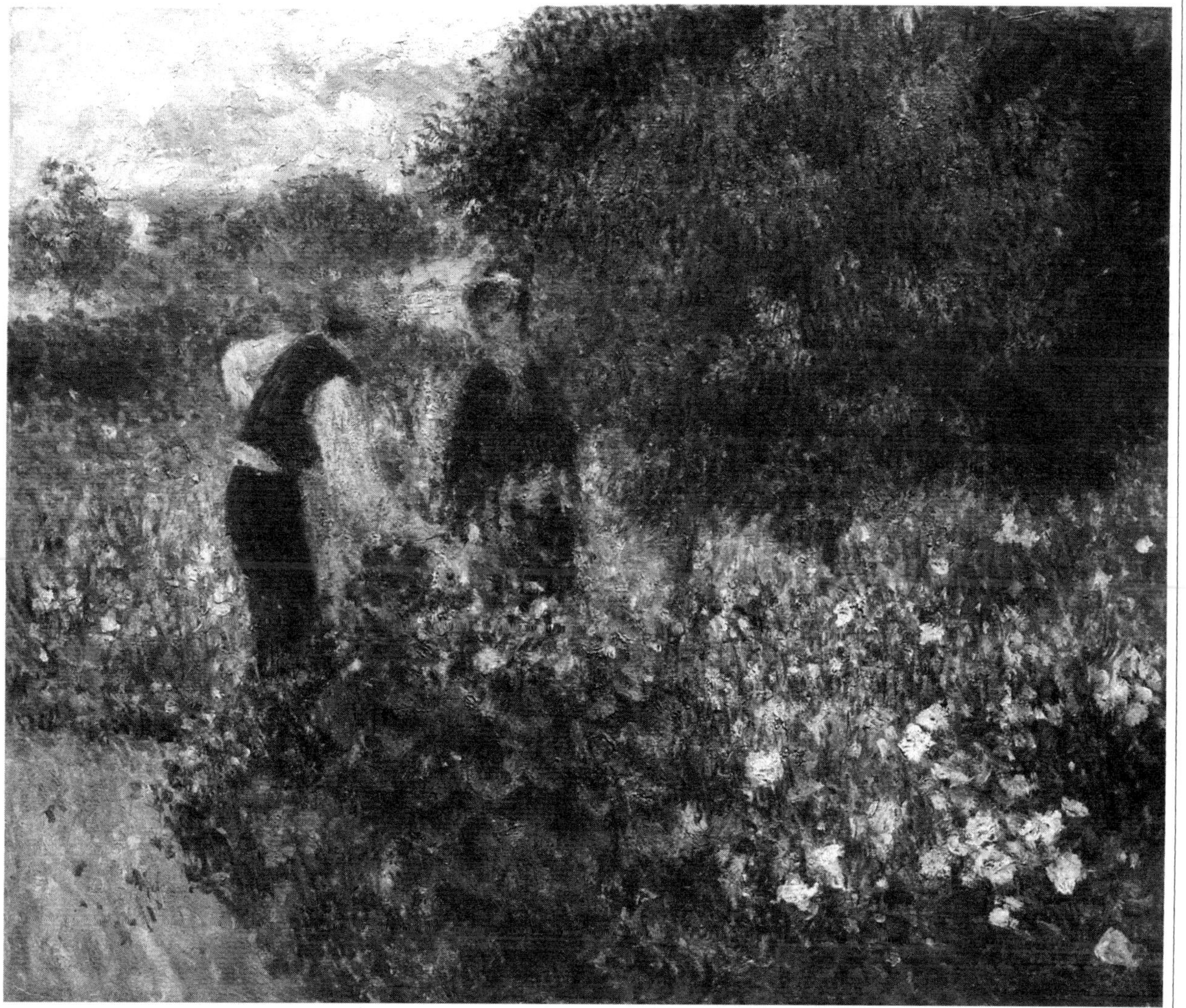

Figure 38
Picking Flowers, 1875
Auguste Renoir

Impressionistic style are *Moulin de la Galette,* a crowded dance floor with people on the sidelines, eating, drinking, and talking; *Madame Monet and Her Son,* a portrait (see Figure 37); *At the Milliner's,* a woman selecting a hat; and *Picking Flowers,* a man and woman in a flowery landscape (see Figure 38). These paintings show sunlight, bright colors, brushy paint strokes, and limited detail. A later painting done in 1881, *Luncheon of the Boating Party,* shows more detail and individualized faces, perhaps because the young woman holding the dog at the left later became Renoir's wife.

The artist continued to pick up commissions and to make portraits, for which there was some demand. After the Salon of 1879 Renoir made a trip to Algiers and Italy. He saw the art of Venice, and in Palermo made a portrait of the composer Wagner. These and later travels seemed to confirm his feeling that one could see just as much and paint just as well back in France. At this time he was 41, and had begun to experience his first problems with the **arthritis** that would gradually cripple him.

With plenty of work to keep him financially secure, and an increasing dissatisfaction with Impressionism, Renoir did not exhibit with the group from 1879 to 1881. He was impressed by Raphael's paintings during a trip to Rome in 1882. He also became interested in a book written by a follower of Giotto that described the process of egg tempera painting. No doubt his training in the classical tradition by Gleyre had its effect. Although the style he developed next kept some Impressionist elements, his forms became more distinct and their edges and details more visible. He kept the bright, joyful color of his previous style, though some call this middle period of his art more "harsh."

By the end of the 1880s, Renoir was moving back to a style closer to Impressionism and to his beginnings. There was more control, perhaps, than in the early years; the brush strokes were more pronounced. The colors he loved were there, the forms looked more solid, and the edges had softened. The subject matter still included many women, girls, groups, nudes, and landscapes.

Renoir had married in 1880. His son Pierre was born in 1885; the second son, Jean, was born in 1893; Claude, the third son, was born in 1901. (Jean Renoir became a famous director of films in France in the first half of the twentieth century.)

In the 1890s the Renoir family and two servants lived in an old house in Montmartre. He went to the seashore to work in the summers and spent the winters in Paris. As the decade wore on, his arthritis became more of a problem and he spent more time in the south of France, hoping for some relief in a warmer climate. His life, on the whole, was as tranquil after the early days as Monet's was troubled. Renoir reached a point at which his financial postion was secure. He had the comfort of a loving wife and family and the admiration of the public. He was a kindly man. A story is told of his treatment of a forger: The man brought him an obviously forged painting with Renoir's signature. Renoir touched it up, signed it himself, and, since the man seemed down on his luck, gave it back to him.

In later years, the forms of his figures became heavier and the brushwork more loose. This is common in painters who live and work to an advanced age. With Renoir the arthritis probably contributed; he could not hold his paintbrushes and had to have one fastened to his hand in order to paint. During the last 15 years of his life he continued to paint still lifes, landscapes, and portraits. Often he painted members of his family and servants. He painted until the very end, though in a wheelchair, dying on December 17, 1919, at 78.

Glossary

Renoir pronounced ren-wahr´

compatible in harmony with or agreement with another person or idea

arthritis inflammation of the joints that causes pain and stiffness

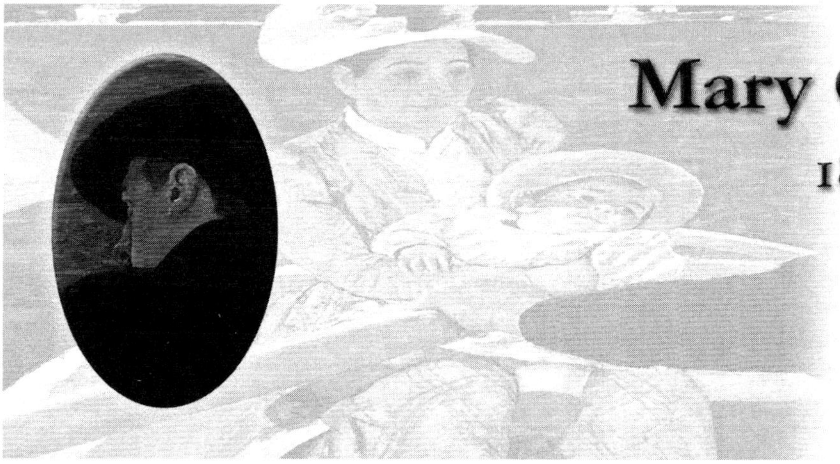

Mary Cassatt
1845 – 1926

ANOTHER PAINTER in the Impressionist style was a woman and an American. Her name was Mary **Cassatt.** She was born in Allegheny City, Pennsylvania on May 22, 1845. Her father had various business interests and was inclined to move about. The family moved to and from various cities in Pennsylvania. In 1851, when Mary was seven, Robert Cassatt took his wife, Katherine, and their children to Europe. They lived first in Paris and then in Germany. The son, Robert, died in Darmstadt, Germany in 1855. The family then moved back to the United States and settled in Philadelphia. In the fall of 1861 Mary was 17. She decided to beome an art student at the Pennsylvania Academy of Fine Arts, one of the few art schools in the country at that time. After four years there she knew that she had gone as far as possible with the instruction offered.

Mary had made up her mind to study in Europe. Her father believed that no young woman of good family and means should even think of a career, particularly one in art. Mary was as strong-willed as her father, and finally received his permission to go. It was arranged for her to live with friends of the family. She studied at the Chaplin studio, but after a while thought she could work better on her own. During the war between France and Prussia, Mary was told to come back to Philadelphia.

By 1872 she returned to Europe. She wanted to study the old master painters of Italy and spent some time in Parma. There she also learned engraving, studying with the man who was head of the engraving department of the art academy. Later in her life her prints were an important part of her work. She traveled to Spain, where she was influenced by the paintings of Rubens in the Prado.

Mary Cassatt had lived in Paris off and on since she was seven and probably felt more at home there than anywhere else in Europe. That city had become the center of the art world, and she chose to settle there. Her parents lived there with her during her middle age. Sometimes one or more of her brothers, and always her sister, Lydia, stayed with Mary and their parents. She had the problems of her mother's poor health and her sister's illness. She had to take time from her work to find areas to live where they were comfortable and

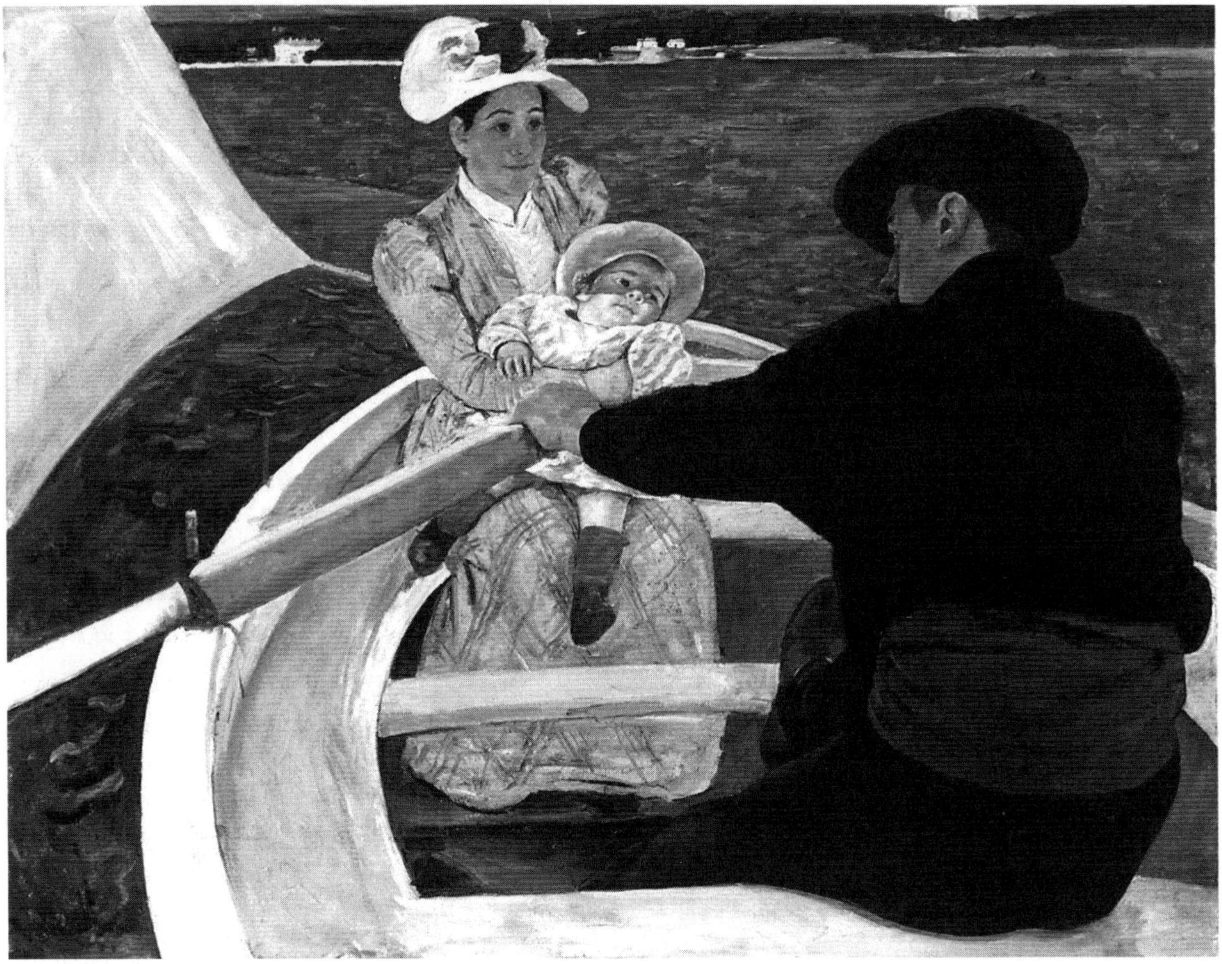

Figure 39
The Boating Party, 1893–1894
Mary Cassatt

where their health might improve. Some stories of her life assume that the family was wealthy. This is not altogether true. While they were better off than many Americans, her father was not always successful in his business dealings. Living in Europe allowed them to live better than they might have in America.

Mary was influenced by the Impressionists as well as by other artists. Most artists do find that their work reflects the work of those whom they admire and study. But they want to develop their own personal style, and that is what Mary spent her life doing. Her best-known paintings are those of women and children, for example, *The Boating Party* (see Figure 39). This theme had been suggested to her by the painter Edgar **Degas,** a longtime friend and advisor. Mary had met Degas and other Impressionists and had exhibited her work with theirs in their first independent exhibition. Throughout her life she upheld their ideas and she, too, rebelled against the Salon system, believing there should be no awards or medals for art. Late in her life, when she refused an award, she said that she felt awards of money were more sensible but should be given only to young painters or students.

Some believe that Mary Cassatt and Degas were romantically involved, but there is no evidence of this. She was a very proper woman of a very proper time in history, the Victorian era. Codes of behavior then were strict, especially for girls and women. She was more concerned with her progress as an artist than with anything else, though her obligations to her family were important. She lived at a time when it was unusual for a woman to work for a living if her family could support her or if she had married. She was irritated if people said such things as "Good painting—for a woman," or "How can a woman paint so well?" She worked hard. Each morning she was in her studio by eight. By evening, when daylight was gone and she had to depend on artificial light, she worked on her printmaking. Printmaking did not depend as much on daylight as painting did.

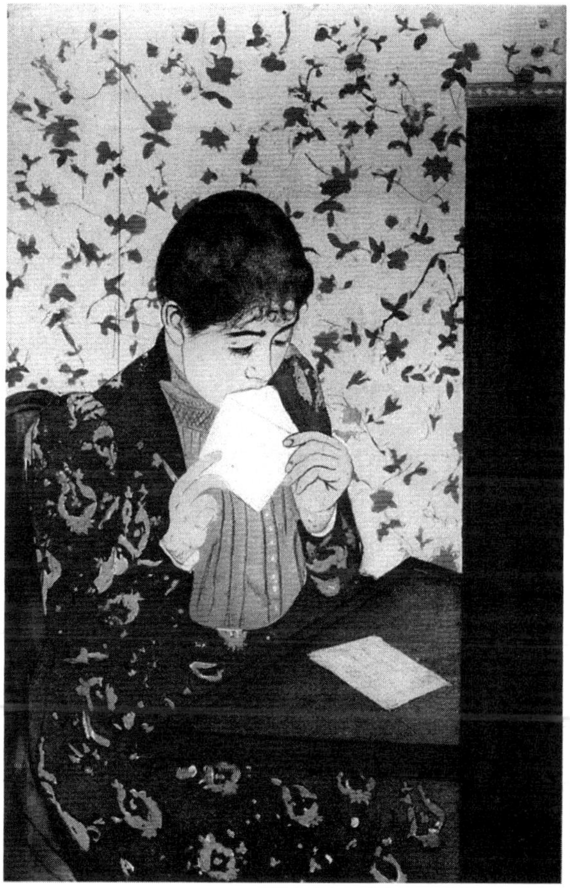

Figure 40
The Letter, 1891
Mary Cassatt

Mary's family was pleased that her art could bring in the money that it did, but they never really appreciated what she did. She was devoted to her parents and saw to it that they had any help they needed. She willingly took time from her work to find houses or apartments that suited them. She was also always devoted to her brothers and sister, nephews and nieces. Some of the relatives did not get on well with Mary; she had a sharp tongue and usually said just what she thought. This became even more true as she grew older.

The first paintings exhibited by Mary Cassatt were in that April exhibit by the Impressionists in 1879. *La Loge* shows a young woman in a theater. The colors are rich and dramatic: The woman with red hair wears a pink gown. The critics were complimentary. Before long she began to be recognized for her work. The portrait *Miss Mary Ellison* (see Color Plate 13) is a noteworthy work from this period in Cassatt's career. She exhibited in the Salons of 1872, 1873, and 1874. In 1875 one of her entries was rejected but accepted at the next Salon after she toned down the color. She was rejected the next year and never submitted entries again. She painted in oils and did **pastels,** engraving, etchings and aquatint. *The Letter* (see Figure 40) is a well-known etching with aquatint.

Mary Cassatt also helped influence artistic interests at this time. She had helped her brother find paintings by the best artists for his private collection. She also bought a number of paintings for herself. Since she knew Americans who were visiting Europe, many of whom were wealthy, she could advise them in their collections of art. When these paintings were brought back to America, more people could learn about some of the best art in Europe. Many of these works of art found their way into museums.

Except for a few visits to America, Mary Cassatt spent her adult and professional life in Europe. She might have traveled to America more often if air travel had been possible. (She became violently seasick on several of her voyages.) She did love to travel by car, though. In 1906 one of her wealthy friends gave her a car. She hired a driver and traveled over much of Europe.

By 1893 Mary had bought and moved into a house in the country. After the death of both her parents, she no longer had the responsibility of looking after them and had more freedom to live as she liked. She had made many friends over the years: other artists, politicians, and wealthy Americans who traveled to Paris. In the community where her chateau, or country house, was located, she contributed to the village school, helped young women find work, and often "borrowed" children and mothers to model for her pictures. She felt strongly about the rights of women at a time when such ideas only flickered on the horizon. She liked children and got on well with them. She found that babies were good models, if held in a woman's arms. Toddlers were a bit too active to be good models. Older children modeled well, and apparently liked working with her. Ample goodies and rewards probably helped.

Mary Cassatt's style was thoroughly developed by her middle years. At about this time Japanese prints had been introduced in Europe and were popular. Mary's prints were influenced by the Japanese block prints. In 1893 her work was exhibited by the Durand-Ruel galleries, some 98 pieces including *A Cup of Tea, At the Opera,* and *The Bath*.

The artist's health gave her problems as she grew older. She developed diabetes. By 1915 cataracts began to affect her eyesight. In spite of several operations, her sight was failing. Her disposition, which had never been particularly sunny, became more irritable. She had passed the peak of her artistic powers, and did not get along well with those left in her family. The work of the newer artists such as Matisse, van Gogh, and Picasso horrified her. Cézanne's work was as "modern" as she could tolerate.

With her servants taking care of her, Mary Cassatt spent her last years in her country home. She was frustrated by her loss of sight and by illness.

During World War I she was evacuated to Grasse, where she had a vacation home. The waste of war further depressed her spirits. Her life came to an end on June 14, 1926. She was 82. Pictures that were left to the remaining members of her family were at first just considered family heirlooms. Her nieces and nephews were surprised later to find out how valuable Aunt Mary's artworks were.

Glossary

Cassatt pronounced cas-saht´

Degas pronounced day-gah´

pastels mediums made from powdered pigments mixed with a binder and formed into chalk sticks

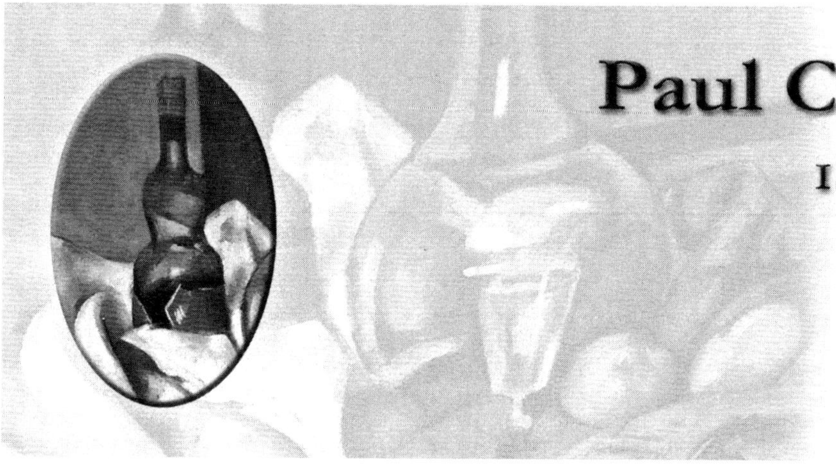

Paul Cézanne

1839 – 1906

THE TERM Postimpressionism is used for the work of artists who moved on from Impressionism into new ways of painting. One outstanding Postimpressionist was Paul **Cézanne.**

Paul Cézanne was born in Aix-en-Provence on January 19, 1839. It is probable that his ancestors came to southern France from Italy in the seventeenth century. His father, Louis-Auguste, who was a strong force in his life, had begun as a hatmaker. He was a clever businessman. After developing his own hatmaking business, he went into banking. He married one of the shop girls from his business. Paul had two sisters. Louis-Auguste was an ambitious man and an assertive and domineering father. Paul was forever in fear of him, and turned to his mother and sisters for help when he felt he had to go against his father's wishes.

Paul Cézanne grew up to be an insecure, timid man. On one hand he longed for success, recognition, and friendship; on the other hand, he had a violent temper, feared failure, and could not handle relationships with others well. During his school days he liked to write poetry and planned to become a writer. All his life, books were important to him. One of his boyhood friends was Emile Zola, who also wanted to write. They roamed the countryside around Aix during vacations and remained friends well into their adult lives. Zola did become a writer and was one of the best-known novelists in France.

Cézanne's father insisted that Paul go to law school. Not the first artist who was sent to law school by an ambitious parent, Paul made the effort, but found that law was not for him. He decided on a career in art, possibly because he did not want to compete with his friend Zola. While he was still studying law, he was allowed to set up a studio at home and receive lessons from a local painter. His mother apparently encouraged his painting and probably was the one who made these arrangements. However, Paris was the place to study art in those days, and Paul wanted to go there. Zola had moved to Paris with his family, and now urged Paul to come. By spring of 1861 his father relented and allowed him to try it.

Cézanne began his studies at the Académie Suisse, where there were models but there was no instruction. Several other well-known artists had worked there at one time or another, including Courbet, Delacroix, Monet, and Pissarro. Pissarro was in the group of Impressionists and became a friend of Cézanne's, giving him as much help and encouragement as possible.

Cézanne at first admired the paintings of the Salon exhibits and tried to follow that path himself. Contact with fellow painters who were looking for new directions also gave him new ideas. In visits to the Louvre he discovered the old masters, especially Giorgione, Rubens, and Michelangelo. He was also influenced by Courbet and that painter's method of using his palette knife with thick paint.

Cézanne's early paintings show solid forms, dark outlines, and visible brush strokes. He often used dark colors with strong light contrasts. The themes were often violent and strange: *The Autopsy, The Murder, The Abduction, The Orgy,* and *The Strangled Woman*. His uncle Dominique obligingly posed for portraits wearing parts of costumes; in one he is painted as a monk.

Cézanne did not have the kind of early genius we have seen in Dürer, nor did he fill his copy books with drawings as Monet did. He felt that he was far behind his fellow painters in learning technical skills in painting and drawing. He worked very hard, trying to catch up and to develop his own style. Often he shut himself into his studio and saw no one for weeks at a time. He did not fit into the group of young artists who became the Impressionists and who socialized together. He simply did not find that he could have easy, comfortable contact with people. His mood swings were extreme, changing from calm to sudden anger in an instant. He was often on the defensive, made fun of elegant manners, and was generally disagreeable. The painter Pissarro tolerated him best. He insisted that Cézanne's paintings be included in the first Impressionist exhibit. He worked with him and invited him to stay at his home in Pontoise. Cézanne later said that Pissarro was "like a father to me." Cézanne did have the advantage of a wealthy father who, though he did not approve of his son's career in art, was still willing to support him. Cézanne cared little for material things and could live comfortably on his allowance from his father.

Following his early, rather dark and heavy style, Cézanne came closer to the Impressionistic style, lightening his color. One painting from that period, *The House of the Hanged Man,* was exhibited in the first Impressionist show and was sold. Its title suggests his early macabre themes, but the painting is actually of houses in a landscape, done in warm, light colors. The textures of the thatched roofs are created with short brush strokes. The heavy outlines seen in earlier works are gone. His other paintings in the exhibit, though, received the same kinds of harsh criticism that the others did.

Cézanne moved on, developing his style. He did not want to paint a fleeting moment as the Impressionists did. He wanted to show solid forms, not flickering color. He wanted balance and order in a painting. He was willing to distort shapes or even tilt objects to achieve this balance. All of his life as a painter was spent solving these problems. He began a painting by looking intently at whatever he was going to paint. He tried to understand all he could about it, whether it was a landscape, a person, or a still life. From that point the painting was begun. Cézanne wanted to be, as he said, "faithful" to nature. His expression of nature was different from Dürer's, for example. Both men, however, were "faithful" to nature in their own ways. For Cézanne, it was not a matter of reproducing what he saw, but of using that as a starting point. He did not always use local color (the actual color of an object). Similarly, he left off details, often stripping the object down to its basic form. He said that all nature could be seen in the cylinder, the sphere, and the cone. While Cézanne did not begin the abstract style in art, his work was a factor in the later development of Cubism.

Since the fifteenth century, artists had been working out methods of perspective (ways to show space and depth in a painting or drawing). This had been one of Dürer's interests. Cézanne was not concerned that the two-dimensional canvas be made to appear three-dimensional. He discarded methods of linear perspective as well as atmospheric perspective (in which colors are less intense in the distance). To preserve the sense of balance in his paintings, each color was equally bright. This eliminates sunlight in a painting, for that would make bright areas and shadowed areas. Where he needed to show distance and depth, he used overlapped forms and warm colors with cool colors for strong contrasts. He also tilted objects and distorted shapes, most noticeably in his still lifes.

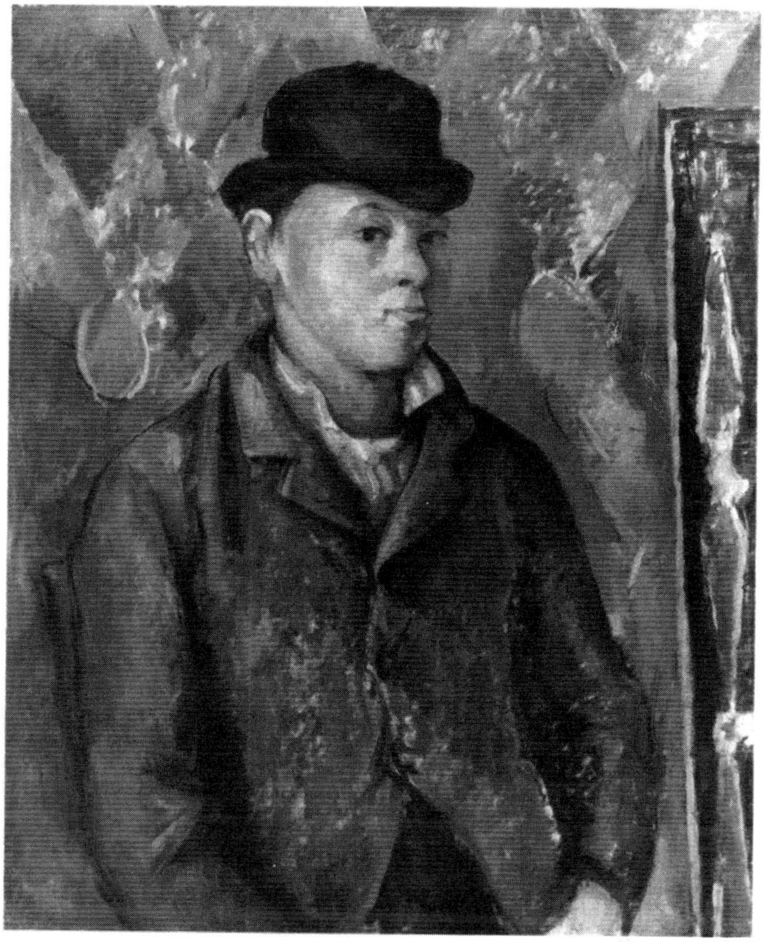

Figure 41
The Artist's Son, Paul, 1885–1890
Paul Cézanne

To begin a painting, Cézanne drew the parts that would be in shadow, placing the darker areas on the outside edges of the forms. If you have studied **positive space** and **negative space** in drawing, you know that he was actually drawing the negative space first. He might spend as much as a week on just this part of a painting. He worked slowly and carefully. For someone who could so easily become enraged and frustrated, we marvel at his patience. He did, however, discard many paintings that displeased him. The art dealer Julien Tanguy collected paintings from Cézanne, many of which he had been ready to destroy. Tanguy was able to convince him that they were worth saving. While Renoir painted from love of painting, Cézanne painted from some compulsion.

Not far from Cézanne's home in Aix was Mont Sainte-Victoire. This mountain was the subject of many of his paintings. In the later ones, the houses at the foot of the mountain became more and more abstract, hardly more than geometric forms. Earlier paintings of the same subject show us houses, trees, roads, and fields.

Cézanne lived and worked in villages on the outskirts of Paris as well as in Aix, L'Estaque, and Gardanne near the Mediterranean. Most of the time he lived and worked alone. Though he had married and had a son, Paul, he did not always live at home. His wife was the model for many portraits and Cézanne did a number of self-portraits. He was not an easy man for whom to model. He required long periods of time to work and became very upset if the model became tired or moved. This may explain why he often painted his patient wife or did self-portraits. His son Paul modeled for a few paintings, including *Mardi Gras,* in which he and a friend dressed as the familiar **harlequin** and a clown, and *The Artist's Son, Paul* (see Figure 41).

In another well-known painting, *Cardplayers,* some of the workers from his father's estate modeled in their working clothes. Three men sit at a table engrossed in a card game, while a fourth stands to watch. He tried the same theme in several other paintings, using different numbers of players and onlookers, trying to discover the arrangements that suited him best.

By the 1890s Cézanne lived in Aix. He had inherited money after his father's death and was well off. He continued to paint and spent more and more time alone. His mother and sister quarreled with each other and with his wife. His wife

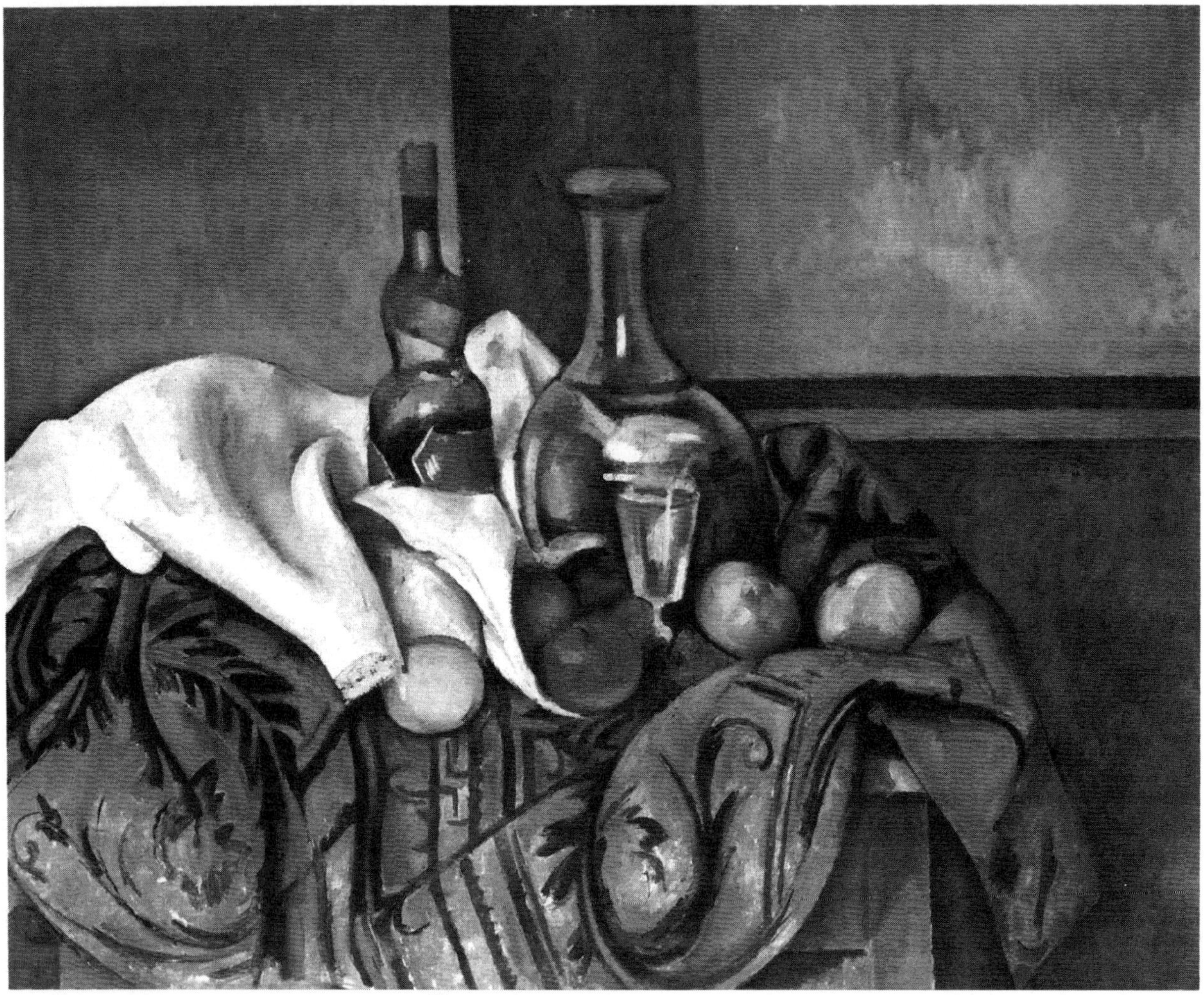

Figure 42
Still Life with Peppermint Bottle, c. 1894
Paul Cézanne

lived in one home and his mother, sister, and often Cézanne himself lived on the old family estate. The younger sister had married and lived far away. Cézanne seemed to be very fond of his son Paul, even though they did not see each other for months at a time. The boy was often at school in Paris or with his mother. During the last years of Cézanne's life, Paul acted as an **agent** for his father's work with art dealers and helped with other practical matters. While his older sister was alive, Cézanne had depended on her for advice; Paul now took her place. During his last years he became even more difficult in his relationships and dealings with people. Most of the artists he used to know had lost patience with him, though they had admired his work. *Still Life with Peppermint Bottle* dates from this period in the artist's life (see Figure 42).

By 1895 four fellow artists (Monet, Renoir, Pissarro, and Fuillaumin) convinced the art dealer Vollard that he should organize an exhibit of Cézanne's work. Cézanne had never put on a one-man show before. Vollard bought five paintings from Tanguy and asked Cézanne to send some of his paintings from Aix. He sent 150 canvases that had never been displayed. Many were sold at the exhibit and became the beginnings of collections of his work. Up to this point he had spent almost 20 years working, with little contact with the rest of the world. From time to time his name was mentioned, or he came to Paris, but most people had forgotten about him. After the exhibit his reputation bloomed, and by 1904 he was regarded as a leading artist in France. At this time he produced one of his last works, *Le Château Noir* (see Color Plate 14).

Fame did not change his way of life. His emotional state became even more strange. He had developed diabetes and he suffered from fits of depression. The people of Aix had no more respect for him after he became a well-known painter than they'd had before. They did not recognize him for the artist that he had become. They continued to think of him as an eccentric.

The artist's health became worse, and toward the end of October 1906 he collapsed on the road as he walked home. He developed pneumonia and died on October 22.

Cézanne could not have known that he was to influence almost every art style for the next 50 years. He told young artists to make their own discoveries instead of trying to repeat his.

Glossary

Cézanne pronounced say-zahn´

positive space the object itself

negative space the space around the object

harlequin in French and Italian pantomime and comedy, a traditional clown who wears a mask and a colorful costume

agent a person who transacts business for another

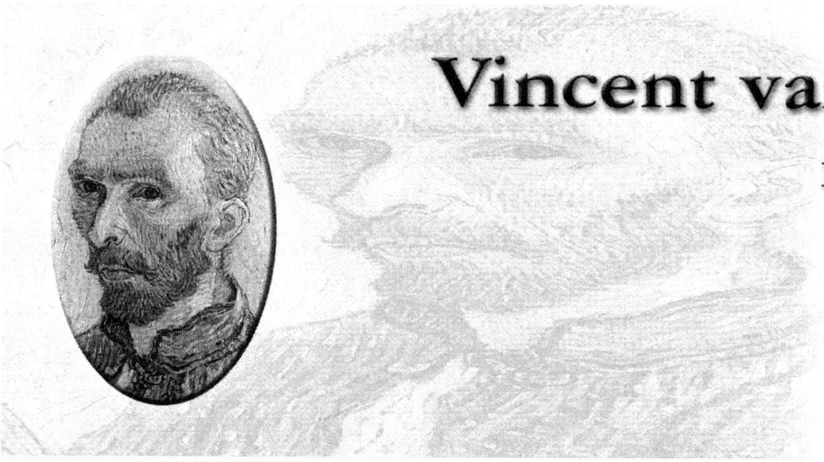

Vincent van Gogh

1853–1890

VINCENT VAN GOGH studied and worked with the Impressionists in Paris but moved on to develop a powerful style of his own. He is considered a Postimpressionist. He died in his thirty-seventh year two days after an attempt to take his own life. Van Gogh had worked as an artist for ten years. His life had been a struggle between his need to help and relate to others and his need to find himself and express his own feelings through his art.

Van Gogh was born on March 30, 1853, at Zundert, a Dutch village near the Belgian border. His father was the village pastor. There were two other boys in the family and three girls. Behavior codes in the village were strict; religious principles were stressed. Vincent grew up with deep sympathy for others who were troubled. He loved the countryside of the area and spent hours exploring it alone. His independent nature and moodiness caused problems for him. Members of the family said that he lived among them "as if he were a foreigner." Throughout his life, however, his brother Theo, who was four years younger, was his best friend and greatest source of help.

Vincent loved to draw as he grew up but did not decide on a career as an artist until he was 27. His first job was with art dealers. He was a salesman in an art gallery, first at The Hague, then in London, and lastly in Paris. He was evidently not cut out to sell art. For one thing, he refused to encourage sales of paintings or prints that he himself did not like. He was eventually dismissed.

While he was in London he fell in love for the first time but was rejected by the young woman. In his disappointment over this, and in losing his job, he turned to his religion. He read the Bible over and over. He attended religious worship at various churches and **synagogues.** He was an assistant schoolmaster at Ramsgate in England, and then a lay minister for a Methodist pastor at Ilesworth. By 1875 he returned to his parents' home, now in Etten. He found work in a bookshop. Still thinking of a religious **vocation**, he went to Amsterdam in May 1877 to study for admittance to a theological college. At the end of a year he gave up his studies. His father may have been at a loss to understand this son who could not hold a job and who now could not stay with his studies. Vincent, though, still filled with religious fervor, went to Belgium as a missionary to the miners in the Borinage district. He had become extremely sympathetic toward the poor. He worked hard, helping the sick, teaching the children, trying to preach, and giving all of his own possessions to the poor. His efforts were so excessive that he made not only the miners and their families suspicious of him, but also the church officials. He was dismissed.

Vincent kept up a correspondence with Theo. It is through these letters that we've been able to learn of his life. At this point, Theo visited him and suggested that he find some other profession. He reminded Vincent that the family was concerned about him, and that he needed to be able to support himself.

By the summer of 1880 van Gogh emerged from the confusion he felt and decided to give up organized religion, helping the downtrodden, his family, and his country. He said that in the future his country would be "painting, books, and the works of art." He settled in Brussels. His father sent him a small allowance each month; Theo sent him money and books. Vincent had begun to take lessons and worked hard at his drawing. When he came back to his family the next year, they were pleased to see his new efforts and dedication.

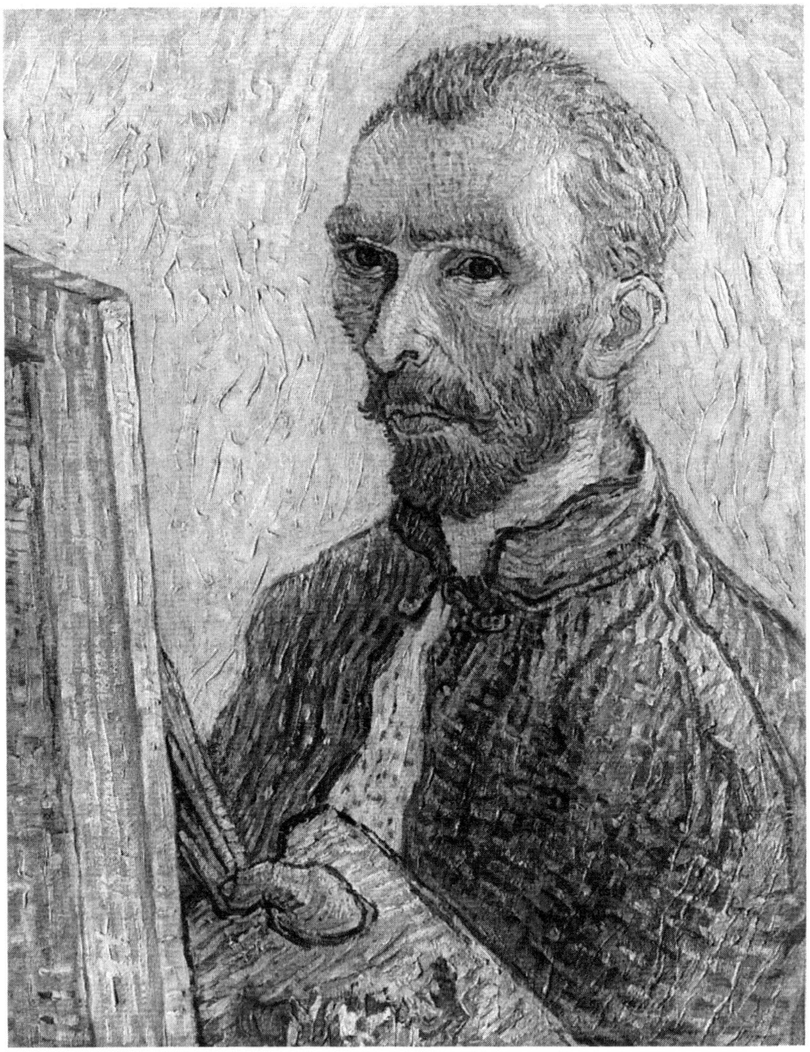

Figure 43
Portrait of van Gogh, c. 1925–1928
Imitator of Vincent van Gogh

This new harmony was soon destroyed when Vincent fell in love with a cousin, who also rejected him. In demanding to see her he held his hand over the flame of a lamp until she agreed to the meeting. He fainted from the pain. It was the beginning of a pattern of self-punishment. Not surprisingly, this upset his family.

From this point Vincent was interested in little but his art. He did not try to build a career, support himself, or marry. He became isolated; he had few friends. His only family relationship was with his brother, Theo, and much later, Theo's wife and son. He seemed to want to have friends, but most of the time his attempts at socializing were clumsy and unproductive.

Van Gogh's first drawings and paintings were of the peasants he had known and the places they lived. One of his earliest paintings, *The Potato Eaters,* shows five dark figures under pale lamplight, eating their evening meal. In a letter to Theo, Vincent said that he wanted the viewer to see ". . . these people [who are] eating their potatoes under the lamp, and putting their hands in the plate, have also tilled the soil, so that my picture praises both manual labor and the food they themselves have so honestly procured."

Van Gogh studied from time to time with other artists, but seems to have preferred to find his own way much of the time. He learned from the work of Rubens, Millet, Rembrandt, and Hals. He also read the writings of Balzac, Dickens, Zola, and Hugo. He made many still lifes and drawings. He used charcoal, chalks, pencils, and ink. He often made pens from the reeds that grew in the marshes, cutting them to form the kind of line he wished to draw.

By 1885 Theo was living in Paris and had discovered the work of the Impressionists, which he liked. He encouraged Vincent to use less of the dark colors and to try the light and pure colors the Impressionists used. Vincent began to study color and to think about ways past and present artists used it. He went to Paris in 1886 to live with Theo. There he met Gauguin, Degas, Pissarro, and Seurat. He studied the work of the Impressionists, and also became interested in the Japanese art that had come to Europe. He bought oriental printed silk fabric and hung it on the walls of his room, often using it as a background for portraits. In Paris he felt comfortable. His behavior did not need to conform to that which was expected at home in Holland.

The last four years of van Gogh's life saw a tremendous output of paintings and drawings. His colors began to take on the light, warm color that we most associate with his work. The very visible brushwork for which he is known appeared. His drawing skills became sure in line and contour. The hatch lines, dots, dashes, and swirls seem to repeat the brushwork of his painting style. Many drawings were landscapes, some were portraits. Some were studies for later use in paintings; others were final works of art. Sometimes Vincent drew because he could not afford painting materials.

His constant work began to tire him; his paintings were not selling. He was unhappy about having to accept money from his brother. He began to be irritable, restless, and quarrelsome. Theo worked for the same art dealers, the Goupils, who had earlier fired Vincent. He was forbidden to bring any of Vincent's paintings to sell. His employers called them "horrors." The art dealer and supplier Tanguy did take some of Vincent's work to sell, and supplied him with oils and canvas in exchange for paintings.

Theo was now engaged to be married. Vincent left Paris for Provence in the south of France. He settled in Arles in February 1888. He was just ahead of the spring season, and the glory of spring in Provence thrilled him. It is here he painted *Farmhouse in Provence, Arles* (see Color Plate 15). He painted the orchards in bloom, the soldiers in uniform, little girls going to First Communion; everything delighted him.

He was really discovering color for the first time. He found it was not necessary to use local color; he could use color in an individual way. A sky could be a color other than blue and trees didn't always have to be green. The colors around him—yellows, blues, reds, and greens—all seemed ready-made for the kind of paintings he loved to make. As the summer progressed, the ever-brighter sun seemed to call for more intense color in his work. His popular sunflower series was begun that summer. Yellow became a favorite color. Even *The Starry Night* uses a lot of yellow in the whirling stars. He painted many landscapes; some people became friends and posed for portraits. He made six paintings of the postman, Roulin, who became a loyal friend.

When van Gogh left Paris, his plan had been to establish a studio in Arles at which artists could work together and learn from each other. He had talked about this dream with Paul **Gauguin**. In the fall of 1888 Gauguin arrived to share the house and start the studio. It was a short-lived venture. Gauguin assumed direction immediately, and began directing van Gogh's work as well as doing his own. At first Vincent accepted this direction, but soon it became like having a teacher instead of a fellow artist sharing the studio. Vincent had become exhausted from the work he'd done since arriving in Arles. He often did not eat well or get enough rest. Soon he and Gauguin argued about everything. Vincent's only interest in life was his art. Gauguin had begun as a bank clerk and his goal was to become a famous and wealthy painter. A final quarrel on Christmas Day resulted in Gauguin's moving out. Then van Gogh cut off the lobe of his left ear (a well-known

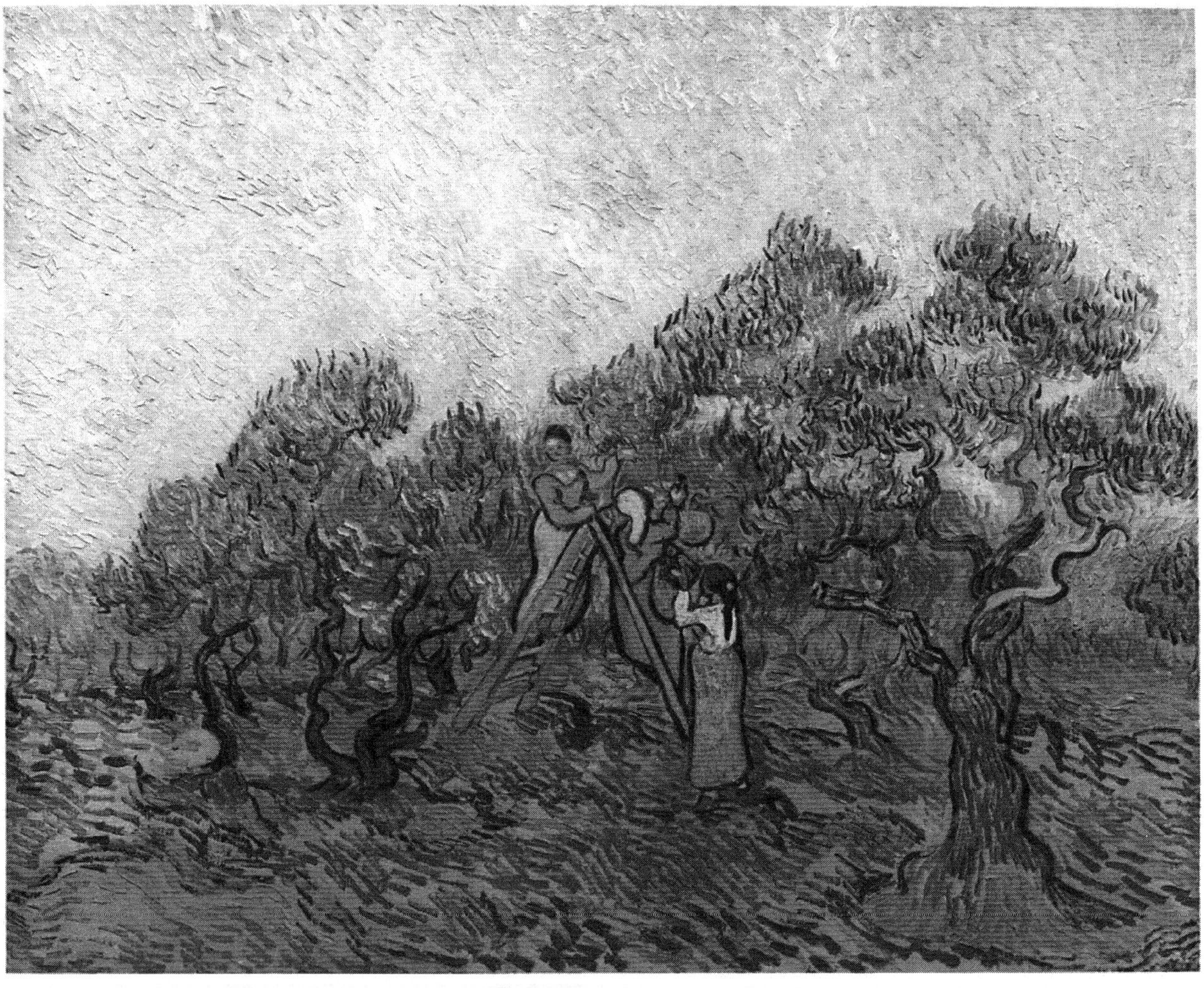

Figure 44
The Olive Orchard, 1889
Vincent van Gogh

story). This was the second time he had injured himself following rejection. He was taken to a hospital, where he experienced his first bout of mental illness.

Sent home in January, Vincent was back in the hospital in February. From that point on he could never be sure when he would experience a violent episode. He was allowed to draw and paint while in the hospital. He worked on a fourth portrait of Madame Roulin called *La Berceuse* and painted the trees in blossom as he had the year before. By the end of April he had decided to enter the Asylum of St. Paul in St. Remy. He did not feel safe living alone, not knowing when he would have an attack. There he was able to work outside much of the time.

Van Gogh's style changed toward the end of his life. His brush strokes became more free, curving, twisting and active. The paintings *Two Women and Cypresses* and *The Olive Orchard* (see Figure 44) are good examples of these new developments. It was believed that the well-known portrait of van Gogh was painted around this time (see Figure 43). The painting was once thought to be a self-portrait. Now, however, many scholars think the portrait was actually painted by an unknown imitator of van Gogh around 1925. Van Gogh's last paintings are disorganized, reflecting his mental state.

In January 1890, art critic Albert Aurier wrote enthusiastic praise of van Gogh's work. But Vincent felt uneasy about this praise. He asked Theo to ask Aurier ". . . not to write any more articles about my painting. Try to make him understand that he is mistaken about me, for I really feel too exhausted by my misfortunes to stand publicity . . . to hear others discuss my painting is more painful to me than he realizes."

By the spring of 1890 Vincent was well enough to go to Paris for a visit. Theo was now married and had a son named for Vincent. After staying a few days, Vincent moved on to Aubers-sur-Oise to be treated by a Dr. Gachet. The physician was interested in painting and had friends who were painters. Van Gogh found a room to rent and found he liked the countryside. It reminded him of the area in which he had grown up. He and Gachet became close friends; he painted several portraits of the man.

This period held some happier times for Vincent. He made some friends in the community, including other painters. This was followed by strain in his relationship with his brother. Theo was in poor health, and his wife and child were also not well. Vincent was no doubt uneasy about the money that Theo had given him over the years, money that Theo now needed for himself and his family. Vincent became more and more depressed and irritable. On Sunday, July 27, he shot himself. The bullet could not be removed and he died two days later. He was buried in the cemetery at Auvers.

Glossary

van Gogh pronounced van-gō´

synagogues buildings used by Jews for worship services

vocation a strong impulse to enter a specific career, particularly a religious one

Gauguin pronounced gō-gan´

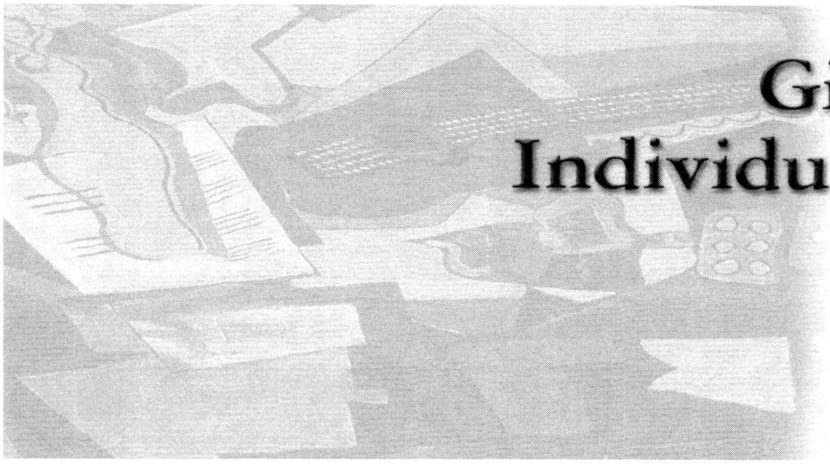

Giants of Individual Style

IN THE LATE NINETEENTH CENTURY and well into the twentieth, Europe was headed for disaster. Still, artists were able to express their life and art in new forms that reflected the contradictions of the age. In this section we look at the lives and works of four of these artists: Käthe Kollwitz, Henri Matisse, Pablo Picasso, and Marc Chagall.

Kollwitz was born in east Prussia. Her parents were concerned with the living conditions of the working class. Her husband, a doctor, tended the unfortunate. Her graphic art told of the misery of the poor and downtrodden. Matisse shielded himself from the events of the world by concentrating on pure form and color. Picasso didn't like to address particular issues in his paintings. His *Guernica* shows the horror of a Spanish village destroyed by war. Still, he preferred the painting *Three Musicians* because it is a pure exercise in painting, free from outside concerns. Chagall, a Russian Jew by birth, had to flee the German occupation of Paris in the 1940s. World War II had a great effect on his personal life. Kollwitz and Matisse were born within two years of each other. Their art careers began before those of Picasso and Chagall.

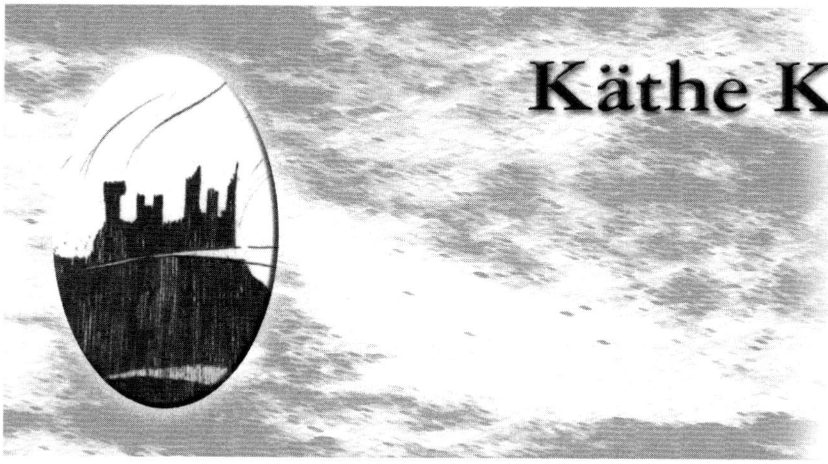

Käthe Kollwitz

1867–1945

BEFORE THE Industrial Revolution began in the middle of the nineteenth century, people in Europe were roughly divided into two groups. The aristocracy owned the land. The peasant classes worked the land for the owners. They were not paid in money. Instead, they were allowed to live on the land. They also kept a small share of the crops they grew. This system had been in place for generations. The invention of mechanical ways to do some jobs disrupted the old system. First came a cheaper way to make steel. Then came a boom in building railroads, bridges, and taller buildings . . . the list goes on and on. Peasants flocked to industrial centers. They were eager to earn actual money instead of only a share of what they produced. The old aristocracy had to start making room for rich factory owners. However, the thousands who came to the cities were worse off than they had been as peasants. There was no longer a master to help out when they were in need. The population of Europe had more than doubled. Fewer wars increased the numbers of people. Scientific discoveries helped keep more people alive. Cities and industrial areas became overcrowded. Living conditions were terrible, with little sanitation. Housing was put together hastily, and was poorly built.

Käthe Kollwitz was born in 1867, when the Industrial Revolution was in full force. She became an artist who drew attention to the plight of the poor through her dramatic portrayals of the underclass.

Kollwitz was born in Konigsberg, in east Prussia. Her grandfather on her mother's side, Julius Rupp, was a **nonconformist** pastor. Her father, Karl Schmidt, a lawyer, was an activist in the Social Democratic Worker's Party and a follower of Karl Marx. He had become dissatisfied as a lawyer. He gave up law and trained as a stonemason, and went on to run his own construction company.

Schmidt did not want his daughters to have to follow traditional roles. He wanted them to develop their individual talents. Käthe was seen to have artistic ability. She was sent to have private lessons with an engraver, Rudolf Maurer, and a local painter, Emile Neide. She was allowed to roam the streets of the town. An especially favorite place was the waterfront, where she watched the Russian and Lithuanian dockworkers. The movements of their bodies as they did their work gave her an early appreciation of the human form. Their wide gestures and expressions were beautiful to her.

Käthe was a reserved person. However, the journals she kept daily from 1908 give us information about many aspects of her life.

As Käthe grew up, her older brother, Konrad, was an important person in her life. Like their father, he was involved in socialist causes and was a member of the Social Democratic Worker's Party. Through him she learned about the writers Dostoevsky, Tolstoy, Ibsen, Zola, Marx, Goethe, and August Bebel. Bebel had helped start the Worker's Party. He had written a book, *Women and Socialism*. He believed that women could be free of the traditional narrow domestic life. They could also have economic independence and contribute to the world. Käthe was influenced by these ideas.

Käthe met Karl Kollwitz through his friendship with her brother, Konrad. Both were interested in socialist causes. Käthe's father thought her involvement with Karl would interfere with her studies. She was sent to Berlin to study. Her ability as a graphic artist was recognized by her first instructor there, Karl Stauffer-Bern. He acquainted her with the work of graphic artist Max Klinger. Klinger's style was naturalistic. For his subjects he chose the working class, the poor and downtrodden. He believed that some subjects should be depicted in black and white, rather than in color.

After Berlin, Käthe studied for a year at the Women's School of Art of the Munich Academy. Her fellow students there were serious and committed young women. They felt that marriage meant giving up careers. Their attitudes made Käthe rethink her own plans to marry Karl. She also knew her father's attitude. However, Karl had completed his medical studies. He had a job with a health insurance plan for workers. He was to be stationed in Berlin; they were married in 1881.

Since Käthe Kollwitz was a graphic artist, this is a good time to find out just what the term means. A graphic artist is one who uses line to create the forms, shapes, or shaded areas of a picture. Lines can be made by pencils, pen and ink, chalks, or charcoal, usually on paper. (Charcoal was a medium Kollwitz often used.) These drawn lines obviously leave a single picture, not multiple copies.

Printmaking allows an artist to make more than one copy of a graphic. Relief prints created from a single drawing are made using wood or linoleum. The lines are left on the surface; the material around the lines is removed. Ink is rolled on the lines, paper is pressed on the inked lines, and the printed picture is removed. In engraving, the lines are cut (engraved) into the printing block. Wood and copper are commonly used. Ink is rolled on the surface and into the lines. Then it is wiped off, leaving the ink in the engraved lines. The paper then is pressed onto the printing plate, picking up the image of the inked lines. The lithography process was discovered in 1798. A Bavarian named Aloys Senefelder found that if grease was applied to a limestone surface, it would retain ink. Areas around the ink, if wet, would resist it. Today materials other than stone are used, such as aluminum or zinc. Still, many artists prefer a smoothed slab of limestone. The drawings are made with greasy crayons; then chemicals are applied. The crayon drawings adhere only to the paper in the printing process using a lithographic press. The artists Rembrandt, Hogarth, and Goya had produced engravings, which enthralled Käthe. Hogarth did scenes of street people in London. They contain the same critiques of conditions that Käthe herself would create later. Ernst Barlach, a sculptor and graphic artist, was another

Expressionist whose work she admired. He later encouraged her to try wood engraving.

In 1892 the Kollwitzes' first child, Hans, was born. Käthe's husband did all he could, while taking care of his patients, to see that she had time for her work. A second son, Peter, was born in 1896. She was in the middle of her first large production, *The Revolt of the Weavers*. Käthe wrote that she was "passionately interested" in everything during this period.

The Revolt of the Weavers was inspired by the Gerhart play *The Weavers.* It told of a rebellion in 1844 of linen weavers trapped between the new **capitalism** and their old situation in a feudalistic world. Kollwitz had first intended to use engraving for the series of prints. She gave that up and used lithography for part of it. The project took five years. Plate one is titled "Poverty," plate two is "Death," plate three is "Conspiracy." They are dark lithographs, both in terms of style and subject matter. She expresses her strong feelings about the situations in which people were finding themselves. Light elements are used for contrast to emphasize the symbolism she sought. Plate number five is "Attack." In this plate, the workers stone the home of the mill owner. The series created great excitement when it was shown at the Great Berlin exhibit of 1898. Kaiser Wilhelm refused to honor her with a medal, calling her a "gutter artist." However, two years later the King of Saxony gave her a gold medal. From then on, Kollwitz was seen as one of the most important artists in the country. She was asked to teach at the Women's School of Art, which she did for two years. In 1918 she became the first woman asked to a professorship at the Prussian Academy of Arts. Ten years later, she was the first woman to head a department there.

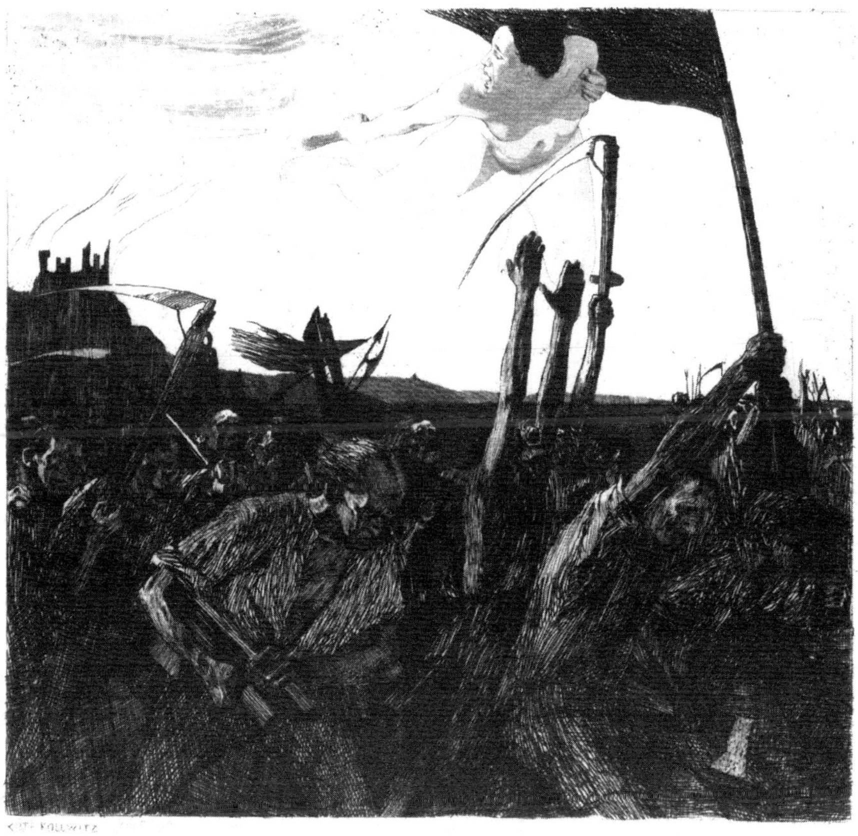

Figure 45
Uprising, 1899
Käthe Kollwitz

Whether Kollwitz used charcoal, the lithograph crayon, or engraved line to express the dramatic qualities of her drawings, she was able to make statements about misery, squalor, and hopelessness. Charles Dickens' novels told his stories of these times. Kollwitz provided pictures. In *Harnessed to the Plow,* a man is harnessed to a plow while a woman behind guides it. His body leans far forward. The light areas of his back, shoulder, and head contrast with the black shaded spaces that pick out the furrows and the bowed-down body of the woman. Her hands gripping the plow and her head bent forward are in lighter focus. It was not until the early 1900s that farmworkers in Europe or Britain were given much relief. Nor was it unusual for them to be harnessed to a plow if need be.

Kollwitz was always concerned for women, whether for fellow artists striving for recognition, or those who faced the daily struggles of the lower classes. In her journal she wrote: "Frau Pankopf was here. She had a black eye. Her husband had flown in a rage. . . . For the woman the misery is always the same. She keeps the children . . . the man drinks." She knew a lot about the sick and injured through the work of her physician husband. At least two of her pictures were of a husband mourning a dead wife. Another showed a mother watching over a sick child. She was familiar with scenes like those. Another comment from her journal: "All my life I carried on a conversation with death."

Etchings often seem to contain a line quality that fits dramatic scenes of protests, anger, and riots. A good example is the etching *Uprising* (see Figure 45). As haggard men scream, they wave axes, scythes, and banners. The use of the etched lines emphasizes the feelings of the crowd.

The softer quality of charcoal and crayon seems to fit the softness of child figures and faces as well as those of the mother. The lithograph *Mother and Child by a Wayside Shrine* shows a mother bending over a child. Both faces and stance show a feeling of wonder as they look at the holy shrine. The shading of the crayon shapes the mother's form and emphasizes that of the child, whose face and figure are a much lighter value than the mother's.

Following World War I, the theme of mothers and children was a recurring one: mothers and children suffering the tragedies of the war, mothers trying to shelter and protect children. Käthe began to use sculpture more than she had before. Her son, Peter, was killed in the early days of the war. Käthe was never able to put it behind her. As often has happened, an artist tries to go forward from grief by plunging into the creative process. For Käthe it meant making a large sculpture as a monument to Peter's memory. The huge figure shows a mourning father on his knees with clasped arms and a crouched figure of the mother. These granite cast forms overlook the graves in a cemetery for soldiers near Roggevelt, Belgium, where their son is buried. Käthe worked on the sculpture for 15 years.

Her last lithograph took its title from a Goethe novel. *Seeds for the Planting Shall Not Be Ground Up* was completed in 1942, two years after her husband's death. War was again raging in Germany. Before the end came, her grandson, Peter, was also "ground up," another victim of war. The lithograph shows us a grim and determined mother, her strong arms extended and bent over the children beneath to protect and restrain the huddled figures. Speaking about the meaning she gave the lithograph, Kollwitz told a friend: "The old mother says, 'No: You stay here:—get ready for life, not for war again.'" Kollwitz died in 1945 at the age of 74, still retaining her strong ideals and ability to transmit them to those who would listen.

Glossary

nonconformist a person who does not conform to a generally accepted pattern of thought or action; a person who does not conform to an established church

capitalism an economic system characterized by private or corporate ownership

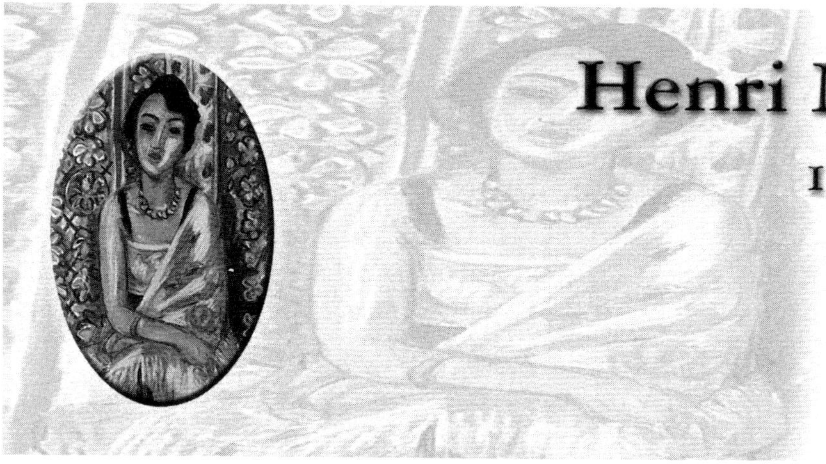

Henri Matisse

1869 – 1954

HENRI MATISSE has been called one of the two most important painters of the first half of the twentieth century. He was born on December 31, 1869, in Bohain-en-Vermandois in northern France. His father was a successful grain merchant who wanted his son to become a lawyer. He is not the first father of a future artist to have this dream. Henri's mother had artistic interests and liked to paint decorations on china. Henri was sent to school in St. Quentin when he was ten and at eighteen he went to Paris to study law at the University.

Henri had little real interest in law. He did enjoy going to the Louvre to see the art. When he received his diploma he returned home. He worked as a clerk in a law office, copying page after page of legal papers. He began to attend drawing classes taught by a local artist. He had to get up early enough to go to class before he went to his office. In the summer of 1890, he was ill in the hospital. To help him pass the time, his mother gave him a box of paints. He began copying pictures of paintings. One of his first paintings on canvas is a still life of books, a candle on a newspaper, and a table cover.

Like some other fathers of aspiring artists, Emile Matisse did not want Henri to give up a sensible and secure career in law to become an artist. Like other artists, Henri insisted on following his own path. In the end his father agreed that his son could attend the Académie Julian in Paris, which was run by the painter Bouguereau. He was back in Paris, then, in the winter of 1891.

Matisse had little respect for the work of Bouguereau. It represented the height of the artistic style popular in the mid to late nineteenth century. Overly sweet, with beauty that lacked sincerity, it was the kind of art against which such artists as Delacroix, Courbet, Géricault, and the Impressionists had rebelled earlier.

Matisse rebelled also, and quit the Académie Julian. He began working in the courtyard of the École des Beaux-Arts, making drawings of sculpture. An artist and teacher at the school, Gustave Moreau, noticed Matisse's work and invited the young artist to study with him. Moreau did not try to impose his style on his pupils, but encouraged each to find his or her own style. He told his students to study the art in the Louvre and to look at the people and events around them. Matisse made many copies of paintings in the museum, partly to study them and partly in hope of selling them. This was a common way for artists to earn a little money. Matisse received a small allowance from his father, but always needed more money.

In 1890 a new, more liberal Salon had been organized. It was called the Societé Nationale des Beaux-Arts. Matisse submitted paintings in 1896; four of them were accepted, and Matisse was elected as an Associate Member. This was high praise for a young artist (he was then only 27). Now he could show his work at a Salon without having it first accepted by the jury. It increased his chances of selling his paintings.

Matisse painted many still lifes in his first years. In 1897 he had become committed to an impressionistic style, encouraged by Pissarro, who even suggested that Matisse go to London to study Turner's work. Matisse also studied and was influenced by the work of van Gogh, Cézanne, and Renoir. He did go to London, but on his honeymoon. He had married Amelie Payrayre, and they had begun their 40 years of marriage.

At this point, Matisse could have chosen a safe path. He had developed a style that was popular and that he knew could be sold. Instead, he chose to experiment with different styles. This continued throughout his career. In the last years of his life he continued to try new methods of expression. He had tried impressionism. He tried **pointillism,** using tiny dots of color that together register with the viewer as mixed color. Next he began to concentrate on all the possibilities of color. He did not use it to describe a particular object, as one can use local color. Nor did he use color values to describe a shape.

In the painting *Madame Matisse (The Green Line)* Matisse used dark blue for the hair and the lines of the dress. He used pinks for the right side of the face and yellow ochre for the left side. In the background are violet, greens, and red-orange. Down the center of the face is a wide yellow-green line. In this picture Matisse was not painting a portrait of his wife, but an abstract painting. In abstract art the shapes and forms are stripped of details, leaving lines, or shapes, often with little regard for realistic appearance. We can see that this is a woman's face, but details are missing. At this time many African sculptures and masks had found their way to Europe, and many artists, including Matisse, were fascinated by the simplified forms. We can see elements of the mask style in this painting.

Matisse had clearly chosen the experimental path. In the early years of the century he struggled to earn enough money to support himself and his family. He worked at other jobs, doing such things as painting decorative interiors. One such work was the ceiling of the Grand Palais.

The **Fauve** period of Matisse, and other artists who shared that style, began around 1905. He had exhibited paintings in the Salon d'Automne of that year. That Salon was so named to contrast with other Salons, which were held in the spring and not the fall. Just as the Impressionists had rebelled against the styles at the Salons of the Academy, these artists, whom critics called Fauves (wild beasts), rebelled against the styles popular at that time. Color was the most important element of their paintings. They used it in its purest form, not mixed with other colors and often just as it came from the tube (without diluting it with oils). Matisse believed that painting combined the feelings of the painter toward the things he painted with the way he used paint to translate those feelings into color and forms. This belief continued throughout his career, not just during his Fauve period. He wanted art that could be enjoyed by everyone who needed to rest busy or troubled minds.

Fauvism as a style did not last long and in a few years had been replaced by a new style, Cubism.

But it had started a movement that would lead to abstract art.

Matisse had begun to find patrons who bought and collected his work and who introduced it to others. He no longer had financial troubles, and could spend all his time on his own work. He enjoyed travel and was able to go to Germany, Italy, and Algeria. He also wrote an article on painting, "Notes d'un Peintre," in 1908. Besides painting he also did sculpture, etchings, engravings, and some ceramic plaques and plates. For a time he was the instructor in the Académie Matisse, which gathered admiring students from Europe, Great Britain, Scandinavia, and the United States, where his work was now exhibited. Teaching took too much of his time, however, and he gave it up by 1911.

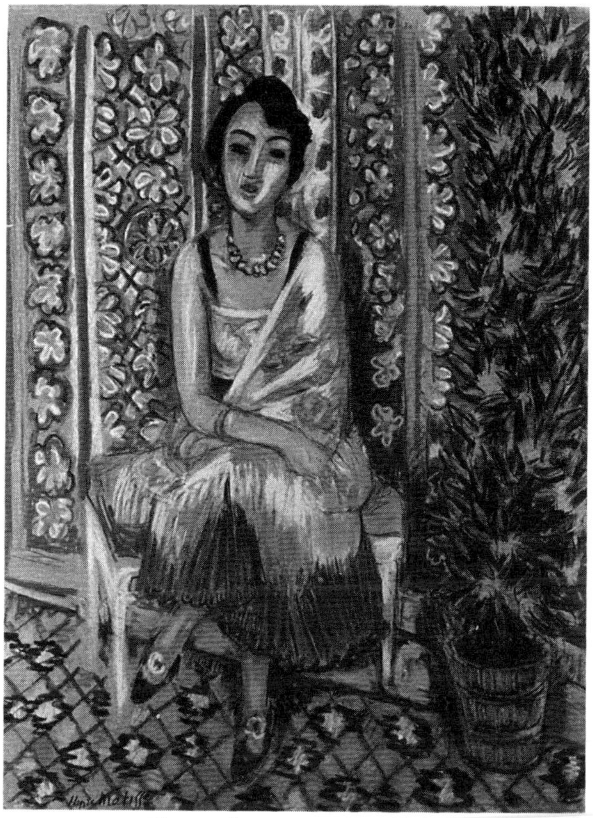

Figure 46
Woman with Exotic Plant, c. 1925
Henri Matisse

The paintings in which Matisse portrays the human figure have been compared with Cézanne's landscapes. Cézanne eliminated detail from landscape and Matisse eliminated detail from the human figure. He also used color as it suited him, and we see orange, blue, and red as well as flesh tones used in his nudes. The forms in his paintings are two-dimensional, with little use of shading or modeling. There is little sense of perspective except for forms that overlap or are higher or lower in the picture to indicate space. He made many studies for each painting, instead of simply changing the first day's work again and again. In each study he worked over the relationships of all the parts and tried to finish with a harmonious whole. He left nothing to chance. In a Matisse painting, the background was just as important as the subject. Sometimes forms were distorted. The paint was always used thinly, never in thick **impasto.** The brush was often used like a pencil to draw the forms.

Matisse repeated several themes in his art. One of these was the human body. "What interests me most is not still life, or landscapes, but the human form. It is here that I can best express the almost religious feeling that I have about life." Most often the female form was the one he painted and drew. Usually women in his paintings are not involved in any particular activity. They are sometimes nude, sometimes dressed in elegant dresses or oriental costumes. Even in portraits, the faces are simplified to the basic lines to show us the essence of the person. Often the space around the person is filled with the decorative flowers and patterns that delighted him (see Figure 46). Although Matisse kept birds, cats, and dogs, these rarely appear in his pictures. He did use goldfish swimming around in their bowls, letting us see through the water to the surrounding objects.

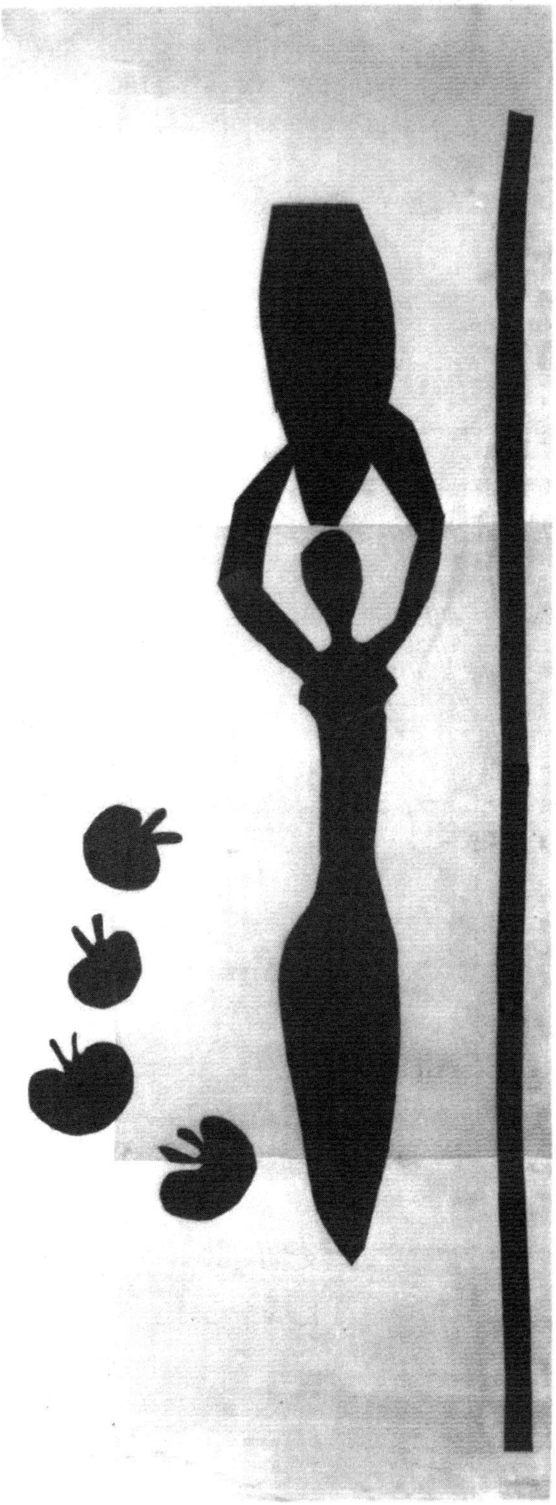

Figure 47
Woman with Amphora and Pomegranates, 1952
Henri Matisse

Matisse did paint some landscapes during his career. They were most often a part of an interior, a view from a window or through a doorway, often with shutters around the doors or windows. Still, life often became a part of an interior but was seldom the most important element. Sometimes he included parts of his own pictures within other paintings of an interior. Matisse said, "I have a great love for pure, clear, sparkling color . . . a great modern victory is that the secret of expression rendered by color has been found."

During the 1920s Matisse painted more three-dimensional and realistic paintings, but by the middle and late 1930s he was again making flat, two-dimensional forms that were rather abstract. In 1929 he was spending most of his time making prints, sculpture, and drawings. He was a perfectionist and spent many hours over a small problem if it developed in his work. After going back to the two-dimensional style he made no further stylistic changes.

He spent much of his life in Nice in the south of France. In a nearby town, Vence, his friendship with a Dominican nun led to one of his last and most important works. He designed a chapel and its furnishings for the Dominican convalescent home. He'd had a serious illness and had been nursed back to health by the Dominican nun. He was not a religious man, but had been impressed by her devotion to her faith. He spent four of his last years working on the designs for the interior, the altar, the crucifix, stained-glass windows, the priests' vestments, and the spire.

The walls of the chapel of Notre Dame du Rosaire are white ceramic tile with black line drawings. The stained-glass windows are in bright yellows, blues, and greens. He wanted the chapel to create feelings of joy. In his usual careful way, he spent two years just making sketches, sometimes as many as 3,000 for one mural. He worked on this project from 1948 to 1951. He believed it to be his best piece of work.

After his illness in 1941 he was not physically able to be active. He spent much of his last seven years either in bed or in a wheelchair. During this time he developed still another technique that he called "carving in color." His assistants painted sheets of paper in flat gouache paints. From these, Matisse cut forms. Some were decorative shapes, some were human figures, flowers, leaves, birds, and geometric forms. These were fastened to the walls so he could study them and decide on their final arrangement on background colors (see Figure 47). Matisse said that in this way an object's form was reduced to its **essence.**

Matisse did worry that young painters would see his work as too simple, too easy. In 1948 he thought they might see it as an excuse to ". . . do away with certain exercises that I believe to be necessary." He thought he saw this in some of the young painters who seemed to be avoiding the ". . . slow and painful preparation necessary to construct with colors alone."

Matisse died at the age of 85. He had been a painter for 62 years. In Nice the Musée Matisse contains nine rooms of his paintings, drawings, prints, cutouts, and sculptures. It is the memorial he wanted. His family carried out his wishes.

Glossary

Matisse pronounced mah-teese´

pointillism pronounced pwan´-til-ism

Fauve pronounced fōve

impasto the thick application of a pigment in painting; the body of pigment applied

essence that which makes a thing what it is; the true nature of a person or a thing

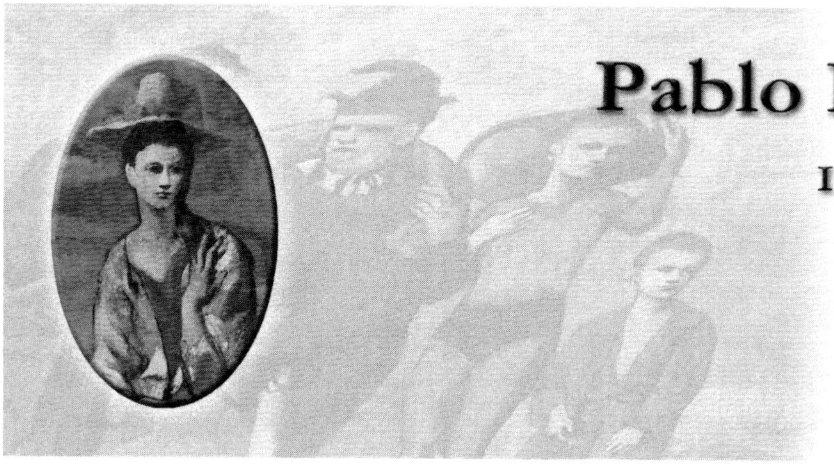

Pablo Picasso

1881 – 1973

PABLO **PICASSO** was born in Málaga, Spain, in the area along the Mediterranean coast called the Costa del Sol. This area was once part of the Roman Empire, and was later conquered by the Moors. It is now part of a section called Andalusia, famous for flamenco dancing, bullfights, hot sun, and a blue sea.

When Picasso was born on October 25, 1881, his father was a teacher in the School of Arts and Crafts in Málaga. Picasso was another artist whose artistic abilities were apparent when he was a youngster. He once said, "When I was 12, I drew like Raphael." He worked in some of his father's classes and even finished some of his father's paintings. The story goes that when Pablo was about 13 his father came home and saw a still life of his that Pablo had just finished. He then gave his son his brushes and paints and did not paint again.

By 1895 the family had moved to Barcelona. The father had become a professor at the Academy of Fine Arts. At 14 Pablo took the examination for admission to the Academy. In one day he finished the examination drawings, which most students took a month to complete. He was not satisfied with the Academy for long. Restless, he moved to Madrid to begin studies at the San Fernando Academy. An uncle had given him enough money to make this possible. It was the first time the 16-year-old boy had been on his own. Often he skipped his classes, spending time at the Prado, studying the paintings of such masters as Velázquez, Rubens, El Greco, and Titian.

While in Madrid he became ill with scarlet fever and had to return to Barcelona. He began to find friends there among other artists, intellectuals, and writers. He also saw art from the Romanesque period that had been placed in museums in Barcelona. Later this art style would be noticed in his own work.

At 19 Picasso went to Paris for the first time. He shared a studio with a fellow artist and found buyers for some of his paintings. At this time he was influenced by the work of Toulouse-Lautrec, who painted the nightlife and cafes of Paris. Picasso's early paintings show concern for realistic forms, though much detail is left out. His brush strokes remind us of Impressionism. He painted street people and entertainers. At about this time he used lots of cool color, particularly blue; it is called his Blue Period. Often he painted the destitute and unhappy (see Figure 48). He spent time in both Paris and Barcelona during the three years of his Blue Period.

By 1904 Picasso settled again in Paris, this time in a new studio. His friends included Matisse, Braque, and Henri Rousseau. The colors in his paintings brightened and became warmer; the moods became happier. His interest in the life of the circus led to paintings that needed more lively color. An example of his fascination with circus life is *Family of Saltimbanques* (see Figure 49). These next three or four years are called his Rose Period. An example is *Boy with Bouquet,* painted in 1905.

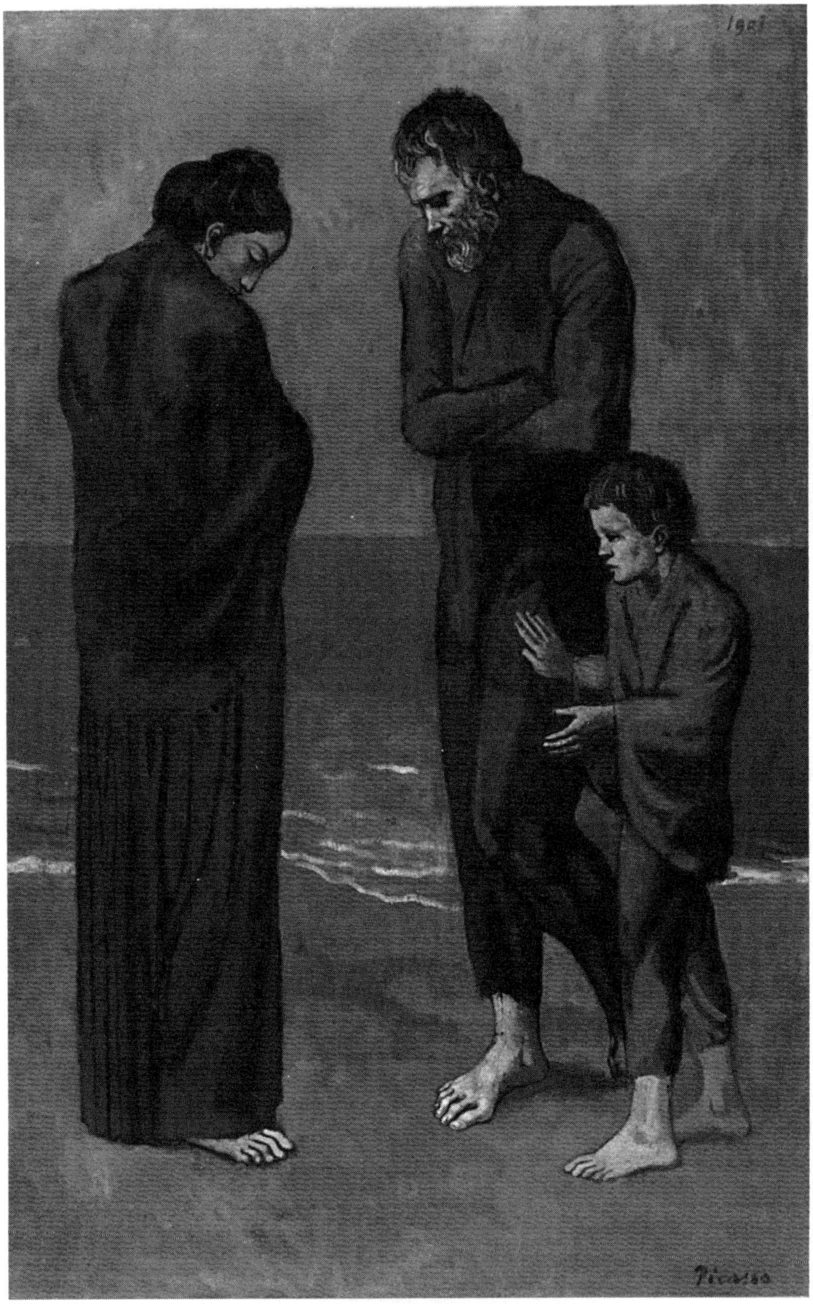

Figure 48
The Tragedy, 1903
Pablo Picasso

In 1907 Picasso painted *Les Demoiselles d'Avignon,* the most important early Cubist painting and one of his major paintings. The five young women featured in the painting are not conventional beauties. The two on the right have the sturdy, stiff forms of archaic Greek sculpture, while the two on the right have faces that may remind us of African masks. Picasso was familiar with the archaic sculpture of the Roman era in Spain. At this time many African masks and primitive sculptures had found their way to Europe, and were admired by many artists for their geometric yet natural forms. Picasso's first Cubist work caused much comment when it was finally bought by Jacques Doucet in 1920. Up to that time, it had been kept rolled up in the studio and only shown to an occasional visitor. Many in the art world were disappointed with this painting of unlovely female nudes. Matisse thought it was a scheme to discredit the new kinds of art.

The term Cubism was created by Louis Vauxcelles in 1909. He heard that Braque had submitted some paintings to the Salon d'Automne that were rejected. Matisse told him that some of the pictures were "entirely made up of little cubes." Vauxcelles then invented the word "Cubism."

Cubism was influenced by Cézanne. In 1907 an exhibit of much of Cézanne's work was held at the Salon d'Automne. Picasso saw the exhibit, and painted many landscapes and still lifes in which the essential forms are the important elements. At the same time Picasso painted these early cubist forms, Georges Braque was also painting landscapes in another part of France. Both were stirring the beginnings of Cubism, and their early cubist paintings have many similarities.

Up to this time artists had used the principles of perspective to show depth and space on a two-dimensional surface. The cubist painter tries to show all the sides of an object at the same time. The original object is destroyed with distortions used to show the "fourth" dimension; it is splintered into many small planes. The colors used are often subdued tones: browns, greens, grays, and tans. Early Cubism is called "analytic." A later, more modified style is called "synthetic." This latter style allows the artist more freedom of choice in color and form. Objects may retain more of their original shapes; detail is removed and the appearance is generally abstract. Synthetic Cubism lets the artist set his or her own limits. An example of a work in the Synthetic Cubism style is *Still Life* (see Color Plate 15).

Collage was developed as an offshoot of Synthetic Cubism. Its actual origins are not certain, but we know that at about the same time both Braque and Picasso began to paste such things as ticket stubs, paper, cloth, and tobacco labels onto their paintings. In his first collage, Picasso painted a still life that was framed by a piece of rope curved into an oval shape. He also used a piece of oilcloth that was imprinted with the pattern of chair caning; this was pasted onto the painting. In another collage, *Man with a Hat,* he used several kinds of paper, including newspaper, and charcoal lines along with black ink.

Picasso was never satisfied to stay with one style for long. He was very energetic. The quantity of art that he produced during his long life was more than several artists might have done. He never felt that a painting was really finished. Over the years he often brought out an old painting and worked on it again; he also went back to styles that he had given up years before. He tried the ideas of others and invented new styles himself.

At about the time Picasso tried collage, he also worked in another painting style. He drew and painted human forms that were like classic forms, but were much heavier and more monumental. Some examples are *Mother and Child, Three Women at a Fountain,* and *Maternity.*

A well-known painting done in 1921 shows Picasso moving from collage to painting that looks like collage. In *Three Musicians* we see shapes painted as though they were pasted paper forms. The three figures, Harlequin, Pierrot, and a monk, are masked and costumed for a carnival. Each one holds a musical instrument. Picasso painted two versions of this theme. In *Three Dancers,* done in 1925, the female nudes are painted with a background that appears to be cutout materials (such as patterned cloth) and wallpaper. The figures are also like cutout shapes with details painted on.

In the 1920s Picasso began to include the painter himself in his compositions. This theme is dropped and picked up again several times. During the next decade his work shifts from one style or period to another, and often back again. In the painting *Girl Before a Mirror* we see heavy black swirling outlines and circles with bright colors like stained glass. The girl looks into the mirror but sees an entirely different image in the reflection. Psychology had begun to attract a following and people invented many theories about the meaning of this painting. This style is also present in *Still Life on a Pedestal Table,* done in 1931, and *The Mirror,* 1932.

Sometimes Picasso created paintings and sculpture full of the joy of living; at other times he expressed his sadness and horror over the cruelty and tragedy of life. He knew what was happening in the world of politics and in the governments of the world. These happenings affected him and were expressed in his work. His many love affairs and wives are also present in his art. The joy he felt in the presence of his children is captured. He loved the bullfights of his native Spain. He enjoyed having animals and gave them the run of the house—dogs, birds, and a goat. Though Picasso's art was the most important thing in his life, it was interwoven with the rest of his life.

The Civil War in Spain began in the summer of 1936. It led to one of Picasso's best-known paintings. He was living in Paris. The Spanish republican government commissioned him to make a painting, a very large one, for the Spanish section of an exhibition scheduled in Paris in 1936. While searching for a theme for the painting, Picasso heard of the bombing of the town of Guernica in northern Spain. He painted ***Guernica*** on three panels, one large center panel with a smaller one on each side. Its message is the horror of war. The painting is done in dark blues, blacks, purples, and grays on a cream-colored background. The human figures and animals are screaming and dying. Their forms are distorted and grotesque. There is nothing beautiful about the suffering of the population of the little village as everything is laid waste. Picasso was expressing his loathing not only of war but also of the governments that bring war about.

Some elements of the *Guernica* style crop up from time to time in Picasso's later work. In *Weeping Woman,* done in 1937, we see the same kind of distortion, though with bright colors. These are repeated in *Still Life with a Red Bull's Head.*

World War II followed closely behind the Spanish Civil War. Picasso decided to stay in Paris. He wanted to continue working, and was not looking for a place to escape. Many of his fellow artists came to America. Picasso's work had just been exhibited in a large show in November 1939 at the Museum of Modern Art in New York. It was called Picasso: 40 Years of His Art. He could have easily found refuge in many countries, but decided to stay in France, which had been his home for most of those 40 years. When Paris was occupied by the Germans, he refused to collaborate (cooperate) with them. Instead, he kept on making paintings, sculpture, and drawings and coping with the difficulties everyone experienced.

Picasso had worked in sculpture as early as 1912, making works of bronze and trying constructions. One of his first constructions was a guitar made first of cardboard and then from sheet metal and wire. He did little sculpture, however, until the end of the 1920s, when he again made constructions using a variety of materials. From that point he continued to use sculpture as an additional art form, along with painting, printmaking, and ceramics.

In much of his sculpture he used "found objects"—commonplace materials. *Construction with Glove (By the Sea)* is created from plaster and wood on canvas, covered with sand. *Figure,* 1939, is made from string, wood, two garden tools, and other objects. Some figures are like small dolls, made from wood and cloth. *Bull's Head,* 1943, is made from a bronzed bicycle seat and handlebars. Many bronze sculptures were made as well as ceramic ones. The found objects were set into clay or fastened together in order to make the model for the bronze casting. *Baboon and Young* is a bronze sculpture in which a toy automobile and large cooking pot are used with other found objects to form the animals.

After the war Picasso spent an increasing amount of time in the south of France. The climate along the Mediterranean was like that of his native Spain. Bullfights were held in Provence. Though he had decided never to return to Spain as long as Franco was in power, he could still attend bullfights. He lived in one house after another around Cannes and Antibes and at last settled in a farmhouse close to Mougins.

In 1947 Picasso visited the village of Vallauris, where local potters were trying to revive a ceramics business that had been forced to close during

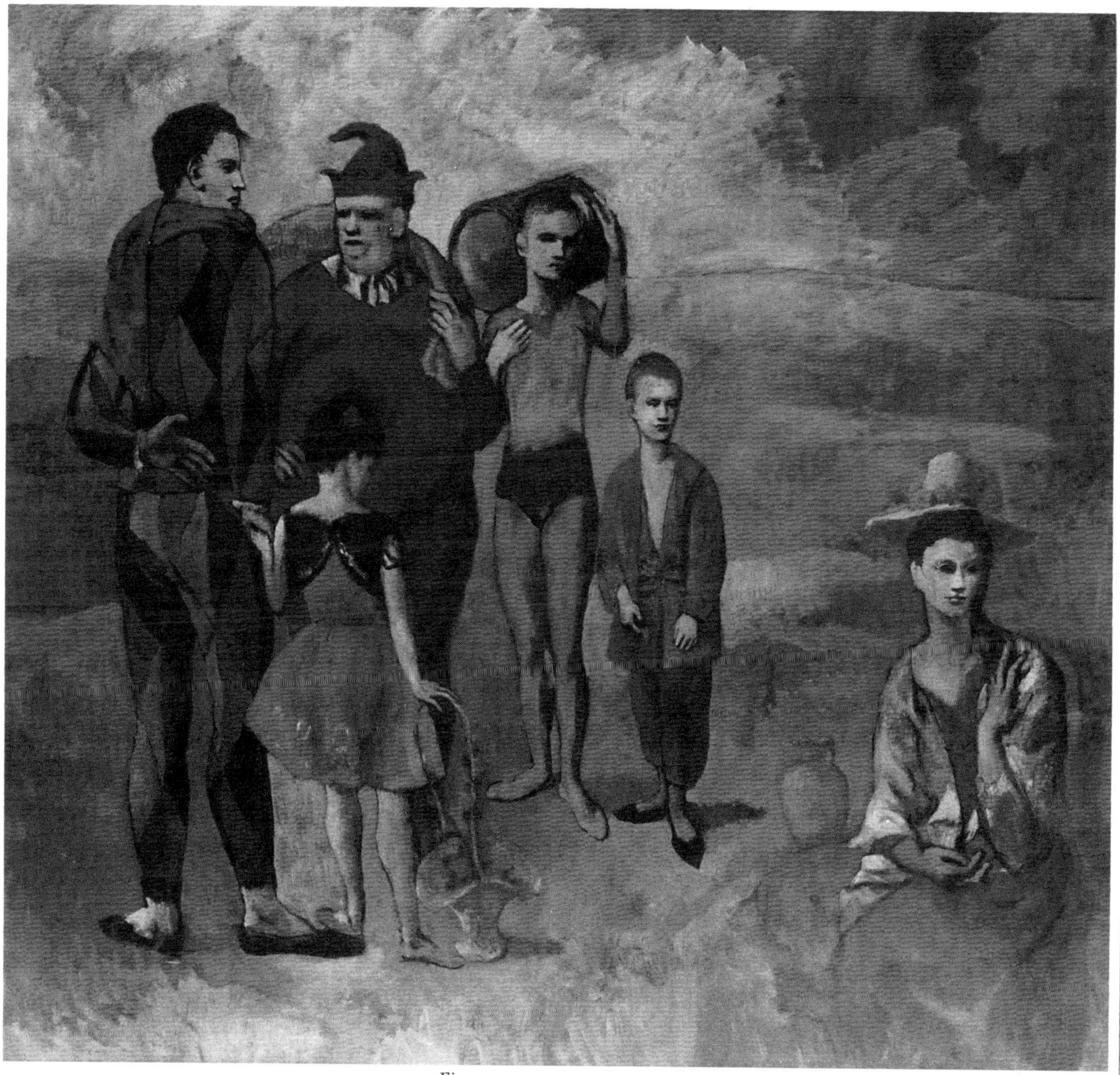

Figure 49
Family of Saltimbanques, 1905
Pablo Picasso

the war. He began to experiment with clay, and became fascinated with its possibilities. He made plates with a bullring design, plates with a blazing sun motif, and vases and pitchers with human forms or designs. In one year he made about 2,000 pieces. He liked the idea of people actually using his work, for he wanted his art to be available to everyone.

Vallauris made Picasso an honorary citizen and gave him an old chapel to use as he wished. He made it into a temple of peace, and painted two large ceiling paintings in the building: *War* and *Peace*. The colors are stronger and brighter than those in *Guernica*. The message of *War* is that of horror and death, while *Peace* shows people who experience happiness, joy, and warmth. The chapel is a popular place for visitors. Nearby is the sculpture *Man with a Sheep,* which Picasso gave to the town, asking that it be placed in the town square where children could play near it.

Picasso remained a productive artist throughout his later years. He continued to go back to themes and ideas that he had used earlier. He painted harlequins, circus performers, masks, artists and models, landscapes, and still lifes. He studied the old masters and painted many versions of their works. Among these are Delacroix's *Women of Algiers* and 44 paintings of Velázquez's *Las Meninas*. Some paintings were details (parts) of others' masterpieces.

Picasso had always signed the date of each painting; at first, the date was painted on the back of the picture. Later he painted the date on the front, along with his signature. As he grew older he seemed more aware of time—both of recording it and needing to hold it fast. His style continued to feature strong outlines, usually dark lines, with strong, often bright contrasting colors filling in the shapes. Sometimes he limited himself to only a few colors—grays, blues, or browns. He continued to use distorted, imaginative shapes.

One of the last exhibits of his work before his death was held in Avignon in 1970. (Centuries before, Avignon had been the temporary seat of Christianity; the Papal Court was located there.) In the summer of 1970, however, the old Palace of the Popes was filled with 165 paintings that Picasso had done the year before. One estimate is that he painted one every 52 hours. All were medium to large in size and show a fast-moving brush. The colors were bright and glowing. Some of the paintings were *Man with Gun; Harlequin Arlequin; Adolescent;* and *Kiss*.

Picasso did not like to think about growing old or dying. His natural good health and energy probably helped him to seem younger than his years and to work vigorously far longer than the average person does. He died at his home on April 8, 1973, at the age of 91. His life had been dedicated to his art. His work has influenced generations and will continue to influence generations of artists to come.

Glossary

Picasso pronounced pe-cah´-sō

collage pronounced cō-lahge´; an art method in which paper, cloth, wood, and miscellaneous materials are arranged and glued on a base or background

Guernica pronounced gwear´-nee-ca

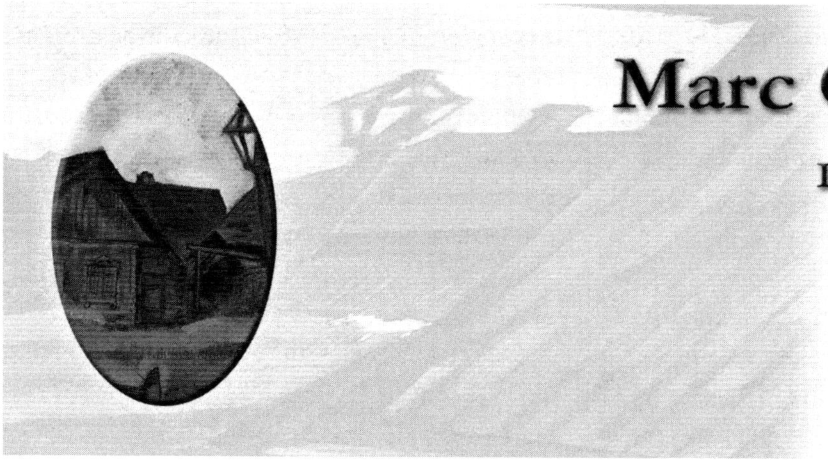

Marc Chagall

1889 – 1985

Marc Chagall painted a kind of fantasy that has been called the beginnings of **Surrealism.** Often-used themes are family, children, love and marriage, and religious symbols, both Judaic and Christian. These themes are made lively by the use of bright and glowing colors, floating figures, and houses that appear upside-down, with gravity ignored. Flowers, fairy tales, birds, and animals, sometimes combined with human forms, fill spaces. The people and villages are often those of his childhood in Russia. He remembered the old Russia of the czars, not the later communist state.

Chagall was born in the small city of Vitebsk on July 7, 1887. His family was Jewish and lived in the section of the city in which all Jews lived. His father worked in a factory packing herring into barrels. Chagall remembered how tired his father was when he came home at night to his family of nine children, and how his religious faith helped him. Chagall's mother was small and lively. She opened and ran a small grocery shop, which helped to support the family. She was outspoken; her husband was quiet. Marc and the other children were wrapped in the love of a close-knit extended family that included grandparents, aunts, uncles, and cousins.

As a child, Marc Chagall was not strong. He was of slight build and pale coloring, with blue eyes and very curly hair. He did not like school and did not do well there. He was the object of teasing and torment by other children. What he liked best in school was music and singing. At home he spent his time playing with his animals and with toys he had made.

In his last year of school, Chagall discovered drawing. He got books from the local library and drew pictures from them. He found that there was an artist in the city who taught painting. His parents were reluctant, but finally allowed him to study with the painter Judah Pen. While he studied painting, he also worked in a photographer's shop.

One of Chagall's friends was going to St. Petersburg to study art. Chagall decided to go there for study as well. Times were hard. He had little money and could not live as comfortably as he did at home. He was often hungry and without a decent place to sleep. At last he was accepted by the school of the Imperial Society for the Protection of the Arts. The director of the school was able to get a scholarship for Chagall; then he was at least able to eat once a day. There he first saw the art of the West, in particular that of Matisse, Gauguin, and van Gogh.

In 1910 Chagall had the opportunity to go to Paris. He was to work for a designer of stage sets for the Ballets Russes. Chagall was entranced with life in Paris. He saw all the exhibits and museums, and was able to see the work of all the great artists of the past. He found a studio where he could live and paint. He spent four years in Paris at this time. One painting from this period was *I and the Village,* in which he used fantasy and childhood themes. *The Poet, or Half Past Three,* painted in the same year, was an experiment with Cubism. The Salon des Indépendents accepted Chagall's paintings in 1911, and in 1912 he was invited to exhibit at the Salon d'Automne. He began to find himself accepted in the groups of artists, writers, poets, and critics that were the heart of the art world of Paris.

He went back to Vitebsk to marry Bella Rosenfeld. They had been engaged since his days in St. Petersburg. Her family was wealthy (her father was a jeweler). Her family did not approve of

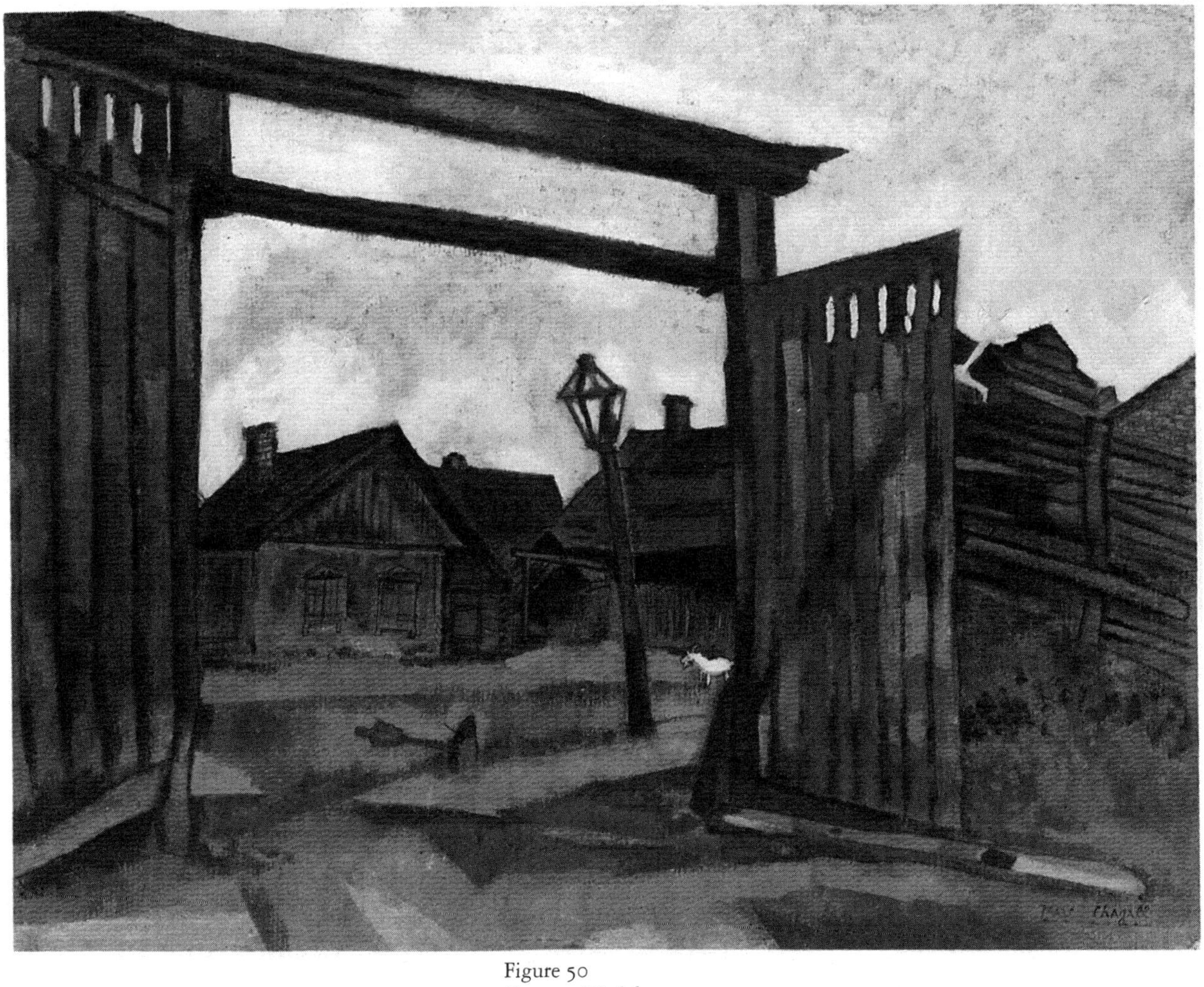

Figure 50
Houses at Vitebsk, 1917
Marc Chagall

the match. However, it was a strong and happy marriage that lasted 30 years, until Bella's death. She was an excellent businesswoman and a great help to Chagall in keeping his profession a profitable one. He left all sales and business arrangements to her.

In 1917 the rulers of Russia were overthrown and the revolution followed. Artists were given work to do but later, under Stalin, there was little freedom for the arts. The new government wanted realistic paintings only. Anything "modern" was definitely not allowed. During 1917 Chagall painted *Houses at Vitebsk* (see Figure 50).

Chagall, with Bella and their daughter, Ida, had moved to Moscow in hope of finding better conditions. Food was scarce everywhere. Black markets and profiteering were common. Chagall found work with the Jewish Theater designing sets; he continued to do his own paintings when he could. Discouraged and disillusioned, he made the decision to leave Russia. Taking his wife and child, he went first to Berlin. His work had been shown there when he'd lived in Paris, and he was still a recognized artist there. Berlin was just a stopover on the way to Paris. By September 1923 they arrived there.

Chagall's work was taken by the gallery of Vollard, the same dealer who had sold the work of Cézanne, Renoir, Matisse, and Picasso. Chagall was also commissioned by Vollard to do etchings and engravings to illustrate a book of fables by La Fontaine, Gogol's *Dead Souls,* and the Bible. In Paris Surrealism had been popular but had been replaced in popularity by Cubism. Chagall rejected Surrealism, although many felt that his imaginative paintings had actually inspired it. Chagall tried Cubism a few times but did not stay with it.

From this period until the beginning of World War II, Chagall lived in France. He explored the country from north to south. Some of his most joyous paintings were made during this time, which was also probably one of the happiest periods of his long life. The colors were bright and **luminous;** besides flowers and lovers there appeared a new interest that would be seen again—the circus.

When World War II was in full swing, Chagall had to leave France. The Germans had occupied the country and Jews were being arrested and sent to the death camps. He and his family were able to get out with special passports, though they were first arrested by the Gestapo. An American official was able to get them released and on their way to the United States.

Chagall, Bella, and Ida, with her husband, managed to get to New York City. They settled in a section of the city near Central Park. Chagall found other artists in the area. Some of the other artists who had escaped put down roots and stayed in America. Chagall probably never intended to stay. He did not try to learn English. He said that learning French after leaving Russia had been difficult enough. His not speaking the language could have added to his feeling that he was not "at home."

He began painting again. Some of his work had been brought over, with great difficulty, by his daughter. During this period he painted bright and cheerful pictures as well as some more sober, serious ones. Among them were: *Yellow Christ, Crucifixion and Candles, Song of the Cock, Red and Green Cock, Turtle Dove,* and *Feathers and Flowers.*

One of his best paintings was done at this time. It is *Between Darkness and Light,* a portrait of Bella and the artist with a snow-covered background.

Six weeks after Chagall and Bella heard the good news of Paris' liberation, Bella was dead. She had contracted a virus and died of the infection. Chagall's life seemed to go to pieces for a time, for she had helped him with so much of his life and work. His grief subsided; he began to work again.

He did the set design for a production of Stravinsky's *The Firebird* by the American Ballet Theatre (then known as the Ballet Theatre). There were several **retrospectives** of his work, among them one in the Museum of Modern Art in New York City that later went to Chicago. It went to Paris the following year.

In 1948 Chagall returned to France. By 1952 he had remarried. His new wife, Valentine, had been introduced to him by his daughter. Valentine became as indispensable to him as Bella had been. He continued to work, and even tried working in stained glass and ceramics. In his later years he came to appreciate the paintings of Monet, and the color Monet used. He spent his time between Paris and Provence. Chagall in his old age was compared to Picasso. There are some similarities: both lived long and productive lives, both worked in a variety of media, both lived in the south of France, and both married young women in their later years. The two were actually on friendly terms for some of the time Picasso lived in the south, but the friendship cooled when Chagall grew irritated with the jokes Picasso made at Chagall's expense.

The last retrospective of Chagall's work was held first in London in early 1985 and in the Philadelphia Museum of Art in May of that year. It was the first large showing of his work in either country in 30 years. At the age of 90, Chagall became the first living artist to be exhibited at the Louvre. The basic themes of his work had not changed greatly by the end of his life. Some critics complain about that, but his work continues to be familiar and popular, and is often reproduced. Chagall died in the spring of 1985 in his home in the south of France.

Glossary

Surrealism an art movement in which the subject matter is dreamlike, or looks as though it comes from the subconscious mind

luminous seeming to give off light

retrospective a look backward. A retrospective show of an artist's work is a collection of his or her work from the past to the present.

Two Nineteenth-Century American Greats

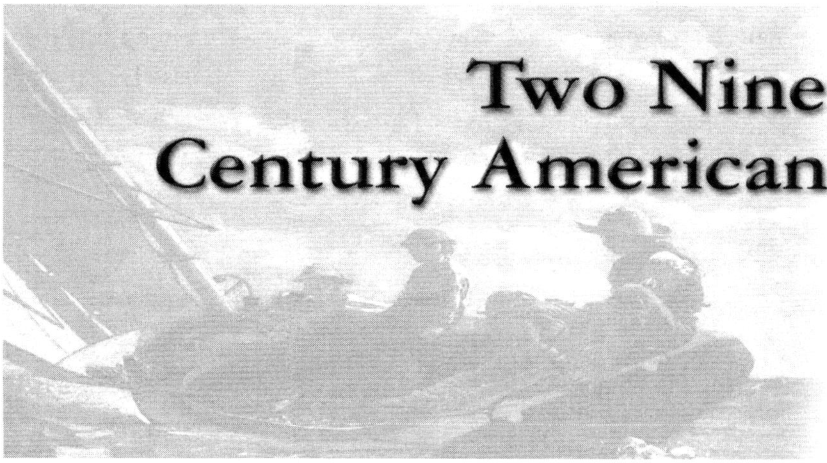

In Winslow Homer and Thomas Eakins we have two people who tried as hard as Wilbur and Orville Wright to get an American invention off the ground. These artists were almost as successful as the Wright brothers. They did manage to give American painting a running start, and their successors saw it take off early in the twentieth century.

Homer and Eakins worked separately to create the art of America while ignoring the art of Europe. In many other nineteenth-century American endeavors, that tactic seemed to be working. After the Civil War, Americans had a lot to do. In 1869 the transcontinental railway was completed. Manufacturing grew, the telephone and other modern amenities were invented, and settlement kept pushing westward. American literature came into its own with the talents of Poe, Melville, Whitman, Thoreau, Emerson, and others. United States involvement in foreign affairs was far from what it is today.

Yet, European influence still had the upper hand when Americans were choosing art to hang in their new homes. Only newspaper editors were interested in American artists: Since the camera had not then been perfected, newspapers needed artists to provide illustrations.

Like America's new literary giants, Homer and Eakins stubbornly stuck to native themes and urged younger artists to do the same. Although both men spent time in Paris and saw the Impressionists' work, they did not like its fuzzy mood and blurred detail. They were determined to get at the truth, no matter how awkwardly, according to one art historian.

Though Homer and Eakins sometimes made a living from their "American" art, it would still be a while before this country's art escaped measurably from European influence and matured on its own. When that happened two generations later, it was well worth the wait.

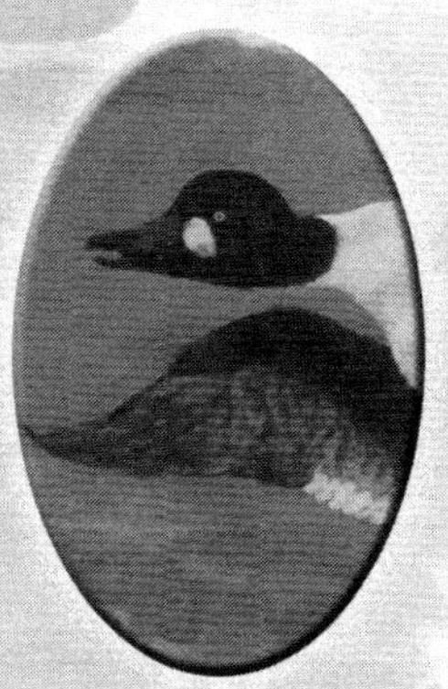

Winslow Homer
1836–1910

AMERICAN PAINTER Winslow Homer was born in Boston, Massachusetts, on February 24, 1836. He was born within a few years of such artists as Manet, Monet, Renoir, Cézanne, and fellow American Mary Cassatt. Homer began as an illustrator. By middle age he'd developed his own realistic style of painting, while he shared with the Impressionists a love of painting the outdoors, and experimented with ways to paint light.

Homer's father was a businessman who tried one kind of moneymaking scheme after another, even prospecting for gold in the gold rush of the mid-1800s. His mother was an accomplished painter of decorative watercolors. Many young women in those days learned to paint while waiting for marriage; after the wedding the paints were usually put away. Henrietta Maria Benson Homer continued to paint, however, and is considered to have encouraged her second son Winslow, who loved to draw.

Homer's earliest known watercolor is a landscape with a farmhouse and trees. An early pencil drawing shows a boy daydreaming as he lies on the grass. Another sketch done when he was 13 shows his father riding on the back of a giant bug flying over the mountains to join the gold rush miners and crashing among them.

Winslow's first job was in a printmaking shop when he was 19. His father urged him to answer an ad in the newspaper. Winslow' s drawing skills were good enough for him to be signed on as an apprentice. He worked there for two years. He hated the job. He did not like being confined in the shop all day long. He liked to fish, and often got up early enough to go fishing for an hour or so before going to work. When he had spent his two years there, he vowed never to work for someone else, but to always be his own master.

Homer learned lithography. He drew on a smooth, prepared stone with a greasy crayon. When the stone plate was inked, the ink stayed on the crayon lines as the print was made. He made **illustrations,** among them title pages for sheet music. Magazines, books, and advertisements also needed pictures to illustrate their messages.

When Homer left the print shop, he rented a studio. He had decided to become a painter but knew he needed to support himself with other work. He learned to make woodcuts, and soon sold them to various publications. There was a demand for artists who could make drawings for woodcuts. *Harper's Weekly* accepted some of Homer's work. He decided to move to New York City to be closer to the market for his work. His themes were often "genre" scenes (pictures of ordinary people going about their lives). He also did many drawings of Civil War scenes, visiting the battlefields to draw the troops in battle and at rest.

By the time he was 25 he began to explore oil painting. He began by learning how to arrange the paint on the palette and how to mix the colors. He got this information from a French artist, Frederic Rondel. This seems to have been the only instruction he received. He acquired the rest of his knowledge of painting on his own. His first known oil painting was of a Civil War **sharpshooter** in a tree. This was followed by other paintings of soldiers, which sold well.

In 1866 Homer went to visit Paris. His painting *Prisoners from the Front* was hung in the Universal Exposition. Many American painters were going to Paris at that time to study. Homer, however, is not known to have had much to do with the art academies. He made sketches at the Louvre, many of which included the artists at work or others looking at the art. He was not interested in the styles promoted by the Academy; the Impressionists had not yet become known. After ten months in Paris he went back home. He continued to paint, but also went back to making illustrations to earn his living.

Homer had always enjoyed the outdoors. His paintings of people often included landscape. He liked to paint nature when unusual and dramatic contrasts could be portrayed. Since he had not had formal training as a painter, he had to develop his own techniques to show the subject matter as he intended. Some of the compositional methods used in his black-and-white prints could be used in his paintings.

Just as the Impressionists had struggled with the idea of light, Homer, too, worked with the problem of light outdoors. He worked on portraying light as it comes directly from the sun, around the clouds, and as it is reflected from one object to another. In 1873 he began to work in watercolor, the medium he had first seen his mother use when he was a child. An advantage to watercolor was that he could work more quickly and catch some of the outdoor effects that he wanted. He could produce watercolors in less time and sell them at a lower price than the oils. Since they sold well, he could rely on those sales instead of illustrating for a living. He worked outside in the summer with watercolor, and in the winter often tried to reproduce some of the watercolors as oil paintings.

Homer's oil paintings sold slowly. However, he refused to cater to the critics by painting what was currently popular. His style was criticized for its lack of "polish." He eliminated much detail and emphasized shape, mass, and light. A well-known oil from this period of Homer's work is *Breezing Up (A Fair Wind)* (see Figure 51). At this time the Impressionists were also called "crude," although their style and Homer's were not alike.

In 1881, following a few years of frustration, he went to England. He lived in a cottage along the North Sea. There he watched the dramatic action of the North Sea and the people who lived beside it. The work he did there was the beginning of his later, most successful style. It was also better received by the critics and public, which may indicate some new thinking about painting. Some of the paintings done in this period are *Wreck of the Iron Crown, Watching the Tempest, Gale,* and *Lifeline.*

In 1883 Homer moved from his New York City studio to Maine. His brother had bought property in Prout's Neck, a fishing village, and had built a summer home. Winslow converted a stable into a home and studio, and lived there the rest of his life. Just as in England, he lived beside the sea and with the people who worked the sea.

By 1884 Homer was ready for a holiday. He sailed to the Bahamas (in the Caribbean). The tropical sunshine made a difference in color and in his response to it. Some of his most exciting watercolors were painted in the Bahamas and in Florida. He found ways to let the whiteness of the paper reflect back light and color. Instead of making a colored-in drawing, he worked freely with the brush. While his earlier watercolors disappointed some of the public, who wanted them to look like oil paintings, his watercolors of the tropics were popular at once and sold well.

Since Homer never married, his family was especially important to him. His two brothers, their wives, and their children spent the summers at Prout's Neck. His father spent the summers with his children and the winters in Boston. Henrietta Homer had died in 1884. The elder Homer was an extroverted fellow who often created problems for his sons with his outlandish behavior. Winslow, on the other hand, needed privacy and solitude; he was glad when the summer people left the area.

The places Homer most often painted were at Prout's Neck, the Caribbean (for tropical themes), and the Canadian North Woods and Adirondack Mountains, where he went hunting and fishing with his father and brother Charles. Some of Winslow's best-known watercolors are *Osprey's Nest, An October Day, On the Trail,* and *Shooting the Rapids.* Most of his watercolors from the tropics were not repainted in oil, but one that was is *The*

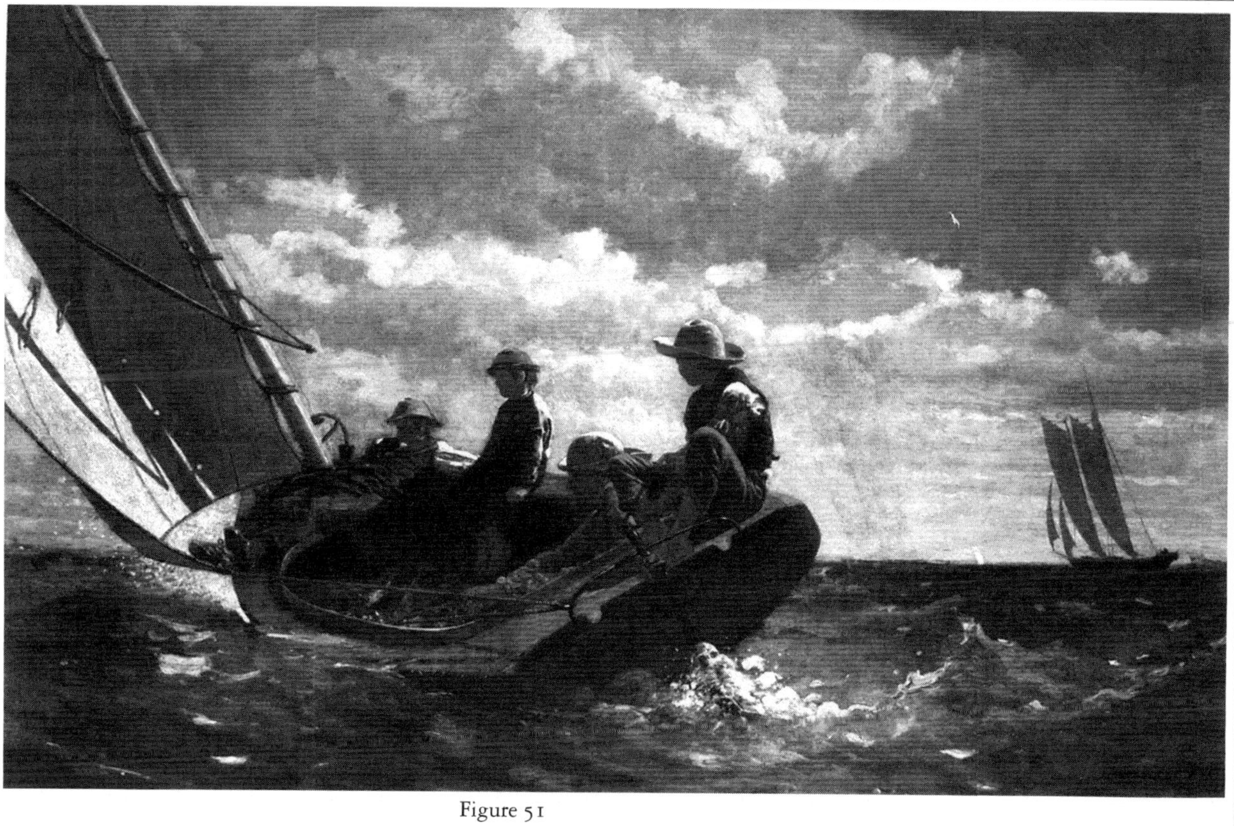

Figure 51
Breezing Up (A Fair Wind), 1876
Winslow Homer

Gulf Stream, in which sharks menace a young black man on a damaged sailboat. His paintings were not **contrived** and were seldom sentimental. He did not make up situations for a painting, but observed real life closely to find scenes that interested him. His later years are thought to have produced his best work. His later seascapes do not include people. He liked the sea best when it was wild and dramatic, with crashing waves and salt spray.

By the 1890s Homer was regarded as the leading American artist. In 1890 he was awarded a gold medal that he cherished by the Paris International Universal Exhibition. In 1896 he was awarded a $5,000 prize by the Carnegie Institute. Though he received recognition, he still longed for popularity with the common people and never quite felt that he'd achieved it.

In 1909 he painted two of his greatest oils, *Driftwood* and *Right and Left* (see Color Plate 17). The next year, when he was 74, he became blind. He refused to leave his home, however, and died there on September 29, 1910. At a time when Americans were still looking to Europe for great art, one of their own had helped establish American painting.

Glossary

illustrations pictures used in books, newspapers, magazines, or other printed materials

sharpshooter a good marksman

contrived artificial

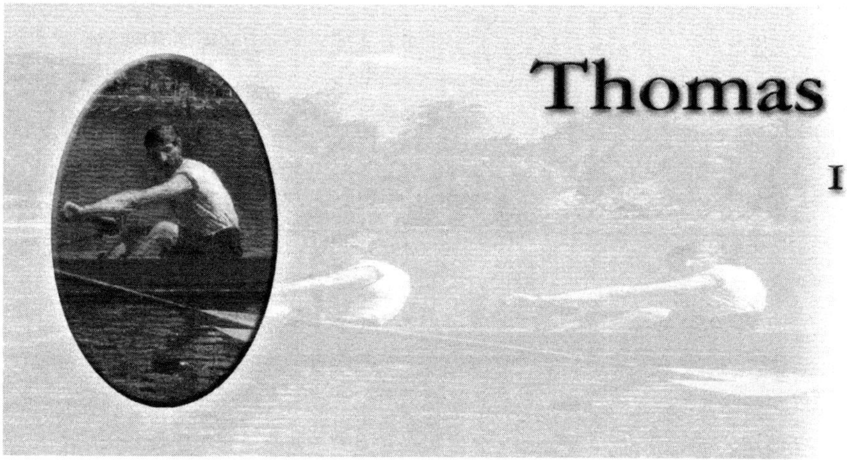

Thomas Eakins
1844–1916

PHILADELPHIA, in Thomas Eakins' time, was a thriving city in the process of recovering from the Civil War (as was the rest of America). The West was attracting hordes of settlers, and the Industrial Revolution was changing the social structure of the country. Philadelphia was a conservative city. The kind of art that was approved by the expanding middle and upper classes of the city was idealized, comfortable, and often overly pretty. It was not the kind of art Thomas Eakins chose to make.

Eakins was born in Philadelphia on July 25, 1844. His father was a writing master who taught and also made copies of certificates, deeds, diplomas, and other records in beautiful, ornamental writing and lettering. This is an art known as calligraphy. He was a domineering man, with the kind of strength and stubbornness that Thomas would exhibit in his own life. He recognized his son's ability and encouraged him. He was also able to give him financial help.

Eakins graduated from Central High School in 1861 with a B.A. degree, which was the equivalent of a college degree today. He loved mathematics, music, and languages. He was **fluent** in French and knew Latin well. As a boy he had built a steam engine that ran; in high school he had enjoyed making mechanical drawings of machinery.

After graduating from high school, Eakins entered the Pennsylvania Academy of Fine Arts and also studied **anatomy** at Jefferson Medical College. He was very interested in the way human and animal bodies work, and had thought of becoming a doctor. Later in his life he did research on the structure and action of muscles. He also made experiments in the photography of moving athletes that were later important in the development of the movie camera.

In 1866 Eakins went to Europe to study art. He enrolled in the École des Beaux-Arts. His teacher was the popular Jean-Léon Gérôme, who was a stickler for technical detail. Eakins was not interested in the museums; he seemed to have discovered the old masters only when he arrived in Madrid. There he admired Velázquez and Rembrandt most, and disliked Rubens' work intensely.

By 1870 Eakins returned home. He began to paint, making portraits of family, friends, and

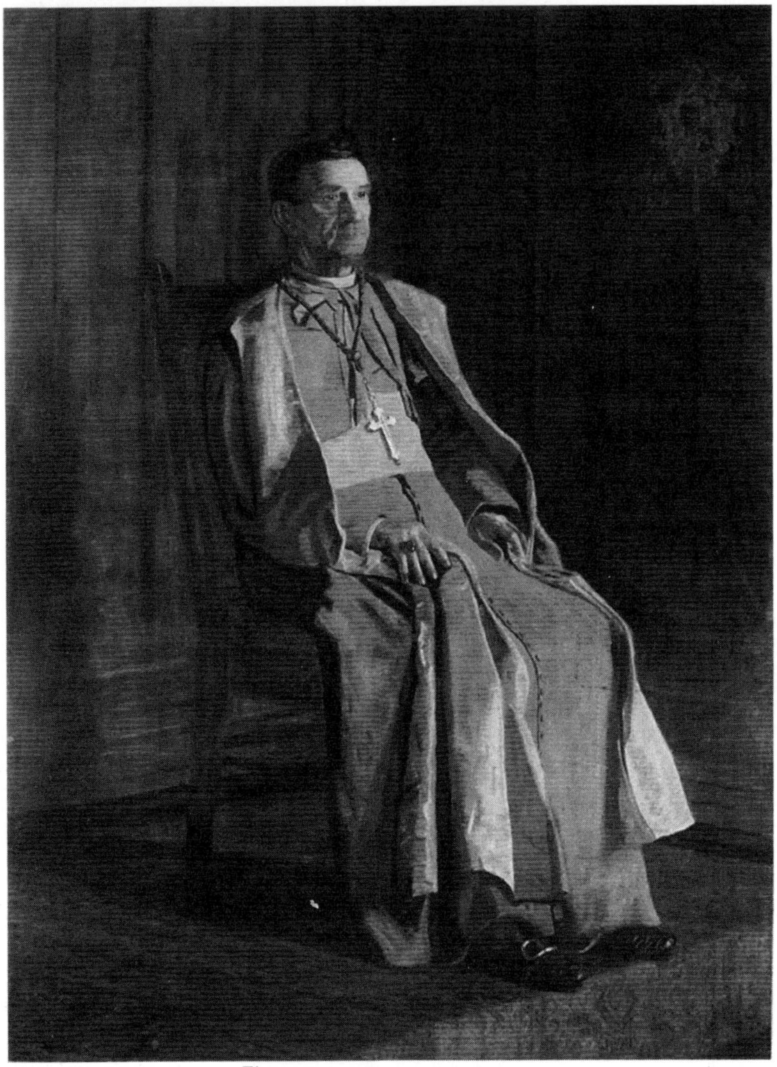

Figure 52
Archbishop Diomede Falconio, 1905
Thomas Eakins

the "pretty" style, and people who posed for his portraits were not flattered by them. His clinging to the absolute truth was part of his undoing: He would not compromise, even to save a commission.

After a beginning that was nevertheless favorable in his home city, Eakins painted his first controversial pictures. He painted *The Gross Clinic* and *William Rush Carving His Allegorical Figure of the Schuylkill River* for the Philadelphia Centennial Exhibition of 1876. Both paintings offended critics and the public. *The Gross Clinic* shows Samuel Gross, a famous doctor and teacher, with other surgeons, conducting an operation. One is reminded of Rembrandt's *The Anatomy Lesson of Dr. Nicolaes Tulp;* Eakins may have been thinking of that painting when he decided to do the *Clinic* picture. To Philadelphians it contained too much blood, flesh, and suffering. The other painting submitted showed an early American sculptor working from a nude model to produce a draped form.

acquaintances. Some were in outdoor settings, featuring people hunting, rowing, and sailing (see Color Plate 18). He could not paint idealized figures. To him, to **idealize** meant to change or distort what was real, and therefore to create ugliness instead of beauty. His pictures were carefully put together. A model was placed in the same position each day, and sessions could go on for a good number of days. His study of anatomy made it necessary for him to paint the human body as he knew it to be put together. His style was far from

Even the back view of the female model was too much for the times. People were shocked.

By 1879, however, Eakins was a professor of drawing and painting at the Pennsylvania Academy of Fine Arts, and later was its Director of Instruction. The classes were intended for those who had a serious professional interest in learning to make art. Eakins taught drawing and painting as he thought they should be taught. This included classes in anatomy and drawing, using live and often nude models. By 1886 rumors were flying about the "moral character" of the classes. As a teacher, Eakins had made the mistake of believing that he could get away with using nude models in mixed classes of men and women students in Victorian Philadelphia. He made no exceptions for the women. He was ahead of his time on this issue, and was asked to resign. He did. He had a loyal following of students who left with him. They established an Art Students League that Eakins taught without pay for six years.

Eakins had married when he was 40. His wife was an accomplished painter who met him when she enrolled in his classes after seeing *The Gross Clinic*. She was a help and comfort to him in times of crisis.

After leaving the Academy, Eakins concentrated on portraits. Perhaps he felt that in making portraits he could paint honestly yet avoid controversy. He went to meet Walt Whitman, asked to do his portrait, and became a good friend. Whitman came to like his portrait and to understand Eakins. He found that under Eakins' lack of social grace and concern for what was "proper" there was an appealing honesty and concern for truth.

Although commissions were not always plentiful, Eakins' father had provided enough money for him to live on. The painter did many portraits of men and women in the area, and also a series of paintings of Catholic clergy whom he met through a friend (see Figure 52). Eakins liked to visit St. Charles Borromeo Seminary in Overbrook. Although he was an atheist, he apparently liked to talk with these men, who had an intellectual insight not found among his contacts in Philadelphia

In 1878 the Jefferson Medical College had bought *The Gross Clinic* for $200. In 1889 the graduating class of the University of Pennsylvania Medical School commissioned Eakins to paint a portrait of the retiring professor of surgery, Dr. D. Hayes Agnew. Eakins decided to paint not only the doctor, but the entire graduating class. In the large (6' × 13') painting, Dr. Agnew is to the left, lecturing during an operation. The class of students looks on from the background, while surgeons and a nurse work to the right. The medical team and Dr. Agnew are bathed in light and light colors. Surgeons no longer wore business suits during an operation, as shown in *The Gross Clinic,* but were now aware of the importance of a more sterile environment and dressed in white clothing. Dr. Agnew refused to let Eakins paint blood on his hands; Eakins changed the hands. But the painting was received by critics with as much dislike as the earlier work had been. The graduating class liked the painting, but the Society of American Artists refused to hang it in the 1891 Exhibition. Following that, Eakins wrote a

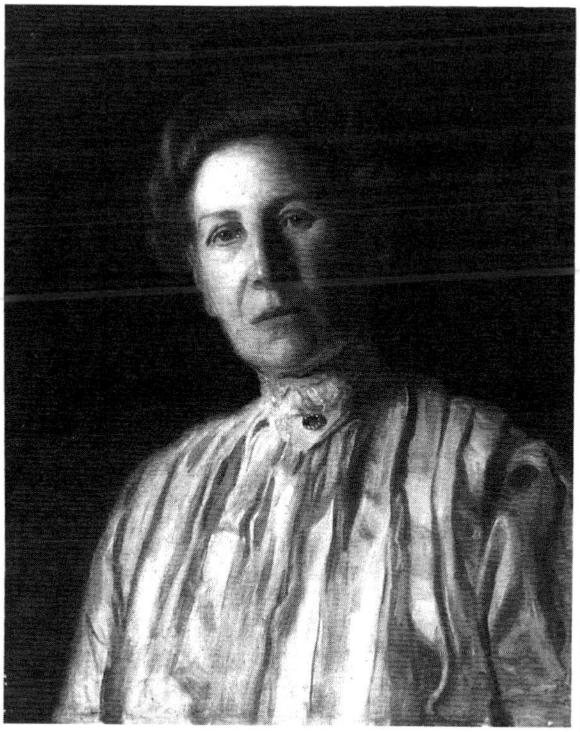

Figure 53
Mrs. Louis Husson, c. 1905
Thomas Eakins

bitter letter to the Society, severing all ties with the group.

During his middle age Eakins continued to paint portraits, revealing much about the personality and character of the subjects (see Figure 53). He was heavyset and gray-haired. He dressed in whatever suited him at the moment. He usually wore flannel shirts and baggy, unpressed trousers and coats. In the summer he might have worn only an undershirt and trousers. Sometimes he seemed to dress inappropriately on purpose to irritate the proper Philadelphians.

A few honors came to him before the end of his life. He was elected to the National Academy in 1902; he also taught at the National Academy of Design in New York from 1888 to 1894. In 1914 the study he'd made for *The Agnew Clinic* was sold for $5,000, three times more than the original painting had brought. By 1910 Eakins' health had begun to fail. He had spells of weakness, unusual fatigue, and unsteadiness. His eyesight left him and he died on June 25, 1916. His wife lived until 1938, long enough to see her husband's work finally appreciated by critics and the public. Some pieces were given to the Philadelphia Museum of Art, and many more were bought for private and public collections. His work was exhibited in the Museum of Modern Art and the Whitney Museum. Many of the clerical portraits are now at St. Charles Borromeo Seminary.

Glossary

fluent able to use words easily and smoothly

anatomy the study of human, animal or even plant bodies to determine how the various parts are put together and function

idealize to portray as more perfect than is true

Outstanding Modern American Painters

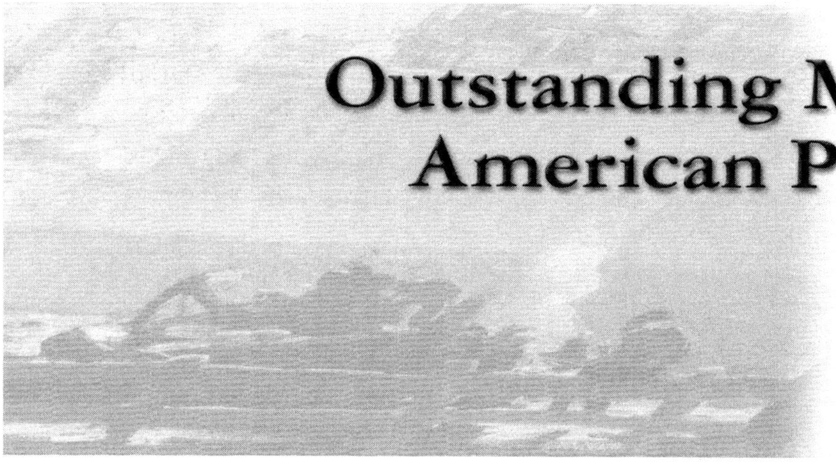

It is hard to categorize the American art scene beginning in the 1930s. It began as the first expressions of American style. After World War II, it exploded in a riot of ideas.

The artists of this period had little in common. For some, "art" meant highly personal visions. For others, it meant realistic pictures of American life. And still others painted everything in between. This revolution in art did not occur quite so quickly as it might seem. The United States endured some ugly times in the 1920s and 1930s. The country's involvement in World War I had brought democracy to some countries. Conditions improved for a few minority groups. But around 1920 America retreated into itself. The nation isolated itself from others' problems. As a backlash against the growth of communism in Russia and Europe, the U.S. government tried to get rid of all European ideas. It reacted with violence to the formation of labor unions.

For a while, postwar wealth continued. Then, in 1929, the stock market collapsed. The hopes of many went with it. People lost their jobs as manufacturing slowed. President Roosevelt provided some help. He set up a program called the New Deal. This provided jobs in many areas. This help extended into the arts. For the first time in American history, art was seen as vital to the nation as a whole.

After World War II, Europe's energies were scattered. It was then that American art really began to come into its own. The country grew in every way during the postwar boom. The conflicts that come with this kind of growth provided more inspiration for America's increasingly creative artists.

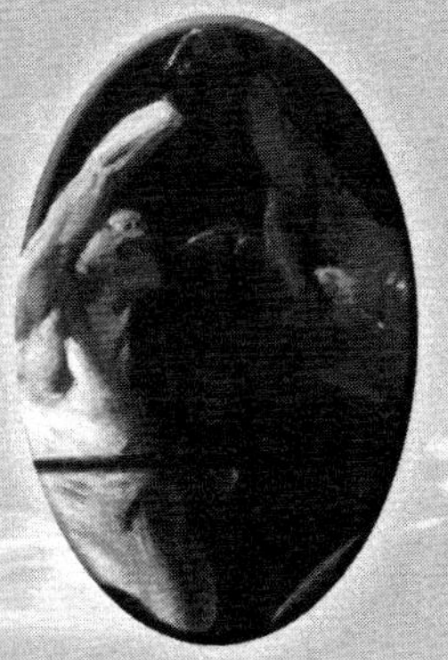

George Bellows

1882 – 1925

THE EARLY 1900s were years of great change and revolt in the American art world. The National Academy of Design in New York had set up restrictive standards for the acceptance of new art. Several groups of artists, united behind new ideals in artistic expression, revolted against such institutions as the Academy. One such group was called "The Eight." This group, and others who shared some of their ideas, have also been referred to as "The Ash Can School." Some of the subjects they painted—city streets, dilapidated tenements, and even trash bins—led to that label.

The Eight was led by an artist named Robert Henri, whose **charisma**, energy, and encouragement of young artists had an immediate—and often unwelcome—effect on the art establishment during his day. Henri opened the gates for the uniquely "American" artists who were to follow.

George Bellows studied with Henri, and was closely allied to The Eight in spirit. He never truly joined the group, however. He blazed his own trail. And, if never leaving the United States were the only qualification for being called an American painter, Bellows qualified for the title. But there are other reasons why he is considered one of our finest, truly authentic American artists.

George Bellows was born in Columbus, Ohio, in 1882. His parents were Methodists, and Sundays were days when George was allowed either to read or to draw. George often drew while his mother read to him. She hoped her son would become a bishop. George's father, who was a building contractor, hoped his son would be a banker. George, however, had other ideas.

The boy grew up to be a tall, handsome young man, more than ready for the challenges of his college years at Ohio State. He was good at both basketball and baseball, but he selected the "national sport" of baseball as his game. He chose to play shortstop and was considered the finest shortstop Ohio State had ever had. At six feet two inches, he was also by far the tallest.

He was a rambunctious, energetic student. He played ball, sang in the glee club, made cartoons of his professors, and illustrated some college publications. Those who assumed Bellows would go on to play professional baseball assumed incorrectly. He already knew he wanted to be an artist. He left school after his junior year, took himself to

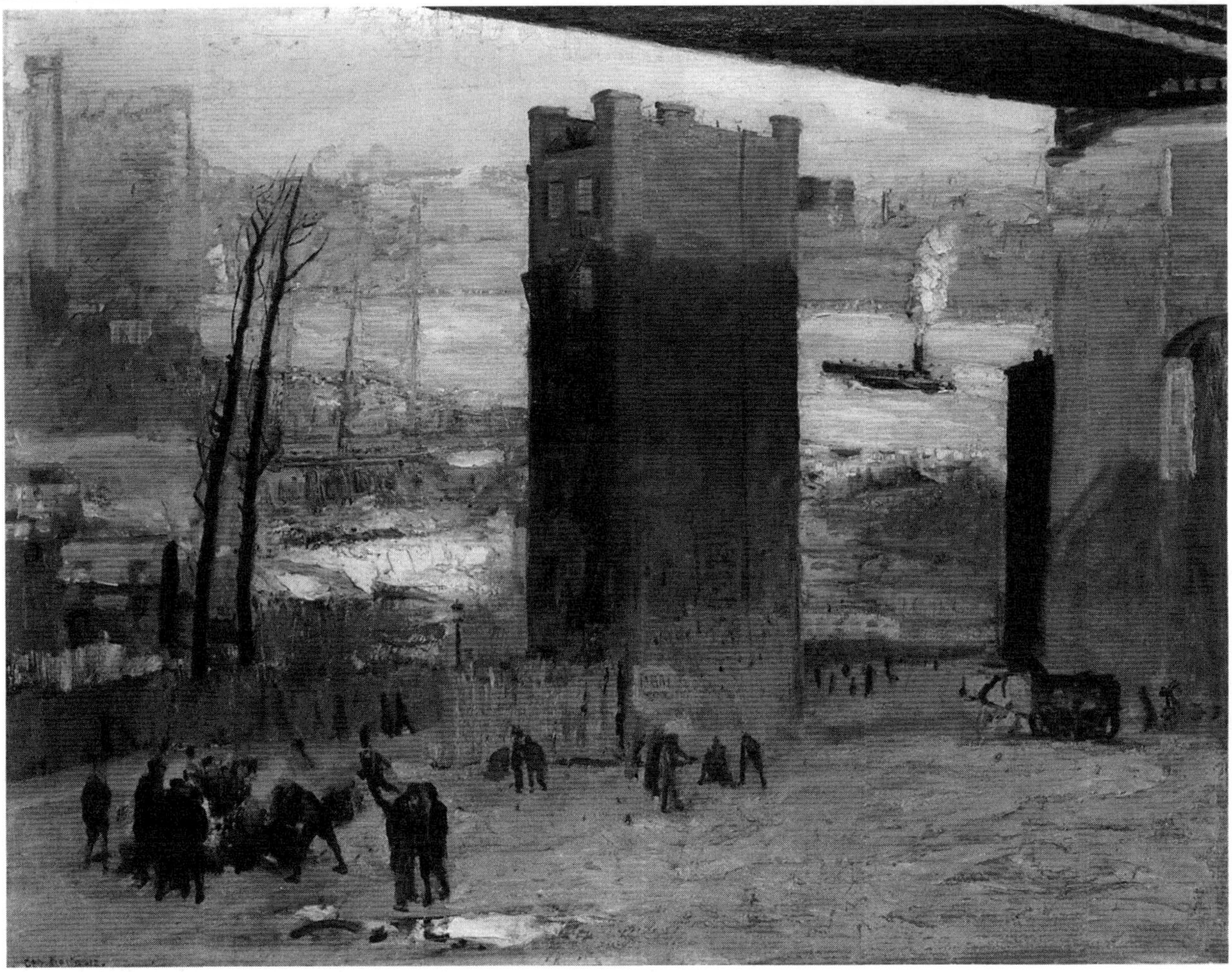

Figure 54
The Lone Tenement, 1909
George Bellows

New York, and began to study with Robert Henri at the New York School of Art.

Bellows participated to a limited extent in The Eight's stand against the art establishment in New York. They had their own shows of their own works, in defiance of the National Academy. They advertised their shows all over the city, and they succeeded in getting the public's attention. Bellows enjoyed taking part in this rebellion, but above all, he painted. He didn't mind participating in both worlds—The Eight's rebellion and the Academy's traditions. He entered a painting called *Forty-Two Kids* in the Academy's annual exhibit in 1909. It was a realistic, somewhat humorous portrayal of a group of city kids swimming off a dock in Manhattan. It won an award, and Bellows was elected an associate of the Academy. At age 27, he became the youngest member of the Academy.

In that same year, Henri formed his own school of art in Manhattan, and Bellows continued to work with him. All of Henri's students were encouraged to get out on the streets and paint life just as they saw it. Bellows painted the riverfront, the docks, and other everyday scenes that no one could have thought were exceptional, or worth the honor of being painted. Such paintings as *Blue Morning* (see Color Plate 19) and *The Lone Tenement* (see Figure 54) captured the gritty essence of the city.

Bellows used broad brush strokes and new symbols in his form of realism. Some of his most famous paintings are of the prizefighters he watched at Tom Sharkey's Athletic Club, which was across the street from Henri's school. Prizefighting was illegal at the time, and private clubs were formed so that the sport could be carried on "privately"—and illegally. *Both Members of This Club* (see Figure 55) and *Stag at Sharkey's* are depictions of a sport, the savageness of which is reflected in the eerie, cartooned faces of the spectators in the paintings. Yet the power and immediacy of these works is a triumph of artistry that seems to **transcend** the ugliness, or violence, of the subject.

Bellows painted many events and scenes of high action, but he felt free to take on many other subjects, as well. He and his wife, Emma, had two daughters, Anne and Jean, and the family portraits Bellows painted are well-loved for their tenderness and aptness of form. One such portrait, *Lady Jean,* is of his younger daughter playing dress-up in her mother's clothes. He painted portraits of his aunt and his mother that express a deep sensitivity to the wisdom and grace of old age, and all that it brings.

Bellows produced two important paintings that arose from his indignation and outrage at World War I. In *The Murder of Edith Cavell,* Bellows showed the British nurse going to her execution. She was killed by the Germans for aiding wounded prisoners, even though she had also tended to German soldiers. Here, again, was Bellows at work capturing a scene of dramatic impact. The other painting, called *Return of the Useless,* was of French peasants who were ill-used and broken by the Germans, then released because they were no longer fit to work.

Bellows traveled within the United States, but never went to Europe, unlike so many of his **compatriots** at the time. He had a Manhattan home and one in Woodstock, New York. He traveled to Maine and out West, and he broadened his subject matter over the years. He was an excellent

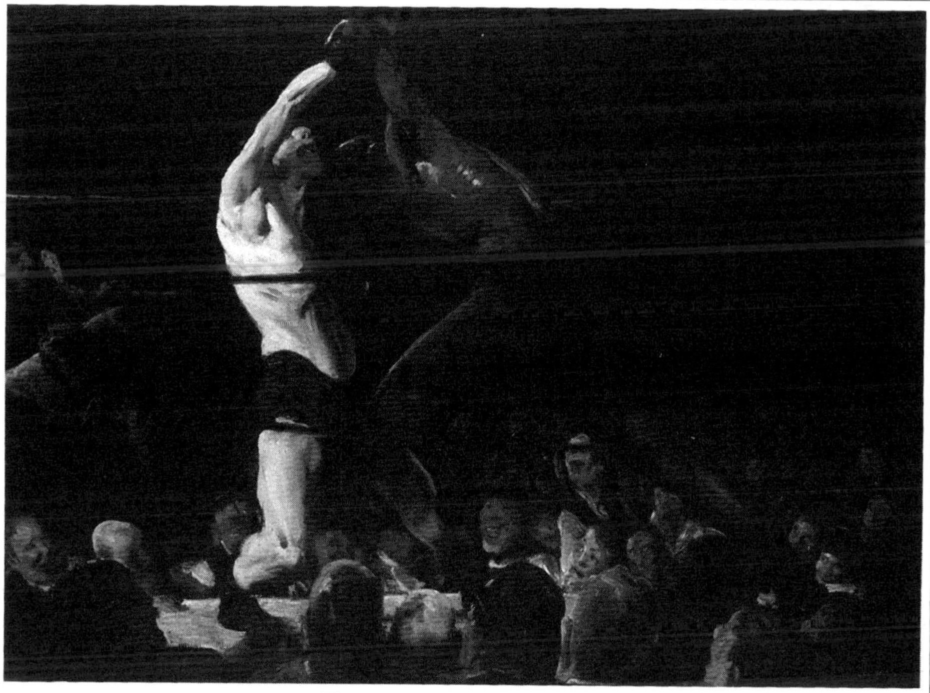

Figure 55
Both Members of This Club, 1909
George Bellows

lithographer and illustrator, and tirelessly pursued these disciplines in addition to his painting.

It is historically unusual for an artist's work to be so well received from the early works on. Many of Bellows' works were bought at popular prices, but he also had a considerable number hanging in art museums and institutions when he was still in his twenties. At the same time, he taught composition and life classes to art students, organized a new painting society, and spent time with underprivileged city children at a New York school.

The White Horse is a powerful landscape set in the Catskill Mountains. Bellows painted it three years before his death. The horse, in the foreground of the painting, stands still looking out at a horizon brimming with eerie and threatening storm clouds. The charged atmosphere of the moment, the use of color that so aptly reflects the strange light of a storm, and the attitude of the horse, in silent but alert observance, all come together in one of the finest examples of Bellows' mastery of his realistic art.

Bellows' death was tragically early. He died of a ruptured appendix in a hospital at the age of 43. A memorial show was held at a New York museum, where the crowds were awestruck by the immense and powerful body of his work displayed together in the show. Bellows had once said, "The ideal artist is he who knows everything, feels everything, experiences everything, and retains his experience in a spirit of wonder and feeds upon it with creative lust. . . . The ideal artist is the superman."[1] Though dismayed by the loss of this vital and dynamic artist, Americans may also feel grateful that his energy produced such a legacy of fine works.

1. *The Paintings of George Bellows,* compiled by Emma Bellows, (N.Y.: Alfred A. Knopf, 1929), p. *x*.

Glossary

charisma a magnetic quality in a person that draws other people to him or her

transcend to pass beyond

compatriots fellow countrymen, or members of the same group of people

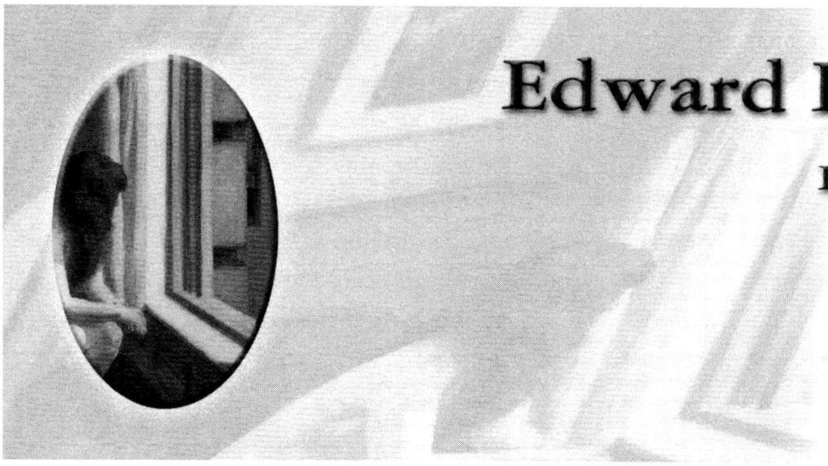

Edward Hopper

1882 – 1967

EDWARD HOPPER WAS BORN in the same year as George Bellows, and he, too, studied with Robert Henri. There, for the most part, the similarity between them ends. Bellows is often remembered for capturing a dramatic moment. Hopper may be thought of as creating drama from the very starkness of his paintings—in many cases, from the **stark** portrayal of emptiness and loneliness.

Hopper was born and brought up with his sister in Nyack, New York, where his father had a **dry goods** business. He went to a local private school, and then to Nyack High School. Nyack was a boatbuilding community, and Hopper spent many hours at the local shipyards watching the boats. He loved to draw what he saw, and he knew he wanted to be an artist. His parents enrolled him in a school for illustrators at the age of 17. A year later, in 1900, Hopper went to the New York School of Art to study with Robert Henri.

It was difficult for Hopper to share all that Henri's Realists were doing. They seemed at times too emotional, too dependent on a theme, and too lacking in design or form for Hopper. He left Henri's school in 1906, feeling the need to get away and see more of what other painters were doing. He went to Paris.

Hopper taught himself to speak French, and he painted on his own while in Paris, not joining an art school. He experimented with painting light—how it rested on a building, the way it changed colors. He often painted a work in one sitting. Of the French painters, Hopper most admired Manet and Monet and their Impressionist views. They used **palettes** of paint with lighter colors; Hopper lightened his palette.

By 1910, Hopper had made several visits to Paris, but now he came back to the United States to stay. Like so many artists, he needed to work in commercial art to make a living. He worked in an advertising agency three or four days a week and painted when he could. He was a successful illustrator, but his early paintings were not very popular. He sold his first painting at a big show in New York in 1913. *The Sailboat* was priced at $300 but sold for only $250. And it wasn't until ten years later that he sold another painting. At the same age, George Bellows was winning prizes and distinction, but Hopper couldn't even get his paintings considered by the juries at the National Academy of Design.

Many people have said that Hopper, angry and hurt by his lack of success, withdrew from the art scene for the next several years. Hopper later insisted that wasn't the case at all. He simply felt it wasn't necessary to actually live and work among the other popular painters of the day. He illustrated and he painted, especially during the summers (which he spent in Gloucester, Massachusetts and Ogunquit, Maine). He got his own printing press and did many etchings during this time.

The paintings of this period, both oil and watercolor, were often of New England scenes of boats or the ocean. They included New England houses and architecture. In 1923, the Brooklyn Museum bought one of his paintings, *The Mansard Roof,* for $100. The next year, an important art gallery held an exhibition of his watercolors. *All* of them sold! Hopper was 42 years old when, finally, he became a recognized artist.

That same year, Hopper married his wife Jo, who had also been an art student of Henri's. The two of them enjoyed a simple life. They never had children. They lived in New York and summered

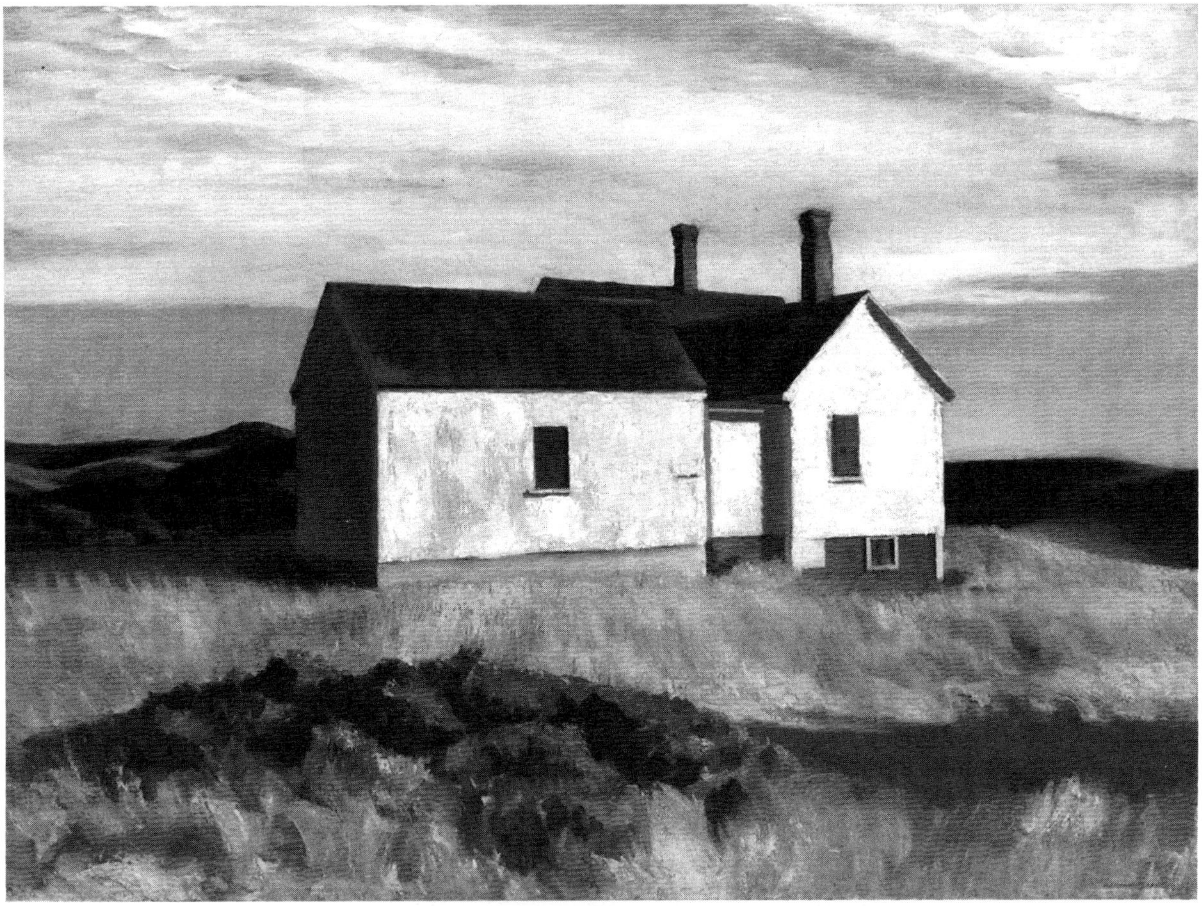

Figure 56
Ryder's House, 1954
Edward Hopper

in Cape Cod. Jo became the model for most of the female figures in Hopper's paintings.

The painting *Eleven A.M.* (see Color Plate 20) is representative of many of Hopper's symbols and themes. He did a series of paintings of women in city interiors. Their faces are often hidden or otherwise obscured. They are depicted alone, perhaps dressing to go out, often gazing out the almost ever-present window. *Eleven A.M.* invites the observer to think about this woman. What is she feeling? Is she lonely? Sad? What does the hour of the day mean? Doesn't she have some place to go? The painting that seems so **static** at first glance is actually provoking dozens of questions.

Light that streams through a window is almost a constant in Hopper's work. Here, the light from the window is the only connector, or bridge, between the woman and the city outside. When Hopper had to work as an illustrator to make a living, it was not a happy time in his life. He said later about this period, "What I wanted to do was to paint sunlight on the side of a house." And, indeed, he spent a lifetime with the question of how light *looks*—at different times of the day, on houses, in the countryside, and in the city.

In *Ryder's House* (see Figure 56) we're shown a cloudy sky, yet light is coming in from somewhere behind us. The house, isolated and weathered, seems somehow noble in its sturdiness. The light that moves toward it enhances that feeling.

Hopper painted "lonely" houses, with empty or nearly empty rooms. Often the viewer is separated from the subject itself—by railroad tracks or some other barrier in the foreground. Yet Hopper did not like the critics who always had the word "lonely" in their reviews. He thought they stressed it too much. He was interested in facts, in how things actually were—at eleven in the morning or at twilight. He painted scenes with no one there as if to ask, "How does it look when no one's there to see it?"

In 1933, Hopper wrote, "My aim in painting has always been the most exact **transcription** of my most intimate impressions of nature."[1] One extension of this is that the painter recorded what was there, and left it for the viewer to fill in the story line.

Hopper lived to be 85 years old. In his long life, he recorded for us the life of a still-young country that was growing at an incredible rate of speed. Cities sprouted up and became overcrowded. Houses were built, grew old, and came down. People came to the cities and later fled from them.

Edward Hopper was less "modern" than some artists, yet he didn't hesitate to try techniques that were previously untried. In many ways, his large following was gathered because he could appeal to everyone. We appreciate his work for its inherent "truth," and for the logic, care, and careful "transcription" that went into it.

1. *America and Alfred Stieglitz,* Waldo Frank, et al., eds. (N.Y.: The Literary Guild, 1934), p. 4.

Glossary

stark harsh in appearance; barren or grim

dry goods textiles, clothing, and other such articles

palettes the boards on which artists mix colors, or the ranges of colors that artists use

mansard a roof with two slopes on all four sides

static having no motion

transcription the process of recording, in one form or another, what one observes

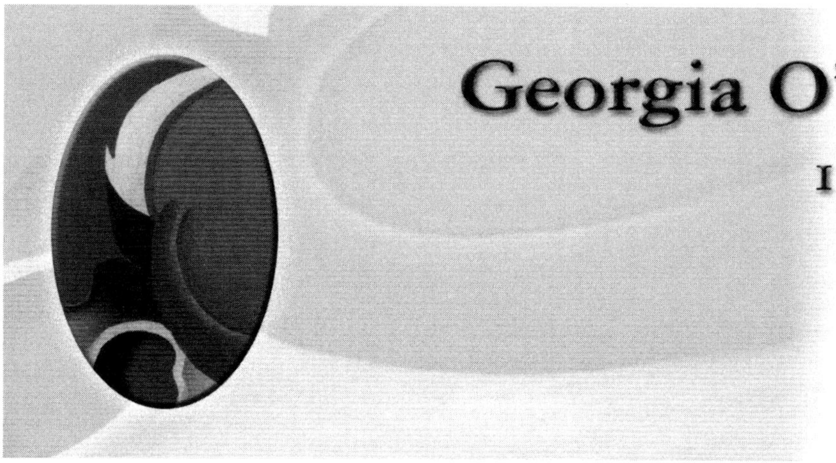

Georgia O'Keeffe

1887 – 1986

THE TURMOIL OF THE ART WORLD in the early part of this century caused artists to take many different paths. There were traditionalists, realists, regionalists—and now abstractionists. A realist might paint a refrigerator that one could immediately recognize as a refrigerator. An abstractionist painter, when asked to paint a refrigerator, might paint his or her idea of the *essence* of a refrigerator. That might be a rectangular or boxy form shrouded in icy colors— blue or white, perhaps. The abstractionist's object was to express ideas through form or color, not to paint a realistic portrait of the subject or theme. Though she did not consider herself an abstract painter, Georgia O'Keeffe was one of this country's abstractionists.

"Pioneer" is a term often applied to O'Keeffe, and rightly so. Hers was a long life of thinking for herself and expressing those thoughts in a manner no one, except her, could ever have imagined. She took the world by surprise again and again. She lived and painted on her own terms.

O'Keeffe was born in Sun Prairie, Wisconsin, in 1887, the daughter of Francis and Ida O'Keeffe. She and her six brothers and sisters grew up on a large farm in an old-fashioned country house. Georgia knew at the age of ten that she wanted to be an artist. She was lucky enough to have private drawing lessons in addition to the art classes at school.

The family moved to Virginia when she was 15 years old. She entered the Art Institute of Chicago at the age of 18 and went on to the Art Students League of New York in 1907. O'Keeffe was a fine student, even winning a prize for a still life she had painted—a realistic work. But she was thoroughly dissatisfied with what she was learning. It seemed to her that all the students were doing was painting the same ways other artists had already painted.

Was there nothing new to do? She left school after one year, destroyed her work, and went back to Chicago to make a living drawing embroidery and lace for advertisements (truly an exercise in realistic representation). That, too, was a frustrating experience. She left Chicago and went back to Virginia to see her family.

In 1912, one of her sisters took her to an art class at the University of Virginia. The teacher was a follower of Arthur Dow, who was known for teaching art based on some of the principles of oriental art. O'Keeffe saw a ray of hope for herself. There *was* something different to be done. She just knew it.

For the next three or four years, O'Keeffe made her living by teaching art. She spent two of those years in the Amarillo, Texas, public schools. She saw the harsh climate as a challenge to be borne. The vast, empty countryside, with warm colors of sandstone against the wide blue sky, later led her to portrayals of the West. She helped her students find beauty in the surroundings that they had always thought desolate and to appreciate simple objects. On her part she gained an appreciation of children. She was remembered as an understanding teacher.

In addition, O'Keeffe was pursuing the "new" direction in art that Dow had pointed out to her. In fact, she went to study directly with him. Dow taught the concept of using lines to draw outlines of different shapes, and then showing the relationship of one shape to another. Often these lines and shapes imitated those found in nature, but they didn't necessarily depict natural things in a realistic fashion.

O'Keeffe began a series of abstract drawings in charcoal that she sent to a friend in New York. Against O'Keeffe's wishes, the friend took them to Alfred Stieglitz, who promptly proceeded to exhibit them without the artist's knowledge or permission.

Stieglitz was a leading figure in the New York art world. He was both an artist and a photographer, and a **patron** of the arts as much as a participant in them. He encouraged the "new—particularly the abstract—art theories among the artists who flocked around him. He hung show after show of the works of his **protégés,** never minding the ruckus he was creating in an established art society that was not interested in change.

When O'Keeffe heard that her works were hanging in Stieglitz's gallery on Fifth Avenue, she charged down to see him and angrily insisted that he take them down. Stieglitz refused, and the drawings stayed up. A year later, Stieglitz held a one-woman exhibition of O'Keeffe's works (this time with the artist's permission). A friendship had started with an argument, proceeded to a working-and-learning association, and, in 1924, Stieglitz and O'Keeffe were married.

Their early years were spent in an exciting rush of shows and exhibitions among a wide circle of friends. O'Keeffe was favorably reviewed by the critics for the most part. She had started painting in oils, then in watercolors, and she produced works that amazed the public. She painted abstractions with names such as *Blue and Green Music* and *Orange and Red Streak,* and a series of paintings all called *Black Spot.* (She would go on to paint many series of paintings with the same subject; that, too, was something that oriental artists often did, showing different versions and angles of one idea or theme.) O'Keeffe used color in bold ways—as she felt it, not in the established ways. Her style was not one anyone could put a label on: flowing lines, bold curves of color, and lots of "spaces." Space was as important as the lines that defined it.

O'Keeffe did do some painting that approached reality. For example, in a painting called *Lake George with Crows,* the viewer can actually identify a lake, trees, and circling crows. But the composition of the painting, with its exaggerated roundness of forms, is only O'Keeffe's. She painted the city, also, in works that look true to the urban scenery in a way, and yet not. She had no wish to paint buildings as they looked in a photograph, but as what they represented to her. In *River, New York,* smokestacks and chimneys on both sides of the river are busily sending smoke up to the sky. One has the feeling that O'Keeffe thought these man-made structures were bringing a great haze down on the city.

One of the subjects for which O'Keeffe is well-known are her giant flowers. One can certainly recognize them as flowers, but their giant scale is far from realistic. In *An Orchid* and *The White Trumpet Flower,* and many others, one enormous flower covers the entire canvas. In the rounded, sometimes velvety petals and the dark shadows within the flower, O'Keeffe seems to repeat some of the forms she was always painting in earlier works. It is as if she had been endowed with an instinct for what was deep in nature.

O'Keeffe and Stieglitz at first spent their summers at Lake George, with some visits to Maine. In 1929, O'Keeffe discovered New Mexico for the first time, and she fell in love with the mountains and desert there. After that first trip, she went back every year. She would bring pieces of the desert back with her to New York to paint—skulls and partial skeletons of desert animals, in which she found a kind of peace and beauty. *Goat's Horn with Red* (see Figure 57) is just one of the many such paintings she did. In reality, the bones and skeletons were probably bleached white by the sun, but O'Keeffe often added bright colors to them when the bright colors seemed to her to somehow belong to the bones.

Twenty-two years after they married, in 1946, Alfred Stieglitz died. In those years, he and O'Keeffe had given encouragement and new challenges to each other. They had had numerous exhibitions and shared great acclaim for their work. After his death, O'Keeffe prepared two exhibitions of his photographs. Then, she moved to New Mexico to be in the country that felt a part of her.

There, she lived in an area called the Ghost Ranch, west of Taos. She was at home with a desert that was itself painted with flowers, cliffs, hills—and bones. She continued to paint her bones, her ranch, and the views she had from the ranch.

The interest of the art public in O'Keeffe's work had slackened. However, in the 1960s O'Keeffe's paintings, with their bright, exciting colors,

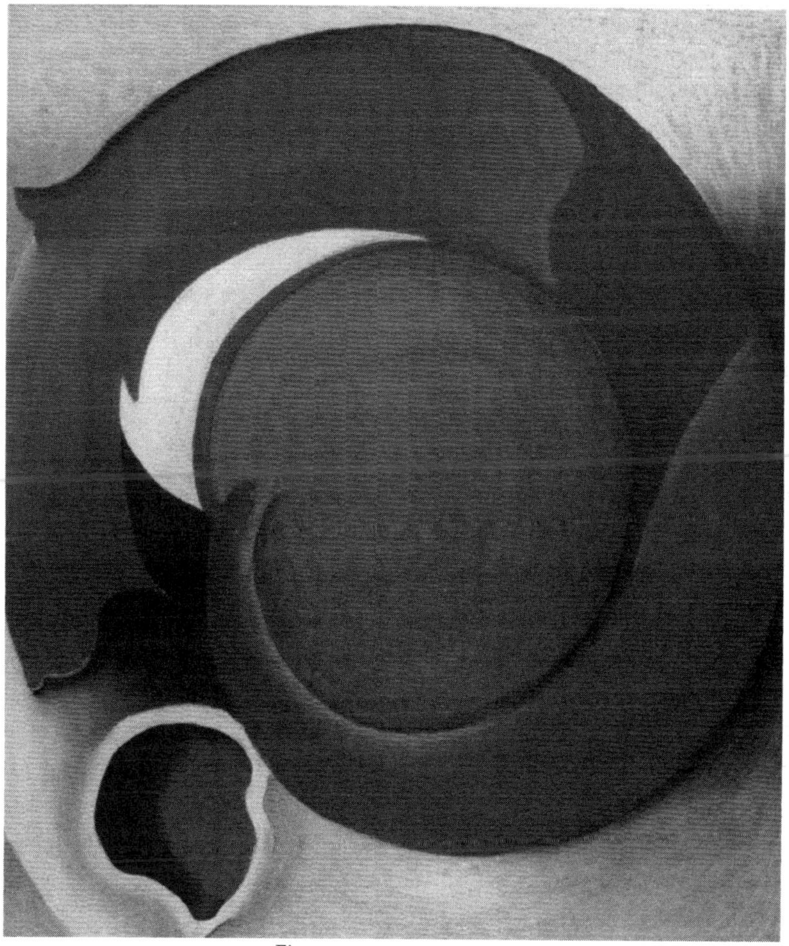

Figure 57
Goat's Horn with Red, 1945
Georgia O'Keeffe

appealed to those who had of late been introduced to psychedelic colors. In 1958 the Metropolitan Museum of Art had an exhibit, "Fourteen American Masters," in which O'Keeffe's work had its own exhibition room. In 1960 the Worcester Art Museum, in Massachusetts, held a one-woman show of her art. Her early paintings looked so in tune with the times that people thought she was imitating, until the dates on the paintings showed otherwise. Her lifestyle was very appealing. She lived independently out on the desert, raised her own produce, wore long skirts—though she always had, sometimes with men's jackets—in black or white or subdued colors.

Like Bellows, O'Keeffe never studied abroad. Until she was in her sixties, all her traveling was in the United States or in Mexico. Then jet travel changed all that. With a friend or a relative she traveled to Europe, the Far East, and around the world. She brought her experiences of flying back home in a series of paintings, one of which was called *Sky Clouds*. The last of this series is an enormous painting, 24 feet wide, of cloud upon cloud in the vast infinity of space. The clouds are white pools under a rosy horizon that seems to go on forever. The canvas would not fit in her studio and had to be set up in the garage. She worked on it from morning till night, wanting to finish before winter in the unheated garage.

She had another reason to work quickly on the huge canvas. Her eyes had been bothering her, making her vision blurred at times. When she finally consulted her doctor, she was told that she had macular degeneration. This disease gradually destroys the central vision, leaving the outer rim with some sight before the person becomes totally blind. It is easy to understand how devastating such a diagnosis was for O'Keeffe. She faced up to it as she had faced up to other tough situations. She had always had people tending the houses and ranch areas, and was able to continue to keep their help. She was not an easy person to work for since "her way" was the only way. Friends and relatives also were willing to stay, although O'Keeffe was used to being alone, working alone. She gradually experienced the physical failings of old age in addition to her loss of sight, and was less and less able to cope. As artists in the past, she left priceless gifts.

Georgia O'Keeffe, whom we call a pioneer, really never stopped uncovering new territory. She lived a long life, rich in her own resources and proud to express what was within her. She died in New Mexico in 1986. She was in her late nineties. She once said, of the paintings she did of the bones in the desert, "I have used these things to say what is to me the wideness and wonder of the world as I live in it."[1] It is fitting for a pioneer not to be afraid of wideness and wonder, but to embrace it, and call it her own.

1. *Georgia O'Keeffe,* Goodrich and Bry, (N.Y.: Praeger Publishers, 1970), p. 25.

Glossary

patron a supporter or benefactor

protégés people whose training or careers are helped along by an influential person or by a patron

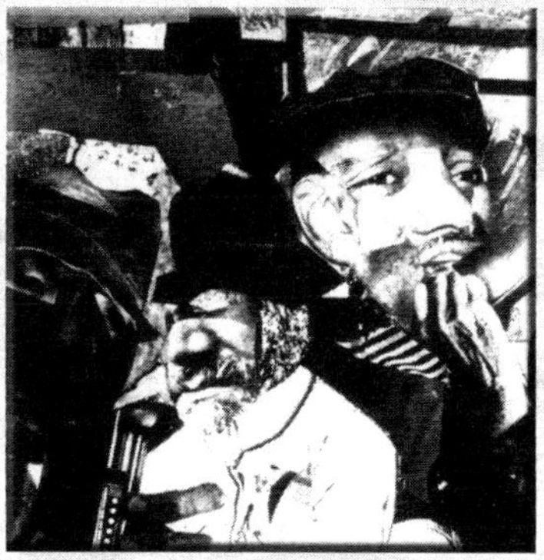

Romare Bearden

1914 – 1988

After the Civil War, both the North and South slowly began to heal. Blacks who were freed from slavery now had opportunities to make lives of their own. Many were able to go to school. Some found jobs as skilled workers. Some became ministers, doctors, teachers, or lawyers. However, they still had to fight against prejudice. Laws, known as "Jim Crow" laws, restricted the rights of African Americans. Some of these laws kept blacks from voting. Some kept them from using public facilities that were available to anyone else. Many of these restrictions lasted until the 1960s when civil rights legislation was passed.

Romare Bearden's great-grandparents are thought to have been born into slavery. His great-grandfather was Henry B. Kennedy; his great-grandmother, Rosa Catherine Gosprey. They were married in 1863, when he was 18 and she was 16. Their only child, Rosa Catherine, Romare's grandmother, was born in 1865. By 1870 they had settled in Charlotte, South Carolina. There Kennedy was a railroad mail agent. Within eight years, they saved enough money to buy a quarter acre of land that had several houses on it. After another ten years, Kennedy owned the family home, two more houses, and a grocery store. He was regarded as a member of the middle class in Charlotte.

Romare's parents were college-educated. His father, Howard, attended Bennett College in Greensboro. When he went north to find work, he met Bessye Johnson Banks, who lived in Atlantic City. She had graduated from Virginia Normal and Industrial Institute in Petersburg. They were married in Philadelphia in 1910 and lived in Charlotte for several years. Their son, Romare, was born on September 9, 1914. However, the black population in Charlotte was no longer prospering. Opportunities for young blacks were fewer. When Romare was three years old, the family moved north. His father had difficulty finding a stable job. For about five years the family lived in Canada while he worked as a railroad steward. The family settled in New York City, in Harlem, in 1920. Romare and his parents often spent summers in Charlotte. He was influenced by the atmosphere, way of life, and family relationships there. Many of these memories later surfaced in his art, from drawings to abstract paintings to cartoons. These all led up to his final works that began in the 1960s—his treatment of the collage medium, for which he is best known.

One could compare Romare Bearden's life and career to his work in collage—layer upon layer of media, developing final relationships and form. His mother, Bessye, was a dynamic woman. She was the New York editor for the *Chicago Defender* in the 1920s. She served on countless boards and committees. The family home in Harlem entertained an assortment of well-known people—artists, musicians, writers, politicians, entertainers. These successful people in an assortment of fields must have influenced young Romare.

He graduated from New York University in 1932. He also attended Boston University in Massachuestts for two years, where he was a star pitcher on the varsity baseball team. His freshman year had been at Lincoln College in Pennsylvania. He preferred the curriculum at the Boston school and transferred there.

The next layer of Bearden's life was a stint as a cartoonist. This began with cartoons for the Boston University student paper. When he went to New York University, he hoped to be closer to career opportunities. As an undergraduate there, he did cartoons for the *New York University Medley.* He became the art editor in 1934. This was a publication on the order of the *New Yorker.* His cartoons fitted that mold. Only once did they show the situations of the blacks during those times.

After his graduation, Romare spent a year and a half at the Art Students League, studying with George Grosz. This artist's work had been suppressed in his native Germany, so he immigrated to the United States. With Grosz as teacher and mentor, Bearden learned the basics. He studied the work of Dürer, Ingres, Hans Holbein, Brueghel, and Daumier. They were all master draftsmen; the latter two were noted satirists. From 1935 to 1937, Bearden did weekly cartoons for the *Baltimore Afro-American.* His work was on the editorial page. It was often critical of the black condition and of the impending war in Europe. The country was in the Depression years. Workers were jobless. Most artists found it hard to support themselves, no matter what kind of art they did. The WPA Federal Art Project was created in 1935. This program helped people in the arts find work and get more training in their fields. Romare took a job as a caseworker for the New York City Department of Welfare in 1938. He worked out of the Harlem office. This provided a reliable income and a chance to paint during his off-hours. Also, his experiences as a caseworker added images of the lives of people in the cities to his memories of the rural South.

Bearden's work was in two exhibitions in 1941. *The Visitation* and *Woman Picking Cotton* were in a show titled "Contemporary Negro Art" at the McMillen Building in New York City.

The Bridge and *After Church* were displayed in a large exhibit of American Negro Art at the Downtown Gallery on East 51st Street. The latter exhibit had two purposes. The first was to show the contribution of black artists in the nineteenth and twentieth centuries. The second was to encourage the purchase of these works and their donation to museums and other institutions.

The United States had plunged into war after the bombing of Pearl Harbor, Hawaii, on December 7, 1941. Romare Bearden joined the U.S. Army, 1st Headquarters, 15th Regiment, the 372nd Infantry Division, an all-black unit. He spent his entire service time in the United States. Like other black servicemen, he experienced prejudice during his years on duty.

Bearden was discharged from the service in 1945. By October 1945 his *The Passion of Christ* series was exhibited at the Samuel Kootz Galleries. The series included 11 oils and 11 watercolors.

In four days, ten watercolors and seven oils had been sold. Two months later The Museum of Modern Art purchased *He Is Risen* from the same series. These works received great acclaim from art critics. During this period we seem to see the influence of Cubism, of flatness, of the African masks Picasso had admired, and his arrangements of forms and lined patterns. After *The Passion of Christ* series came a series of paintings motivated by the poet Garcia Lorca's "Lament for a Bull-fighter: Ignacio Sanchez Mejias." Hemingway's novel, *Death in the Afternoon,* about the civil war in Spain, and Picasso's *Bullfight* or his *Guernica* could also have shaped the interests of artists like Bearden. His *The Bull Bellowed Like Two Centuries, You Are Dead Forever, Bull with Bullfighter, Formed of Tears,* and *Banderillas of Darkness* made up the new series. There were twelve oil paintings and nine watercolors. Bearden was ever looking for ways to control his medium, the colors he wanted to use, and the feelings of frustration that can occur in a creative person.

In May 1949, a good friend proposed that Romare spend time in Paris. Paris was again the place for artists and writers. As a former soldier, Romare could take advantage of the G.I. Bill. This bill gave veterans money for tuition, books, supplies, and living expenses at government-approved schools. Veterans used these grants to begin or complete their educations in every area of study. Many would never have had the opportunity otherwise. The nation benefited just as much. It gained a huge force of educated citizens who could take their places in the artistic, professional, and technical fields.

Bearden studied philosophy at the Sorbonne. He also enrolled in French language study at the Institut Britannique and plunged into the study of art, past and present. He made friends with a number of well-known artists. He also visited all the art galleries and exhibits, doing little painting himself, but just absorbing everything he saw and heard. He left for the United States at summer's end, then returned to France for a few months the next year.

In the mid-1950s, Abstract Impressionism had begun to displace Cubism. Painters did not try to show any particular subject with any realism. They were interested in color relationships; their work contained large swaths of color contrasting with others. Bearden found it difficult to work with this improvisational kind of painting.

Around this time, Bearden also explored his interest in music. As he grew up, there were always musicians in the house. He knew some songwriters, and talked to them about learning how to compose popular music. He thought it might be a good way to make some money. Working with two musician friends, he had some success, but not as much as he had hoped.

Bearden was drifting. Fellow artists told him that he had to get back to painting. He had a period of serious depression. This was relieved by medication, rest, and taking better care of himself. In September 1954 he married Nannette Rohan, who was a positive influence in his life. Besides helping him to regain mental and physical health, she encouraged him to go back to his painting. In 1952 he returned to his job for the Department of Welfare. This meant that, as before, he could concentrate on his art when not at work.

Changes in Romare's use of color had begun. He found that trying nonrepresentational forms with new color methods gave him a path away from Cubism. He used flat, strong, primary colors for figures, which contrasted with **collage** additions. Increased use of oils made for more experiments. He tried gluing down layers of various kinds of papers such as rice paper, brushing paint over the paper, then ripping off layers. He was creating strips and shapes of light visible through varied colors.

Bearden's first one-man show since 1949 was held in November 1955 in the Barone Gallery. His oils and watercolors were favorably reviewed by critics. They praised his new use of layered oils and brighter watercolor washes. He had become acquainted with a Chinese man, Mr. Wu. Mr. Wu ran a bookshop, and knew a great deal about traditional Chinese calligraphy and painting. Bearden learned about characteristics of Chinese landscape painting—the flatter space, for instance, and the far distance appearing larger, not smaller, as in Western art. He began to use oils in a more translucent way. He washed layers of turpentine over an oil surface to build up transparent layers of color. The process was in a way similar to his layering of rice papers.

In 1960 his large abstractions of the 1950s were given an exhibit at the Michel Warren Gallery. By April 1961, Bearden was asked to present his work for a one-man show at the Cordier-Warren Gallery. This gallery was relatively new. It had works of such well-known artists as Dubuffet, Noguchi, and Duchamp. Bearden's submissions were all nonrepresentational and untitled. They used the controlled, thinned-paint techniques that he had developed.

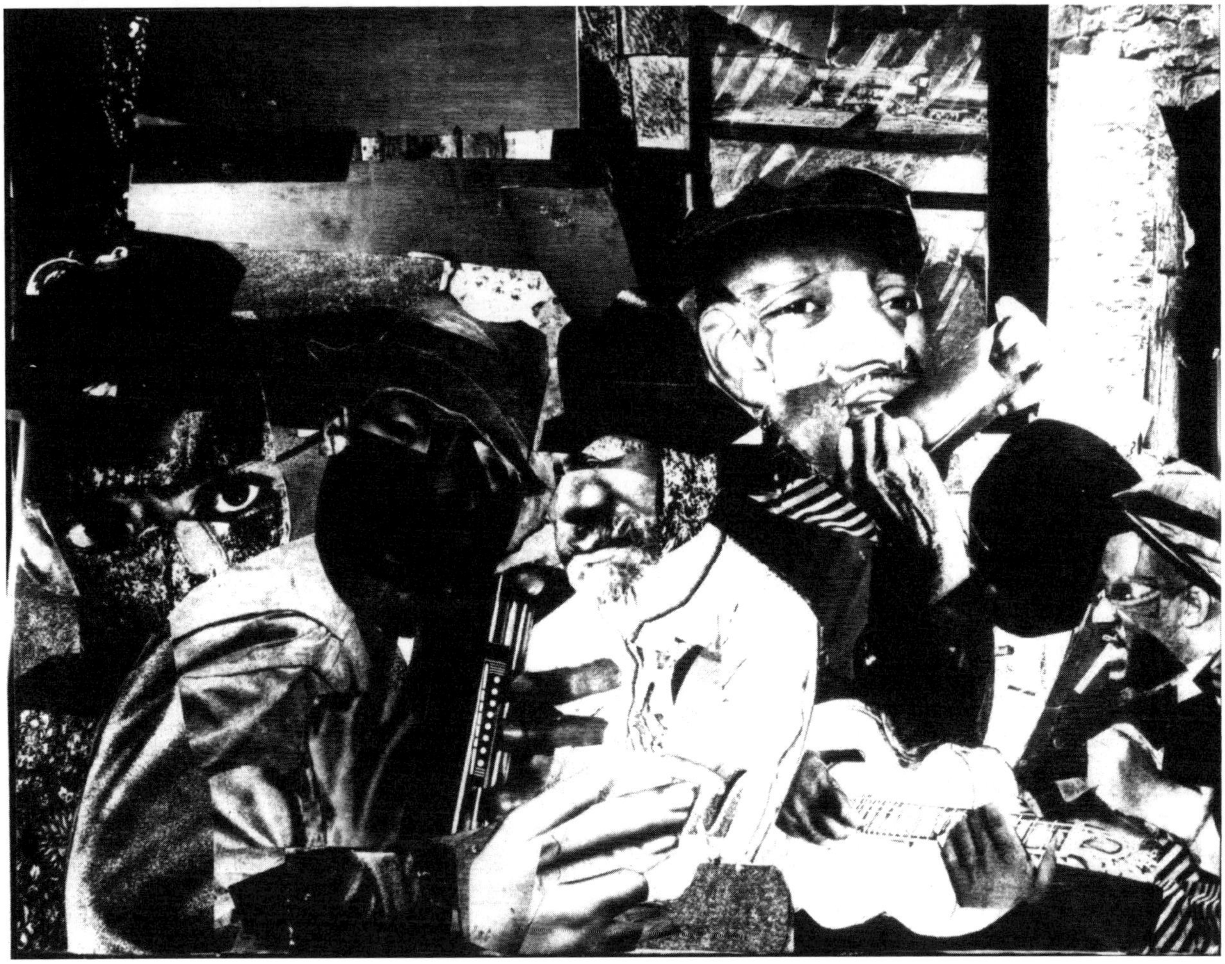

Figure 58
Train Whistle Blues #1, 1964
Romare Bearden

Again, he received much favorable notice from the critics.

Bearden's collection, "Projections," including the **photomontage** *Train Whistle Blues #1* (see Figure 58), was shown in October 1964 in the Cordier-Eckstrom Gallery. This work grew from his concern with the position of black artists and the political condition of the country in the early 1960s. His concerns were shared by other black artists with whom he formed the Spiral Group. Bearden suggested that the group collectively create a photomontage of photographs that he had collected. This would be an expression of the position of blacks in America. Nothing came of his idea as a group piece, but he acted on his own with montages measuring about 8" × 11". These were later enlarged to 6' × 8'. Later, Eckstrom saw the enlargements. He wanted to use them in an exhibit, providing that Romare could create 20 more. Eckstrom suggested the title for the collection: "Projections." They were shown first at the Cordier-Eckstrom Gallery in October 1964. The next year they were shown in the Corcoran Gallery in Washington, D.C.

As Bearden developed his collage techniques, various themes appeared. These included life in the South; Harlem, which had been his home for many years, and the jazz scene there; steel mills; the island of St. Martin in the West Indies, where Nannette's parents and relatives lived; and the people he met through his work in the Welfare Department. His collages were often grouped together. For example: *The Prevalence of Ritual, Of the Blues, Of the Blues: Second Chorus, Rituals of the Obeah, The Odysseus Collages, Profile/Part I: The Twenties, Profile/Part II: The Thirties.* The earlier collages tended to have more people and objects. The later ones had fewer. As he cut out pieces, they were reassembled into parts of faces, bodies, objects, surrounding structures and landscapes—all related through use of color. He knew from experience the importance of keeping open to new ideas and concepts. He had learned that getting stuck in one method can harm an artist's career. He kept in mind artists of the past who did not stagnate. As he tried one method after another, he went forward. His "reinvention" of collage developed from abstract paintings in which he tried new methods and developed textures and layered tones. He seemed seldom at a loss for new approaches. The later collages were often done in vivid, splashy colors, like *Family,* done in 1986 (see Color Plate 21). Bearden also used fewer figures in dramatic surroundings. In the *Of the Blues* series, singers, musicians, and instruments are arranged so that one can easily connect with the subject matter.

Toward the last years of Bearden's life his health was poor. Still, this did not prevent his steady contributions to the art world. His work continued to be exhibited in shows and galleries. He received recognition that would have gratified any artist. By spring of 1988 he was hospitalized for the last time; he died on March 12. A memorial service was held for him in the Cathedral Church of Saint John the Divine. There were speeches, prayers, music, and dancing, reminiscent of the kind of enjoyment that he and his art had given to so many.

Glossary

collage an art method in which paper, cloth, wood, and miscellaneous materials are arranged and glued on a base or background

photomontage similar to collage, but made up of photographs of related things, people, and ideas, trimmed and glued to a background

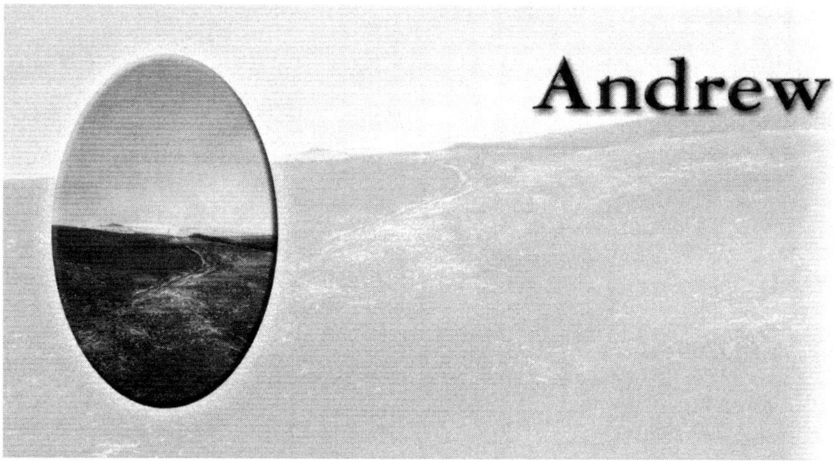

Andrew Wyeth
b. 1917

Andrew Wyeth combines a realistic style with an element of abstraction. His paintings have been called nineteenth-century realism, abstract realism, magic realism, and just plain realism. Wyeth himself calls his style abstract. We know what the subject of the painting is, but the composition and use of colors are designed to create a particular mood. He uses some elements and omits others. Wyeth's favorite media are watercolor and egg tempera. He was not caught up in the art of the 1930s, in which regionalism or social comment played a part. His art is highly personalized—an expression of the people, the landscapes, and objects that have meaning for him. Such diverse things as a bucket of blueberries, old soldiers, a coat hung on a wall, walking boots, and interesting people have all appeared in his paintings. He likes to paint the landscape in winter and early spring when colors are subtle and the trees are bare. The colors suit his tempera palette, **low-key** and subdued. In many paintings the space around the objects or people becomes an important element of the composition. Wyeth does not want people to look at his painting just to see how well he has painted the fine details. He prefers that, through his paintings, people be reminded of memories of their own past or experience new feelings in the present. Not shallow nostalgia but depth of emotion is his goal.

Wyeth has been influenced by the watercolors of Winslow Homer and the work of Piero della Francesca (in the Italian Renaissance) and Albrecht Dürer. Dürer's greatest work, to Wyeth's thinking, is *The Large Piece of Turf.*

In making a watercolor, Wyeth begins with splashes of color laid on in the background, and then adds forms and careful detail with dry-brush technique. Watercolor allows him to get an idea for a painting down on paper quickly. He feels this lets him express the freer side of his nature. Then, with smaller brushes, he dips into the paint, squeezes out excess paint, and separates the bristles to make a fan-like shape. As the brush moves on the paper, separate lines of paint in various widths are created. One of his first dry-brush paintings was *Faraway,* a painting of his son Jamie when he was a child. The boy wears a coonskin cap and is sitting on the grass. It was begun as a watercolor, with the dry-brush technique used for the fur of the cap. Wyeth believes that Dürer must have used dry brush in his watercolors.

In the 1940s Wyeth turned to tempera. He prefers egg tempera. He likes its dryness, its flatness, and the way it forces him to tighten up his technique. His most detailed, controlled paintings are done in egg tempera on panels that are first coated with gesso. In preparing the paint, dry pigments, which he often grinds himself, are mixed with egg yolk and then diluted with water. He uses mineral pigments from all over the world, and likes using natural materials. His colors are very low-key; some paintings are almost **monochromatic.** The quality of the tempera pleases him. Before beginning a picture, he often makes a watercolor sketch of his ideas. Tempera paint is applied in thin layers, one upon another. As in watercolor, the broad areas go on first, with the objects and details painted last. Egg tempera is a very tough surface. After drying for six months it can even be scrubbed.

Wyeth was born in 1917. He grew up as the youngest in a family of five children. His father, Newell Convers Wyeth, was a well-known illustrator. His best-remembered pictures are found in the series of children's books published by Charles Scribners Sons. N.C. Wyeth loved fantasy and shared with the family not only that love, but also a love of music, poetry, and literature. Part of the time the older children were educated at home by tutors because N.C. did not believe in the structured teaching of the schools. He wanted his children to have the freedom to create art, music, and indeed whatever caught their interest. The holidays were especially exciting. For example, the painting studio was decorated with pumpkins, corn, lanterns, and candles to make an autumn scene for the family Halloween parties. At Christmas, N.C. dressed as a Father Christmas figure. He climbed onto the roof of the house, stamped about with jingling bells, and then climbed down to distribute presents. He believed in becoming totally involved in whatever he did, and wanted his children to do the same. Taking his youngsters on hikes across the countryside around Chadds Ford, Pennsylvania, where they lived, he urged them to really see their surroundings. He wanted them to see the colors, shadows, and textures, hear the sounds, and smell what they saw. Even the fury of thunderstorms, wind, and blizzards was seen as high drama and excitement.

Though the older children had the experience of going to school, Andrew did not. His health was poor. He was educated entirely at home. He did not have formal instruction in drawing and painting until he was 15, although he had been doing both on his own since childhood. He had made his first pen and ink drawings when he was about ten, drawing the islands in Maine where the family vacationed. At about this time he began using watercolors. He was allowed the freedom of using the media and methods that appealed to him.

Andrew's formal training began, with his father as his only teacher. At first it was hard to accept the discipline. His first drawing task was to draw an old flintlock pirate pistol. His father had chosen something that would catch Andrew's interest. He drew it over and over, first in one position, then another, for five months. It did not take long for him to become intensely interested in the task. The next project was making drawings of cubes and a sphere. Following that, he painted in oil from a still life of apples on draped cloth. Next he made paintings of a copy of Beethoven's death mask, then a large cutlass against drapery. His father taught without pressure, helping him to make steady progress. By the time Andrew was 18 some of his watercolors were taken by a New York art dealer and sold in his gallery. Andrew knew he needed more knowledge and experience. His father helped him study anatomy, beginning with drawings of a skeleton. Then they hired local people to model for drawings. His father seemed to know when to help his son move on to the next phase of his training. Andrew learned to really "get inside" the object or person he was painting.

By the early 1940s Wyeth had to make the decision whether to become an illustrator, like his father, or to continue as a painter in the fine arts sense. Some of his pen drawings had been published as illustrations when he was only 12. In 1943 other work had been sold as illustrations. He was offered a contract to illustrate for *The Saturday Evening Post.* He decided to concentrate on painting. He knew that his father had not been able to find the time for painting while he worked in illustration. Wyeth had married Betsy James in 1940. She, too, wanted him to stay with painting. She has been a valuable asset to Wyeth during their life together. She arranges their schedule to allow him the time he needs to be alone to paint, take walks, and gather ideas for his paintings.

The death of N.C. Wyeth in an accident in 1945 grieved Andrew profoundly. His relationship with his father had been deeper and more intense than what most sons and fathers experience. N.C. had been father, teacher, and friend. Andrew believes that the turning point in his career came after his father's death. He wanted to use all his father had taught him to become all he could as an artist. His first tempera painting done

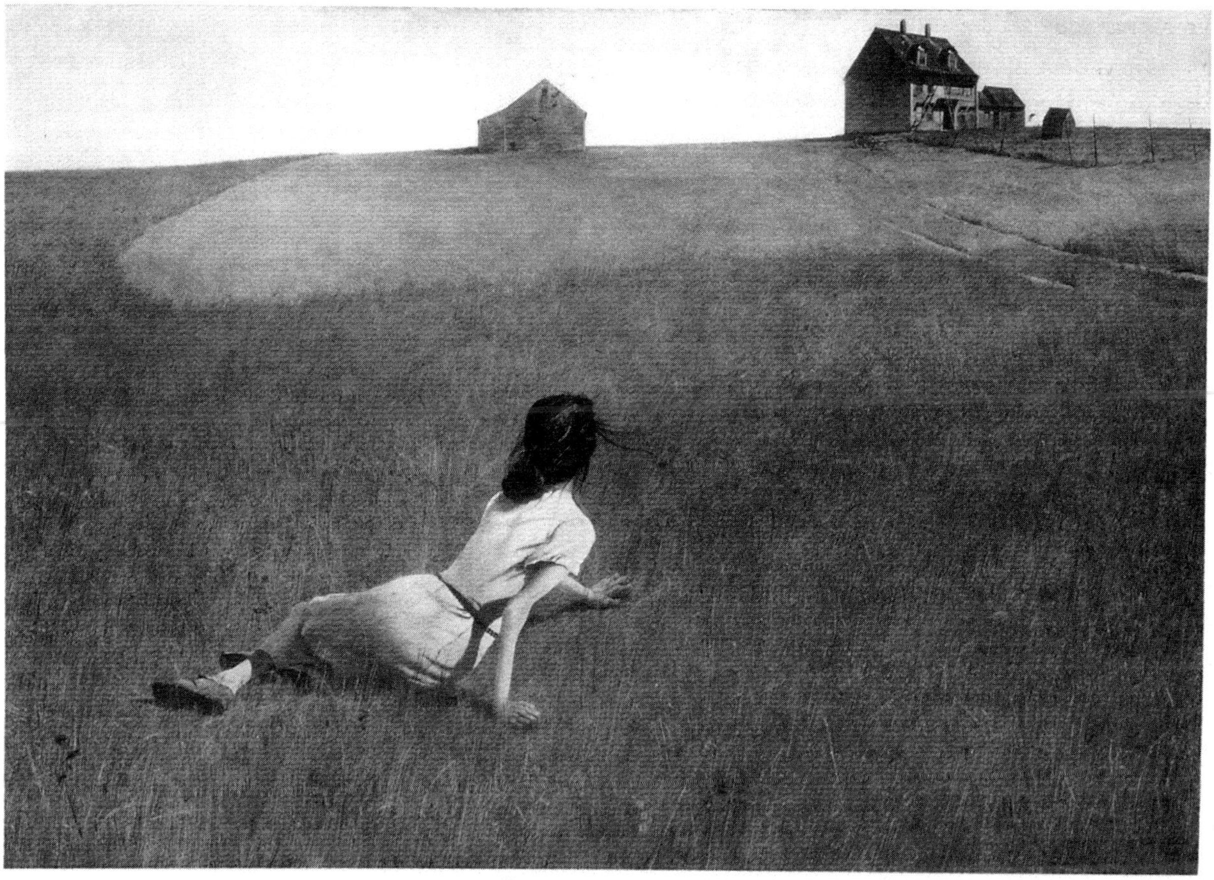

Figure 59
Christina's World, 1948
Andrew Wyeth

after this was *Winter 1946,* a picture of a boy running down a bare hill in winter. Behind that hill is the railroad track on which his father's car had been struck. Other paintings made during that decade reflect both the gloom of that wartime period and the emotional stress Wyeth felt.

The artist spends his year between Chadds Ford and Cushing, Maine. As he grew up, his family had also lived in those areas. Wyeth and his wife have restored the buildings of an old grain mill in Chadds Ford. They live in the miller's house. The legend built up around Wyeth portrays him as a solitary painter who paints the countryside and seldom leaves it. It is true that he spends much of his time at home, but he certainly is part of the modern world. He does value **solitude** for his work. This includes rambling about the countryside, developing ideas for his paintings. He has a lively imagination. On long walks he likes to think about what his environment was like long ago—who lived there, and how—the kind of personal involvement his father had encouraged in his children on other long walks. To strangers Wyeth may appear to be shy and reserved. To those who know him better, he is outgoing and **congenial.** When he paints he hates to have someone watching or talking to him. He likes to become absorbed in his work without being distracted.

Some of Wyeth's best-known works have involved two families and their farms. In Chadds Ford, Karl and Anna Kuerner lived close to the Wyeths. As a boy Wyeth used to visit them to talk to Karl about his experiences in World War I as a German soldier. The Kuerner house, farm buildings, and animals (and the Kuerners themselves) have often been subjects of Wyeth paintings. Among these are *Lamplight, Brown Swiss, Spring Fed, Groundhog Day, Karl, Anna Kuerner, The Kuerners,* and *The German.* The painting *Karl* is the one Wyeth considers his best. The man is seated in the third floor of his house. Above him are hooks on which sausages were hung in the winter. A landscape of wide open space and hills called *Snow Flurries* (see Color Plate 22) is also from the Kuerner series.

Paintings of the Olsons and their seaside farm and buildings probably came about because Betsy Wyeth had known the Olsons since she was a little girl. She introduced Wyeth to them shortly after she and Andrew first met in Cushing, Maine. Christina and Alvaro were sister and brother. Alvaro had been a fisherman until his sister's health made it impossible for her to be left alone on the farm for long periods. She had been crippled by polio when she was a child. Wyeth came to spend much time at their house, talking, sketching, and painting. An upstairs room was turned into a place for him to work. One of his best-known paintings from the Olson group is *Christina's World* (see Figure 59), done in 1948. Her world was a small one, limited to the house and grounds around it. Other paintings include *Anna Christina, Miss Olson and a Kitten, Christina Olson,* and *Oil Lamp,* in which Alvaro sits beside a lamp—the only painting of Alvaro. Pictures of the house and farm include *Wind from the Sea, Breakfast at Olsons, Weather Side,* and the final painting, *End of Olsons.*

In 1986, a trove of secret Wyeth paintings of another local model was revealed by the artist, creating a sensation in the art world. The model, Helga Testorf, had been a nurse to Karl Kuerner, and had worked for Wyeth's sister in Chadds Ford. Wyeth produced 240 drawings and paintings of Helga over a period of 15 years, and had kept the existence of almost all this work completely hidden.

Wyeth's works are not, of course, limited to the models mentioned above. He has painted other people in Cushing as well as in Chadds Ford. The sea and the countryside provide continually changing subject matter. While realism in painting gained in popularity and acceptance in the 1980s, Wyeth's work shows greater depth of feeling than is often found in the photo-realism styles of the 1980s.

Glossary

low-key low in intensity or value

monochromatic from **mono** (meaning one) and **chroma** (meaning color): a color plan limited to one color with its value changed by adding black or white, or its intensity changed by using its complement

solitude the state of being alone

congenial friendly

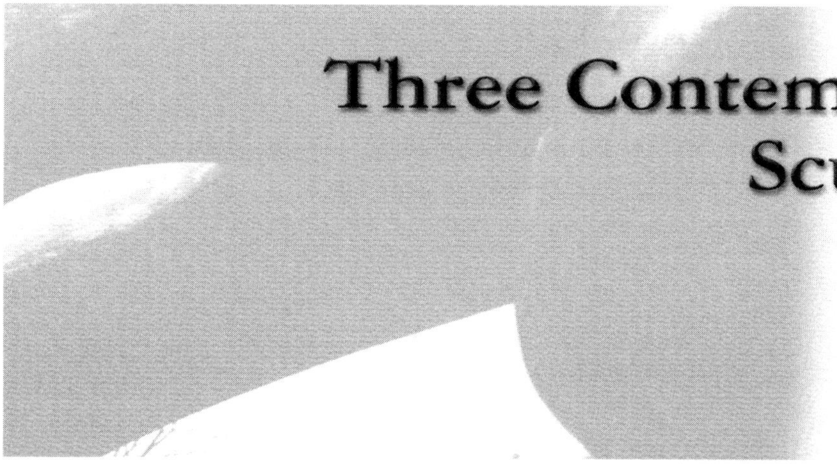

Three Contemporary Sculptors

SCULPTURE, along with painting, has undergone radical changes in our modern era. The territory defined by the word "sculpture" can now include a $5\frac{1}{2}$' reclining squeezed toothpaste tube as well as the more recognizable animal and human figures artists have been making for thousands of years.

How did this come to be? Well, mostly it is the result of tremendous change during the last hundred years. The twentieth century saw the rapid growth of science and technology, along with two global wars and numerous other conflicts. To many people it seems that nothing is certain anymore, and that technology has changed our lives forever (perhaps not even for the better). While such major change can be upsetting, it can also open up a world of possibilities, especially for artists. In the twentieth century, sculptors helped in our efforts to adjust to—or resist—the apparently "unnatural" environment being thrust upon us.

Like much of modern painting, modern sculpture may seem baffling when we first see it. An average person in sixteenth-century Florence looking at Michelangelo's *David* could easily admire the statue for its fine representation of courage and beauty, as well as its accomplishment in the carving of marble. An average person today, however, might well be mystified by a construction of wire and papier-mâché that has ears, feet, screwdrivers, and gears sticking out at every angle. A set of glossy black rectangles arranged vertically can be even more puzzling.

Anyone with a real desire to understand—or just enjoy—new sculpture should not be discouraged. It is exciting that "sculpture" now encompasses just about every natural and man-made material we have, and can be as small as a teacup or big enough to dominate a city square.

In this section we will meet three of the world's most admired sculptors: Henry Moore, Barbara Hepworth, and Alexander Calder. Moore and Hepworth were born within a few years of each other in Yorkshire, England. Calder was an American, born in Pennsylvania the same year as Moore. Hepworth and Moore were among the first to break with the classical tradition of sculpture, creating organic forms of simple beauty. Calder, after attending engineering school and joining the Art Students League in New York, experimented with a variety of materials, combining the two kinds of training. His moving abstract sculptures, "mobiles," are possibly his best-known works. Through knowing about the works of these artists, you may begin to expand your vision of art in the twentieth century.

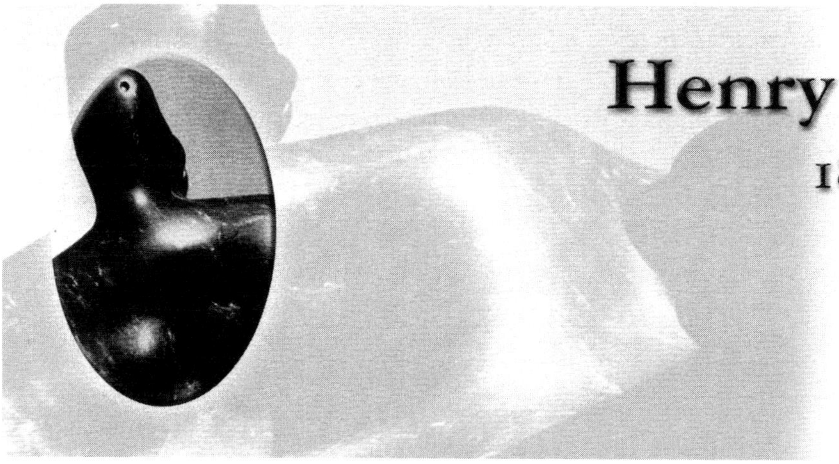

Henry Moore

1898 – 1986

THE SCULPTURE OF HENRY MOORE is closely related to natural forms. He found ways to use **negative** space or volume with **positive** space or volume. He saw that a hole in a sculpture seemed to connect one side with another. Much of his work is larger than life, and meant to be placed outdoors in natural settings.

Henry Moore was born on July 30, 1898, in the village of Castleford in Yorkshire, England. It was a coal mining town. His father was a miner who was self-educated, and wanted all his children to go to school. He believed that by getting an education each child would have a better chance in life than he'd had. He never allowed them to go into the mines with him.

Henry Moore decided to be a sculptor at age 11. He had heard about Michelangelo's sculpture. He also liked stopping by an old Gothic church near his village to look at the sculpture it contained. At school he enjoyed his art classes and was encouraged to pursue a career in art by his teacher, Alice Gostick.

When Moore returned from serving in the army in World War I, Miss Gostick helped him apply to the Leeds School of Art for admission. Some of the returning servicemen were eligible for grants for study. Moore was able to get such a grant. At the school Moore's sculpture instructor was a man who had just come from the Royal College of Art. Moore was his only pupil. In a year's time Moore had finished a two-year course and had received a scholarship to the Royal College of Art in London.

It was exciting for Moore to be on his own in London. He enjoyed visiting the British Museum and spent hours there studying the sculpture that had been brought from other countries. He went to Paris for the first time in 1923 and saw some of the art of Cézanne. In 1925 he was awarded a scholarship for six months of travel in Italy and France. During these early years Moore was influenced by two different kinds of art. He liked the nobility of styles of the old masters. He was also drawn to the more primitive art from Egypt, the Greek sculpture from the Cyclades, Sumerian sculpture, and ancient Mexican stone sculpture. In Paris in 1925 he saw the *Chac Mool,* a sculpture of a Mayan rain spirit in a reclining pose. The next year Moore made the first of his reclining figures, a style for which he became famous.

Moore's work was shown in exhibition for the first time in 1928. Thirty drawings were sold, along with a few sculptures. The public was slow to appreciate his work. Even some of his fellow teachers at the Royal College of Art, where he now taught, threatened to quit unless Moore was dismissed. At about that time his contract was due to end, and he accepted a position at the Chelsea School of Art in London. He was a teacher there on a part-time basis until World War II. Like most artists, he had to have other employment for many years to earn a living while he worked on his own art. On days when he did not teach, he worked in his studio. By the 1930s, he and his wife, Irina, owned a cottage with a sculpture studio on a few acres of land near Canterbury in Kingston.

Moore continued to work in the style he'd developed and gradually won acceptance by the art world and the public. In the years following World War II, he had become one of the world's leading sculptors. It was his aim to combine the abstract elements with the human elements of a figure. Most of his sculpture uses the female figure. Other familiar themes are mother and child, reclining figures, and family groups of mother, father, and child. He strove for an organic form that has warmth and a strong relation to its material. Early in his career he stressed "truth to material," by which he meant carving directly on the material, and using material that was appropriate for the ideas used. His sculpture is in the round (meant to be seen from all sides); it has a different appearance from each point of view. He wanted it to be created "from pressure from within." Sometimes faces are natural; often, however, only an eye, or nose, or other feature is suggested. He used stone, wood, and bronze. He also used open spaces within the material to create a negative space; the surrounding material formed the postive space. In order to make thinner forms that would still be strong, Moore used bronze in later years.

Drawing was always important in Moore's work. He sketched ideas for sculpture, although he stopped short of drawing a three-dimensional picture. He believed that drawing in too much detail would rob him of the excitement of actually creating the sculpture itself. Some of his best-known drawings were done during the bombing raids on London during World War II. The city was being bombed night after night. People began taking blankets and going to the subway tunnels, where they slept on the platforms. The subways became giant air-raid shelters. Moore visited the tunnels during the nights and spent a year developing drawings from his sketches of the sleeping forms. At that time sculpture materials were difficult for him to get, and drawing became a substitute for sculpture. He also visited the coal mines where his father had worked and drew the miners.

Usually an artist has a particular size in which he or she likes to work. A painter may paint anything from a few inches to many feet in height and width. Sculptors also like to work within a particular scale. Moore liked a scale just over life size. Since he wanted his work to be placed and seen outdoors, he tried to fit a sculpture to an open space.

A sculptor may do his or her own bronze casting of pieces that are small enough to be managed. Larger sculptures are taken to foundries and often cast in pieces, which are then assembled. Freshly made, they are bright and shiny. As bronze is exposed to air and moisture, the color usually turns shades of green. An artist may use chemicals on the surface to control the color and get reds, black, or various greens as the metal weathers.

To get ideas for his sculpture, Moore collected rocks, bones, shells, driftwood, and found objects, which he kept in a small studio. He also kept

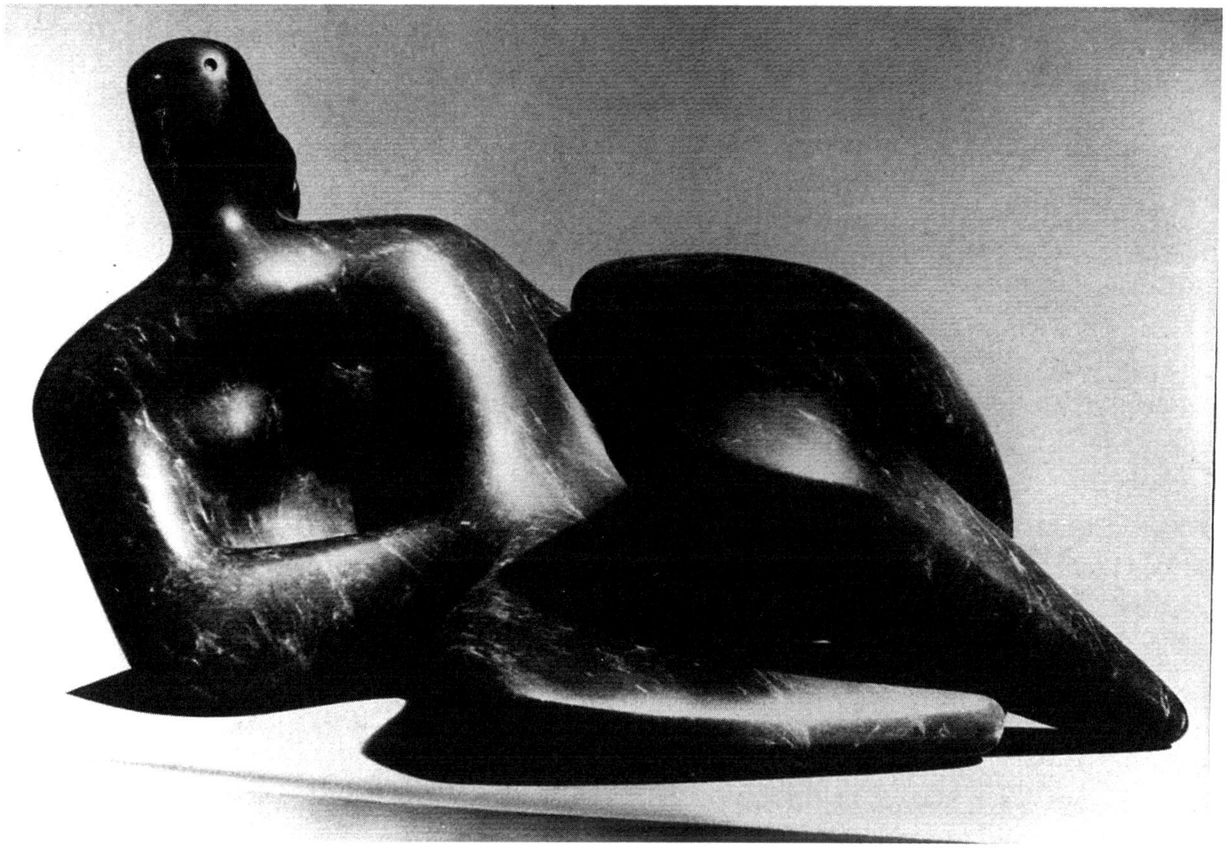

Figure 60
Reclining Figure: Curved, 1977
Henry Moore

sketchbooks that he filled with drawings, doodles, and sketches. He worked out his ideas in small models, or maquettes, perhaps no larger than his hand, using clay or plaster. He imagined the model in the actual size it would be when it was made in the final size. When a sculpture was commissioned, Moore sometimes reached an agreement to make more than one casting. In this way, several sculptures were made of the same design, and could be kept by the artist, sold, or given away.

The *Madonna and Child* for the Church of St. Matthew in Northampton was done in 1943. Before Moore decided to take this commission, he made sketches and small models of ideas for the work. He wanted to create a work of nobility and grandeur, devoid of sentimentality. The Madonna is seated with the Child on her lap. Her face wears a sadness and dignity that reminds one of the expression of another Madonna's face—that in Michelangelo's famous *Pietà*. The sculpture styles are entirely different; Moore's Madonna seems to look into the future of the Child she holds.

Other family themes followed, notably *Family Group* in 1944. Moore's mother died in 1944; his only child, a daughter, Mary, was born in 1946. The family themes may have been related to Moore's personal feelings at that time about his own family.

In 1951 Moore visited Greece. This trip was followed by two sculptures that seem to have been influenced by what he saw there. *Fallen Warrior* and *Warrior with Shield* are two of his rare uses of male figures other than in his family groups. *King and Queen* was also made at about this same time. He began *Warrior with Shield* after finding a pebble on the beach. It reminded him of a stump of a leg. He thought of battle scenes, and began working on ideas. It was the first male figure he did as a single and separate figure.

In 1957–1958 Moore was commissioned to make a sculpture for the United Nations Educational, Scientific and Cultural Organization (UNESCO) headquarters in Paris. At first he planned to make a reclining figure in bronze, but decided that it would become too dark for the place where it would be seen as it weathered. He chose to use **travertine** instead. He took his plaster models to Italy and worked there. The sculpture weighs 39 tons and is more than 16' long. With the help of local stone carvers, he worked on the sculpture for almost a year. The travertine matches the stone at the top of the UNESCO building and is weathering to the kind of color Moore had in mind.

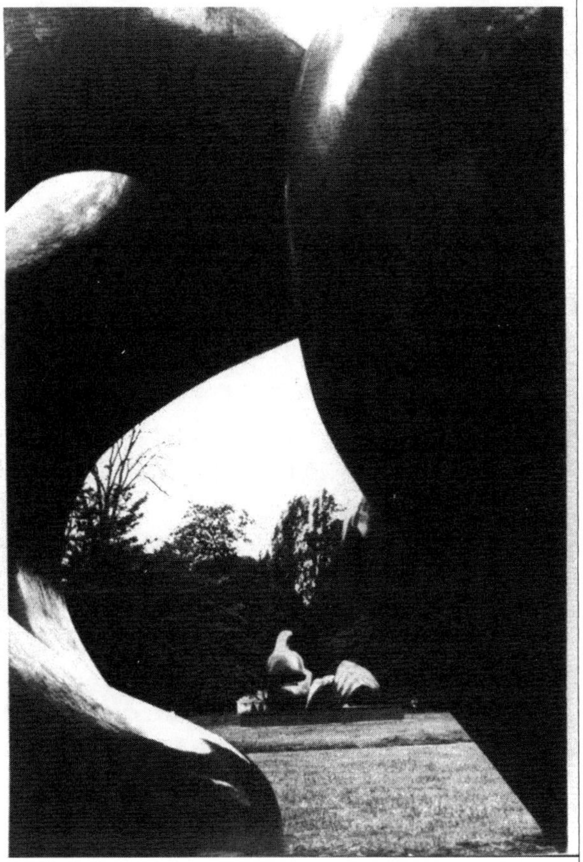

Figure 61
Three Piece Reclining Figure: Draped, 1975
Henry Moore

Other later pieces are *Atom Piece* (1966) for the University of Chicago, which is a reminder of the splitting of the atom with a mushroom cloud formation at the top; *Locking Piece* (1964); and *Knife Edge Two-Piece* (1965).

Moore was honored in the United Kingdom and other countries. He received honorary degrees from Cambridge and Oxford in his own country, and from Harvard in the United States. The Order of Merit was presented to him in 1963; it is the highest distinction that can be given to a British subject. Henry Moore never lost touch with his beginnings. He was proud of his working-class background, of his farm-laborer ancestors, and of his coal miner father. In later years he lived simply and employed young sculptors and office help, working with them in the morning and alone in his studio in the afternoons. From this late period in his career come *Reclining Figure: Curved* (see Figure 60) and *Three Piece Reclining Figure: Draped* (see Figure 61). His art collection—including works by Corot, Degas, Renoir, Rodin, and Cézanne—was the most visible sign of his wealth and success. From 1940 until his death on August 31, 1986, his permanent home was at Perry Green, Much Hadham, in Herefordshire, about 20 miles from London.

Glossary

positive/negative shapes and forms (positive space) and the space around the shapes and forms (negative space)

travertine a light-colored limestone quarried in Italy

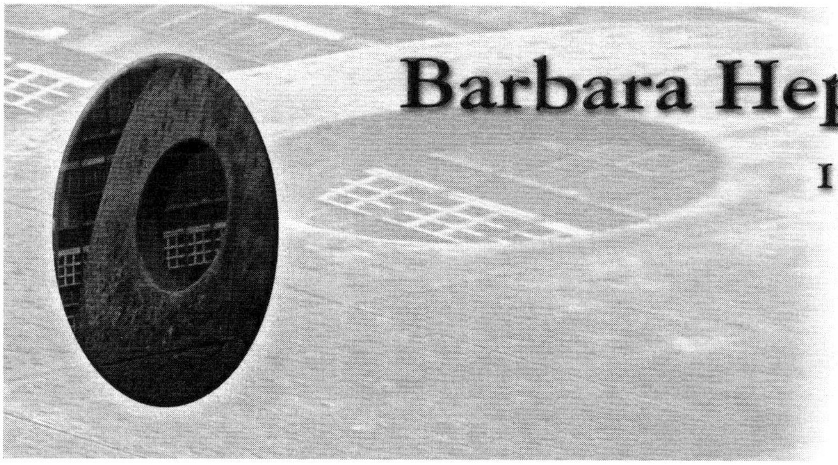

Barbara Hepworth

1903 – 1975

Barbara Hepworth was born in 1903 in Yorkshire, England. Her childhood years were spent in Wakefield with her parents, and sometimes in Dewsbury with relatives. It was a bleak and dreary area, typical of Britain's harsh manufacturing towns, as the Industrial Revolution slowly eased to a stop. When Barbara began school, she was amazed and delighted to see the reproductions of paintings by the old masters that hung on the walls of the classrooms. Her first introduction to sculpture, to pictures of the three-dimensional forms, came through a program by a speaker who used slides to illustrate the presentation. How different these were from the paintings on the school walls! When she was older, she accompanied her father as he drove around the Yorkshire dales. Here began her lifelong love and appreciation of hills and valleys, of texture and color, proportion and movement, gestures and rhythm, of relationships between one form and another.

Hepworth's mother was a frugal homemaker, but she managed for Barbara and her sisters to study music and dance. Her father was an engineer and a very gentle and thoughtful person. He did not give preference to boys; he thought that his daughters should have the same chance for an education as his son. Hepworth has said that she learned a great deal from him. She inherited his aptitude for form and construction; he did not "teach" her, but just let her absorb it.

Barbara was enrolled in the Wakefield Girls' High School. The headmistress, Mrs. McCroben, recognized and encouraged her talent. She won a scholarship to the Leeds School of Art and left home at 16 to study there. Within a year she won a scholarship to the School of Sculpture at the Royal College of Art in London. She had met the sculptor Henry Moore when he was attending the Leeds School; now they were both attending the Royal School of Art at the same time. (In later years, when both were established sculptors, their styles were thought to have similar qualities.) Within three years both had received their diplomas and had been granted West Riding traveling scholarships for a year's study abroad.

Hepworth chose to go to Italy. There she was entranced by the light and warmth and color, perhaps as she had been fascinated by the rolling forms in the Yorkshire dales. During the first year, she lived in Florence. From there she explored Tuscany and saw the Romanesque architecture, the landscapes bathed in sunlight, Perugia, Assisi, Siena, and the works of Cimabue, Giotto, and Michelangelo. She sketched and soaked up all that the area offered. During the following 18 months, she stayed on in Italy, living in Rome, and continued her exploration and study of art in that country.

During this time she met and married John Skeaping, who was also a sculptor. Hepworth learned carving from an Italian master carver named Ardini. At one point he told her that "marble changes color under different people's hands." This led her to think of greater coordination between the head and the hand. She has said that this thought recurred again and again and helped develop her greatest interests.

Not long after Hepworth and her husband, Skeaping, came back to England, their son, Paul, was born. Having a baby apparently put stress on their relationship. She wanted to put her energies into her work, her child, and home, but her husband wanted his freedom. Others had warned her that she couldn't possibly handle her work, husband, and family, but she had thought otherwise.

In 1930 Hepworth met Ben Nicholson and saw his paintings. In them she saw a movement like that in her sculpture, ideas of color and form and approaches to the object in landscape. In 1931 they entered a marriage that was to last 20 years. She sharpened his sense of form. He helped her see the world of color. Each served the role of esteemed critic to the other. They traveled and had contacts with the **avant-garde** of art in Europe. Back in the United Kingdom, they were active in moving some English artists into more modern styles.

In 1934 Hepworth and her husband had triplets—two girls and a boy, named Rachel, Sarah, and Simon. They were living in a small basement flat near their studio. The arrival of three babies instead of one meant that immediate and inventive changes had to be made. Their income was limited to what Nicholson's paintings and reliefs brought in, and the sales of her carvings. The experience of children, though, seemed to deepen their sense of direction and purpose. Hepworth found combining home, children, husband, and working in her studio environment a great inspiration. She arranged the day-to-day routines so that she could go back to her studio and go on from where she had stopped a project. Her husband was involved in his own work, too. They let the children grow up amid all that their parents did. Hepworth said the most difficult times were when someone was ill; she used to work out of the anxiety and strain by concentrating on a new work. She found that if she thought positively, good work could result. If she let herself become overcome by the worry, bad work came from it. She found time to do some work every day, even at midnight, because that was the professional way. Also, Hepworth didn't want to be in competition with male artists. She felt the contribution of both men and women to the field of art was complementary and had nothing to do with being male or female.

Hepworth's sculpture was **organic,** connected to human forms and nature, yet abstract. She carved smaller forms in the beginning—as small as 10"–12". If one is most familiar with some of her large works, it is a surprise to compare them with the small forms. In 1931, she was the first sculptor to cut through the stone. She preferred carving hard materials to modeling or shaping a less resistant substance. She liked to touch the material for the physical pleasure of direct contact with the form. She knew before she started what she wanted to create, and let her intuition guide her on to the completion. It was satisfying to think of the sculptures and their relationships with the people who came to see them, the way people studied each one, walked about, looked through the open spaces, and thought of the forms that stood singly or grouped together. She thought of the spectator as someone who was involved in the sculpture, too.

Hepworth chose basic geometric shapes—spheres, cones, rectangles, and cylinders. She enjoyed their simplicity and the ease with which one shape could combine with another. Often a large form would flow into a smaller one, like a mother and child together. Scooped-out shapes with flowing curves seem to serve as metaphors for the land and sea meeting together, blown by the wind.

The art historian Herbert Read has called Hepworth's sculpture "vitalist" because of the vitality she brought into the sculptural tradition that had remained relatively unchanged since Rodin. She was influenced first by the early Greek and Roman sculpture, then by that of Arp and Brancusi. She believed in "truth to materials"—the need to act honestly in working with a material and its intrinsic qualities. The materials she preferred included walnut, elm, yew, stone, slate, bronze, Nebrasina teak, alabaster, aluminum, and Guarea wood. She sometimes used **maquettes** (small models of a planned sculpture). However, she thought the model was either larger or smaller than the finished work would be. She found it less satisfying in the long run than to see the piece develop in the size she had in mind. When she began work on a new piece, she had a mental picture of what she wanted.

In 1934 Hepworth finished a 14¼" carving called *Large and Small Form.* The "large form" reminds one of one of Henry Moore's reclining figures. The "small form" is slightly raised from the opposite end, facing the larger shape, as though a relationship existed between them.

A 1938 sculpture in teak is titled *Two Forms.* The lower form is like half a solid sphere that has been slightly scooped out to balance the ovoid resting on the top. On that form are carved out three round hollows; the largest is in the lower side, with the other two smaller ones in the upper half, one above the other. The teak is perfectly smooth. One can imagine the hours Hepworth spent working to achieve that surface.

A yew tree was the source of the material for Hepworth's sculpture in 1958. It is titled *Nanjizal,* and is 98" tall, a vertical, elongated shape, open through the center, with its height making it appear slender. It is joined at the top and above the base, the long central area adding to the organic feeling, as though it could have first been found in a forest. The wood is smooth in the Hepworth manner, adding to its feeling of elegance.

As Hepworth began opening up parts of her sculptures, she also thought of adding color to the inner surfaces, not bright or strong color, but more subtle tones, such as whites, blues, and black. Another innovation at about this time was the addition of string or wire stretched across an opening, blending the developed string forms with the open form. An example is *Curved Form (Orpheus),* in which the strings form their pattern across the grain of the wood surface beneath.

In 1957 she found a way to personalize a method of working with bronze. She had large bronze sheets cut to shape, then textured them with files and abrasive tools. The work *Figure (Archaean)* is an illustration of textures tooled into the surface. She created large linear constructions that literally soar into space. At about the same time, she began combining string with brass, blending openness with light, elegance, and dignity. An early sculpture using this technique is titled *Winged Figures I and II.*

Possibly Hepworth's best-known sculpture is *Single Form,* which stands in the plaza of the United Nations (see Figure 62). Dag Hammarskjöld, the late secretary-general of the United Nations, admired and collected her work. He commissioned the sculpture for the plaza in New York City. It has since become a memorial to him following his death in a plane crash. The form is 21' tall, a size that presented many problems. Hepworth had to cope with the stress caused by wind velocity, height, and width. She used the engineering knowledge learned from her father to deal with these problems. Seven pieces were cast to have somewhat diagonal seams to contrast with the huge form.

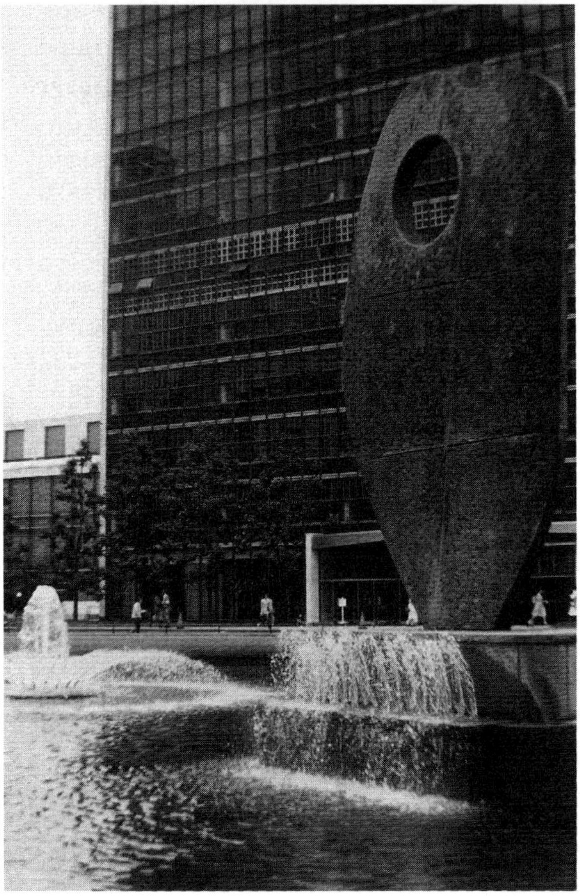

Figure 62
Single Form, 1961–1962
Barbara Hepworth

Creating some of the large works involved special challenges. Hepworth needed to find clients to finance them and appropriate settings for the completed pieces. The group of sculptures *Family of Man: Nine Bronzes,* which Hepworth completed late in her career, resulted after many years of waiting for the money, time, and space. The largest of the group is 11' tall. The other eight bronze pieces are done in variably smaller heights. They are often arranged on a grassy slope; the two tallest are like parent figures, the others placed here and there behind them. Their forms are made up of various sizes of bronze that are like rectangles or cubes with rounded-off edges, hollowed-out sections that may or may not cut through the entire shape. These pieces are welded together, one atop another. The two tallest are made up of four sections, while the smaller ones are constructed of two or three.

By early 1939 the threat of war in Europe began to divert interest away from art. Artists who had lived and worked in France and surrounding countries started to migrate to the United Kingdom and the United States. By the time the war began in the fall of 1939, it was more and more difficult to sell sculptures or paintings. Artists were barely able to earn a living. Hepworth took the children with her to Cornwall just five days before Britain declared war against Germany. In the beginning they stayed with friends. Among her baggage, Hepworth carried with her a maquette for her first sculpture using color, along with her hammer and stone carving tools. Still in Cornwall in early 1940, they were able to find a small house. There she set up a nursery school that she ran for three years. She wasn't able to work on her carvings in the daytime. Still, she did make maquettes for sculpture she planned to do in the future. As most artists do, she had always made sketches and drawings. She could pursue these works using pencil and **gouache** for abstracts, finding ways to use color with form. This activity was best suited for the evening hours. Many of their artist friends had come to Britain from Europe. Some lived in Cornwall, and some came to them for weekend rests from the turmoil in the London area.

Perhaps because she could not work on her sculptures during the war, Hepworth became more and more involved in abstract drawing. She found that drawing with pencil on a hard paint surface was like pressing lines into slate. Unlike life drawing, the lines are twisted, tightened, repeated, added, moved in repeated patterns, allowing the artist free rein. Someone suggested that she might like to do some drawings in an operating room. She did not expect to like it! However, she became totally engrossed. She saw a perfection of concentration and gesture, a "special grace" close to what she tried to achieve in her own work. These drawings are fascinating. They show a rather cloudy, misty surface through which one sees the simple outlined forms of the men and women working in the operating room. Only the eyes seen above the surgical masks and the gloved hands coming through the sleeves of the gowns are drawn in careful detail. Hands may hold surgical tools or a needle threaded to stitch the patient. The contrast between the unarticulated space and the beautifully-depicted eyes and hands is engrossing to a viewer. Hepworth made more than three groups of lithographs. Those who could not afford an expensive sculpture could have the pleasure of owning a drawing through a lithograph.

During the mid-1940s Hepworth and her family moved to a larger house that overlooked St. Ives Bay, from the island to Godrevy lighthouse. Living in that area, she discovered what she called a "pagan landscape" that lay between Land's End, St. Ives, and Penzance. Thereafter it had a very strong effect on her life as an artist. This landscape affected her feelings about sculpture in landscape, light and color as it is affected by the sea, the sky, and winds coming onto the shores. She spent most of her remaining years at St. Ives. She delighted in her surroundings there. She was awarded the Grand Prix for plastic art at the Bienal of Modern Art in Sao Paulo, Brazil in 1959. In addition, she was made a Commander of the British Empire in 1958, and a Dame, a title equivalent to a knighthood, given by the queen.

Barbara Hepworth died in a studio fire in 1975. In her will she had asked that her studio be kept the way it had been in her lifetime. In 1976 the studio was dedicated to her memory.

Glossary

avant-garde those who develop new or experimental concepts, especially in the arts

organic forming an integral part of a whole; coordination of parts

maquettes pronounced ma-'ket; small preliminary models of sculptures

gouache pronounced 'gwash; a method of painting with opaque watercolors; the pigment used in gouache painting

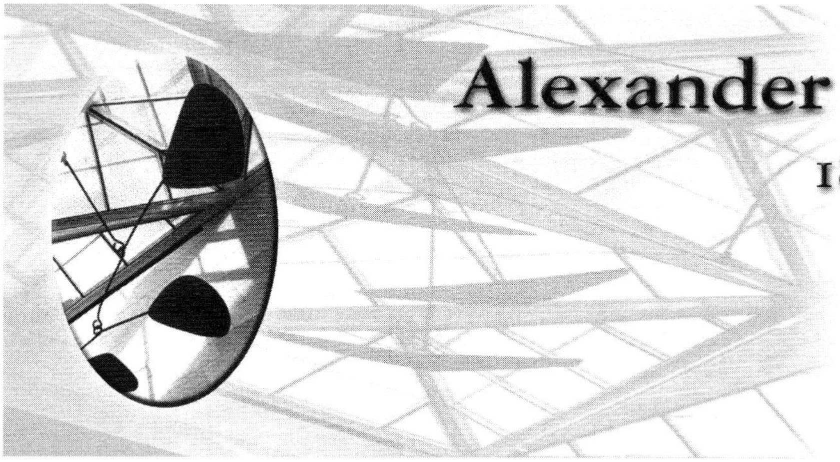

Alexander Calder

1898 – 1976

ALEXANDER CALDER, or "Sandy," is one who has seemed, like many of his moving sculptures, never to be still for a moment. In his wire circus figures, he brought us humor and fancy. He has given us, in his "mobiles," an entirely new definition of sculpture. In his giant abstract outdoor sculptures, he brings us our link between the earth and the sky—the great connection between being a human being and having a boundless, immortal imagination.

Calder was born in Pennsylvania, in the same year as Henry Moore. Both his father and grandfather were sculptors, his mother a painter. But, even **nurtured** as he was by artistic parents, he had no early drive to be an artist himself. He did like to make things, and he was fascinated by gadgets of all kinds.

Sandy decided, in an offhanded sort of way, to go to engineering school. He succeeded there, but the work that followed seemed a great bore to him. He took a drawing class at night. He quit work and hopped a ship to the West Coast to see his sister. He worked in a couple of logging camps. Then, something told him he must go to New York and study to be a painter. In 1923, he went and he, too, joined the Art Students League.

New York fascinated Calder. He was taken with the work of the Ash Can School, and with the sights and sounds of the booming metropolis. Here he discovered the circus. In connection with his work as an illustrator, he went to see the circus every night for the two weeks the circus was in town. During this time, also, he made his first representation of an animal done in wire. Combining engineering and artistry, he made a clock in the form of a rooster.

When he was 28 years old, Calder decided to go to Paris to learn and to work. That was the beginning of his living on two continents. It wasn't long before he had his own studio in Paris, where he began making animals out of wood and wire. These were both ingenious and humorous, and he sold some of them as toys. But he was also making his own "circuses," complete with trapeze artists and animal cages and all the odd characters to be found at a circus.

He began to show his circus to the public, which took an immediate liking to the life and humor in the small wire **caricatures**. Calder began to go back and forth between Paris and the United States, constantly working on and refining his circus, and designing other sculptures that stood on pedestals in order to be admired from all sides. On one of his trips he met Louisa James, whom he married in 1931. They proceeded to establish homes (and studios for Calder) in both France and Connecticut.

Calder experimented with motors for his sculptures. The figures turn and move of themselves, and around each other. Once, during a visit to Mondrian's studio, Calder was suddenly struck with the full meaning of "abstract art." He had an urge to take the rectangular shapes Mondrian had painted and set them in motion. And he wanted to create abstract "things" himself.

He started working with plastic rather than wood; plastic seemed more abstract than wood. He took plastic pieces, shaped them as he wanted, and suspended them on wires, balanced by spheres and other objects. A breath of air would move the shapes around one another.

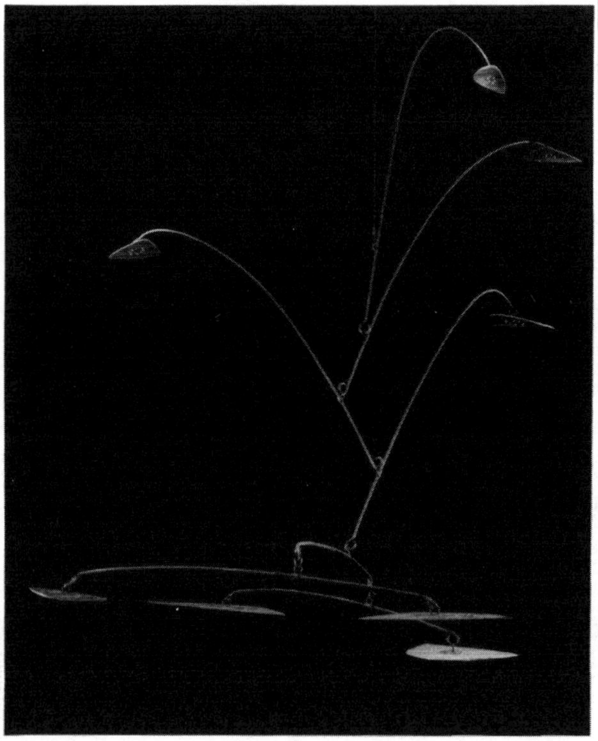

Figure 63
Stainless Stealer, 1966
Alexander Calder

These sculptures became increasingly complex. When Calder asked the artist Marcel Duchamp what to call these artistic balancing acts, Duchamp immediately said, "mobiles." And so they became. An example of one of Calder's mobiles is *Stainless Stealer* (see Figure 63). In the same year, the surrealist painter Jean Arp suggested to Calder that if the moving sculptures were "mobiles," then Calder's other works (which didn't move) would have to be called "stabiles." And so they were.

The mobiles included a group of white disks that balanced off wires and moved around each other. Calder originally called it *Snow Flurries.* There were birds that unfolded their feathers and whirled around. There were dancers and fish, and many more abstract shapes that called on the observer for definition. The stabiles had names like *Nymph, Apple Monster,* and *Shark and Whale.* They may not have moved, but they often had to do with opposites brought into balance. This was often accomplished with a small form balanced on a large form, or a large, gawky figure resting on slender "legs."

Calder and his wife traveled extensively. They shuttled from France to the United States and much farther afield, often and tirelessly. Calder was often referred to as a great bear. A large and friendly man, he had a multitude of friends and supporters wherever he went. Not one to be interested in speaking of art in spiritual terms, he was happy when his friends did the talking for him. Jean-Paul Sartre, Fernand Léger, André Breton, and many other famous artists and writers were often able to put the beauty of the sculptures into words. In an introduction for a New York exhibition, Sartre wrote:

> The "mobiles," which are neither wholly alive nor wholly mechanical . . . may be likened to water grasses in the changing currents . . . they are . . . lyrical inventions, technical combinations of an almost mathematical quality and sensitive symbols of Nature . . .
>
> "Calder's Mobiles," Buchholz Gallery, 1947

Calder, of course, had far more going on than just the mobiles, which were earning him great fame. Starting from the time he made his wife's wedding ring, Calder made jewelry. He made stage sets. He painted for a few months in each year, and dabbled in printmaking and silk-screening. He had a great knack for finding materials for his work in just about anything. During World War II, when aluminum was hard to come by, he cut up his aluminum boat. He created a piece from an old boiler he found in a junkyard. He insisted that outdated Connecticut license plates were excellent raw material for his art. He worked almost entirely in metal in the 1940s.

After the war, Calder's ideas about the size of his work began to get bigger and bigger. So did his work. His mobile *Untitled,* for example, is 29'-10 ½" × 76' (see Figure 64). He started working in plaster and had pieces cast in bronze. He regained an interest in stable sculptures, but these were larger than any he had done before. He began to live most of the time in France, because there was a **foundry** nearby, and he could work with the men who helped him make his giant outdoor

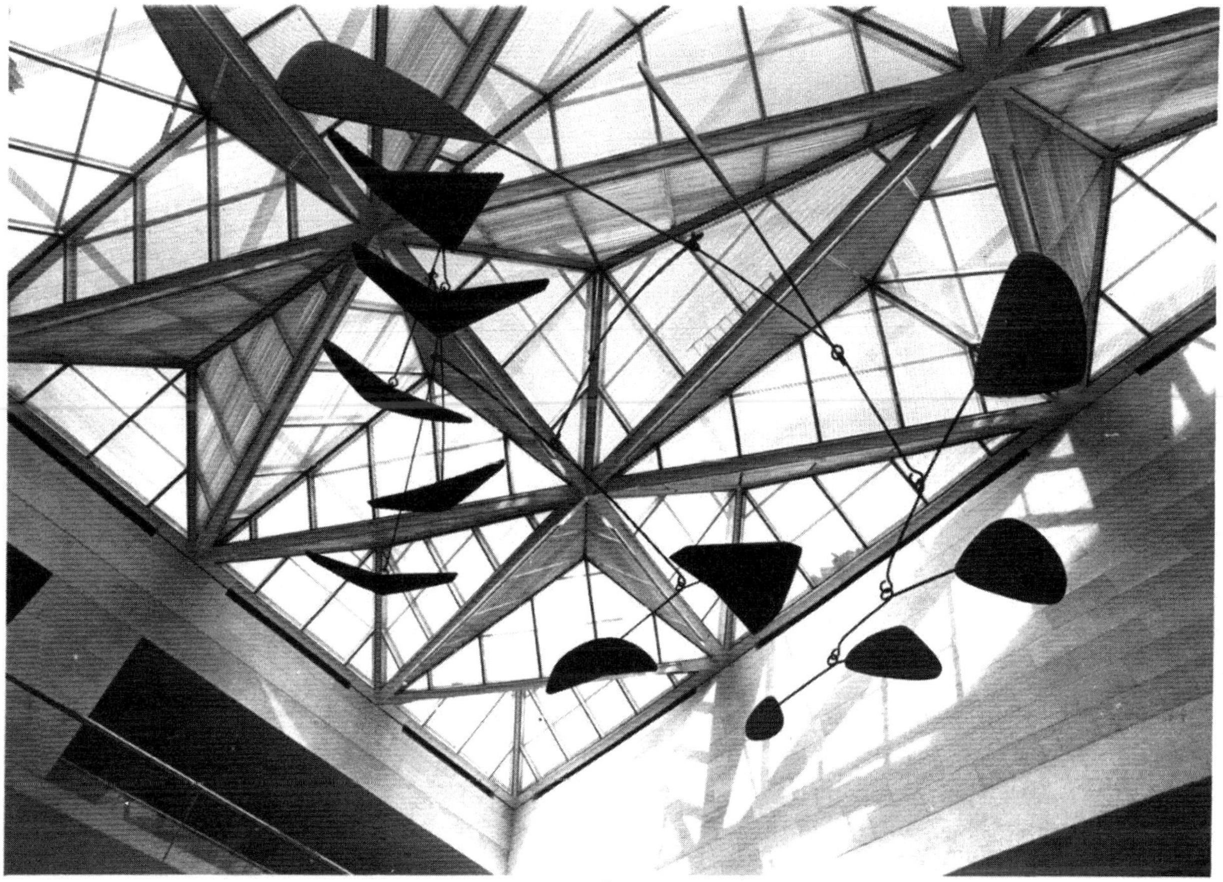

Figure 64
Untitled, 1977
Alexander Calder

sculptures. He made a huge "standing mobile" called *The Spiral* for the UNESCO building in Paris. He had shows of large stabiles in both Paris and New York in the late 1950s. *Crossed Blades,* which is in Sydney, Australia, is 36' high. *Morning Cobweb,* like so many of the large stabiles, is a work that people can walk through, under, and around.

Calder's reputation early on was almost that of an entertainer. He made people laugh with his delightful, spinning sculptures. He rather enjoyed that reputation, but he was also gratified when, over the years, critics and the public accepted him as a "serious" artist. He was commissioned to do grand works for schools, cities, and various institutions. His shows drew enormous crowds of people who thrilled to the now-giant mobiles overhead and the huge, balanced iron structures that pointed to the sky while being firmly planted on the ground.

Poems were written to Calder, the great bear of a man who always spoke in short, abrupt sentences. He is an American bear, but he is loved the world over for the great gifts he brought to the medium of sculpture. Once, when he was asked whether he considered himself a realist, Calder replied, in essence, that if you can imagine something, you can make it, and then automatically, you're a realist. He said, "The universe is real, but you can't see it." Yet Calder imagined it, and made many sculptures called *Universe.* They had globes of wire with spheres that circled around each other and the globes. Calder imagined the universe, and he made it, several times over. So, yes, by his definition he was a realist.

Glossary

nurtured nourished or sustained; promoted development

caricatures representations of a subject or theme in which features are distorted or exaggerated, often producing a comic effect

foundry a place in which metal is melted, put into molds, or cast

Photo Credits—Black and White

Figure 1
Madonna and Child
Giotto di Bondone, c. 1320–1330
National Gallery of Art, Washington
Samuel H. Kress Collection.
Wood; $33\frac{5}{8}$" x $24\frac{3}{8}$"

Figure 2
Christ in Limbo
Giotto di Bondone, c. 1320–1325
Pinakothek, Munich
Tempera on panel; $17\frac{3}{4}$" x $17\frac{1}{4}$"

Figure 3
Giuliano de' Medici
Sandro Botticelli, c. 1478
National Gallery of Art, Washington
Samuel H. Kress Collection
Wood; $29\frac{3}{4}$" x $20\frac{5}{8}$"

Figure 4
The Adoration of the Magi
Sandro Botticelli, early 1480s
National Gallery of Art, Washington
Andrew W. Mellon Collection
Wood; $27\frac{5}{8}$" x 41"

Figure 5
Ginevra de' Benci
Leonardo da Vinci, c. 1474
National Gallery of Art, Washington
Ailsa Mellon Bruce Collection
Wood; $15\frac{1}{4}$" x $14\frac{1}{2}$"

Figure 6
The Virgin of the Rocks
Leonardo da Vinci, c. 1506
Reproduced by courtesy of the Trustees,
The National Gallery, London
Wood; 486" x 307"

Figure 7
Pietà
Michelangelo Buonarroti, 1498–1500
St. Peter's Basilica, The Vatican
Marble

Figure 8
The Creation of Adam (detail),
Michelangelo Buonarroti, 1508–1512
The Sistine Chapel, The Vatican

Figure 9
The Alba Madonna
Raphael Santi, c. 1510
National Gallery of Art, Washington
Andrew W. Mellon Collection
Oil on wood transferred to canvas; $37\frac{1}{4}$"
in diameter

Figure 10
Bindo Altoviti
Raphael Santi, c. 1515
National Gallery of Art, Washington
Samuel H. Kress Collection
Wood; $23\frac{1}{2}$" x $17\frac{1}{4}$"

Figure 11
The Annunciation
Jan van Eyck, 1434–1436
The National Gallery of Art, Washington
Andrew W. Mellon Collection
Transferred from wood to canvas;
$36\frac{1}{2}$" x $14\frac{3}{8}$"

Figure 12
The Arnolfini Marriage
Jan van Eyck, c. 1434
Reproduced by courtesy of the Trustees,
The National Gallery, London
Wood; $23\frac{1}{2}$" x $32\frac{1}{4}$"

Figure 13
Madonna and Child
Albrecht Dürer, c. 1505
National Gallery of Art, Washington
Samuel H. Kress Collection
Wood; $19\frac{3}{4}$" x $15\frac{5}{8}$"

Figure 14
Portrait of a Clergyman
Albrecht Durer, c. 1505
National Gallery of Art, Washington
Samuel H. Kress Collection
Parchment on canvas; $16\frac{7}{8}$" x 13"

Figure 15
The Meeting of Abraham and Melchizedek
Peter Paul Rubens, c. 1625
National Gallery of Art, Washington
Gift of Syma Busiel
Wood; 26" x $32\frac{1}{2}$"

Figure 16
Self-Portrait
Rembrandt van Rijn, 1650
National Gallery of Art, Washington
Widener Collection
Canvas; $36\frac{1}{4}$" x $29\frac{3}{4}$"

Figure 17
Saskia van Uilenburgh, the Wife of the Artist
Rembrandt van Rijn, c. 1633
National Gallery of Art, Washington
Widener Collection
Wood; $23\frac{3}{4}$" x $19\frac{1}{4}$"

Figure 18
Christ Cleansing the Temple
El Greco (Domenikos Theotokopoulos),
c. 1570
National Gallery of Art, Washington
Samuel H. Kress Collection
Wood; $25\frac{3}{4}$" x $32\frac{3}{4}$"

Figure 19
Saint Martin and the Beggar
El Greco (Domenikos Theotokopoulos),
1597–1599
National Gallery of Art, Washington
Widener Collection
Canvas; $76\frac{1}{8}$" x $40\frac{1}{2}$"

Figure 20
The Needlewoman
Diego Velázquez, c. 1640
National Gallery of Art, Washington
Andrew W. Mellon Collection
Oil on canvas; $29\frac{1}{8}$" x $23\frac{5}{8}$"

Figure 21
Pope Innocent X
Diego Velázquez, c. 1650
National Gallery of Art, Washington
Andrew W. Mellon Collection
Oil on canvas; $19\frac{1}{2}$" x $16\frac{1}{4}$"

Figure 22
Condesa de Chinchón
Francisco de Goya, 1783
National Gallery of Art, Washington
Ailsa Mellon Bruce Collection
Canvas; $19\frac{7}{8}$" x $26\frac{3}{4}$"

Figure 23
Maria Luisa, Queen of Spain
Francisco de Goya, c. 1799
National Gallery of Art, Washington
Andrew W. Mellon Collection
Oil on canvas; $18\frac{1}{4}$" x $11\frac{3}{4}$"

Figure 24
Wivenhoe Park, Essex
John Constable, 1816
National Gallery of Art, Washington
Widener Collection
Canvas; $22\frac{1}{8}$" x $39\frac{7}{8}$"

Figure 25
A View of Salisbury Cathedral
John Constable, c. 1825
National Gallery of Art, Washington
Andrew W. Mellon Collection
Oil on canvas; $28\frac{3}{4}$" x 36"

Figure 26
Self-Portrait
Joseph Mallord William Turner, c. 1800
The Tate Gallery, London
Oil on canvas; $29\frac{1}{4}$" x 23"

Figure 27
Venice: Dogana and San Giorgio Maggiore
Joseph Mallord William Turner, c. 1834
National Gallery of Art, Washington
Widener Collection
Canvas; 36" x 48"

Figure 28
Columbus and His Son at La Rabida
Eugène Delacroix, 1838
National Gallery of Art, Washington
Chester Dale Collection
Canvas; $35\frac{5}{8}$" x $46\frac{5}{8}$"

Figure 29
The Horse Fair
Rosa Bonheur, 1853–1855
The Metropolitan Museum of Art
Gift of Cornelius Vanderbilt, 1887
(87.25). All rights reserved, The
Metropolitan Museum of Art
Oil on canvas; $96\frac{1}{4}$" x $199\frac{1}{2}$"

Figure 30
Colonel William F. Cody
Rosa Bonheur, 1889
Courtesy of the Buffalo Bill Historical
Center, Cody, Wyoming
Oil on canvas; $18\frac{1}{2}$" x $15\frac{1}{4}$"

Figure 31
A Young Woman Reading
Gustave Courbet, 1868–1872
National Gallery of Art, Washington
Chester Dale Collection
Canvas; $23\frac{5}{8}$" x $29\frac{3}{4}$"

Figure 32
Landscape Near the Banks of the Indre
Gustave Courbet, 1856
National Gallery of Art, Washington
Gift of the W. Averell Harriman Foundation in memory of Marie N. Harriman
Canvas; 24" x $28\frac{7}{8}$"

Figure 33
Gare Saint-Lazare
Édouard Manet, 1873
National Gallery of Art, Washington
Gift of Horace Havemeyer in memory of
his mother, Louisine W. Havemeyer
Canvas; $36\frac{3}{4}$" x $45\frac{1}{8}$"

Figure 34
The Plum
Édouard Manet, 1877
National Gallery of Art, Washington
Collection of Mr. and Mrs. Paul Mellon
Canvas; 29" x $19\frac{3}{4}$"

Figure 35
Bazille and Camille
Claude Monet, 1865
National Gallery of Art, Washington
Ailsa Mellon Bruce Collection
Canvas; $36\frac{5}{8}$" x $27\frac{1}{8}$"

Figure 36
The Artist's Garden at Vétheuil
Claude Monet, 1880
National Gallery of Art, Washington
Ailsa Mellon Bruce Collection
Canvas; $59\frac{5}{8}$" x $47\frac{5}{8}$"

Figure 37
Madame Monet and Her Son
Auguste Renoir, 1874
National Gallery of Art, Washington
Ailsa Mellon Bruce Collection
Canvas; $19\frac{7}{8}$" x $26\frac{3}{4}$"

Figure 38
Picking Flowers
Auguste Renoir, 1875
National Gallery of Art, Washington
Ailsa Mellon Bruce Collection
Canvas; $21\frac{3}{8}$" x $25\frac{5}{8}$"

Figure 39
The Boating Party
Mary Cassatt, 1893–1894
National Gallery of Art, Washington
Chester Dale Collection
Canvas; $35\frac{1}{2}$" x $46\frac{1}{8}$"

Figure 40
The Letter
Mary Cassatt, 1891
National Gallery of Art, Washington
Rosenwald Collection
Etching and aquatint; $13\frac{5}{8}$" x $8\frac{5}{16}$"

Figure 41
The Artist's Son, Paul
Paul Cézanne, 1885–1890
National Gallery of Art, Washington
Chester Dale Collection
Canvas; $25\frac{3}{4}$" x $21\frac{1}{4}$"

Figure 42
Still Life with Peppermint Bottle
Paul Cézanne, c. 1894
National Gallery of Art, Washington
Chester Dale Collection
Canvas; 26" x $32\frac{3}{8}$"

Figure 43
Portrait of van Gogh
Imitator of van Gogh, c. 1925–1928
National Gallery of Art, Washington
Chester Dale Collection
Canvas; $23\frac{1}{4}$" x $19\frac{1}{8}$"

Figure 44
The Olive Orchard
Vincent van Gogh, 1889
National Gallery of Art, Washington
Chester Dale Collection
Canvas; $28\frac{3}{4}$" x $36\frac{1}{4}$"

Figure 45
Uprising
Käthe Kollwitz, 1899
Courtesy Galerie St. Etienne, New York
Etching on paper; $11\frac{5}{8}$" x $12\frac{1}{2}$"

Figure 46
Woman with Exotic Plant
Henri Matisse, c. 1925
National Gallery of Art, Washington
Chester Dale Collection
Pastel; 26" x $20\frac{1}{4}$"

Figure 47
Woman with Amphora and Pomegranates
Henri Matisse, 1952
National Gallery of Art, Washington
Ailsa Mellon Bruce Collection
Paper/canvas (collage); 96" x $37\frac{7}{8}$"

Figure 48
The Tragedy
Pablo Picasso, 1903
National Gallery of Art, Washington
Chester Dale Collection
Wood; $41\frac{1}{2}$" x $27\frac{1}{8}$"

Figure 49
Family of Saltimbanques
Pablo Picasso, 1905
National Gallery of Art, Washington
Chester Dale Collection
Canvas; $83\frac{3}{4}$" x $90\frac{3}{8}$"

Figure 50
Houses at Vitebsk
Marc Chagall, 1917
National Gallery of Art, Washington
Gift of Mr. and Mrs. John U. Nef and Mr. and Mrs. William Wood-Prince
Paper/canvas; $18\frac{5}{8}$" x 24"

Figure 51
Breezing Up (A Fair Wind)
Winslow Homer, 1876
National Gallery of Art, Washington
Gift of the W.L. and May T. Mellon Foundation
Canvas; $24\frac{1}{8}$" x $38\frac{1}{8}$"

Figure 52
Archbishop Diomede Falconio
Thomas Eakins, 1905
National Gallery of Art, Washington
Gift of Stephen C. Clark
Canvas; $72\frac{1}{8}$" x $54\frac{1}{4}$"

Figure 53
Mrs. Louis Husson
Thomas Eakins, c. 1905
National Gallery of Art, Washington
Gift of Katherine Husson Horstick
Canvas; 24" x 20"

Figure 54
The Lone Tenement
George Bellows, 1909
National Gallery of Art, Washington
Chester Dale Collection
Canvas; $36\frac{1}{8}$" x $48\frac{1}{8}$"

Figure 55
Both Members of This Club
George Bellows, 1909
National Gallery of Art, Washington
Chester Dale Collection
Canvas; $45\frac{1}{4}$" x $63\frac{1}{8}$"

Figure 56
Ryder's House
Edward Hopper, 1954
National Museum of American Art, Smithsonian Institution
Bequest of Henry Ward Ranger through the National Academy of Design
Oil on canvas; $36\frac{1}{8}$" x 50"

Figure 57
Goat's Horn with Red
Georgia O'Keeffe, 1945
Hirshhorn Museum and Sculpture Garden, Smithsonian Institution
Pastel on paperboard; $31\frac{11}{16}$" x $27\frac{7}{8}$"

Figure 58
Train Whistle Blues #1
Romare Bearden, 1964
© Romare Bearden Foundation
Licensed by VAGA, New York, NY
Photomontage; 29" x $37\frac{1}{2}$"

Figure 59
Christina's World
Andrew Wyeth, 1948
Collection, The Museum of Modern Art, New York
Purchase tempera on gesso panel; $32\frac{1}{4}$" x $47\frac{3}{4}$"

Figure 60
Reclining Figure: Curved
Henry Moore, 1977
Private Collection
Black marble

Figure 61
Three Piece Reclining Figure: Draped
Henry Moore, 1975
Kensington Gardens
Bronze

Figure 62
Single Form
Barbara Hepworth, 1961–1962
UN/DPI Photo
Bronze; 21'

Figure 63
Stainless Stealer
Alexander Calder, 1966
Hirshhorn Museum and Sculpture Garden, Smithsonian Institution
Stainless steel and aluminum; 120" x 180" x 180"

Figure 64
Untitled
Alexander Calder, 1977
National Gallery of Art, Washington
Gift of the Collectors Committee
Painted aluminum and tempered steel; 29' $10\frac{1}{2}$" x 76'

Photo Credits—Color

Color Plate 1
The Virgin Adoring the Child
Sandro Botticelli, c. 1480–1490
National Gallery of Art, Washington
Samuel H. Kress Collection
Wood; $23\frac{3}{8}$" in diameter

Color Plate 2
Saint George and the Dragon
Raphael Santi, c. 1506
National Gallery of Art, Washington
Andrew W. Mellon Collection
Oil on wood; $11\frac{1}{8}$" x $8\frac{3}{8}$"

Color Plate 3
The Descent from the Cross
Rembrandt van Rijn, c. 1655 (altered at a later date)
National Gallery of Art, Washington
Widener Collection
Canvas; $56\frac{1}{4}$" x $43\frac{3}{4}$"

Color Plate 4
Madonna and Child with Saint Martina and Saint Agnes
El Greco (Domenikos Theotokopoulos), c. 1597–1599
National Gallery of Art, Washington
Widener Collection
Canvas; $76\frac{1}{8}$" x $40\frac{1}{2}$"

Color Plate 5
Bartolomé Sureda y Miserol
Francisco de Goya, c. 1803–1804
National Gallery of Art, Washington
Gift of Mr. and Mrs. P.H.B. Frelinghuysen in memory of her father and mother, Mr. and Mrs. H.O. Havemeyer
Canvas; $47\frac{1}{8}$" x $31\frac{1}{4}$"

Color Plate 6
The White Horse
John Constable, c. 1819
National Gallery of Art, Washington
Widener Collection
Canvas; 50" x 72"

Color Plate 7
Norham Castle: Sunrise
Joseph Mallord William Turner, c. 1835–1840
The Tate Gallery, London
Oil on canvas

Color Plate 8
Arabs Skirmishing in the Mountains
Eugène Delacroix, 1863
National Gallery of Art, Washington
Chester Dale Fund
Canvas; $36\frac{3}{8}$" x $29\frac{3}{8}$"

Color Plate 9
Boats on a Beach, Etretat
Gustave Courbet, 1869
National Gallery of Art, Washington
Gift of the W. Averell Harriman Foundation in memory of Marie N. Harriman
Canvas; $25\frac{1}{2}$" x $36\frac{1}{4}$"

Color Plate 10
At the Races
Édouard Manet, c. 1875
National Gallery of Art, Washington
Widener Collection
Wood; 5" x $8\frac{1}{2}$"

Color Plate 11
Woman Seated Under the Willows
Claude Monet, 1880
National Gallery of Art, Washington
Chester Dale Collection
Canvas; $31\frac{7}{8}$" x $23\frac{5}{8}$"

Color Plate 12
A Girl with a Watering Can
Auguste Renoir, 1876
National Gallery of Art, Washington
Chester Dale Collection
Canvas; $39\frac{1}{2}$" x $28\frac{3}{4}$"

Color Plate 13
Miss Mary Ellison
Mary Cassatt, c. 1880
National Gallery of Art, Washington
Chester Dale Collection
Canvas; $33\frac{1}{2}$" x $25\frac{3}{4}$"

Color Plate 14
Le Château Noir
Paul Cézanne, 1900–1904
National Gallery of Art, Washington
Gift of Eugene and Agnes Meyer
Canvas; 29" x 38"

Color Plate 15
Farmhouse in Provence, Arles
Vincent van Gogh, 1888
National Gallery of Art, Washington
Ailsa Mellon Bruce Collection
Canvas; $18\frac{1}{8}$" x 24"

Color Plate 16
Still Life
Pablo Picasso, 1918
National Gallery of Art, Washington
Chester Dale Collection
Canvas; $38\frac{1}{4}$" x $51\frac{1}{4}$"

Color Plate 17
Right and Left
Winslow Homer, 1909
National Gallery of Art, Washington
Gift of the Avalon Foundation
Canvas; $28\frac{1}{4}$" x $48\frac{3}{8}$"

Color Plate 18
The Biglin Brothers Racing
Thomas Eakins, c. 1873
National Gallery of Art, Washington
Gift of Mr. and Mrs. Cornelius Vanderbilt Whitney
Canvas; $24\frac{1}{8}$" x $36\frac{1}{8}$"

Color Plate 19
Blue Morning
George Bellows, 1909
National Gallery of Art, Washington
Chester Dale Collection
Canvas; $31\frac{5}{8}$" x $43\frac{3}{8}$"

Color Plate 20
Eleven A.M.
Edward Hopper, 1926
Hirshhorn Museum and Sculpture Garden, Smithsonian Institution
Oil on canvas; $28\frac{1}{8}$" x $36\frac{1}{8}$"

Color Plate 21
Family
Romare Bearden, 1986
Smithsonian American Art Museum, Transfer from the General Services Administration, Art-in-Architecture Program
© Romare Bearden Foundation
Licensed by VAGA, New York, NY
Collage on wood; 28" x 20"

Color Plate 22
Snow Flurries
Andrew Wyeth, 1953
National Gallery of Art, Washington
Gift of Dr. Margaret I. Handy
Tempera on panel; $37\frac{1}{4}$" x 48"

Bibliography

Andre, Christopher, "Chagall." *Christian Science Monitor,* Vol. 77, No. 54 (Feb. 8, 1985), pp. 20–21.

Arthur, John. *Realism-Photorealism.* Tulsa, OK: Philbrook Art Center, 1980.

Ashton, Dore, and Denise Brown-Hare. *Rosa Bonheur: A Life and a Legend.* New York: The Viking Press, 1981.

Ashton, Dore. *Picasso on Art: A Selection of Views.* New York: The Viking Press, 1972.

Baigell, Matthew. *A History of American Painting.* New York: Praeger Publishers, 1971.

Barnes, Albert C., and Violette De Mazia. *The Art of Renoir.* New York: Minton, Balch and Company, 1935.

Barr, Alfred H. Jr. *Matisse: His Art and His Public.* New York: Arno Press, 1966.

Beam, Phillip C. *Winslow Homer at Prout's Neck.* Boston, Toronto: Little, Brown & Co., 1966.

Berenson, Bernard. *Italian Painters of the Renaissance.* London: Phaidon Press, Ltd., 1952.

Berger, John. *The Success and Failure of Picasso.* New York: Pantheon Books, 1965.

Berman, Avis. "Thomas Eakins: Master of Realist Art." *Saturday Review,* Vol. 9 No. 6 (June, 1982) pp 24–28.

Bishop, Morris. *The Horizon Book of the Middle Ages,* ed. Norman Kother. New York: American Heritage Publishing Company, Inc., 1968.

Bittner, Alan, ed. *Käthe Kollwitz: Drawings.* New York: Thomas Yoseloff Inc., 1959.

Boswell, Peyton, Jr. *George Bellows.* New York: Crown Publishers, Inc., 1942.

Bouret, Jean. *The Barbizon School and 19th-Century French Landscape Painting.* Greenwich, CT: The New York Graphic Society, 1972.

Braness, Alan, ed. *The Sculpture of Barbara Hepworth.* New York: Praeger, 1971.

Brown, Dale, and the editors of Time-Life Books. *The World of Velázquez, 1599–1660.* New York: Time-Life Books, Inc., 1969.

Brown, Milton W. *The Story of the Armory Show.* Greenwich, CT: The New York Graphic Society and The Joseph H. Hirshhorn Foundation, 1963.

Brown, Milton. *American Painting from the Armory Show to the Depression.* Princeton, NJ: Princeton University Press, 1955.

Burchell, Samuel C. *Age of Progress.* New York: Time-Life Books, Inc., 1966.

Cahill, James. *The Distant Mountains: Chinese Paintings of the Late Ming Dynasty, 1570–1644.* New York: Weatherhill, 1982.

Canaday, John. *The Lives of the Painters,* Vols. 1,11. New York: W.W. Norton and Co., Inc., 1969.

Cheng, Francois. *Empty and Full: The Language of Chinese Painting.* Boston: Shambhala Publications, Inc., 1991.

Clark, Kenneth. *An Introduction to Rembrandt.* NewYork, London: Harper & Row Publishers, 1978.

Clark, Kenneth. *Rembrandt and the Italian Renaissance.* New York: New York University Press, 1966.

Clark, Kenneth. *Looking at Pictures.* New York: Holt, Rinehart and Winston, 1960.

Cogniat, Raymond. *Chagall.* New York: Crown Publishers, Inc., 1965.

Corbino, Marcia. "The Art World According to Jack Levine." *American Artist,* Vol. 49, No. 514 (May 1985).

Corn, Wanda. *The Art of Andrew Wyeth.* Greenwich, CT: The New York Graphic Society, 1973.

Crespelle, Jean-Paul. *Chagall.* New York: Coward-McCann, Inc., 1970.

Cuttler, Charles D. *Northern Painting.* New York: Holt, Rinehart and Winston, Inc., 1968.

Daix, Pierre. *Picasso.* New York: Praeger Publishers, 1965.

Davidson, Abraham A. *Early American Modernist Painting, 1910–1935.* New York: Harper & Row Publishers, 1981.

Delacroix, Eugène. *The Journal of Eugène Delacroix,* trans. Walter Pach. New York: Crown Publishers, 1937–1948.

Dorival, Bernard. *Twentieth-Century Painters.* New York: Universe Books, 1958.

Eimerl, Sarel, and the editors of Time-Life Books. *The World of Giotto.* New York: Time-Life Books, Inc., 1967.

Elgar, Frank. *Van Gogh.* New York: Praeger Publishers, 1958.

Feldman, Edmund Burke. *The Artist.* New Jersey: Prentice-Hall, Inc., 1982.

Flexner, James Thomas, and the editors of Time-Life Books. *The World of Winslow Homer.* New York: Time-Life Books, Inc., 1983.

Freedgood, Lillian. *An Enduring Image: American Painting from 1665.* New York: Thomas Y. Crowell Company, 1970.

Gallwitz, Klaus. *Picasso at 90: The Late Work.* New York: G.P. Putnam's Sons, 1971.

Garraty, John A., and Peter Gay. *The Columbia History of the World.* New York: Harper & Row, 1972.

Gaunt, William. *Renoir.* London: Phaidon Press, Ltd., 1962.

Geldzahler, Henry, and The Metropolitan Museum of Art. *American Painting in the Twentieth Century.* Greenwich, CT: The New York Graphic Society, 1965.

Gillette, Henry S. *Raphael, Painter of the Renaissance.* New York: Franklin Watts, Inc., 1967.

Gilot, Françoise, and Carlton Lake. *Life with Picasso.* New York: McGraw-Hill Inc., 1964.

Goodrich, Lloyd, and Doris Bry. *Georgia O'Keeffe.* New York: Praeger Publishers, 1970.

Greenfeld, Howard. *Marc Chagall.* Chicago, New York: Follett Publishing Company, 1967.

Guichard-Meili, Jean. *Matisse.* New York: Praeger Publishers, 1967.

Hale, Nancy. *Mary Cassatt.* Garden City, NY: Doubleday and Company, Inc., 1975.

Hammacher, A. M. *Barbara Hepworth.* London: A. Swemmer, 1959.

Hepworth, Barbara. *A Pictorial Autobiography.* New York: Praeger, 1970.

Hirsh, Dianne, and the editors of Time-Life Books. *The World of Turner.* New York: Time-Life Books, Inc., 1969.

Hodin, J.P. *Barbara Hepworth.* New York: David McKay Company, 1959.

Hogrefe, Jeffrey. *Georgia O'Keeffe: The Life of an American Legend.* New York: Bantam Books, 1992.

Homer, William Innes. *Alfred Stieglitz and the American Avant-Garde.* Boston: The New York Graphic Society, 1977.

Hoving, Thomas. *The World of Andrew Wyeth.* Boston: Houghton Mifflin Company, 1978.

Huyghe, Rene. *Van Gogh.* New York: Crown Publishers, Inc., 1967.

Ives, Cotta Feller. *The Great Wave: The Influence of Japanese Woodcuts on French Prints.* New York: The Metropolitan Museum of Art, 1974.

James, Phillip, ed. *Henry Moore on Sculpture.* New York: Viking Press, 1967.

Kearns, Martha. *Käthe Kollwitz: Woman and Artist.* New York: The Feminist Press, 1976.

Kellogg, Rhoda. *Analyzing Children's Art.* Palo Alto, CA: National Press Books, 1969.

Klein, Mina C., and H. Arthur. *Käthe Kollwitz: Life in Art.* New York: Holt, Rinehart & Winston, 1972.

Legendre, Maurice. *El Greco.* New York: Hyperion Press, 1947.

Lewis, Samella. *Art: African American.* Los Angeles: Hancraft Studios, 1990.

Lewis, Wyndham D.B. *The World of Goya.* New York: Clarkson N. Potter, Inc., 1968.

Lindsay, Jack. *Cézanne: His Life and Work.* Greenwich, CT: The New York Graphic Society, 1969.

Lindsay, Jack. *J.M.W. Turner.* Greenwich, CT: The New York Graphic Society, 1966.

McCoubrey, John W. *American Tradition in Painting.* New York: George Braziller, 1963.

McCoubrey, John W. *American Art, 1700–1960. Sources and Documents.* Englewood Cliffs, NJ: Prentice-Hall, Inc., 1965.

Michiletti, Emma. *Botticelli,* trans. Peter Cook. Milan: Arti Grafiche Ricordi, 1964.

Mount, Charles Merrill. *Monet: A Biography.* New York: Simon and Schuster, 1966.

Mulas, Ugo, and H. Harvard Arnason. *Calder.* New York: The Viking Press, 1971.

Muller, Joseph-Emile. *Fauvism.* New York: Praeger Publishers, 1967.

Munsterberg, Hugo. *A History of Women Artists.* New York: Clarkson N. Potter Inc., 1975.

Murphy, Richard W., and the editors of Time-Life Books. *The World of Cézanne.* New York: Time-Life Books, Inc., 1969.

Nagel, Otto. *Käthe Kollwitz.* Greenwich, CT: The New York Graphic Society, 1971.

Nemser, Cindy. *Conversations with Twelve Woman Artists.* New York: Charles Scribner's Sons, 1975.

Nicolaides, Kimon. *The Natural Way to Draw.* Boston: Houghton Mifflin Co., 1969.

O'Doherty, Brian. *American Masters: The Voice and the Myth.* New York: Random House, Inc., 1976.

O'Keeffe, Georgia. *Georgia O'Keeffe.* New York: The Viking Press, 1976.

Pagano, Grace. *Contemporary American Painting.* New York: Duell, Sloan, and Pierce for Encyclopaedia Britannica, 1945.

Partridge, Loren, et al. *Michelangelo—The Last Judgment: A Glorious Restoration.* New York: Harry N. Abrams, Inc., 1997.

Peacock, Carlos. *John Constable: The Man and His Work.* Greenwich, CT: The New York Graphic Society, 1965.

Penrose, Roland. *The Sculpture of Picasso.* New York: The Museum of Modern Art, 1967.

Perlman, Bernard B. *The Immortal Eight.* Westport, CT: North Light Publishers, 1979.

Porter, Fairfield. *Thomas Eakins.* New York: George Braziller, Inc., 1959.

Prideaux, Tom, and the editors of Time-Life Books. *The World of Delacroix.* New York: Time-Life Books, Inc., 1966.

Reynolds, Graham. *Turner.* New York: Harry N. Abrams, 1985.

Rose, Barbara. *American Art Since 1900: A Critical History.* New York: Praeger Publishers, 1967.

Rosenzweig, Phyllis. *The Fifties.* Washington, DC: Smithsonian Institution Press, 1980.

Russell, Frances, and the editors of Time-Life Books. *The World of Rubens.* New York: Time-Life Books, Inc., 1967.

Russell, John. *The Meanings of Modern Art.* New York: The Museum of Modern Art and Harper & Row, 1981.

Sandler, Irving. *The Triumph of American Painting.* New York: Praeger Publishers, 1970.

Schafer, Edward H., and editors of Time-Life Books. *Great Ages of Man Series,* Vol. 17, *Ancient China.* New York: Time-Life Books, 1967.

Schickel, Richard, and the editors of Time-Life Books. *The World of Goya, 1746–1828.* New York: Time-Life Books, Inc., 1968.

Schiff, Gert, ed. *Picasso in Perspective.* Englewood Cliffs, NJ: Prentice-Hall Inc., 1976.

Schinneller, James A. *Art/Search and Self-Discovery.* Scranton, PA: International Text Book Company, 1968.

Schneider, Pierre, and the editors of Time-Life Books. *The World of Manet, 1832–1883.* New York: Time-Life Books, Inc., 1968.

Sims, Lowery Stokes. *Romare Bearden.* New York: Rizzoli Publications, 1993.

Sloan, John. *The Gist of Art: Principles & Practices Expounded in the Studio & Classroom.* New York: Dover Publications, Inc., 1977.

Stearns, Monroe. *Rembrandt and His World.* New York: Franklin Watts, Inc., 1967.

Sweet, Frederick A. *Miss Mary Cassatt, Impressionist from Pennsylvania.* Norman, OK: University of Oklahoma Press, 1966.

Wallace, Robert, and the editors of Time-Life Books. *The World of Rembrandt.* New York: Time-Life Books, Inc., 1968.

Young, Hahonri Sharp. *The Eight.* New York: Watson-Guptill Publications, 1973.

Vasari, Giorgio. *The Lives of the Artists,* trans. George Bull. Great Britain: Penguin Books, 1965.

Warner, Malcolm. *Portrait Painting.* New York: Mayflower Books, 1979.

Wentworth, Richard L. "Controversy Clings to Sistine Chapel Ceiling." *The Christian Science Monitor,* Wednesday, June 1, 1994, p.16.

Williams, William J. *A Heritage of American Paintings from the National Gallery of Art.* New York, NY and Maplewood, NJ: The Rutledge Press and Hammond Incorporated, 1981.